# The History of POPULAR CULTURE

## To 1815

# The History of
# POPULAR CULTURE

## To 1815

&§ Edited by Norman F. Cantor
and Michael S. Werthman

**THE MACMILLAN COMPANY**

**COLLIER-MACMILLAN LIMITED**
London

# SOURCES AND ACKNOWLEDGMENTS

The selections anthologized in this book are listed below in the order in which they appear in the book. The title and author as listed at the head of the selection are followed by the precise bibliographical reference. This in turn is followed by the permission copyright credit in parentheses. Where no permission credit is given, the work cited is in the public domain.

## Part One / The Classical World, to A.D. 450

### 1. GREEK ATHLETICS AS SPORT AND RITUAL

Games the Greeks Played    E. Norman Gardiner
    E. Norman Gardiner, *Athletics in the Ancient World*, Oxford: Clarendon Press, 1930, pp. 1–2, 32–33, 222, 223–229. (By permission of the Clarendon Press, Oxford.)

### 2. POPULAR ASPECTS OF GREEK DRAMA

The Audiences of Greek Drama    A. E. Haigh
    A. E. Haigh, *The Attic Theatre*, Oxford: Clarendon Press, 1855, pp. 361–363, 364, 366–368, 387–388.

### 3. SEX AND MARRIAGE IN ANCIENT GREECE

The Greek Double Standard    Hans Licht
    Hans Licht (pseud. for Paul Brandt), *Sexual Life in Ancient Greece*, London: G. Routledge & Sons, Ltd., 1932, pp. 332–334, 338–340. (By permission of Barnes & Noble, Inc. Inc. By permission of Routledge & Kegan Paul, Limited.)

Engagement, Wedding, and Divorce in Ancient Greece    Robert Flacelière
    Robert Flacelière, *Daily Life in Ancient Greece at the Time of Pericles*, tr. by Peter Green, London: George Weidenfeld & Nicolson, Ltd., 1965, pp. 60–66, 71, 72. (Reprinted with permission of The Macmillan Company from *Daily Life in Ancient Greece at the Time of Pericles*, by Robert Flacelière. Translated from the French by Peter Green. © Librairie Hachette, 1959. English translation Copyright © 1965 by George Weidenfeld & Nicolson, Ltd. By permission of George Weidenfeld & Nicolson, Limited.)

Varieties of Prostitution    Hans Licht
    Hans Licht (pseud. for Paul Brandt), *Sexual Life in Ancient Greece*, London: G. Routledge & Sons, Ltd., 1932, pp. 332–334, 338–340. (By permission of Barnes & Noble, Inc. By permission of Routledge, Kegan and Paul, Limited.)

Homosexual Love    Robert Flacelière
    Robert Flacelière, *Love in Ancient Greece*, tr. by James Cleugh, New York: Crown Publishers, 1962, pp. 62–63, 64–65, 66, 67–70. (From *Love in Ancient Greece* by

Seventh Printing, 1972

Library of Congress catalog card number: 68–10355

THE MACMILLAN COMPANY
866 Third Avenue, New York, New York 10022

COLLIER-MACMILLAN CANADA, LTD., TORONTO, ONTARIO

*Printed in the United States of America*

Robert Flacelière. © 1962 by Frederick Muller, Ltd., and James Cleugh and Crown. Used by permission of Crown Publishers, Inc. By permission of Frederick Muller, Limited.)

## 4. IN THE ANCIENT MARKETPLACE

The Agora of Athens    Robert Flacelière
Robert Flacelière, *Daily Life in Ancient Greece at the Time of Pericles*, tr. by Peter Green, London: George Weidenfeld & Nicolson, Ltd., 1965, pp. 4–5, 35, 184. (Reprinted with permission of The Macmillan Company from *Daily Life in Ancient Greece at the Time of Pericles*, by Robert Flacelière. Translated from the French by Peter Green. © Librairie Hachette, 1959. English translation Copyright © 1965 by George Weidenfeld & Nicolson, Ltd. By permission of George Weidenfeld & Nicolson, Limited.)

A Tour of Antioch in the Fourth Century A.D.    Glanville Downey
Glanville Downey, *Antioch in the Age of Theodosius the Great*, Norman, Okla.: University of Oklahoma Press, 1962, pp. 16–22. (From *Antioch in the Age of Theodosius the Great*, by Glanville Downey. Copyright 1962 by the University of Oklahoma Press.)

## 5. TRAVEL IN THE ROMAN WORLD

Reasons for Travel    Ludwig Friedländer
Ludwig Friedländer, *Roman Life and Manners Under the Early Empire*, 4 vols., London: G. Routledge & Sons, Ltd., and New York: E. P. Dutton & Co., 1908–1913, vol. 1, pp. 316, 317, 318, 320, 321, 322.

The Quality of Land Travel    Ludwig Friedländer
Ludwig Friedländer, *Roman Life and Manners Under the Early Empire*, 4 vols., London: G. Routledge & Sons, Ltd. and New York: E. P. Dutton & Co., 1908–1913, vol. 1, pp. 287–288, 289–290, 292, 293, 294–295, 296, 297.

Travel by Sea    Ludwig Friedländer
Ludwig Friedländer, *Roman Life and Manners Under the Early Empire*, 4 vols., London: G. Routledge & Sons, Ltd. and New York: E. P. Dutton & Co., 1908–1913, vol. 1, pp. 282, 283, 286.

The Embattled Driver in Ancient Rome    Kenneth D. Matthews
Kenneth D. Matthews, "The Embattled Driver in Ancient Rome," *Expedition* (Bulletin of the University Museum of the University of Pennsylvania), vol. 2, no. 3, 1960, pp. 23–24, 27. (By permission of *Expedition*.)

## 6. LUST AND BLOOD LUST AS ROMAN POPULAR ENTERTAINMENTS

Legalized Prostitution    E. Royston Pike
E. Royston Pike, *Love in Ancient Rome*, London: Frederick Muller, Ltd., 1965, pp. 197–204. (By permission of Frederick Muller, Limited.)

Bread and Circuses    Jerôme Carcopino
Jerôme Carcopino, *Daily Life in Ancient Rome*, H. T. Rowell (ed.), tr. by E. O. Lorimer, New Haven, Conn.: Yale University Press, 1940, pp. 202–203, 210, 211, 212–213, 215, 218, 231–232, 237–239. (By permission of Yale University Press. By permission of Routledge & Kegan Paul, Limited.)

## 7. THE ROMAN BATHS AS POPULAR RECREATION

The Importance of the Roman Baths    Lawrence Wright
Lawrence Wright, *Clean and Decent, the Fascinating History of the Bathroom and the Water Closet*, New York: Viking Press, 1960, p. 14. (From *Clean and Decent, the Fascinating History of the Bathroom and the Water Closet*, by Lawrence Wright. Copyright © 1960 by Lawrence Wright. Reprinted by permission of The Viking Press, Inc. By permission of Routledge & Kegan Paul, Limited.)

The Baths and Bathers    Jerôme Carcopino
Jerôme Carcopino, *Daily Life in Ancient Rome*, H. T. Rowell (ed.), tr. by E. O. Lorimer, New Haven, Conn.: Yale University Press, 1940, pp. 254, 256–257,

258, 260–261, 262–263. (By permission of Yale University Press. By permission of Routledge & Kegan Paul, Limited.)

## 8. ROMAN HOMES AND BANQUETS

The Houses in Rome    Jerôme Carcopino
  Jerôme Carcopino, *Daily Life in Ancient Rome*, H. T. Rowell (ed.), tr. by E. O. Lorimer, New Haven, Conn.: Yale University Press, 1940, pp. 22–23, 32–33, 35–36, 38. (By permission of Yale University Press. By permission of Routledge & Kegan Paul, Limited.)

Country Villas    Samuel Dill
  Samuel Dill, *Roman Society from Nero to Marcus Aurelius*, 2d ed., London: Macmillan & Co., Ltd., 1920, pp. 174, 175, 178–179. (By permission of Macmillan & Co., Limited.)

Roman Banquets    Jerôme Carcopino
  Jerôme Carcopino, *Daily Life in Ancient Rome*, H. T. Rowell (ed.), tr. by E. O. Lorimer, New Haven, Conn.: Yale University Press, 1940, pp. 264–270, 271. (By permission of Yale University Press. By permission of Routledge & Kegan Paul, Limited.)

## 9. THE DIVERSIONS OF THE LEGIONARIES

The Off-Duty Roman Soldier    Ramsay MacMullen
  Ramsay MacMullen, *Soldier and Civilian in the Later Roman Empire*, Cambridge, Mass.: Harvard University Press, 1963, pp. v–vi, 82–85, 98. (Reprinted by permission of the publishers from Ramsay MacMullen, *Soldier and Civilian in the Later Roman Empire*, Cambridge, Mass.: Harvard University Press, Copyright, 1963, by the President and Fellows of Harvard College.)

## 10. CLASSICAL RELIGIOUS PRACTICES AND EARLY CHRISTIANITY

The Eleusinian Mysteries    George Thomson
  George Thomson, *Aeschylus and Athens: A Study in the Social Origins of Drama*, London: Lawrence & Wishart, Ltd., 1941, pp. 121–124, 129. (By permission of Grosset & Dunlap, Inc., and Lawrence & Wishart, Ltd.)

Mithraic Practices    Franz Cumont
  Franz Cumont, *Mysteries of Mithra*, tr. by T. J. McCormack, La Salle, Ill.: Open Court Publishing Co. (By permission of The Open Court Publishing Company, La Salle, Illinois.)

Early Christian Practices    Louis Duchesne
  Louis Duchesne, *Early History of the Christian Church,* 3 vols., London: John Murray, Ltd., 1957, vol. 1, pp. 34–37, 143, 145. (By permission of John Murray [Publishers] Limited.)

The Success of Christian Fervor    Edward Gibbon
  Edward Gibbon, *The Decline and Fall of the Roman Empire*, 6 vols., New York: Collier, 1899, vol. 1, pp. 523, 536–541.

# *Part Two / The Medieval World, 450 to 1350*

## 1. NATURE, MAN, AND TIME IN THE MIDDLE AGES

The Medieval World View    Marc Bloch
  Marc Bloch, *Feudal Society,* tr. by L. A. Manyon, Chicago: University of Chicago Press, 1961, and London: Routledge & Kegan Paul, Ltd., 1961, pp. 72–75. (Reprinted from *Feudal Society* by Marc Bloch, translator, L. A. Manyon, by permission of the University of Chicago Press. © Routledge & Kegan Paul, Ltd. 1961. By permission of Routledge & Kegan Paul, Limited.)

## 2. GERMANIC LIFE IN THE EARLY MIDDLE AGES

At Home with the Barbarians    R. H. Hodgkin

R. H. Hodgkin, *A History of the Anglo-Saxons*, 2 vols., 3d ed., London: Oxford University Press, 1952, vol. 1, pp. 217, 218, 220–221, 225, 226. (By permission of the Clarendon Press, Oxford.)

## 3. THE DIMENSIONS OF POPULAR RELIGIOUS LIFE

Popular Aspects of Worship   J. A. Jungmann
    J. A. Jungmann, *Pastoral Liturgy*, New York: Herder and Herder, 1962, pp. 53, 55, 56, 57, 64, 66, 69, 70, 71. (By permission of Herder Book Center, Incorporated.)

Hysterical, Superstitious, and Apocalyptic Mass Religion   Norman Cohn
    Norman Cohn, *The Pursuit of the Millennium*, Fairlawn, N.J.: Essential Books, 1957, pp. 29–30, 35–40. (From *The Pursuit of the Millennium*, by Norman Cohn. Oxford University Press, 1957. Reprinted by permission. By permission of Martin Secker & Warburg, Limited, Publishers.)

Popular Vernacular Preaching    G. R. Owst
    G. R. Owst, *Literature and Pulpit in Medieval England*, New York: Barnes & Noble, Inc., 1961, pp. 110, 114, 117. (By permission of Barnes & Noble, Inc. By permission of Basil Blackwell & Mott, Limited.)

The Impact of the Friars    David Knowles
    David Knowles, *The Religious Orders in England*, 2 vols., New York and London: Cambridge University Press, 1960, vol. 1, pp. 180, 184–185, 188, 192–193. (By permission of Cambridge University Press.)

The Gothic Cathedral As an Instrument and Expression of Popular Religion   Allan Temko
    Allan Temko, *Notre Dame of Paris*, New York: The Viking Press, 1955, pp. 5–6, 199–201, 202, 203, 204–206. (From *Notre Dame of Paris*, by Allan Temko. Copyright © 1952, 1955 by Allan Temko. Reprinted by permission of The Viking Press, Inc. By permission of James Brown Associates, Incorporated.)

The Cult of the Virgin   G. G. Coulton
    G. G. Coulton, *Five Centuries of Religion*, 4 vols., London: Cambridge University Press, 1929, vol. 1, pp. 142, 145–146, 170. (By permission of Cambridge University Press.)

Relic Worship   G. G. Coulton
    G. G. Coulton, *Five Centuries of Religion*, 4 vols., London: Cambridge University Press, 1929, vol. 1, pp. 88, 106, 107. (By permission of Cambridge University Press.)

*Piers Plowman:* The Quest for Perfection   Morton W. Bloomfield
    Morton W. Bloomfield, *Piers Plowman As a Fourteenth Century Apocalypse*, New Brunswick, N.J.: Rutgers University Press, 1961, pp. 3–4, 5–6, 104–105, 107. (By permission of Rutgers University Press.)

## 4. POPULAR SUPPORT FOR THE CRUSADES

The Penetration of the Crusading Ideal   Steven Runciman
    Steven Runciman, *A History of the Crusades*, 3 vols., London: Cambridge University Press, 1951, vol. 1, pp. 106, 107–108, 112–115, 121; vol. 2, pp. 139–143, 123. (By permission of Cambridge University Press.)

## 5. THE ROYAL CORONATION AS GRAND SPECTACLE

Coronation Ritual and Festivities   Percy E. Schramm
    Percy E. Schramm, *A History of the English Coronation*, tr. by Leopold G. Wickham Legg, Oxford: Clarendon Press, 1937, pp. 31–32, 89, 90–92, 93–94. (By permission of the Clarendon Press, Oxford.)

## 6. ARISTOCRATIC DIVERSIONS AND ENTERTAINMENTS

Chivalry and Courtly Love   Sydney Painter
    Sydney Painter, *French Chivalry: Chivalric Ideas and Practices in Medieval France*, Ithaca, N.Y.: Cornell University Press, 1957, pp. 95–96, 102–104, 110,

111–112, 134–136. (Copyright, 1940, Johns Hopkins Press. By permission of The Johns Hopkins Press.)

The Profit and Glory of Tournaments   Sydney Painter
   Sydney Painter, *William Marshall: Knight Errant, Baron, and Regent of England,* Baltimore, Md.: Johns Hopkins Press, 1933, pp. 1, 30, 37–43. (By permission of The Johns Hopkins Press.)

## 7. ELEANOR OF AQUITAINE: EUROPE'S FIRST JET-SETTER

I Wonder What the Queen Is Doing Tonight   Amy Kelly
   Amy Kelly, *Eleanor of Aquitaine and the Four Kings,* Cambridge, Mass.: Harvard University Press, 1950, pp. 4, 5, 6–7, 32–33, 34, 35, 38–39, 55–56, 59, 60, 61–63, 77, 100–102, 103. (Reprinted by permission of the publishers from Amy Kelly, *Eleanor of Aquitaine and the Four Kings,* Cambridge, Mass.: Harvard University Press, Copyright, 1950, by the President and Fellows of Harvard College.)

## 8. PEASANT LIFE AND AMUSEMENTS

Village Pleasures   H. S. Bennett
   H. S. Bennett, *Life on the English Manor: A Study of Peasant Conditions, 1150–1400,* London: Cambridge University Press, 1960, pp. 259–267. (By permission of Cambridge University Press.)

## 9. POPULAR PARTICIPATION IN MEDIEVAL COMMON LAW

Instant Justice   Frederick Pollock and Frederick W. Maitland
   Frederick Pollock and Frederick W. Maitland, *The History of English Law Before the Time of Edward I,* 2d ed., 2 vols., London: Cambridge University Press, 1923, vol. 2, pp. 578–580. (By permission of Cambridge University Press.)

## 10. UNIVERSITY LIFE

Reading, Writing, and Rioting   Hastings Rashdall
   Hastings Rashdall, *The Universities in the Middle Ages,* 3 vols., F. M. Powicke and A. B. Emden (eds.), London: Oxford University Press, 1958, vol. 3, pp. 352–355, 378–380, 419–426, 437–438. (By permission of the Clarendon Press, Oxford.)

## 11. THE ARTHURIAN LEGEND AS POPULAR ROMANCE

Arthur Lives!   R. S. Loomis
   R. S. Loomis, *Arthurian Literature in the Middle Ages,* R. S. Loomis (ed.), Oxford: Clarendon Press, 1959, pp. 64, 65, 66–71, 553–559. (By permission of the Clarendon Press, Oxford.)

## 12. THE IMPACT OF THE BLACK DEATH

The Plague Conquers Europe   Hans Zinsser
   Hans Zinsser, *Rats, Lice, and History,* Boston: Little, Brown and Company, 1935, pp. 80–84, 88–91, 197–200. Copyright 1934, 1935, © 1963, by Hans Zinsser. (From *Rats, Lice, and History* by Hans Zinsser, by permission of Atlantic–Little, Brown & Company.)

## *Part Three / The Early Modern Era, 1350 to 1700*

## 1. THE SURVIVAL OF MEDIEVAL ATTITUDES

Fascination with the Dance of Death   Johann Huizinga
   Johann Huizinga, *The Waning of the Middle Ages,* London: Edward Arnold & Co., 1927, pp. 129–132, 133–134. (By permission of Edward Arnold [Publishers] Limited.)

The Heyday of Witchcraft   Aldous Huxley
   Aldous Huxley, *The Devils of London,* London: Chatto & Windus, Ltd., and Toronto: Clarke, Irwin & Co., 1952, pp. 140–142, 143–147. (Copyright 1952 by

## 2. REFORMATION AND COUNTER-REFORMATION ZEAL

## 3. THE COARSENESS AND SPLENDOR OF COURT LIFE

## 4. THE MODE OF ARISTOCRATIC LIFE

## 5. POLITICAL ACTIVITY AS POPULAR DIVERSION

## 6. THE LIFE OF THE RICH BOURGEOIS IN AN ARISTOCRATIC SOCIETY

1956, pp. 4–7, 26–27, 29, 31–32, 36–37. (By permission of the Clarendon Press, Oxford.)

## 7. POVERTY AND INSECURITY IN TOWN AND COUNTRY

Town Life   M. St. Clare Byrne
   M. St. Clare Byrne, *Elizabethan Life in Town and Country*, 5th ed., London: Methuen & Co., Ltd., 1947, pp. 51–52, 59, 74–78. (By permission of Methuen & Co., Limited.)

The Magnitude of French Poverty   Cecile Augon
   Cecile Augon, *Social France in the XVII Century*, London: Methuen & Co., Ltd., 1911, pp. 168–169, 170–173, 189. (By permission of Methuen & Co., Limited.)

## 8. POPULAR ASPECTS OF ARMY LIFE

The Extramilitary Activities of Cromwell's Army   C. H. Firth
   C. H. Firth, *Cromwell's Army*, London: Methuen & Co., Ltd., 4th ed., 1962, pp. 293–295, 296–300, 301, 329–331. (By permission of Methuen & Co., Limited.)

French Corruption and Incompetence   W. H. Lewis
   W. H. Lewis, *The Splendid Century*, Garden City, N.Y.: Doubleday Anchor, 1957, pp. 125–129, 139–141. (Reprinted by permission of William Morrow and Company, Inc. Copyright, 1953, by W. H. Lewis. By permission of Eyre and Spottiswoode.)

## 9. FROM RENAISSANCE TO BAROQUE: THE ENRICHMENT OF POPULAR CULTURE

The Advent of Printing   Henry J. Chaytor
   Henry J. Chaytor, *From Script to Print*, Cambridge: W. Heffer & Sons Ltd., 1945, pp. 135–138. (By permission of W. Heffer & Sons, Ltd. With acknowledgment to Sidgwick & Jackson Ltd., publisher of the present paper edition.)

The Passion for Discovery   J. H. Parry
   J. H. Parry, *The Age of Reconnaissance*, London: Weidenfeld & Nicolson, Ltd., 1963, pp. 33, 279. (By permission of The New American Library, Inc. © 1963 by J. H. Parry. By permission of Weidenfeld & Nicolson Limited.)

America and the Appearance of Venereal Disease   Will Durant
   Will Durant, *The Renaissance*, vol. 5 of *The Story of Civilization*, New York: Simon & Schuster, Inc., 1953, pp. 534–536. (Copyright 1953, by Will Durant. Reprinted by permission of Simon & Schuster, Inc.)

The New World's Impact on English Culture   A. L. Rowse
   A. L. Rowse, *The Expansion of Elizabethan England*, New York: St. Martin's Press, 1955, pp. 233–234, 235, 236–237. (By permission of St. Martin's Press, Inc. By permission of Macmillan & Co., Limited.)

The Power and Influence of the Florentine Humanists   Lauro Martines
   Lauro Martines, *The Social World of the Florentine Humanists*, Princeton, N.J.: Princeton University Press, 1963, pp. 12, 14–15, 278–280. (Reprinted by permission of Princeton University Press. © 1963 by Princeton University Press.)

The Thirst for Learning   Lawrence Stone
   Lawrence Stone, *Crisis of the Aristocracy, 1588–1641*, Oxford: Clarendon Press, 1965, pp. 672–675, 676–677. (By permission of the Clarendon Press, Oxford.)

Civic and Private Art in Florence   August C. Krey
   August C. Krey, *A City That Art Built*, Minneapolis, Minn.: University of Minnesota Press, 1936, pp. 38–40, 42–43. (By permission of University of Minnesota Press.)

Popular Art Exhibitions   Francis Haskell
   Francis Haskell, *Patrons and Painters*, New York: Alfred A. Knopf, 1963, pp. 125, 129, 130. (From *Patrons and Painters*, by Francis Haskell. © Copyright 1963 by Francis Haskell. Reprinted by permission of Alfred A. Knopf, Inc. By permission of Chatto & Windus, Limited.)

The Popular Appeal of Mannerism    Jacques Bousquet
    Jacques Bousquet, *Mannerism, The Painting and Style of the Late Renaissance,*
tr. by Simon W. Taylor, New York: George Braziller, Inc., 1964, pp. 62, 64–67.
(George Braziller, Inc.—from *Mannerism, The Painting and Style of the Late
Renaissance,* by Jacques Bousquet; translated by Simon W. Taylor; reprinted with
permission of the publisher. English translation © 1964.)

Baroque Aesthetics As a Reflection of Social Change    Hugo Leichtentritt
    Hugo Leichtentritt, *Music, History, and Ideas,* Cambridge, Mass.: Harvard Uni-
versity Press, 1938, pp. 115–116, 124–125. (By permission of Harvard University
Press.)

## Part Four / Enlightenment and Revolution, 1700 to 1815

### 1. THE ENJOYMENT OF VIOLENCE AND DEATH

Blood Sports    E. D. Cuming
    E. D. Cuming, "Sports and Games," in *Johnson's England,* 2 vols., A. S. Turber-
ville (ed.), Oxford: Clarendon Press, 1933, vol. 1, pp. 372–378. (By permission of
the Clarendon Press, Oxford.)

Upper-Class Devotion to the Hunt    G. M. Trevelyan
    G. M. Trevelyan, *English Social History,* London and Toronto: Longmans, Green
& Co., Ltd., 1942 and 1946, pp. 279–281, 406–407. (By permission of Longmans,
Green & Co., Limited.)

The Attractions of Popular Executions    Leon Radzinowicz
    Leon Radzinowicz, *A History of English Criminal Law and Its Administration
from 1750,* 3 vols., London: Stevens & Sons, Ltd., 1948, vol. 1, pp. 176–179, 187–
191, 186. (By permission of Stevens & Sons, Limited.)

Popular Responses to the Guillotine    Alister Kershaw
    Alister Kershaw, *A History of the Guillotine,* London: John Calder, 1958, pp. 64–
65, 69–70. (By permission of Calder and Boyars, Limited.)

### 2. THE EXTENT OF DRINKING AND GAMBLING

The Twin Vices of the Leisure Classes    A. S. Turberville
    A. S. Turberville, *English Men and Manners in the 18th Century,* Oxford:
Clarendon Press, 1936, pp. 84–86. (By permission of the Clarendon Press, Oxford.)

Hard Drinking in London    M. Dorothy George
    M. Dorothy George, *London Life in the 18th Century,* Harper Torchbook, 1964,
Copyright, 1925, by Kegan Paul, Trench Trubner & Co., Ltd., from Chapter One,
pp. 27–28, 30–31, 33–35. (By permission of Routledge & Kegan Paul, Limited.)

### 3. THE POPULAR MANIA FOR FINANCIAL SPECULATION

The Big Bubble    John Carswell
    John Carswell, *The South Sea Bubble,* Stanford, Cal.: Stanford University Press,
1960, pp. 101–102, 121, 153–156, 191, 194–195. (Reprinted from *The South Sea
Bubble,* by John Carswell, with the permission of the publishers, Stanford University
Press. © Copyright 1960 by John Carswell. By permission of Cresset Press Limited.)

### 4. THE CLUBS, COFFEEHOUSES, AND SALONS

The Golden Age of Clubs    Donald McCormick
    Donald McCormick, *The Hell-Fire Club,* London: Jarrolds, 1958, pp. 11–16, 17–
18, 19–23, 24–25. (By permission of Jarrolds and David Higham Associates,
Limited.)

The Significance of the French Salons    Albert Guérard
    Albert Guérard, *France, a Modern History,* Ann Arbor, Mich.: University of
Michigan Press, 1959, pp. 205–207. (Reprinted from *France, a Modern History* by
Albert Guérard by permission of the University of Michigan Press. © by the University
of Michigan, 1959.)

## 5. THE CHARACTER OF EIGHTEENTH-CENTURY TRAVEL

The Grand Tour    J. H. Plumb
  J. H. Plumb, *Man and Centuries*, Boston: Houghton Mifflin Company, 1963, pp. 56–66. (By permission of Houghton Mifflin Company. By permission of J. H. Plumb.)

Touring England    Dorothy Marshall
  Dorothy Marshall, *English People in the Eighteenth Century*, London: Longmans, Green & Co., Ltd., 1962, pp. 131–133. (By permission of Longmans, Green & Co., Limited.)

English Inns    E. W. Bovill
  E. W. Bovill, *English Country Life, 1780–1830*, London: Oxford University Press, 1962, pp. 136–138. (By permission of Oxford University Press.)

## 6. THE EXPANSION AND TRANSFORMATION OF THE READING PUBLIC

The Growth of the Popular Press    Raymond Williams
  Raymond Williams, *The Long Revolution*, New York: Columbia University Press, 1961, and London: Chatto and Windus, Ltd., 1961, pp. 179–185. (By permission of Columbia University Press. By permission of Chatto and Windus, Limited.)

The Novel As a Reflection of Middle-Class Attitudes    David Daiches
  David Daiches, *A Critical History of English Literature*, 2 vols., New York: Ronald Press, 1960, vol. 1, pp. 700, 701–702, 705–708, 710. (David Daiches—*A Critical History of English Literature*. Copyright © 1960 The Ronald Press Company, New York. By permission of Martin Secker & Warburg, Limited, Publishers.)

## 7. THE NEW POPULARITY OF OPERA

Composers and Audiences    Donald J. Grout
  Donald J. Grout, *A Short History of Opera*, 2d ed., New York: Columbia University Press, 1966, pp. 199–200. (By permission of Columbia University Press.)

The New Paris Opera    Norman Demuth
  Norman Demuth, *French Opera*, Sussex: Artemis Press, 1963, pp. 225–226, 227–228. (By permission of the Artemis Press, Limited.)

## 8. PROLETARIAN LIFE IN THE NEW INDUSTRIAL TOWNS

Adjustment and Survival in the Early Machine Age    J. L. and Barbara Hammond
  J. L. and Barbara Hammond, *The Town Laborer, 1765–1832*, London: Longmans, Green & Co., Ltd., 1920, pp. 39–41, 43–44, 45–46, 48–53. (By permission of Longmans, Green & Co., Limited.)

## 9. EVANGELISM: THE RELIGION OF EXPERIENCE AND EMOTION

The Fervent Popular Response to Methodist Preaching    R. A. Knox
  R. A. Knox, *Enthusiasm, A Chapter in the History of Religion*, Oxford: Clarendon Press, 1950, pp. 520–526. (By permission of the Clarendon Press, Oxford.)

The Great Revival in America    Bernard A. Weisberger
  Bernard A. Weisberger, *They Gathered At the River*, Boston: Little, Brown and Company, 1958, pp. 20–22. (Copyright, © 1958, by Bernard A. Weisberger. From *They Gathered at the River*, by Bernard A. Weisberger, by permission of Little, Brown and Co.)

## 10. SOLDIERS AND SAILORS OF THE REVOLUTIONARY ERA

The Morale of the Napoleonic Armies    David G. Chandler
  David G. Chandler, *The Campaigns of Napoleon*, New York: The Macmillan Company, 1966, pp. 155–157, 159–161. (Reprinted with permission of The Macmillan Company from *The Campaigns of Napoleon* by David G. Chandler. Copyright © David G. Chandler 1966.)

The British Sailor    Arthur Bryant
  Arthur Bryant, *The Fire and the Rose*, London: Collins, 1966, pp. 129–134. (From *The Fire and the Rose*, by Arthur Bryant. Copyright © 1965 by Sir Arthur Bryant. Reprinted by permission of Doubleday & Company, Inc. Reprinted by permission of A. D. Peters & Co.)

## 11. POPULAR UPRISINGS

Eighteeth-Century Mobs    George Rudé
  George Rudé, *The Crowd in History*, New York: John Wiley & Sons, Inc., 1964, pp. 49–52. (By permission of John Wiley & Sons, Incorporated.)

The Rising of the Paris Masses    Alfred Cobban
  Alfred Cobban, *A History of Modern France*, rev. ed., 2 vols., London: Jonathan Cape, Ltd., 1961, vol. 1, pp. 153–154, 157–158, 160–162. (George Braziller, Inc. —from *A History of Modern France* by Alfred Cobban; reprinted with the permission of the publisher. © 1965 by Alfred Cobban. By permission of Jonathan Cape, Ltd., Publishers. By permission of Penguin Books, Limited.)

## 12. THE NEW SENSIBILITY

The Coming of Romanticism    David Daiches
  David Daiches, *A Critical History of English Literature*, 2 vols., New York: Ronald Press, 1960, vol. 1, pp. 858–862. (David Daiches—*A Critical History of English Literature*. Copyright © 1960 The Ronald Press Company, New York. By permission of Martin Secker & Warburg, Limited, Publishers.)

Napoleon As a Romantic Hero    Pieter Geyl
  Pieter Geyl, *Napoleon: For and Against*, New Haven, Conn.: Yale University Press, 1949, pp. 23–24. (By permission of Yale University Press. By permission of Jonathan Cape, Ltd., Publishers. By permission of the Executors of the Pieter Geyl Estate.)

# Contents

# *Introduction*

Man's culture is the complex of all he knows, all he possesses, and all he does. His laws and religious beliefs, his art and morals, his customs and ideas are the content of his culture. The dimensions and forms these various elements take determine the nature and quality of a culture. A society whose dominant concern is warfare will be quite different from one in which religious devotion is uppermost in the lives of the people. But cultures differ not only one from the other; every culture is divided into numerous subcultures with patterns of thought and behavior which distinguish the life of the hunter from that of the shopkeeper, the customs of the city dweller from those of the farmer, the manners of the child from those of the adult. And cutting across cultural and subcultural boundaries is the fundamental distinction between work and play: between what is done of necessity and what is done by choice.

George Santayana, writing about the distinctions between work and play, indicated the importance of the things men do when they are not engaged in the fight for survival or in the avoidance of pain. He said:

> We may measure the degree of happiness and civilization which any race has attained by the proportion of its energy which is devoted to free and generous pursuits, to the adornment of life and the culture of the imagination. For it is in the spontaneous play of his faculties that man finds himself and his happiness. Slavery is the most degrading condition of which he is capable, and he is as often a slave to the niggardness of the earth and the inclemency of heaven, as to a master or an institution. He is a a slave when all his energy is spent in avoiding suffering and

death, when all his action is imposed from without, and no
breath or strength is left him for free enjoyment. . . . Work and
play here take on a different meaning and become equivalent to
servitude and freedom. . . . We no longer mean by work all that is
done usefully, but only what is done unwillingly and by the spur
of necessity. By play we are designating, no longer what is done
fruitlessly, but whatever is done spontaneously and for its own
sake, whether it have or not an ulterior utility.

Popular culture may be seen as all those things man does and all those
artifacts he creates for their own sake, all that diverts his mind and body
from the sad business of life. Popular culture is really what people do
when they are not working; it is man in pursuit of pleasure, excitement,
beauty, and fulfillment.

This book is an anthology describing and discussing all elements of
popular culture from ancient times to 1815. The selections show the relations of the various facets of popular culture with one another and
trace the impact of popular culture itself on the whole pattern of social
interaction and change. The extracts are drawn from serious studies in
social history, from the works of historians, sociologists, and critics
whose concern is human behavior and the nature of human society.
Each of the four parts covers an historical era whose cultural components distinguish it from all others. The book presents a panorama
of the content and quality of popular culture over more than twenty
centuries.

This examination of the myriad of human pursuits reveals that no
single aspect of popular culture controls or determines the course or
composition of all others. No general rule indicating that culture moves
from the rich and powerful classes downward to other social groups is
evident. Influences seem to move in all directions with varying degrees
of force. A preoccupation with military prowess and courage may have
been fundamental to the culture of medieval noblemen, but the impress
of these elements upon the amusements and diversions of the peasants
was minor. Religious fervor, on the other hand, can explode over the
entire social spectrum, instilling in men of all classes the desire to use
their time and energy in the creation of suitable instruments for the
fulfillment of their devotion and inspiring them into acts of high purpose touching their faith. Even the cultural components of social groups
whose power and influence in society would seem logically to be strictly
limited may be taken up by members of more influential segments of
the community or even be incorporated into the popular culture of the
general society itself. Thus, in the contemporary era, the subculture of
the young has been adopted by the adult population, putting suburban

matrons into miniskirts, getting diplomats to dance to rock and roll bands, and making the jargon of teenagers a source for the rhetoric of academicians. Similarly, the tastes and standards of the very lowest elements of society can find their way eventually into the customs and manners of the very highest status groups. Fashions and attitudes that in one era were to be found only in the house of ill repute filter through the social system, capturing entertainers, socialites, working people, and even the young, who may well have no knowledge of the origins of their behavioral patterns. And so high school girls in the middle of the twentieth century can wear clothes and makeup which in the eighteenth century would have been suitable only for a Fanny Hill.

Changes in popular culture often depend on the exposure of the members of a social group to external influences which shape their taste and behavior. It is obvious, therefore, that as technology has increased the potential of communication, the expansion and enrichment of popular culture has been facilitated. When people play out their lives in limited geographical areas, the possibility of cross-cultural contacts and influences is greatly diminished. Similarly, when the vast majority of humankind are illiterate, the dissemination of cultural information is circumscribed. But printing, railroads, steamships, radio, and television make it easy for people and ideas to move about with great speed and relative facility. This means that in the modern era the forms of popular culture have multiplied enormously, and at the same time the possibility for people of divergent backgrounds to share the same cultural experience has become a reality.

The vastly increased occasions for entertainment provided by mass transportation and mass media and by the provision of money and leisure for more and more people have had the effect not of satiating man's hunger for diversion, but of amplifying it. Man's need and desire for enjoyment, excitement, and beauty seem to be unlimited. The more intense and varied the cultural offerings, the greater his demand for yet more amusement. Participation in leisure activities is equated with the good life, with a man's desire to do with his time and energy what he will. It is in popular culture, in the organized, structured, and institutionalized activities of play, that man learns and practices social interaction in a manner least threatening to his position and well-being. In games and leisure activities he can work out his aggressions, indulge his fantasies, and test his abilities without risking serious scorn or censure. There is a freedom and spontaneity in play not permitted man in his workaday existence. Involvement in and enjoyment of popular culture permit the participant freedom to be himself.

Play is not frivolous; it is a serious matter centering on how men treat one another, a reflection of man's needs, aspirations, and nature.

The rules which regulate the games people play differ from those prescribed for most human activities inasmuch as a man may choose to play or be a spectator or absent himself altogether. These choices are not open in the larger, more public game of life that depends on political and economic compulsion. The quality of volition therefore informs the whole history of popular culture. In that history is described what men have done and are doing with their capabilities, and further, it measures human potentiality not by showing what man can be forced to do, but by demonstrating what he can do when left to his own devices, free to follow the inclinations of his mind and spirit.

# Part One. THE CLASSICAL WORLD, TO A.D. 450

Life in the ancient world, for all but the tiny minority of the richest and most powerful, was extremely harsh and often quite short. The earth yielded its fruits reluctantly, disease cut a wide swath through populations possessed of little more than the rudiments of medicine and public hygiene, and political unrest, class struggle, and war made existence seem an unending cycle of violence and death. But the limitations in technology and the urgency of the fight for subsistence did not mean life in the classical world was devoid of popular amusements and private relaxation. No aspect of life is lacking in opportunities for converting otherwise serious activities into celebration and entertainment. And ancient men, perhaps for the very reason that their lives were so circumscribed by work and worry, tapped every resource to find occasions for play. Furthermore, when society has not yet reached the degree of complexity that supplies entertainment as a specialized facet of life, the most basic elements of the civilization are the material for popular culture.

Ancient tribal, religious, political, military, commercial, agricultural, and familial interactions were carried on with the embellishments of ceremony which made their performance occasions for the diversion of the participants and spectators alike. Beauty and entertainment, excitement, and the chance for a respite from toil were found everywhere. And those who performed the diverting social acts as well as those who watched or assisted were seldom professional entertainers; they were people with other full-time occupations for whom such cultural activities were a secondary but eagerly awaited portion of life—the portion adding spice and verve to an existence marked by strain and dreariness.

Ancient Greek athletics involved sport, ritual, training for war, and the opportunity for glory without death. In the Olympic Games the Greeks found a way for the representatives of all the Greek states to meet and compete under a single, binding set of rules. These games were the sole occasion of unreserved Panhellenism in the classical era. Not even the invasion of Greece by the Persians could bring the various states together, but every four years the Greeks met at Olympia to play games—games whose seriousness is indicated by the very fact of their perpetuation throughout the epoch. It seems logical, then, to begin Part One with a discussion of Greek athletics and the ancient Olympic Games.

The remainder of Part One touches upon Greek and Roman popular culture in the ancient era. The chapter on the Greek drama captures the spirit of those festivals, picturing what it was like to see the plays and parades, and commenting on the nature of the audiences, actors, and playwrights. The various aspects of sexual and marital life are given extensive treatment, and the proliferation of prostitution and homosexual love is carefully discussed. Roman popular culture, as the selections contained here demonstrate, involved more state support and participation than did that of Greece. The great amphitheaters, the marketplaces, and the baths were the creations of the state, built at public expense for the diversion of the populace. The private lives of the wealthy Romans were marked by luxury and self-indulgence. Because of the elitist nature of Roman society, the habits and home life of the aristocrats have an even greater significance for ancient popular culture than do the personal diversions of the common people. Similarly, the feasting and revelry of the villas was in striking contrast to the rather crude circumstances of the garrison troops on the Empire's frontiers.

The final chapter of this part serves to explain the transition between the ancient and medieval cultures. The selections trace the major and typical religious forms and practices of the classical world, highlighting the degree of popular involvement in these rituals and mass commitment to them, a commitment which superseded and survived the collapse of classical culture.

# 1.  Greek Athletics As Sport and Ritual

## Games the Greeks Played
&§ E. Norman Gardiner

The story of ancient athletics is the story of Greek athletics. The Greeks, as far as we know, were the only truly athletic nation of antiquity. To them we owe the word 'athlete' and the ideal that it expresses. This does not mean that the Greeks were the inventors of the various sports and games that we describe as athletic. The love of play is universal in all young things. Running, jumping, throwing various objects, fighting are common to children of all races and all times. But play is not athletics, though the instinct of play is undoubtedly one of their motives, and recreation is an important element therein. The child plays till he is tired and then leaves off. The competitor in a race goes on after he is tired, goes on to the point of absolute exhaustion; he even trains himself painfully in order to be capable of greater and more prolonged effort and of exhausting himself more completely. Why does he do this? Why does he take pleasure in what is naturally painful?

The idea of effort is the very essence of athletics as the Greeks understood the term and as we understand it; it is indeed inherent in the word itself. For the Greek word from which athlete is derived has two forms, a masculine form . . . usually meaning a contest, and a neuter form . . . usually denoting the prize of the contest. Of these two meanings there can be no doubt that the idea of contest is the earlier and root-meaning, for it determines the meaning of the words derived from it. The word is used by Homer to describe the ten years' struggle of the Trojan War; it is used of the labours of Heracles. This meaning of the word is clearest in the adjective . . . formed from it, which from meaning 'struggling,' 'contesting' comes to mean 'miserable,' 'wretched.'

We find this same feeling in Homer when he describes boxing and wrestling as 'grievous' ..., an epithet which he also uses of war and battle. Yet the Homeric warrior delights in these grievous contests, and Pindar describes the athlete as one 'who delights in the toil and the cost.' We too have the same feelings. The game that appeals to every true athlete, the game that he delights in, one that he remembers when his playing days are over, is 'the hard game', the game that puts to the utmost test all his physical powers and all his skill.

But why does the athlete delight in the grievous contest? Why do we enjoy a hard game? The athlete is one who competes for something, but it is certainly not the material value of the prize that attracts him. The prize may be an ox, or a woman skilled in fair handicraft, a tripod, or a cup, but the most coveted prize in the Greek world was the wreath of wild olive which was the only prize at the Olympic Games. The real prize is the honour of victory. The motive that turns his effort into joy is the desire to put to the test his physical powers, the desire to excel. It is not every people any more than every individual that feels this joy in the contest, in the effort. The athletic spirit cannot exist where conditions of life are too soft and luxurious; it cannot exist where conditions are too hard and where all the physical energies are exhausted in a constant struggle with the forces of man or nature. It is found only in physically vigorous and virile nations that put a high value on physical excellence: it arises naturally in those societies where the power is in the hands of an aristocracy which depends on military skill and physical strength to maintain itself. Here are developed the love of fighting and the love of glory, and here we find the beginnings of athletics in wrestling, boxing, and other forms of combat which are the training of the young and the recreation of the warriors. Such were the conditions among the Homeric Achaeans, and probably among many of the tribes of central Europe. But for the tradition which the Greeks inherited from the Achaeans the later development of Greek athletics would have been impossible. And we may doubt whether the modern athletic movement would ever have taken place but for the spirit handed down to us by our Anglo-Saxon ancestors. ...

In the case of some festivals founded in historical times we know that athletic sports were instituted from the first. We know too that in other cases games were added later. Thus athletic competitions were not introduced into the Pythian festival till the sixth century, though the festival itself and the musical contests were many centuries older.

Festivals arose from various origins. Many, and those the oldest, were connected with vegetation rites and the farmer's year, others were connected with the worship of some particular god or hero at some particular place. Many festivals originated in funeral games in honour of some chieftain, or soldier, or of those who fell in battle fighting for their country, a practice which we have seen goes back to Homeric times. Others were founded in commemoration of victory. Of this we have an example in Pindar's legend about Heracles at Olympia. In all these festivals games might be added, but there was no ritual meaning in the games themselves which were purely secular. They were added because festivals were times of peace when men gathered together peaceably under the protection of the gods, and the love of competition that characterized the race found its opportunity in such a gathering.

At the same time it may well be that sports were felt to be particularly appropriate to certain festivals. They were appropriate at funeral games where they might be supposed to be pleasing to the spirit of the deceased who had in his lifetime found his pleasure therein. They were appropriate in games connected with victory. The remnant of Xenophon's Ten Thousand celebrated their return to safety by a sacrifice to Zeus Soter and by games. Sports were appropriate to the festivals of certain gods or heroes, e.g. to those supposed to be the special patrons of sport, Apollo, Hermes, or Heracles. If ... the Olympic festival was from the first the festival of Olympian Zeus, the god of hosts, and was a cessation from war, such sports were particularly appropriate there.

But though the connexion between sport and religion was due to the athletic genius of the race rather than to any ritual significance in the games, we must not underrate the importance of this connexion. Thereby sports were definitely placed under the patronage of the gods, and the victorious athlete felt that he was well pleasing to the gods and owed his success to them. Further, the athlete felt that any violation of the rules of the games, especially any unfairness or corruption, was an act of sacrilege and displeasing to the gods. This feeling undoubtedly tended to preserve the purity of sport at Olympia even when corruption was rife elsewhere. Religious conservatism too tended to check any innovations and accordingly, though additions were made to the programme, the events remained essentially unchanged for nearly twelve centuries. It was to religion that Greek athletics and Greek athletic festivals owed their vitality. . . .

THE ANCIENT OLYMPICS. Now let me try to picture a typical festival. I will take the Olympic festival about the middle of the fifth century; it is the greatest of all Greek festivals, and the half-century that followed the Persian wars was its most splendid period. It is thus the festival and the period of which we know most. At the same time it must be remembered that our knowledge of it is very imperfect and often derived from late authors. Many of the details of the festival, the order of events for example, are uncertain, but the

general outlines are clear. We shall see at least that though the actual
competitions are in many respects similar to our own, the Olympic
festival was something very different from any modern athletic meeting,
even from the modern Olympic Games. It was much more than a
mere athletic meeting. It was the national religious festival of the whole
Greek race. Olympia was the meeting place of the Greek world....

The festival took place every four years, on the second or third full
moon alternately after the summer solstice, in the months of August
or September. Some months before the three sacred 'truce bearers of
Zeus' set out from Olympia wearing crowns of olive and bearing
heralds' staves. They travelled through the length and breadth of the
Greek world, and to every state they proclaimed the Sacred Truce and
invited them to the festival. From that time all competitors or visitors
travelling to or from Olympia were under the protection of the god.

Competitors, it seems, had to arrive at Elis a month at least before
the festival; and there they underwent the last part of their training
under the eyes of the Hellanodikai, the official judges of the games.
The training at Elis was noted for its severity: the Hellanodikai
exacted implicit obedience and enforced it unsparingly with the rod.
During this month they could test the capabilities of the candidates,
and satisfy themselves of their parentage, for only those of pure Greek
birth were allowed to compete. Above all, they had an opportunity for
judging the claims of boys and colts to compete as such. Philostratus
tells us that at the close of the training they called together the competitors and addressed them in these words:

'If you have exercised yourselves in a manner worthy of Olympia, if
you have been guilty of no slothful or ignoble act, go on with a good
courage. You who have not so practised go whither you will.'

Meanwhile, visitors of all classes and from every part were flocking
to Olympia. The whole Greek world was represented, from Marseilles
to the Black Sea, from Thrace to Africa. There were official embassies
representing the various states, richly equipped; there were spectators
from every part, men of every class. Men, I say: for the only people
excluded from the festival were married women, and even if unmarried
women were allowed to be present, few probably availed themselves
of the right except those from the neighbourhood. Apart from this
Olympia was open to all without distinction, to hardy peasants and
fishermen of the Peloponnese and to nobles and tyrants from the rich
states of Sicily or Italy. All had the same rights. There was no accommodation for them except such as they could provide or procure
for themselves; there were no reserved seats at the games, indeed there
were no seats at all. The plain outside the Altis [the area in which the
games were held] was one great fair, full of tents and booths. There

you might meet everyone who wished to see or to be seen, to sell or to buy; politicians and soldiers, philosophers and men of letters, poets ready to write odes in honour of victors in the games, sculptors to provide them with statues, perhaps already made, horse-dealers from Elis, pedlars of votive offerings, charms, and amulets, peasants with their wine-skins and baskets of fruit and provisions, acrobats and conjurers, who were as dear to the Greek as to the modern crowd. . . .

The festival lasted five days, from the twelfth to the sixteenth of the month. The first day was occupied with preliminary business and sacrifices, there were no competitions. The principal ceremony was the solemn scrutiny of the competitors in the Council House. There stood a statue of Zeus Horkios, the God of Oaths, who was represented with a thunderbolt in either hand ready to blast any who broke his oath. Before this awe-inspiring statue the competitors, their trainers, their fathers, and their brothers took their stand, and, having sacrificed a pig, swore on its entrails that they would use no unfair means to secure victory. The competitors further swore that for ten months they had trained in a manner worthy of the festival. Then the judges who decided on the eligibility of boys and colts to compete as such swore to give their decisions honestly and not to reveal the reasons for their decisions.

Throughout the day there were many other sacrifices and rites, both public and private, of which we know nothing. Competitors would offer their vows at the altars of the various gods or heroes whom they regarded as their patrons. The superstitious would consult the sooth-sayers as to their chances of success. Others would go off to the Stadium for a final practice. The crowd of sightseers would wander round the Altis, following in the train of some celebrity, athletic or otherwise, admiring the sculptures of the new temple, or listening to some rhapsodist reciting Homer, some poet reading his verses, some orator displaying his eloquence or sophistries. There were friends, too, to be seen, friends from all parts of the Mediterranean, for all came back to Olympia as to their mother-country.

The games started on the second day with the chariot-race and the horse-race. The Hippodrome lay to the south of the Stadium, the embankment of which bounded it on the north. Like the Stadium, it was merely a long rectangle surrounded by embankments, but larger. The actual course was marked by a pillar at either end round which the chariots and horses turned, but there was no wall, like the spina of the Roman Circus, connecting them. Not a trace of the Hippodrome remains and its dimensions are very uncertain. According to a document found at Constantinople, of somewhat doubtful authority, the distance between the pillars was three stades or about 600 yards. Elsewhere the distance was two stades.

At the western entrance of the Hippodrome was a colonnade, the portico of Agnaptos, and in front of it was a most elaborate starting-gate. Pausanius describes it as shaped like the prow of a ship, the sharp end pointing down the course. Its sides were 400 feet long and along them were arranged parallel pairs of stalls in front of each of which a rope was stretched. Here the competing chariots or horses were placed. ... In the centre of the structure was an altar on which stood an eagle with outstretched wings; at the point was a bronze dolphin. When the official starter touched a piece of mechanism the eagle rose in the air and the dolphin dropped. This was the signal for starting, but we may suspect that it was not really given till the chariots were actually in line. The manner of starting was as follows. First the ropes in front of the pair nearest to the base were withdrawn, and the chariots started. As they drew level with the next pair, the ropes in front of these were withdrawn, and so on till when they reached the peak of the prow all were in line. The object of this elaborate arrangement must have been chiefly spectacular, and the racing did not actually start till all were in line. Whether this complicated starting-gate existed in the fifth century, we do not know. In the description of the chariot-race at Delphi in the *Electra* of Sophocles, there is no suggestion of any starting-gate. The chariots were drawn up in a line and started by the trumpet.

Early in the morning the crowds began to gather in the Hippo-drome, occupying every place of vantage, especially at the ends where the chariots turned and accidents were most frequent. There were no seats except for the officials. The spectators sat or stood on the embankments, bareheaded under the scorching sun, often, as the day wore on, suffering severely from thirst and dust. There they waited till the official procession arrived. First came the Hellanodikai, or judges, robed in purple with garlands on their heads, the herald, trumpeter, and other officials, then the competitors, the chariots, and the horses. The judges took their seats and, as the chariots and horses passed before them, the herald proclaimed the name of each competitor, his father's name, and his city, and asked if any man had any charge to bring against him. Then he proclaimed the opening of the games and the chief Hellanodikas or some other distinguished person addressed the competitors.

The first event was the four-horse chariot race, the most brilliant and exciting of all the competitions, the sport of kings in the Greek world; for only the rich could afford the expense of a racing stable. The chariots were light cars mounted on two wheels, with a rail in front and at the sides, and room only for the charioteer to stand. The two middle horses who did the work were harnessed to the yoke attached to the chariot-pole, the outside horses were harnessed only by traces. The charioteer wore a long white robe, he carried a whip or goad, and held the reins in his left hand or in both. . . .

Once more the herald proclaimed the names of the competitors: lots were drawn for position, and the names perhaps were written on a white board. Then the chariots took their places at the start, the trumpet sounded, and the race began. The fields were large, sometimes as many as forty chariots competing. Alcibiades boasted that he himself had on one occasion entered seven chariots. Fortunately the course was long, twelve double laps, 72 stades or nearly 9 miles, and the pace must have been slow at first. But it must have been a thrilling sight to see a field of even ten chariots such as Sophocles describes in the *Electra*, all racing for the turning-post at the far end of the course. For to be first round the turn must have been a great advantage. It is no easy task to turn a team of four horses sharp round a post, but to do so in a field of ten chariots or more, all striving to be first, must have taxed nerve and skill to the utmost. No wonder that accidents were frequent. For it was not one turn only, but twenty-three turns, that the charioteer had to negotiate: and few must have been the chariots that reached the last lap safely. We are not surprised that in the race where forty chariots competed the chariot of Arcesilaus of Cyrene alone survived. When the last lap was reached the excitement of the spectators knew no bounds, they shouted, leapt from their seats waving their garments, wildly embracing one another.

When the race was over the owner of the victorious chariot advanced and bound a fillet round the head of his charioteer. For though in heroic times the heroes drove their own chariots, the rich nobles and princes of the fifth century, like rich owners to-day, employed professional charioteers and jockeys. The owner, however, as he does to-day, received the prize. Leading, perhaps, his chariot, he advanced to the place where the judges sat. Beside them was a table of gold and ivory on which were placed the crowns of olive leaves cut from the sacred wild olive tree behind the temple of Zeus. Then the herald proclaimed the name of the victor, his father, and his city . . . , and the chief Hellanodikas placed upon his head the crown . . . , while the people shouted and pelted him with flowers and branches.

Next came the horse-race. It was started in the same way, but the distance was only one lap of six stades. The jockeys rode without shoes or stirrups. . . . The horse-race and the four-horse chariot-race were the only events in the Hippodrome at the beginning of the fifth century. Early in the century, a riding race for mares and a mule chariot-race were introduced, but these events were discontinued in 444 B.C. In 408 B.C. a two-horse chariot-race was added, and in the next century three races for colts.

When the horse-races were finished the crowd hurried over the embankment to the Stadium to witness the pentathlon. The first four events in this competition, the foot-race, the long jump, the diskos, and the javelin, took place in the Stadium, the last event, the wrestling-match, in the open space in front of the Altar. . . .

The pentathlon occupied the rest of the day. Then in the evening, under the brightness of the mid-month moon, the precinct rang with revelry and song. The victors and their friends, with garlands on their heads, went in joyous procession round the Altis, chanting as they went the old triumphal hymn of Heracles, written by Archilochus, or some new hymn of victory composed by Pindar or Bacchylides. The procession was followed by banquets given by the victors to their friends. Sometimes a rich victor like Alcibiades would feast the whole assembly, and the revelry would last the whole night.

The third day, the day of the full moon, was the great day of the festival, when the official sacrifice was offered on the Altar of Zeus. The procession started from the Prytaneion. First came the Hellanodikai in their purple robes, the seers and priests, the attendants leading the victims for the sacrifice; then the Theoriai, the official deputations from the states of Greece, having in their hands costly vessels of silver and gold; after them the competitors, chariots, horsemen, athletes, trainers, and their friends. The procession moved along the boundary of the Altis, passed between the Council House and the Temple of Zeus, then made its way through the avenue of statues and monuments in front of the Temple of the Great Altar. The priests and seers mounted the ramp that led to the platform in front of the Altar, and there in the sight of all the people a hundred oxen were sacrificed. The thighs were taken to the top of the Altar and burnt, the rest of the flesh was removed to the Prytaneion to be cooked for the feast.

The sacrifice took place in the morning. In the afternoon the competitions for boys took place, the foot-race, wrestling, and boxing, and the evening was given up to revelry. The chief athletic events were reserved for the fourth day. The morning was occupied by the three foot-races in the Stadium, the afternoon by the three fighting events, wrestling, boxing, and the pancration [a combination of boxing and wrestling]. These last took place, not in the Stadium, but in the Altis, in front of the Altar. Here the ties were drawn in the presence of the Hellanodikai. Lots marked in pairs with the letters of the alphabet were put into a silver urn. Each competitor uttered a prayer to Zeus and drew a lot, holding it in his hand but not looking at it till all were drawn. Then the Hellanodikas went round and examined the lots, pairing off the competitors accordingly. The programme ended with the race in armour, and once more there was an evening of revelry.

The last day of the festival was spent in feasting and rejoicing. The victorious paid their vows at the altars of the gods. Of the other rites and sacrifices that occupied the day we know nothing, save that the victors were entertained at a banquet in the Prytaneion.

# 2. Popular Aspects of Greek Drama

### The Audiences of Greek Drama

*A. E. Haigh*

The theatre of Dionysus at Athens, during the period of the Lenaea and the City Dionysia [religious festivals at which the plays were produced], presented a spectacle which for interest and significance has few parallels in the ancient or the modern world. On these occasions the city kept universal holiday. Business and politics were forgotten; the law-courts were closed; even prisoners were released from gaol, to enable them to partake in the general rejoicings. The deity in honour of whom the festivals had been established was Dionysus, the god of wine, and the type of the productive power of nature. The various proceedings were in reality so many religious celebrations. But there was nothing of an austere character about the worship of Dionysus. To give freedom from care was his special attribute, and the sincerest mode of paying homage to his power was by a genial enjoyment of the various pleasures of life. At this time of universal merriment the dramatic performances formed the principal attraction. Each day soon after sunrise the great majority of the citizens made their way to the southern slopes of the Acropolis, where the theatre of Dionysus was situated. The tiers of seats rising up the side of the hill were speedily filled with a crowd of nearly twenty thousand persons. The sight of such a vast multitude of people, gathered together at daybreak in the huge open amphitheatre, and dressed for the most part in white, or in red, brown, yellow, and other rich colours, must have been exceedingly striking and picturesque. The performances which brought them to-gether were not unworthy of the occasion. The plays exhibited at the festivals of Dionysus rank among the very noblest achievements of Greek genius. For beauty of form, depth of meaning, and poetical inspiration they have never been surpassed. The point of unique interest about the Greek drama is the superlative excellence of its productions, combined with the fact that it was essentially a national amusement, designed for the entertainment of the great mass of the citizens. It would be difficult to point to any similar example of the whole population of a city meeting together each year to enjoy works of the highest artistic beauty. It is seldom that art and poetry have penetrated so deeply into the life of the ordinary citizens. Our curiosity is naturally excited in regard to the tone and composition of the audiences before which a drama of such an exceptional character was exhibited. . . .

At the Lenaea, which was held in the winter, when traveling was difficult, the audience consisted almost exclusively of natives of Athens. The City Dionysia came about two months later, at the commencement of the spring, and attracted great crowds of strangers from various parts of Greece. Representatives from the allied states came to pay the annual tribute at this season of the year. It was also a favourite time for the arrival of ambassadors from foreign cities; and it was considered a mere matter of politeness to provide them with front seats in the theatre, if they happened to be in Athens during the celebration of the City Dionysia. In addition to these visitors of a representative character, there were also great numbers of private individuals, attracted to Athens from all parts of Greece by the magnificence of the festival, and the fame of the dramatic exhibitions. Altogether the visitors formed a considerable portion of the audience at the City Dionysia. . . . The audience at the dramatic performances, whether tragic or comic, was drawn from every class of the population. Men, women, boys, and slaves were all allowed to be present. The evidence from ancient authors is too copious to be accounted for on any other supposition. . . . Even the story of the effect produced by the Eumenides of Aeschylus upon the audience—of the boys dying of fright and the women having miscarriages—such a story, though in itself a foolish invention, could hardly have originated unless women and boys had been regularly present at the theatre. . . .

No doubt at first sight it appears a very startling fact that women and boys should have been spectators of the Old Comedy. But it should always be remembered that the comedies performed at the festivals of Dionysus were a portion of a religious celebration, which it was a pious duty to take part in. Ribaldry and coarseness were a traditional element in the worship of Dionysus, handed down from rude and primitive times, and were not lightly to be dispensed with. The Greeks in such matters were thoroughly conservative. It was a feeling of this kind which caused the satyric drama to be developed side by side with

tragedy, in order that the old licentious merriment of the satyrs might
not be utterly forgotten. The coarseness of the Old Comedy, being a
regular part of the celebrations in honour of Dionysus, might be
witnessed by boys and women without degradation, though their
presence at similar scenes in real life would have been regarded in a
very different manner. Where the worship of the gods was concerned,
the practice of keeping women in strict seclusion was allowed to drop
into abeyance. Women and even girls were present at the phallic
processions in honour of Dionysus. Their appearance an such occasions
was regarded as a mere matter of course. It need not therefore surprise
us that women and boys should have been present in the theatre at the
performances of the Old Comedy.

Whether they were ever present in large numbers is a further question. Even those writers who admit that their presence was not prohibited by law, generally add that the more respectable women would
in all probability keep away. But the only authority for such a notion
is to be found in a couple of passages in Aristophanes, which represent the husband as present in the theatre, while the wife was at
home. There is nothing so unusual in an occurrence of this kind as to
warrant any sweeping conclusions. Some people must necessarily have
remained at home, from the mere fact that the theatre would not have
been large enough to contain the whole population of Athens, if men,
women, and children had all been present. But it is hardly probable ... that there was anything disreputable in a woman visiting the
theatre. Reformers like Aristotle were in advance of ordinary public
opinion in their feelings about such matters. There is a passage in
Aristotle's Politics which is of great interest as showing the general
sentiment on the subject. Aristotle expresses a strong opinion that boys
should be prevented from seeing or hearing any piece of coarseness or
indecency. Even if such ribaldry is an essential feature in the worship
of any particular deity, he says that only men should be allowed to
be present. The men should pay the proper homage to gods of this
character on behalf of themselves, their wives, and their children; but
boys should not be permitted to be witnesses of comedies and similar
spectacles. This passage, in which Aristotle is combating the prevailing
practice of the times, is an additional proof that boys were present at
the performance of comedies, and shows clearly that when the worship
of the gods was concerned ordinary public opinion did not consider
such spectacles improper.

Besides women and children it appears that slaves were occasionally
present at the theatre. Plato in the Gorgias mentions slaves as one of
the classes before which the tragic poets will not be allowed to perform
in his ideal commonwealth. The shameless man described by Theo-

phrastus takes the 'paedagogus' to the theatre, along with his sons, and crowds them all into seats which did not really belong to him. It is not, however, probable that the number of slaves among the audience was ever very great. Their presence would depend upon the kindness of their masters. But the two passages just quoted prove that there was no law to prevent their attendance. . . .

AUDIENCE RESPONSE. The Athenians were a lively audience, and gave expression to their feelings in the most unmistakable manner. The noise and uproar produced by an excited crowd of twenty thousand persons must have been of a deafening character, and is described in the most uncomplimentary language by Plato. It was exceedingly difficult for the judges to resist such demonstrations, and to vote in accordance with their own private judgment. The ordinary modes of signifying pleasure or disgust were much the same in ancient as in modern times, and consisted of hisses and groans on the one hand, and shouts and clapping of hands on the other. The Athenians had also a peculiar way of marking their disapproval of a performance by kicking with the heels of their sandals against the front of the stone benches on which they were sitting. Stones were occasionally thrown by an irate audience. Aeschines was hissed off the stage, and 'almost stoned to death,' in the course of his theatrical career. There is an allusion to the practice in the story of the second-rate musician, who borrowed a supply of stone from a friend in order to build a house, and promised to repay him with the stones he collected from his next performance in public. Country audiences in the Attic demes used figs and olives, and similar missiles, for pelting unpopular actors. On the other hand, encores were not unknown, if particular passages took the fancy of the audience. Socrates is said to have encored the first three lines of the Orestes of Euripides.

If the Athenians were dissatisfied with an actor or a play, they had no hesitation about revealing the fact, but promptly put a stop to the performance by means of hisses and groans and stamping with the heels. They were able to do so with greater readiness, as several plays were always performed in succession, and they could call for the next play, without bringing the entertainment to a close. In this way they sometimes got through the programme very rapidly. There is an instance of such an occurrence in the story of the comic actor Hermon, whose play should naturally have come on late in the day; but, as all the previous performers were promptly hissed off the stage one after another, he was called upon much sooner than he expected, and in consequence was not ready to appear. If the tale about the comic poet Diphilus is true, it would seem that even the authors of very unsuccessful plays were sometimes forcibly ejected from the theatre.

A few scattered notices and descriptions, referring to the spectators in the Athenian theatre, show that human nature was very much the same in ancient times as at the present day. Certain types of character, which were generally to be met with among an Attic audience, will easily be recognised as familiar figures. There was the man of taste, who prided himself upon his superior discernment, and used to hiss when everyone else was applauding, and clap when everyone else was silent. There was the person who made himself objectionable to his neighbours by whistling an accompaniment to tunes which happened to please him. There were the 'young men of the town.' who took a malign pleasure in hissing a play off the stage. There were the people who brought out their provisions during the less exciting parts of the entertainment. There was the somnolent individual who slept peacefully through tragedies and comedies, and was not even waked up by the noise of the audience going away. Certain indications show that the employment of the claque was not unknown to Greek actors and poets. The parasite Philaporus, who had recently taken up the profession of an actor, and was anxious about the result of his first public appearance, writes to a friend to ask him to come with a large body of supporters, and drown with their applause the hisses of the critical part of the audience. Philemon, in spite of his inferior talents as a comic writer, is said to have frequently won victories from Menander by practices of this kind.

The character of the Athenian audience as a whole is well exemplified by the stories of their treatment of individual poets. Although they were willing to tolerate the utmost ribaldry upon the stage, and to allow the gods and sacred legends to be burlesqued in the most ridiculous fashion, they were at the same time extremely orthodox in regard to the national religion. Any atheistical sentiments, and any violations of their religious law, were liable to provoke an outburst of the greatest violence. Aeschylus on one occasion was nearly killed in the theatre itself, because he was supposed to have revealed part of the mysteries in the course of a tragedy. He was only saved by flying for refuge to the altar of Dionysus in the orchestra. Euripides also caused a great uproar by beginning his Melanippe with the line, 'Zeus, whoever Zeus be, for I know not save by report.' In a subsequent production of a revised version of the play he altered the line to 'Zeus, as is reported by truth.' In the same way sentiments which violated the moral feeling of the audience were received with intense indignation, and sometimes resulted in the stoppage of the play. The Danaë of Euripides is said to have been nearly hissed off the stage because of a passage in praise of money. On the other hand, wise and noble sentiments excited great enthusiasm. Aristophanes was rewarded with a chaplet from the sacred olive because of the splendid passage in which he counsels

mercy to the disfranchised citizens. Sophocles is said to have been
appointed one of the generals in the Samian expedition on account of
the excellent political wisdom shown in certain passages of the
Antigone. The partiality of the Athenians for idealism in art is shown
by the reception which they gave to Phrynichus' tragedy of the Capture
of Miletus, an historical drama in which the misfortunes of the Ionians
were forcibly portrayed. So far from admiring the skill of the poet, they
fined him a thousand drachmas for reminding them of the miseries of
their kinsfolk, and passed a law forbidding the reproduction of this
particular play.

The enthusiasm of the Athenians for the drama was unbounded.
Nowhere was the theatre more crowded. In the words of one of the old
historians they 'spent the public revenues on their festivals, were more
familiar with the stage than with the camp, and paid more regard to
verse-makers than to generals.' The speeches of Demosthenes are full
of complaints in the same strain.... It was not however till the
middle of the fourth century that the devotion to this and similar
amusements grew to such a height as to become a positive vice, and
to sap the military energies of the people. The Athenians of the fifth
century showed that enthusiasm for art and music and the drama was
not inconsistent with energy of character. As a matter of fact the very
greatest period of the Attic drama is also the period of the political
supremacy of Athens.

As far as intelligence and discrimination are concerned, the Athenian
audiences were probably superior to any audience of the same size
which has ever been brought together. Their keen and rapid intellect
was a subject of frequent praise among the ancients, and was ascribed
to the exhilarating influence of the Attic climate. They were especially
distinguished for the refinement of their taste in matters of art and
literature, and for the soberness of judgment with which they rejected
any sort of florid exuberance. That they were keenly alive to the
attractions of beauty of form and chastened simplicity of style is proved
by the fact that Sophocles was by far the most successful of their tragic
poets. Though Euripides became more popular among the later Greeks,
Sophocles in his own lifetime obtained far more victories than any
other tragic writer. At the same time it is easy to form an exaggerated
idea of the refinement of an Attic audience. They were drawn from all
classes of the people, and a large proportion were ignorant and un-
cultured. Plato speaks in the most disparaging terms of them, and
charges them with having corrupted the dramatic poets, and brought
them down to their own level. His evidence is perhaps rather prejudiced. But Aristotle who had much greater faith in popular judgment,
is not very complimentary. He divides the theatrical audience into two

classes, the refined and cultured class on the one hand, and the mass of rough and ignorant artisans on the other. One of his objections to the profession of an actor or musician is that he must accommodate himself to the level of the ignorant part of his audience. He mentions examples in the Poetics of the low level of popular taste, from which it appears that the average spectator in ancient times was, like his modern counter-part, fond of 'happy terminations.' He cared little for the artistic requirements of the composition; his desire was to see virtue rewarded, and vice punished, at the end of a play. Then again, a large part of the audience, Aristotle remarks, were so ignorant as to be unacquainted with the ordinary facts of mythology, which formed the basis of most tragedies. In judging a play, they paid more regard to the actor's voice than to the poet's genius. At the same time, in spite of depreciatory criticisms, it must be remembered that the true criterion of a people's taste is to be found in the character of the popular favourites. The victorious career of Sophocles, lasting over more than fifty years, is a convincing proof of the fact that, at any rate during the fifth century, the dramatic taste of the Athenians was altogether higher than that of an ordinary popular audience.

# 3. Sex and Marriage in Ancient Greece

## The Greek Double Standard
~§ Hans Licht

It is hardly necessary nowadays to emphasize the fact that the assertion, one often heard, that the position of the Greek married woman was an unworthy one, is fundamentally wrong. This erroneous opinion was bound to arise, since it originated in an incorrect assumption—a perverted estimate of women. However inferior as politicians the Greeks were throughout their short history, they were always admirable artists of life. Hence they assigned to woman as a whole the limits which nature had prescribed for them. The modern idea that there are two types of women, the mother and the courtesan, was recognized by the Greeks in the earliest times of their civilization, and they acted in accordance with it.... No greater honour could be paid to a woman than the Greeks assigned to the mother type. When the Greek woman had become a mother she had attained the object of her life. Then two tasks were allotted to her, which she considered the highest imaginable—the management of domestic affairs and the bringing up of her children, of the girls until they were married, of the boys until the awakening of the spiritual individuality of the soul. Thus marriage became for the Greeks a means to an end, the means of acquiring a legitimate generation to come after them, and an organized and trustworthy management of household affairs. The kingdom of the wife involved the complete control of domestic affairs, in which she was absolute mistress. If we please we can call such a marriage dull; indeed, we must do so, if we think of the part played by the modern woman in social life. But, on the other hand, it was free from the unnaturalness and falsehood which is frequently attached to modern society. It is not by accident that the Greek language has no equivalent for the ideas of "flirt," "gallantry," and "coquetry."

The modern man might feel inclined to ask the question whether the Greek girls and women did not feel desperately unhappy in a life of such retirement. But the answer must be in the negative. It must never be forgotten that what one does not know cannot be missed; then, also, the Greek women took the strictly limited (but for that reason no less noble) tasks which resulted from their household duties so seriously, that they had no time for detailed or painful thoughts about their existence. . . .

### *Engagement, Wedding, and Divorce in Ancient Greece*
✍ Robert Flacelière

Legal marriage between a citizen and the daughter of a citizen in Athens was characterized by the *engyésis* (literally, 'giving of a pledge into the hand') which was something more than a mere betrothal. It was, basically, a pact, an agreement none the less binding for being spoken only, between two persons: the suitor, and the young girl's *kyrios*, who, naturally, would be her father if he was still alive. The two men shook hands and exchanged some very simple ritual phrases: the following piece of dialogue by Menander probably reproduces them fairly faithfully:

> PATAECUS: I give you this girl, that she may bring children into the world within the bond of wedlock.
> POLEMON: I accept her.
> PATAECUS: I agree to provide a dowry of three talents with her.
> POLEMON: I accept that too—with pleasure.

There must have been witnesses present at this ceremony, so that they could, should the need arise, testify that it had in fact taken place. Nothing was set down in writing.

Was the bride-to-be herself present at the *engyésis*? We cannot be certain about this. What *is* certain is that if she was there she played no active part in the proceedings, nor was her consent to them required. It should be remembered that originally the head of a family had the same absolute rights over his children as he did over his slaves: he could even sell them, a custom still prevalent in many places during the fifth century, though not in Attica. In the Homeric Age, moreover, it was the suitor who offered gifts to his prospective father-in-law (he was, in fact, buying the man's daughter); but the roles later became reversed. A girl *could* marry without a dowry in Athens, but this was an exception to the general rule; there are even grounds for supposing that the existence of a dowry was one factor that distinguished legal marriage from mere concubinage.

As soon as the husband-to-be attained his majority he was no longer obliged to let his father represent him, and would carry out the *engyésis* ceremony in person. It is probable, however, that in most cases he would have asked his father's consent before becoming engaged, and that very often he chose his bride in accordance with his father's advice. One plaintiff tells us: 'As I had reached my eighteenth birthday, my father insisted on my marrying Euphemus' daughter: he wanted to see me beget children. My own feeling was that I must, in duty bound, do anything to please him; I therefore bowed to his wishes, and it was thus that I came to be married.' In such a case it is clear that the father would choose his son's wife (either from the family group or elsewhere) in accordance with his own plans for establishing or strengthening various personal relationships—the prime consideration being one of material self-interest.

The *engyésis*, then, was a promise of marriage, but an extremely binding one: it established strong links between the suitor and his future bride long before they were actually married. In order to understand it fully we have to bear in mind the immense importance which the ancients attached to any solemnly pronounced statement or ritual gesture: such words and actions, even if no formal oath was involved, they regarded as fraught with most serious consequences, and one could not repudiate any engagement entered upon under conditions of this sort without exposing oneself to the possibility of divine retribution. It was not only a prayer or curse that possessed this unequivocally magical power: any formula by which one bound oneself in the presence of the gods had a similar efficacy, and there is reason to suppose that the ceremony of *engyésis* took place in front of the domestic altar. Nevertheless, we know of at least one case in the fourth century where *engyésis* was not followed by marriage. Demosthenes' father, before he died, betrothed his daughter( then only five years old) to a relative of his called Demophon. Demophon received the dowry immediately, but was not to cohabit with the girl 'until she was of suitable age, that is, in ten years' time'—which offers confirmatory evidence that fifteen was regarded as a normal age for girls to get married. This betrothal, however, remained inoperative: the wedding was never celebrated.

On the details of the actual wedding ceremony (known as *ekdosis*, the 'giving away' of the bride to the bridegroom) our information is far from complete; but we can draw a fairly clear general picture of what went on. The marriage existed, legally speaking, from the day of the *engyésis*; but cohabitation between the partners remained, neverthe-less, its ultimate avowed purpose, since it was contracted primarily for the begetting of children. It was this consummation of marriage, the *gamos*, which necessitated the transfer of the fiancée to her suitor's house; and the transfer itself formed the central element in the wed-ding. Ordinarily it was meant to take place very soon after the *engyésis*. However, various superstitions made the Greeks marry, for preference, at the time of the full moon, and in winter rather than summer. Weddings were especially frequent during the month Gamelion (January), the seventh month in the Athenian year, since this was sacred to Hera, goddess of marriage, and its very name means 'the wedding-month.'

The sequence of ceremonies began on the evening before the bride's change of abode. First, a sacrifice was offered up to those gods and goddesses who protected the marriage bed: Zeus, Hera, Artemis, Apollo, and Peitho, or Persuasion. The bride offered up her toys, and all other objects associated with her childhood, as we see from the following epigram: 'Timareta, being about to be married, has consecrated to thee, O Artemis of the Marshes, her tambourines, and the ball she was so fond of, and her hairnet . . . ; her dolls, too, she has dedicated in a befitting manner, with her clothes—a virgin's offering to thee, O Virgin Goddess.' We possess a bronze cymbal that has been dedicated in this way—and to Artemis of the Marshes, as the inscription on it reveals.

But the principal rite—a purificatory ceremony—was the bridal bath, for which a procession had to go and fetch water from a special fountain called Callirhoe. We find this procession illustrated in vase-paintings: a crowd of women holding torches, and amongst them a flute-player, marching ahead of one woman who bore a special-shaped receptacle, in which the water for the bath was to be brought back. . . . The bridegroom, likewise, had to take a ritual bath.

On the day of the wedding (*gamos*), the houses of both bride and groom were decorated with garlands made from olive and laurel leaves, and there was a sacrifice and a banquet at the house of the bride's father. The bride herself was present at this feast, veiled and wearing her finest clothes, with a wreath on her head: she had all her girl-friends around her, and at her side the *nympheutria*, a woman whose task it was to guide and help her throughout the marriage ceremony. Similarly, the bridegroom was accompanied throughout by his *parochos*, or best man. It hardly needs saying that in the banqueting chamber the men were seated apart from the women. This wedding-feast included certain traditional dishes, such as sesame cakes, a symbolic guarantee of fertil-ity. A young boy with both parents living . . . went round among the guests, offering them bread from a basket, and repeating a ritual phrase which recalls certain religious formulas in the mystery cults: 'I have eschewed the worse; I have found the better.' When the meal was over the bride received presents. Perhaps she also removed her veil at this point, but we cannot be certain. As one scholar remarks: 'If the purpose of the veil was to protect her against maleficent influences during the dangerous period when she was in the process of changing her status, it would be more plausible to suppose that the unveiling did not take place till she reached the threshold of her husband's house.'

At last, towards evening, the procession formed up to convey the bride to her new home. Originally this change of abode had been carried out as though it were a forcible abduction, a custom still kept up at Sparta:

> Marriage in Lacedaemonia was a matter of the man abducting his chosen bride. The young girl thus abducted was entrusted to the care of a woman called the *nympheutria*, who close-cropped her hair, dressed her up in a man's clothes and shoes, and bedded her on a straw palliasse, alone and without any light. Her bridegroom, who had dined in the common mess, with his companions as usual, now came in, untied her girdle and carried her to the bed. After spending a brief time with her he would go straight back to his communal dormitory for the rest of the night.

In Athens bride and bridegroom were carried from one house to the other in some sort of vehicle, generally a waggon drawn by mules or oxen, with a friend of the bridegroom's to drive it. The bride carried a sieve and a gridiron, symbols of her future domestic activities. The waggon moved slowly along, with relatives and friends following behind on foot, lit by flaring torches: during the procession the marriage hymn was sung, to the accompaniment of flutes and lyres. The bride's mother carried a torch herself. When they reached the door of the bridegroom's house his father and mother were waiting there, the first wearing a myrtle wreath and the second holding a torch. Nuts and dried figs were showered on the bride—a ritual which was also . . . , performed on the entry of a new slave into the household. She was offered a part of the wedding-cake, made from sesame and honey, together with a quince or a date, both symbols of fecundity.

From here the couple proceeded straight to the bridal chamber (*thalamos*), and it may not have been till then that the bride removed her veil. The door was closed and guarded by one of the bridegroom's friends . . . , while the rest of the company sang some nuptial hymn at the tops of their voices, kicking up a tremendous din in order—or so it is believed—to scare away evil spirits. It goes without saying that the pomp and ceremonial of a wedding varied according to the financial resources of the families involved: the wedding-feast was sometimes so sumptuous that laws were passed on several occasions limiting the number of guests.

The day following the wedding there still remained one ceremony to perform: the bride's parents came in solemn array to the newly-wed couple's house, accompanied by flute-players, and bearing gifts. . . . It was doubtless at this point that the dowry promised during the *engyésis* was handed over. At some slightly later date the bridegroom offered a banquet, complete with sacrifice, to the members of his phratry [kin]. He did not introduce his wife to them; instead he chose this way of solemnly notifying them that he was now married—an important point for the future, since his male children would have to be enrolled in the phratry.

Of all the rites connected with the marriage that are known to us, not one appears intended to consecrate, in some visible and tangible fashion, the personal union of two betrothed individuals. Everything seems, rather, aimed at ensuring the prosperity of the *oikos*—the small socio-religious nucleus which the new home represented—and the procreation of children, through which the future of the *oikos* would be assured. For instance, when the bride was required to consume a piece of cake and a quince before her new husband's hearth, she did not—as we might expect—share them with him. In Sparta, we know that all legislation regarding the family, and relations between the sexes, was dominated by a concern for eugenics, which went so far that an elderly husband married to a young wife was allowed to let some young man sleep with her in order to produce healthy, vigorous children. In Athens they did not go to quite such lengths; but it must be said that nothing, either in the preparations for marriage or the ritual which solemnized it, placed any stress on affection or mutual love between husband and wife. . . .

A man always retained the right to repudiate his wife, even though he might be able to adduce no valid cause for so doing. A wife's adultery, if established by the courts, in fact made such repudiation obligatory on the husband's part, and failure to put away a peccant wife might render him liable to *atimia*, or loss of civil rights. Barrenness was in all likelihood a frequent motive for repudiation: and indeed, since a man married primarily to ensure the survival of his family (and, indirectly, of his city), he was doing no more than his bounden religious and patriotic duty when he put away a barren wife. On the other hand, the fact that a wife was pregnant did not make her exempt from repudiation. However, any husband who sent his wife back home had to return her dowry too: this provision was the only check (a very effective one, doubtless, in many cases) on a rocketing divorce rate.

If divorce through the husband's decision was a quite informal process, the wife who sought a separation found herself in a very different position, since legally she was presumed incapable of managing her own affairs. The only course open to her was to approach the archon—the traditional protector of all such 'incapables'—and put before him a written statement, detailing the reasons for her application. The archon was sole judge of what weight should be attached to offences alleged by an appellant wife. It was unlikely that flagrant infidelity on her husband's part would be regarded, *per se*, as justifying a separation, since custom tolerated complete sexual liberty amongst Athenian married men. Violence, however, and indeed any sort of ill treatment, might be taken as valid reasons for seeking a separation if, on enquiry, such charges proved well-founded. Despite this, public opinion was against wives who obtained a separation from their husbands in this way. Medea—whom Euripides makes talk exactly as though she were a contemporary Athenian woman—is quite unequivocal on the point: 'To leave their husbands brings women into ill-repute, and to repudiate them they have no right.'

THE POSITION OF MARRIED WOMEN. It seems fairly clear ... that there was little intimacy, intellectual contact, or even real love between husband and wife in classical Athens. Men constantly met and entertained one another in their homes, in the Agora or the law courts of the Assembly about their business affairs. Women, by contrast, lived a wholly secluded life.... [And] carnal or emotional needs that the Athenian did not satisfy at home (since he saw his wife merely as the mistress of his house and the mother of his children) he tended to find an outlet for elsewhere, in the company of boys or courtesans....

## *Varieties of Prostitution*
⋙ *Hans Licht*

BROTHELS. The whores who were quartered in brothels ... occupied the lowest rank in the social position of *filles de joie*; they were not distinguished as hetairæ, but were called simply "whores"....

In brothels whores stood very lightly clad or even quite naked for show, that every visitor might make his choice according to his personal taste. The statement by itself is quite credible, but there is abundant evidence to prove it. Thus Athenæus ... says: "Do you not know how, in Eubulus's comedy *Pannychis*, it is said of the music-loving, money-enticing bird-catchers, the dressed up foals of Venus, that they stand there in order on parade, in transparent dresses of fine-spun fabrics, like the nymphs on the sacred waters of Eridanus? Amongst them you can buy pleasure for a trifle to your heart's desire and without any risk."

In the comedy *Nannion* ... it is said: "Who watches stealthily for a forbidden bed, is he not of all men the most unhappy? While he can see the girls standing naked there in the bright sunlight," etc.

Further, Athenæus says "But also Xenarchus ... in his comedy the *Pentathlon* blames people who live like you and are keen after expensive hetairæ and free women, in the following words, 'the young people in our city do what is terrible, terrible, and a thing that can no longer be endured.' Where one sees only comely girls in the brothels—one can look at them and see how, with bared breasts in thin dresses of gauze drawn up in a row they exhibit themselves in the sun; any man may pick out the one that pleases him—thin, fat, roundish, lanky, crooked, young, old, moderate-sized, mature—you need not set up a ladder to enter secretly, you need not creep in through the dormer-window, nor cleverly smuggle yourself in in heaps of straw; they themselves drag you almost with violence into the house, calling you, if you are already an old man, 'daddy,' otherwise 'little brother' and 'little youngster.' And you can have any one of them for a small sum without any risk, by day or towards evening."

It appears that admission to the brothel cost but a trifle—according to ... the comic writer Philemon one obol (about 1½d.). This agrees with a passage from Diogenes Laëtius ... where we read: "When Antisthenes once saw an adulterer running away, he said: "You ass, you could have had that without any risk for an obol!" Of course the price of admission was regulated by place and time and must have differed according to the quality of the houses, yet we may be allowed to assume that in no case can it have been very high, since brothels represented the lowest, and hence the cheapest, form of prostitution. It must be added that, of course, in any case besides the entrance-money a "present" had to be given to the girls, the amount of which was determined by the demands made upon them. If the author rightly understands a note in Suïdas, this present varied between obols, drachmæ, and in better houses even starters. ...

The brothels, as well as the whole system of prostitution generally, stood under the supervision of the city officials, the *astynomoi* ..., whose duty it was to maintain public decency, and also to decide disputes. ...

S T R E E T W A L K E R S .   The wandering prostitutes naturally roamed about wherever a lively street traffic invited; hence they were to be

found in specially large numbers in the harbours and in the streets leading to them. They took their customers into their own or hired rooms,
or gave themselves to them in dark nooks and corners ... , or even between the high sepulchral monuments that bordered certain streets ... ,
and also in the public baths. ... There were also houses of accommodation and inns ... , but the taverns and inns also, especially in the
harbour district, afforded shelters at any time for such purposes.

That the light-hearted companies of flute and cithara-players, acrobats, etc., were to be had for love and money, needs no special remark.

THE HETAIRÆ. The hetairæ stand on a much higher level and
occupy a far more important position in Greek private life. They are
distinguished from the girls of the brothel especially by the social
respect they enjoyed and by their education. ... In the life of almost
every more important personality, prominent in the history of Hellen-
ism, the influence of well-known hetairæ can be proved. Most of their
contemporaries found nothing offensive in it. In the time of Polybius
... the most beautiful houses in Alexandria were indicated by the
names of famous flute-players and hetairæ. Portrait statues of such
women were set up in the temples and other public buildings by the
side of those of meritorious generals and statesmen. Indeed, the degraded sense of honour of the Greek free states condescended to honour
those hetairæ who were intimate with influential personalities, with
garlands and sometimes even with altars and temples.

## Homosexual Love
~§ Robert Flacelière

The word pederasty is derived from the Greek *paiderasteia*, meaning
literally the love of boys. In English pederasty has come to signify
almost exclusively the practice of sexual inversion. But in Greek literature *paiderasteia* is used to refer both to pure, disinterested affection
and to physical homosexual relations. ... We shall employ the word in
its Greek sense. ...

In the first place it appears extremely likely that homosexuality of
any kind was confined to the prosperous and aristocratic levels of ancient society. The masses of peasants and artisans were probably scarcely
affected by habits of this kind, which seem to have been associated with
a sort of snobbery. The available texts deal mainly with the leisured
nobility of Athens. But they may give the impression that pederasty
was practised by the entire nation. The subject, however, of the comedy
by Aristophanes entitled *Lysistrata* suggests that homosexuality was
hardly rampant among the people at large. ... It would be an error of

perspective to think so, and the mistake may as well be pointed out here and now. . . .

There was nothing particularly 'Greek' about homosexual feeling. The nation in antiquity was by no means alone in providing illustrations of inversion, which has been practiced at almost all times and in almost all countries. In our own day the productions of Verlaine, Proust and Gide, to mention only French writers, as well as a number of others, are sufficient evidence of the fact. In the pre-Christian era the case of Sodom is well known. Nor were the Persians, the Etruscans, the Celts or the Romans ignorant of homosexuality. But its existence among these peoples was kept more or less secret on account of the discredit which attached to it. But in Greece, though pederasty was forbidden by law in most of the cities, it had become so fashionable that no one troubled to conceal it. On the contrary, such tendencies were respected and even approved. Plato himself recommended their cultivation as a necessary preliminary to the successive stage of a philosophic understanding of Being.

Many Greeks, moreover, did not feel in the least ashamed of admitting that homosexuality was held in more honour among them than anywhere else in the world. They even affirmed that other nations which practised it were their pupils in this field. . . .

It seems quite likely that pederasty was not introduced into Greece, or at any rate did not prevail there to any great extent, before the Dorian invasions. For in historical times, as we shall soon see, it flourished mainly and attracted most attention among the populations of Dorian descent. Homer describes the Achaean and Mycenean civilisations of the thirteenth and twelfth centuries B.C., the age of bronze. To all appearance it was the Dorian invaders of the eleventh century B.C. who introduced into Greece both the use of iron and homosexual practices. . . .

In any case the Greeks themselves considered that pederasty was of relatively recent origin among them. In the *Erotes* attributed to Lucian there is a dialogue in which the defender of homosexuality admits that it is not a very ancient custom.

'At former epochs,' he says, 'male love-affairs were unknown. In those days it was thought indispensable to couple with women in order to preserve the human race from extinction. . . . Only with the advent of divine philosophy did homosexuality develop. We should be careful not to condemn an invention merely because it came late. . . . Let us agree that the old customs arose from necessity, but that subsequent novelties due to the ingenuity of man ought to be more highly regarded.'

In Plutarch's *Erotikos,* on the other hand . . . , the champion of heterosexual love exclaims:

'Homosexuality resembles a son born late, of parents past their maturity, or a bastard child of darkness seeking to supplant his elder brother, legitimate love. For it was only yesterday or at best the day before yesterday that the pederast came slinking into our gymnasia, to view the games in which youths then first began to strip for exercise. Quite quietly at first he started touching and embracing the boys. But gradually, in those arenas, he grew wings—' Eros being always represented winged—'and then there was no holding him. Nowadays he regularly insults conjugal love and drags it through the mud!'

This passage by Plutarch notes an important fact. There can be no doubt that the development of homosexuality was connected with the rise of gymnasia and arenas in which boys practised the five exercises of the *pentathlon,* which comprised wrestling, the foot-race, leaping, throwing the discus and hurling the javelin. Others were boxing and the *pancration,* a mixture of fist-fighting and wrestling. The competitors were always naked and watched by admiring spectators. In the same work . . . Plutarch tells us that Pisias, in love with a certain youth, Bacchon, whom a rich widow wanted to marry, 'imitated ill-conditioned lovers of the ordinary sort in trying to prevent his friend from marrying. The man's only object was to prolong the pleasure he took in watching the boy strip in the arena, while he still retained his virgin beauty.' Most gymnasia contained not only a statue of Hermes but also one of Eros. . . . There was an image of Eros at the Academy, which was the gymnasium in which Plato met his disciples.

The Greeks were at all times . . . most sensitive to physical beauty, whether masculine or feminine. This susceptibility was felt even in the most ascetic of friendships, when the lover desired nothing more from his beloved than the pleasures of the eye. It should be borne in mind that women were almost entirely excluded from Greek social life, which resembled a man's club. This was especially so at Athens, for at Sparta girls and women had more freedom of movement. . . .

Many of the ancient Greeks lavished all their sexually rooted affections upon boys. For they considered members of the other sex inferior beings, lacking all education and refinement, good for nothing but to ensure a posterity. . . .

All the same, at Athens a whole body of laws existed for the purpose of restraining the spread of pederasty. This legislation probably dated back to the time of Solon. It aimed among other things at keeping male lovers out of the schools and exercising arenas so far as possible. . . . But laws can do very little to suppress widely disseminated and inveterate habits.

In most of the Dorian States homosexuality appeared more con-
spicuously than it did at Athens. The reason is easy to understand if
we accept the theory that pederasty originates in the comradeship of
soldiers. . . . For it was in the Dorian cities that preparations for war
were of the greatest importance. Boys from the age of seven upwards
were enrolled in children's 'trained bands' and lived in continuous
contact with their elders at meals and in the dormitories. Plutarch . . .
states: 'It was chiefly warlike peoples like the Boeotians, Lacedemonians
and Cretans, who were addicted to homosexuality.'

According to Ephorus a male lover in Crete would declare his feelings to the relatives and friends of his beloved. If they consented, he
would carry the boy off three days later, just as at Sparta the bridegroom would simulate abduction of the bride. The Cretan lover conducted the lad to his house, gave him a present and then took him to
some rural retreat for two months, on a sort of honeymoon. After this
period the couple returned to the city, where the boy was given by his
lover a military outfit, a drinking cup and a bull, which the youth had
to sacrifice. These customs were no doubt survivals of former puberty
rites.

It was considered shameful in Crete for a well-born boy not to have
a lover. But lads who had already been abducted were subsequently
regarded with great respect.

Xenophon . . . reports that in Boeotia men and boys likewise paired
off in actual marriages.

At Sparta itself 'boys who had reached the age of twelve and had
a good reputation obtained faithful lovers . . . who share in the good
or bad opinion held of the children. It is said that on one occasion
when a boy had let fall a vulgar expression his lover, not himself, was
punished by the magistrates.' . . .

The age of a beloved boy seems always to have been between twelve
and twenty. A Greek epigram declares:

'Desirable is the bloom of a boy of twelve. But that of thirteen is
much more delightful. Even sweeter is the flower of love that blossoms
at fourteen years. Its charm increases still more at fifteen. Sixteen is
the divine age. A boy of seventeen I would not dare to woo. Zeus alone
would have the right to do so.'

As a rule the first signs of down on the chin of the beloved deprived
him of his lover. But there were exceptions to this convention. Plutarch
writes in his *Erotikos* . . . : 'It is generally believed that a single hair
would be enough to cut the amorous connection in two like an egg
and that lovers of boys resemble nomads who set up their tents in green
and flowery meadows in the spring but desert it as if it were hostile
territory once the season is over. Yet we may recall a famous phrase of

Euripides, spoken amid kisses and caresses to the handsome Agathon, who had already grown a beard: "Beauty is still fair even in its autumn".'

This particular Agathon was a tragic poet, like Euripides himself. It is he who, in Plato's *Symposium*, plays host to the guests he has invited to celebrate the success of one of his plays. He was also mocked in the *Thesmophoriazusae* of Aristophanes, one of his guests on that occasion, for his effeminate tastes. He was said to have worn a long robe, a saffron-coloured tunic and a cape, as though he were a woman, also a bust-bodice, a hair-net and tight buskins such as smart women affected. He is alleged, too, always to have had a mirror and a razor on him. The latter implement was in those days a typical accessory of the feminine toilet, rather than the masculine. For men wore beards, while women of fashion shaved off their superfluous hair. Agathon's prolonged love-affair with Pausanias, another of the guests at the *Symposium*, was celebrated throughout ancient times.

As a rule the lover in these associations was a mature man less than forty years of age. But Aeschines was forty-five when he made his speech *Against Timarchus* . . . , observing . . . :

'I myself no more disdain the pleasures of love today than I did formerly. I freely confess it. . . . To be fond of good-looking and well-behaved young people is a natural tendency of all sensitive and liberal minds.'

The poet Sophocles, again, had passed fifty when he attended a banquet in Asia Minor during the expedition to Samos in which he shared the military command with Pericles. According to P. Mazon . . . on that occasion he 'gaily discomfited a certain pedant by teasing a boy cupbearer and turning the joke against himself by swearing he was a better strategist in love than in war'. Pericles himself was not homosexually inclined. He cared for no one but Aspasia. Sophocles, during the same expedition, happened to praise in his presence the beauty of a certain youth. But Pericles sternly rebuked him, so Plutarch reports in his life of the statesman . . . : 'A General, Sophocles, should refrain not only from soiling his hands but from contaminating his eyes.'

If we are to believe Athenaeus . . . , the poet was sixty-five when he experienced the following misadventure. 'One day he left Athens with a handsome boy, intending to take his pleasure with the lad. The boy laid his own shabby cloak on the grass and they covered themselves with the poet's own fine warm woollen cloak. After the consummation of the affair the youth seized the cloak of Sophocles and made off with it, leaving his own in its place.'

This incident, it appears, elicited an exchange of pungent epigrams between Sophocles and Euripides. We need only add that the former's habits by no means prevented him from being considered throughout classical antiquity as a man of exemplary piety, 'beloved of the gods'. The domains of religion and sexual morality were then regarded as completely separate. It was certainly not in the name of religion that Pericles, himself a 'free-thinker', addressed the above-mentioned reproach to Sophocles. The reference was simply to the dignified conduct expected of a high State functionary. In any case the mighty gods of Olympus themselves, from Zeus and Apollo downwards, were represented in classical times as ardent pederasts.

# 4. In the Ancient Marketplace

## The Agòra of Athens
৵§ Robert Flacelière

It was primarily round the focal point of the Acropolis, and its southern annex the Marsh, or Limnae, that urban life developed: from the end of the seventh century B.C. it expanded towards the north-west, forming the workers' quarter known as the Ceramicus, a name sufficiently explained by the large numbers of potteries and kilns found there. It was in this quarter that Athens' public place of assembly, the *agora* of the Ceramicus, was situated: a centre that combined religious, political and economic functions. Here, on the *orchéstra* or dancing-floor, were held the earliest dramatic representations, in honour of Dionysus, god of the theatre. Here too the assemblies of the people took place, in an area originally marked off with ropes stretched across it.... The *agora* was also used as a market for agricultural produce and industrial goods. But the market, and the passers-by cluttered the place up so much that very soon it became highly inconvenient to hold political assemblies or dramatic festivals in so overcrowded a spot. As a result the former were transferred to the Pnyx (to the west of the Areopagus and the Acropolis) and the latter to the sanctuary of Dionysus Eleutherus (on the southern slopes of the Acropolis). Only the market remained *in situ* at the *agora;* though the members of the Council and the *prytaneis* used it as their meeting-place, and a Citizen Assembly could always be held there if occasion ... demanded.

The Agora was ... a favourite resort for every idle layabout in town: and Athens had many such. Demosthenes was to taunt them a century later with the words: 'You are always strolling about asking each other "What's new?"' and the author of *Acts* echoes him: 'No townsman of Athens or stranger visiting it, has time for anything else than saying something new, or hearing it said.' How could such loungers be made to turn up on the Pnyx [for meetings of the Assembly]? The police— a body of public slaves—barricaded the roads leading to the Agora, and herded citizens in the right direction by means of a rope smeared in wet red paint, which they carried stretched across the road. Being smeared with red paint was quite unpleasant enough in itself, and I see no reason to suppose that Athenians to whom this happened were *also* compelled to pay a fine, or found themselves docked of their *misthos ecclésiastikos* [fee paid those attending the Assembly]. . . .

Athenians who daily frequented the Agora and other public meeting-places never lacked for entertainment: this was especially true of the *gymnasia,* where many citizens continued to take exercise throughout their adult years. The most common, but by no means the least popular amusement was to idle one's time away strolling about the streets and the Agora, gossiping in the barber's shop, or indeed any sort of shop or work-room: this was the proper setting for exchanges of news or a good long discussion, and Socrates regularly came here in the hope of meeting people. The Agora was also a 'pitch' for tumblers, jugglers, mimes, conjurors, dancers, and clowns of every description. Athens certainly had its puppeteers, and a 'shadow-theatre' that was a fore-runner of the Oriental Karageuz; Plato may well have had this in mind when he excogitated his famous myth of the Cave, and the shadows that flitted across the rock-face. Concerts were regularly held in the Odeon, mainly on feast-days.

## A Tour of Antioch in the Fourth Century A.D.
≪§ Glanville Downey

The visitor . . . would come first to the heavily fortified gate in the northern wall of the city, on the road which led from Beroea. The road-way, thirty feet wide, was paved with massive blocks of Egyptian granite. As he passed through the monumental entrance with its heavy doors, he found himself in the main thoroughfare of the city, its granite roadway flanked on either side by covered colonnades, each, like the open street, thirty feet wide.

Running through the long axis of the city, north and south, the main street was two miles long. This famous thoroughfare, resembling the colonnaded street at Palmyra; was one of the city's greatest sources of pride, and one of the well-known reasons for its fame. The wide roadway provided ample room for the busy traffic of the city, and the spacious sidewalks on either side of it, each lined with two rows of

columns, provided pleasant accommodation for pedestrians and loungers. The colonnades were two-storied and roofed, with stairs at intervals
leading up to the second-story galleries and the roofs. Under the
colonnades there was shade in the summer and shelter from rain and
snow in the winter. Along the inner sides of the colonnades ran the
walls of houses and public buildings, their entrances opening between
the columns, while on the side toward the street merchants and vendors
often set up booths between the columns. The municipal authorities
found it difficult to control these intrusions.

The street had been built under the auspices of the Emperors
Augustus (23 B.C.–A.D. 14) and Tiberius (A.D. 14–37), with assistance
from King Herod, at the time when the Romans were transforming
Hellenistic Antioch into a Roman city. In Hellenistic times this had
been a graveled roadway running along the outside of Seleucus' city,
but with the growth of Antioch it had become the principal thoroughfare.

The roadway was open to the sky, but since it ran north and south
it was shaded during part of the day, and it caught the breeze which
blew up the Orontes Valley in the summer. It was full of the most
varied traffic. Travelers on horseback or in carriages drawn by mules;
donkeys heavily loaded with burdens of all kinds, singly or in strings,
led by drivers armed with sticks; two-wheeled carts carrying building
materials; porters bearing heavy loads—every kind of activity could be
seen in this thoroughfare and the side streets which opened from it.
Some drivers, in order to escape the sun, led their asses and camels
through the porticoes—"as though they were brides," as someone said.
Farmers brought food into the city in carts or on donkeys, and the
municipal authorities forced them to carry rubbish out of the city as
they left. Women hurried on errands, their children trailing behind
them. Boys walked to school, chaperoned by slaves carrying their books
and wax writing tables secured in leather straps. High officials and
army officers passed on horseback, their harness and uniforms glittering.
Wealthy citizens had the harness of their horses inlaid with gold, and
ladies went about the city in brightly painted wooden carriages. An
important personage, seated in aloof dignity on his white horse, would
have a servant armed with a stick running before him, shouting and
clearing the way through the crowd for his illustrious master. Many
of the great houses of the city had Negro servants whose liveries were
trimmed with gold. The governors of Syria, the Counts of the East, and
the generals of the eastern command when they appeared in public
were escorted by detachments of the archers who served as police.

The streets and the open squares which occurred at intervals throughout the city exhibited all the varied activity of a Mediterranean city,
where in the warm, dry summer, life was largely lived out of doors.

Antioch was not like other cities in which the vendors of different types of goods tended to congregate, so that each commodity could be purchased in only one part of the city. Thus one would buy hardware in one section of the city, leather in another, cloth in a third region. Instead , . . . everything in Antioch was sold in all parts of the city, and people did not have to make long expeditions in order to make their purchases. The shopper could go from shop to shop, or find an open square filled with the bustle of buying and selling in the open air.

The squares served as social centers as well. Citizens paced about in twos and threes, conversing, while children played tug of war, falling backward sometimes as their rope broke in the middle. Beggars danced and piped, and jugglers and acrobats wandered about giving performances wherever they could collect a crowd. Philosophers made their way about, distinguished by the recognized signs of their calling, the long beard (most men were clean shaven), the threadbare cloak, and the staff carried in the right hand. The streets and market places were busy until midnight, and Antioch enjoyed public street lighting, an unusual thing in those days.

There were camps all about Antioch, which had a permanent garrison and was headquarters for the defense of the Persian frontier; and soldiers were to be seen everywhere in the streets dressed in their uniforms, tunics and kilts, with their branch of service—artillery, cavalry, infantry—indicated by the color of their uniforms. All through the slow-moving crowds one could see visitors from remote parts of the empire or from foreign lands, easily identified by their exotic dress. Servants and porters hurried along, balancing bundles on their heads; and men often carried lumber and other heavy burdens, for it could be cheaper to hire a man than to employ an animal.

At the public fountains at the corners of the streets women and children filled tall earthenware water jars, which they carried on the shoulder, balanced with one hand, or on the back, the pointed bottom of the jar resting in a sling which passed around the forehead and down the back. With the abundant water supply of Antioch, there was no quarreling and pushing about the fountains, as there was in some other cities where water was scarce and the supply irregular. Indeed, many of the large private houses in Antioch had water piped into their courtyards from the aqueducts.

Dress had not changed essentially for many generations and would not change for many more. Men customarily wore a one-piece tunic reaching to the knees, and belted at the waist, to give the effect of a kilt. This was of wool in the winter, cotton or linen in the summer. Officials and citizens of substance wore in addition robes reaching to the ground. In winter there would be worn a wool cloak with an attached hood. While workmen and slaves were barefooted, most men who could do so wore sandals, with tight woolen trousers in cold weather. Officials and army officers wore distinctive cloaks as part of their uniform, fastened at the shoulder with ornamental brooches which betokened rank—officers' cloaks were white. The uniform belt was worn as a badge of service in the army or the civil service.

Women wore long robes reaching to the ground, of various colors and materials—wool, linen, silk—depending on the season of the year and the occasion and status of the wearer. Outdoors the hair was covered with a colored scarf. In winter there would be a wool cloak with a hood. Children wore smaller counterparts of their parents' clothing, and carried toys which have been familiar at all times—wooden or rag dolls, hoops, tops.

The long line of the main street was broken at regular intervals by side streets, on one side running up toward the mountain, on the other side across the level area toward the river. Only the more important of these side streets were colonnaded. The city-blocks were of uniform size, about one hundred yards long and half as wide. The lower slopes of the mountain provided choice sites for houses. . . .

Fine villas lined the slopes, with their dining rooms arranged so that guests could enjoy the view over the city.

As he passed along the street the visitor would see ahead of him a distant vista of an open plaza in the middle of which stood a column bearing a statue of the Emperor Tiberius. At this point the direction of the street changed very slightly, so that as one walked along the avenue toward the center of the city, from either direction, one's view came to rest upon an architectural composition, a more pleasing effect than a straight, unending row of colonnades disappearing into the distance would have been.

When he came to this square, the visitor would pause. He was in the center of the city. On his right, at right angles to the main street, he saw a colonnaded street leading to the river and the large island in the Orontes. At the head of this street, all along the side of the plaza, stood a handsome *nymphaeum*, consisting of an ornamental façade of variegated marble and colored mosaic faced with columns between which were fountains enclosed in niches. The water ran out into a marble basin paved with mosaic.

To the visitor's left, a short colonnaded street, running in the direction of the mountain, led to the recently completed Forum named for Theodosius' predecessor, the Emperor Valens (A.D. 364–78), on which stood some of the most important public buildings in the city.

As he walked up the sloping street and entered the forum with its gleaming marble buildings, the visitor would see about him the tokens

of all the varied activities which went to make up the life of the city.
Government, social life, religion, and trade were all represented in this
splendid composition of monumental public buildings grouped about
a vast open area. The forum was a distinctively Roman institution,
taking the place of the agora or market place of the Greeks, such as
the two old agoras in Antioch which had been the centers of the city's
life in the days of the Seleucids. The Forum of Valens at Antioch was
intended to be one of the most magnificent in the Graeco-Roman
world, resembling in its general composition the Forum of Trajan in
Rome.

# 5. *Travel in the Roman World*

### *Reasons for Travel*
*◁§ Ludwig Friedländer*

Not only change of residence, official tours, military marches and commercial voyages, but many professions compelled constant travelling. The absence of posts and a press and ancient customs further increased the need.

Very many travelled to gain knowledge. To learn from one's own eyes was more usual than now; for ancient methods taught much more through actual sight; and book-lore was rarer and less perfect. Hence the learned (such as Posidonius, Diodorus, Strabo, Apio, Pausanias, Dioscorides, Apuleius and Galen (who insists on the need of doctors travelling much) required long tours; and less eminent men, too, would wander far a-field to widen their scope....

But youth was the time to travel and leave home. Young men regularly left their parents' house to be better educated elsewhere.... Every province and district in the more civilized parts had its academic city, to which students came from far and near.... On the other hand, both teachers and students of all kinds led a migratory life. Rhetors and sophists found the nearest road to fame and wealth in educational and lecturing tours....

Artists were mostly always on the road. The craving for the artistic side of life throughout the whole Roman world is evidenced by the countless ruins of artistic work in every province; and the huge demand could only have been satisfied by 'colonies, expeditions, swarms or clouds of artists, and artists hovering about, ready to settle down anywhere'. One inscription of a wandering sculptor, Zeno of Aphrodisias, is extant, who trusting to his art, visited many cities; statues, bearing his name, have been found at Rome and Syracuse. Actors, musicians and athletes made constant tours, in troops, or singly; especially in Greece and Little Asia. . . .

Feasts and spectacles, at Rome or in the provinces, attracted count-less foreign spectators. The Olympian and the Pythian games assembled all Greece, not only as late as the third century, but even under Julian the Apostate: vehicles were scarce at their conclusion. . . .

At such assemblies traders of all sorts, with an eye to profit met. Dio of Prusa says that panders with their girls travelled to the autumn meeting of the Amphictyonic Council at Pylae, and elsewhere. Panders generally travelled much; the wretches go about, says Clement of Alex-andria, by sea, with a cargo of girls, instead of wine. . . .

Further, even the banished and relegated might attend the great festivals, the Mysteries of Eleusis, the Feast of Dionysos at Argos, the Pythia at Delphi, the Isthmian Games at Corinth. . . .

Voyages for health were also very common. Doctors are right, says Epictetus, to recommend a change of air for lingering illnesses. Lunacy, constant headaches, paralysis, dropsy, bladder troubles, and especially incipient lung diseases, and spitting of blood were thought curable by a change of climate: consumptives were sent from Italy by sea to Egypt or Africa. . . .

Bathing resorts were used as much as they are now, and many of the springs had been discovered, such as Baden, near Zürich (as early as 160 A.D. a busy invalid town), and the thermae of Teplitz, Ems, Pyr-mont, Aix-la-Chapelle contain many Roman implements. Bath was visited very soon after the occupation, and richly fitted up. . . . Remains of Roman bathing-resorts, often very gorgeous, can be traced along all the Mediterranean coasts, and in Africa, e.g. in Hamam Rirra in Algeria, the Pyrenees, the Carpathians (Mehadia), the Alps and Auvergne. Some of these were also pleasure-resorts, e.g. Baiae, Aedepsus, Canobus. Men also travelled for distraction and recreation.

It will thus be seen that travelling in the Empire was more extensive than in Europe up to the nineteenth century. . . .


### *The Quality of Land Travel*

✑§ Ludwig Friedländer

Simple wayfarers walked with their mantle pinned up, or with modest baggage bestrode a mule or a horse; but the poorer even seldom with-out one slave at least. If the traveller drove, the slaves followed in a second carriage, at all events on longer journeys. Seneca once was seized with an impulse to make a poor man's journey. He and a friend, Caesonius Maximus, carrying all their luggage on them, went with so

few attendants that one extra carriage was sufficient. They rested on
the bare earth, a mattress under them, and one rain-mantle as sheet
and one as coverlet. Their meals were of the simplest, and were made
ready in less than one hour: dried figs were invariable, and their tablets
always at hand to note down impressions. He drove in a peasant's
waggon, his mules just moving along, the man guiding them barefoot,
not because it was summer, but as his habit. These two days of Arcady
had taught him how superfluous much of ordinary life was. Yet an
uneasy envy overtook him, at the sight of a gorgeous equipage; he
was ashamed that so poor a vehicle should be thought his. These feelings are explicable in this millionaire and consular: for senators and
knights to travel without retinue and piles of baggage was unique: this
luxury obtained even under the Republic. On a journey to Lanuvium
with his wife, Milo took all his singing boys, besides his slaves, male
and female. Caesar, on his campaigns, carried mosaic floors with him:
Antony's journeys were like a travelling circus, with his huge coach,
the carriage drawn by lions, and the ostentation of gold.

This luxury was far exceeded under the Empire. Nero always had a
suite of a thousand carriages; his mules had silver shoes, his muleteers
scarlet liveries, his outriders and runners were gorgeously clad: Poppaea
had her horses harnessed with gold, and had 500 asses with her, so as
to bathe in their milk every day: in the retinue of Eusebia, the wife of
Constantius (353), there were 'coaches of all sorts, inwrought with
gold and silver and bronze'. The upper classes vied in imitating this
luxury, as Seneca shows: many of these fashionable plutocrats were
only rich on their journeys, and deliberated whether, after their in-
solvency, they should hire themselves out as gladiators or fighters with
animals. Gaily-dressed Moors, Numidian outriders and runners cleared
the way. Well-fed mules, if possible alike in colour, or the little fat
but swift Gaulish horses, drew the waggons, and palfreys followed for
riding. The beasts of burden were covered with gold or purple trappings, with golden bridles and bits: the travelling-carriages were filled
with gold or silver figures, and might be worth many estates; curtains
of silk or other rarities, plate of gold and crystal and myrrha; works
of art, too delicate to be shaken, and carried; such was the pomp: and,
of course, a huge court of love-boys, with masks to protect their faces,
and so on. Rich provincials even travelled in this fashion. Polemo, the
sophist of Smyrna, travelled with hundreds of beasts of burden, horses,
slaves, leashes of hounds, and his own Phrygian or Gaulish horses with
silver harness. . . .

Noble ladies generally travelled in palanquins. Antony, according to
a letter of Cicero (49 B.C.), had his mistress Cytheris thus borne beside
him, and seven other palanquins bore the seven mistresses of his friends.

Julia, the daughter of Augustus and wife of Agrippa, was once at night on the way to Ilium, and was almost drowned with her carriers by a rising of the Scamander. Agrippa, furious at the neglect of her by the townsmen, fined them 100,000 *denarii*, though they had not been advised of her approach; but it was remitted at the intercession of King Herod, through Nicolaus of Damascus.

Slavery, and the lack of inns, account for these gorgeous and complete travelling arrangements. The rich man, with hundreds of slaves, could carry his palace with him everywhere, and some service had become habitual to him. Local inn-keepers could not cater for such luxurious tastes, especially as the warm Southern air made such shelter unnecessary. But there also were some good, or even high-class hotels, where the traveller might well stay on. . . . In populous commercial or pleasure cities or seaside resorts, there would be numerous good hotels. . . . But most inns were probably third-rate, but not because they catered for the poorer classes. They are even now inferior in the South, since the southerner is easily satisfied in the matter of lodging; which was perhaps the case even more in ancient times. But travellers who sought only a bed and a meal and shelter were well contented; and on such these inns throve, for the number of people carrying tents and all their own conveniences with them must have been very small. . . .

The ordinary inns . . . did not invite a long stay: the company was low, grooms and muleteers; Vitellius, before ascending the throne, affected affability and frequented them. Plutarch, as a means of health, recommends constant loud speaking, and says that the jeers of sailors, muleteers and hosts at inns should not deter. Apollinaris Sidonius' description of the interior of a 'greasy tavern' could easily be antedated. The smoke from the kitchen filled it, and oppressed incomers; on thyme-wreathed porringers the sausages could be smelt: the steam and clatter of pots and pans and chanting of the guests. The pillows, stuffed with reeds, instead of feathers, teemed with fleas and bugs; from the ceilings lizards and spiders would drop down. Prices might not be overhigh. In the days of Polybius, in the lowlands of Lombardy, inns were cheap; there were no bills, but an inclusive rate of half an *as*(¼*d.*). A relief, dating from imperial times, at Aesernia in Samnium (Isernia), represents a man in touring-costume, leading his mule, bargaining with his hostess: the legend is that the bread is one *as* (¾*d.*), dessert two *asses*, service two *asses*, hay two *asses*, wine free. The two *denarii* paid by the Good Samaritan for one day's expenses, must have been more than sufficient, as they were also meant to cover medical treatment. Possibly travellers (as to this day in Greek khans) brought their own food with them, to be cooked at the inn.

Further, inns were often brothels. Jurists are constantly mentioning that the servants at inns, in town or country, consisted of cheap girls, and that inn-keepers were unprofessed panders. A rescript of Alexander Severus directed that a slave sold on condition of non-prostitution, might not be bought for such an inn. The law that there could be no adultery with barmaids, was made by Constantine in 326 not to apply to the hostess, provided she did not serve the guests herself.

As panders and for other reasons, inn-keepers had an ill-repute. On the lists of the police-soldiers, they were inscribed with thieves and gamblers. They lied and cheated, adulterated the wine (Trimalchio says they were born under the Sign of Aquarius) and stole the oats provided for the mules. According to Artemidorus (a great traveller) to dream of bronze or iron foreheads was a good omen for publicans and toll-keepers; thorns especially good for publicans, toll-keepers and robbers who gave false weights, and stole by force or craft. Galen says that human flesh tasted very much like pork, and was often dished up by unscrupulous publicans; he had been credibly informed of a very palatable dish, in which a finger-bone was found: the travellers left in instant disgust, and the owner had subsequently been convicted of presence at a human slaughter-house. The land-ladies were often reputed witches, as once in Apuleius. St. Augustine says that they would put a Circean drug into their cheese, turning their guests into conscious mules, and restoring them only on conditions. And publicans were liable for loss suffered by guests in their houses.

Toll-keepers were proverbially dishonest; perhaps largely in fact. Smuggling was common and conscientious officials even were obnoxious. ... Worse than the exactions of the tolls and the cheatings of the publicans was the frequent insecurity of travelling.

Brigandage was worst in the frontier provinces. An inscription in Nether Pannonia ... says that Commodus in 185 A.D. fortified all the banks of the Danube against robbers. In the tombs in Dacia, three (near Mehadja and Cernets) record the murder of two men and a woman by robbers; two were revenged. Monuments to persons killed by bandits have been found in Upper Moesia ... Darmstadt and Trèves. The roads in Africa, despite the castles, were often most insecure, as Cyprian, Bishop of Carthage, shows; he says that a report that an inn had been seized by robbers, made travellers avoid it. An engineer of the third legion stationed at Lambessa, summoned to build a tunnel to Saldae (Bougie) in 152 A.D., says he fell on robbers on the way, and was stripped and wounded. Lucian mentions that there were many robbers in Egypt at the time of the Prophet Alexander of Abonuteichos. The Nile swamps near Damietta were the lurking-place of the *bucoli*, a savage people, known to Eratosthenes: the novel of Heliodorus describes their wild life on barks and islets. Under Marcus

Aurelius, they threatened Alexandria, and Avidius Cassius could hardly subdue them. They gave trouble, later on, to the Khalifs....

But even the most civilized and peaceful regions were sometimes harried. In 187 A.D., a deserter, Maternus, formed a band and terrorized the whole of Gaul and Spain, burning villages and farms, even attacking great cities, setting the criminal free, and ravaging at will. He evaded the troops of Commodus, and escaped to Italy, designing to murder the Emperor: he was betrayed and executed.

In Italy insecurity was greatest, after the civil wars: armed highwaymen appeared publicly and made a night-journey from Rome to Tibur perilous. Augustus erected forts at suitable places, but the evil was not altogether allayed, and Tiberius had to extend them. Highwaymen, when caught, were tortured to death, torn asunder by wild beasts; their corpses hanged, as warnings and 'consolation to the victim's kin', at the spots of their evil trade (as was done in the Papal States up to 1819); they were left on the gallows or crucified, or especially in mountainous districts, left by the roadside, as carrion for the birds, or the curious physician. Galen saw a skeleton of a robber, who had fallen at the hands of his intended victim: the inhabitants would not bury him; and in two days, so much flesh had been torn away, as to make the remains very instructive. But, even in Italy, brigandage died hard, if at all. At night torches were used (and thrown away at daybreak: hedges were thus sometimes set on fire), and any bearer of valuables trembled at the shadows....

### *Travel by Sea*
⇜§ Ludwig Friedländer

Sea-voyages were limited to the spring, the summer and the early autumn. In the late autumn, ships came home or harboured abroad. From the 11th November to the 5th March there was no sailing; on that day, by the reformed calendar, the feast of the 'ship of Isis' (the patroness of sailors) was celebrated all along the Mediterranean coast, with solemn processions, the consecration of a ship, and its sailing abroad. Then all the ships, drawn up on to land, were trolleyed out. No one, except in urgency, risked a winter voyage, though the sea was not absolutely uncrossable; for avarice made men continue to court the sea in winter, as of old, when fear of pirates drove them to it. But, apart from mercantile enterprise, official transports of documents, legates or prisoners and relegates must have been considerable, even in the winter....

Voyages were made by preference on clear, starry nights. The steersman steered by the stars, to whom the passengers made worship before starting. . . .

Ships occasionally had contrivances for measuring their mileage, and Vitruvius describes them. There is material enough to estimate the average sailing-speed. Marcian of Heraclea, the geographer, remarks that these sea-distances (in *stadia*) [eighths of a mile] were very diverse; it was best to draw a mean between the highest and the lowest. A ship with a good wind might do 700 *stadia* a day; a swift cruiser even 900. Scylax of Caryanda makes 500 a day the average, on a long journey. The night-time is not included, for Herodotus and others expressly say that, at midsummer, a ship could do 700 *stadia* by day and 600 by night.

## The Embattled Driver in Ancient Rome
≪§ Kenneth D. Matthews

First we must remember that the Romans handled chariots and wagons drawn by horses or mules which required more physical strength than that expected of a driver today. Then too, the city of Rome had grown without the guidance of a city planning commission and a master scheme of streets and byways. . . . A few broad and many narrow streets twisted their way among an intricate mesh of winding alleys and footpaths.

By the time of Julius Caesar, vehicles had become such a potential problem to the citizens and magistrates alike that something had to be done. For quite different reasons a law had been passed at the end of the 3rd century B.C. forbidding women to ride in carriages. This was included in a war measure restricting the display of feminine luxury and we can imagine with little difficulty the feeling which the ladies of Rome had for Gaius Opius, the originator of the law. Twenty years later they forced the repeal of this law but during the 1st century A.D. the same restrictions on feminine riding were again in force. This seems to have been the result of Caesar's legislation of 44 B.C.

The problem faced by Caesar, however, was of much broader scope and it took a man such as he to produce the ultimate solution. At one sweep he outlawed the use of private vehicles on the city streets during the first ten hours of the day. In every Roman day there were twelve hours of daylight adjusted according to the season. This meant that during the last two hours before darkness settled one might begin his driving. It followed that all business deliveries were made at night while heavy, privately owned coaches which carried paying passengers and their baggage left the city very late in the afternoon or early in the morning before the sun rose.

There were certain exceptions as one would expect. Triumphing generals, vestal virgins, and priests could always employ chariots or carriages; one would also find vehicles in the processions prescribed for particular religious festivals. Since the Imperial Roman government was intensely interested in the construction of public buildings, it also granted contractors working on these structures the right to convey their materials by wagons during the day. If work was in progress on an addition to a private home, however, no one would presume to transport the building blocks by day.

One would also find in Rome certain residential streets where vehicles were forbidden both day and night. Signposts were not necessary to indicate this condition as it was far easier to erect stone posts across the roadway. From Pompeii we learn that road construction often involved the provision of stepping stones leading across the street from one sidewalk to the other. Thus pedestrians avoided the streams of water and refuse flowing down streets not adequately provided with underground sewers, and at the same time night traffic was kept at a slow speed so as not to collide with these obstructions. In a similar manner, ruts worn in the paving stones served to guide the wheels of chariots and wagons.

The narrow streets of the capital itself posed quite a problem in regard to the direction in which traffic should move. Some streets offered passage for only one chariot or wagon at a time and yet there seems to have been no official attempt to create one-way streets. In effect, the driver himself accomplished this by sending on ahead a runner who held up traffic at the opposite end until the chariot had passed through. We know that wealthy Romans maintained such runners when they traveled out of the city. If one did not resort to this device there was every possibility of a traffic jam in the middle of the block. Imagine the uncouth words of rough wagon drivers as they kept the neighborhood awake in the darkness of the night while they disputed the right of way among themselves....

Those who planned a trip in advance left the city in their vehicles before sunrise or else very late in the afternoon. Since while traveling one spent the night in an inn or at the home of a friend, it was preferable to cover as much ground as possible before nightfall and so one was less likely to leave Rome late in the day. Early morning was the time when most travelers passed, sleepy eyed, through the dim dawn shadows of the city gates and rattled off awkwardly at first between the trees and tombs along the highway.

Imposing and important as were the famous Roman roads, their effectiveness began and ended at the walls of cities. Unlike our modern speedways they did not convey traffic into the heart of a community. Although many passed directly through smaller towns, yet traffic was halted at the limits of these communities. By a law of the emperor Claudius, the traveler had to descend from his chariot or carriage and go through the town on foot, in a carrying chair, or in a litter. This must have been a great nuisance if the law was seriously enforced. We suspect, however, that officials were not strict. For example, Hadrian, in the early 2nd century A.D., decreed that no horses should be ridden within city limits. Yet, later in the same century, Marcus Aurelius had to issue the same mandate as well as others repeating earlier legislation against riding and driving inside the limits of any city. This obvious repetition of laws reveals a rather lax state of law enforcement. However, the vehicular traffic laws themselves carried the means of their own destruction; from the beginning exceptions were granted other than those relating to religious functions. By the 3rd century A.D. these exemptions had been extended to various state magistrates and were assumed by others of high social station. Pedestrians were no longer free from the threat of injury or even death at the hands of a careless chariot driver.

# 6. Lust and Blood Lust As Roman Popular Entertainments

## Legalized Prostitution

&§ E. Royston Pike

A woman who wished to become a public prostitute, or *meretrix* (from *merere*, "to earn"; whence our word "meretricious", meaning primarily something characteristic or worthy of a harlot, but by extension, flashy or gaudy) was required to make personal application to the aedile [Roman police official]. Standing before his desk she stated her name, place of birth, and age, and also the name under which she proposed to carry on her trade. It was the aedile's duty to try to get her to change her mind, to "go away and think about it" before committing herself to a manner of life which had so many disadvantages and was generally regarded as disreputable. If the woman insisted, however, the aedile was then required to issue her a licence to practice prostitution . . . , ascertain the sum she proposed to charge her clients, and enter her name on the roll of professional prostitutes that was kept at his office.

Sometimes one sees it stated that once a woman's name was on the roll it could never be removed: repentance could never restore her to respectability. But this is disproved by the cases on record of women who had abandoned their profession and returned to respectable life.

Registration at the aedile's office gave the prostitute a legal right to her fee. If a client bilked her she was entitled to make a formal complaint at the office; and the aedile, if he found the complaint proved, was required to compel the man to pay the sum that the woman was entitled to charge.

While her earnings were thus defended by the public official, the prostitute was required to pay an annual tax equivalent to the amount received in one day from a single client. This tax was paid into the municipal treasury, and the local authority could be relied upon to see that it was demanded by the aedile's officers and duly paid. Women who fell behind in their payments were given a black mark in the aedile's book, and if they fell too much in arrear they might be given a good whipping in public and then chased out of town and warned not to show their face there again.

In his biography of Caligula, Roman emperor from A.D. 37 to 41, Suetonius mentions that he augmented his revenues by imposing a number of fresh taxes and imposts, including, as Philemon Holland puts it in his version, "out of the gets and takings of common strumpets as much as they earned by once lying with a man," and furthermore, "that there should be liable to the tribute not only the parties themselves that by the trade of harlotry got their living, but even they likewise who kept houses of bawdry."

When she had been entered upon the aedile's list the meretrix was required to dress in such a manner as to make clear her profession. She was forbidden, by law, to wear the *stola*, the long dress with slits in the sides for the arms, that was gathered up below the breasts by a girdle; this was considered too modest a dress for a woman of loose morals. Instead she was required to wear a robe that resembled the toga of the men. Certain colours that were considered too loud for respectable females were flaunted by the prostitute, who might be as colourful as she pleased. And instead of attempting to hide her figure in gowns with voluminous folds the meretrix went in for dresses of gossamer fineness and transparency. An appropriate name for such material was "windwoven." While the matron modestly veiled her head when she went out of doors, the prostitute faced the world with a brazenly open face. She might not wear shoes but she was allowed sandals, which very often were gaily coloured and perhaps bejewelled. She was not supposed to wear jewellery, but we may suppose that this ban was not strictly enforced. Among other restrictions she was not allowed to wear purple, as this was the colour of robes of honour, nor to wear her hair in fillets, as these were the marks of maidenly modesty. And while on the subject of hair, it should be mentioned that the meretrix paid great attention to her coiffure. There may even have been a regulation that she should dye her hair a flaming yellow or even a raging red, or she may have preferred to wear a brightly coloured wig instead.

When professionally engaged the prostitute commonly went naked, but if she belonged to the superior sort she might perhaps paint the *papillae* or tips of her breasts with gold leaf. . . .

A registered prostitute or meretrix might carry on her profession on her own, taking a room in the suburbs and doing her own soliciting. But more often, it is supposed, she was attached to a "house of bawdry."

The Roman name for a brothel was *lupanar*, and the *lupanaria* were of two main kinds. In one the establishment was owned and managed by a *lupanarius*, the prostitutes were his employees, and all their earnings were his. Generally the fees were collected at the entrance, but anything that the women were given direct was required to be handed over to the manager as soon as the business was concluded. Very often the prostitutes were slaves, actually owned by the brothel proprietor, in which case they were absolutely at his disposal. Even those women who were legally free occupied a position that was only a very little better than slaves, condemned as they were to lead a life of infamy from which there was small hope of their ever being able to make their escape.

In the other sort of lupanar the women's condition may well have been much better. The place was in the nature of an "assignation house," in that it contained a number of rooms which were let by the proprietor to prostitutes on a weekly, monthly, or yearly basis, or it may have been for only a night or even an hour or two at a time. The women made their own financial arrangements with their customers, and after they had paid their rent and their share of the expense of the necessary staff, heating and lighting, etc., everything that they earned was their own to do what they liked with. Thus notwithstanding their occupation, they were still in considerable measure controllers of their own lives and persons.

Lupanaria differed greatly in size, equipment, cleanliness and general conditions, and in their charges. In Rome they seem to have resembled small houses, consisting of a central court or atrium on to which opened a number of small chambers, cells, or cubicles, in which the women operated. In the middle of the court a fountain might be playing, and there was a supply of water laid on. The walls were covered with frescoes of a generally indecent character, including representations of sexual postures and practices that might have an aphrodisiacal effect or perhaps serve as advertisements of the kind of thing that might be indulged in for the appropriate fee. The fittings of the cells were likewise obscene and lust-provoking; thus the lamps might be shaped like a phallus and the chamber utensils figured with suggestive designs.

As for the closets in which the "rites of love" were celebrated, they were dark and gloomy little places, only a few feet square, with one small window high up in the wall or perhaps with no window at all. A curtain was all that separated the cell from the passage, and the only illumination was an oil lamp. The furniture consisted only of a bed or couch. Sometimes this was a wooden frame on which were a mattress and a couple of coverlets, but often it was nothing more than a platform of earth and the pillow a wooden roller. Over the door of each cell was a wooden tablet on which was written the name of its occupant, together with the price of her favours; on its reverse side was the word *occupata*, so that it could be turned round when the woman was going about her business with a customer....

At Pompeii a lupanar has been discovered and restored. It is seen to consist of a ground floor containing a number of cubicles, each just large enough to take a bed, separated by a passage; upstairs a number of discreet little rooms were available for the convenience of clients who preferred some privacy in their "sex." Some of these rooms have balconies over the street. The walls of the passage were covered with indecent pictures; and on the wall of the establishment outside was a large wooden phallus, as a sufficient indication of the kind of activity that was carried on within.

Prostitution in the lupanaria was carried on under the supervision of the aedile, who, in the absence of a proper police force, was responsible for the maintenance of public order. He had a number of men under him to carry out his orders. They patrolled the streets and cleared them of disorderly elements; they had the right of entering a lupanar at all hours, and saw that the places were closed from daybreak until three o'clock in the afternoon; and in the event of brawls, they were empowered to arrest, charge, and punish those responsible. A lupanar-keeper who failed to keep his list of inmates up to date, or who allowed a woman to work in his establishment who had not been properly registered, was liable to a fine and a public whipping. Another of the aedile's duties was to send unregistered whores packing but this was not always easy, since they might be under the protection of influential citizens.

The man who ran the establishment was responsible to the aedile for its proper management. He, or it might be she, had control of a staff of employees, large or small as the case might be. In the best houses these included in addition to the domestic staff a cashier (*villiacus*) who sat at a desk near the entrance, arranged the terms with customers, and took the cash; stewards who supplied the guests with wine and light refreshments, boys who carried water to the cubicles, and runners who kept contact with the outside world and brought in fresh clients. Then on the female side there were chambermaids and hairdressers, *ancillae ornatrices* or tirewomen, who strove to ensure that their charges always looked their best, and needlewomen and dressmakers whose principal job it was to repair the rents in the flimsy garments that the prostitutes sometimes put on so that their customers might experience the sexual "kick" of ripping them off again. In the downtown establishments there was very likely a "chucker-out," a strong-arm man capable of dealing with any client who made himself a nuisance.

Unless the job was undertaken by the manager, there was also a *leno* or bawd, a man or woman charged with the recruiting of fresh brothel-fodder—a matter of constant concern, since in the harsh and humiliating conditions of work not even the sturdiest woman could be expected to last for long.

In the first sort of lupanaria most, if not all, of the women would be slaves, bought in the open market or through private treaty with a slave-raider, but in those that were akin to assignation-houses the whores would be drawn very largely from the class of freedwomen.

All these women were there because they had to be, no other way of life being open to them. But strange as it must appear, there were also women serving in the establishment of their own free will. The career of a meretrix in a lupanar seems, indeed, to have had an extraordinary fascination for some well born and easy circumstanced ladies. There were no psychoanalysts in ancient Rome, or we might have been provided with some intensely interesting human documents explaining why the performance of the most intimate acts in circumstances which even in the best establishments must have been disgusting and degrading, should have had such an appeal.

The fact seems to be well established. Thus we are told by Tacitus in his *Annals* that in A.D. 19 a Roman lady named Vestilia, married to a man of good position, and herself a member of a highly regarded family, went to the aedile's office and demanded to be registered as a prostitute. This example of female profligacy was too much for the Government, and the Senate promptly passed an ordinance that "no woman should be allowed to trade in her body if her father, grandfather, or husband had been a Roman knight," i.e. belonged to the middle class. Vestilia's husband was also called over the coals. How was it that he had not taken action against his guilty spouse? Even if he had not taken the law into his own hands and slain her as had been the custom in the "good old days," he should have at least shown his resentment at her conduct by repudiating her and obtaining a divorce. The husband made the rather feeble excuse that the law allowed sixty days in which to take action, and that time was not yet expired. It was thereupon decreed that if the husband and relatives of a woman found guilty of unchastity were slow to take action against her, the law might be set in motion by a member of the general public. Vestilia was banished to a rocky islet in the Cyclades, but this does not seem to have had much of a deterring effect, if we may believe Juvenal's story of the Empress Messalina repairing to a brothel to gratify her inordinate lust.

Messalina was an extraordinary exception, but from other sources we may learn that Roman ladies were not over nice in their amours. "'Tis the wild extravagance of some women to be in love with filth," the lady's maid in Petronius' novel *Satyricon* tells the narrator, when discussing her mistress's strange infatuation for a man who seems little higher than a servant; "nor can they be raised to an appetite but by the charms, forsooth, of some slave or lacquey. Some can be pleased with nothing but the strutting of a prizefighter with a hacked face, or an actor betrayed to prostitute himself on the stage. Of this sort is my Lady, who indeed prefers the paltry lover of the upper gallery, with his dirty face and oaken staff, to all the fine gentlemen of the boxes."

## Bread and Circuses

ఆ§ Jerôme Carcopino

[Juvenal attacked his contemporaries with] a laconic indictment which throbs more with scorn than anger: "Now that no one buys our votes, the public has long since cast off its cares; the people that once bestowed commands, consulships, legions, and all else, now meddles no more and longs eagerly for just two things—bread and circuses. . . ."

The Caesars had in fact shouldered the dual task of feeding and amusing Rome. Their monthly distributions at the Portico of Minucius assured the populace its daily bread. By the shows and spectacles they provided in various public places, religious or secular, in the Forum, at the theatres, in the Stadium, in the Amphitheatre, in mock sea fights . . . , they occupied and disciplined its leisure hours. They kept the plebs expectantly awaiting the ever-renewed entertainments, and even in lean years, when treasury shortages compelled them to ration their expenditure, they exhausted their ingenuity to provide the public with more festivals than any people, in any country, at any time, has ever seen. . . . The emperors developed skill in canalising . . . mass emotion and directing its currents, and often succeeded in transferring to the multitude the responsibility for acts of vengeance which they had already planned but preferred to execute under an appearance of popular duress. Thus the spectacles of Rome, though not forming an integral part of the governmental system of the empire, helped to sustain its structure, and without becoming incorporated in the imperial religion, fanned whatever flame still burned in it.

Nor was this all: they formed a barrier for autocracy against revolution. In the city there were 150,000 complete idlers supported by the generosity of the public assistance, and perhaps an equal number of workers who from one year's end to the other had no occupation after the hour of noon and yet were deprived of the right to devote their spare time to politics. The shows occupied the time of these people, provided a safety valve for their passions, distorted their instincts, and diverted their activity. A people that yawns is ripe for revolt. The Caesars saw to it that the Roman plebs suffered neither from hunger nor ennui. The spectacles were the great anodyne for their subjects' unemployment, and the sure instrument of their own absolutism. They shrewdly buttressed their power by surrounding the plebs with attentions and expending fabulous sums of money in the process. . . . [Augustus] wanted to enjoy himself with his people, and he spared nothing to give them pleasure, so that the spectacles of his reign surpassed in splendour and in variety anything which had been admired before. . . . And as each Caesar succeeded the last he bettered the example of Augustus, in order that it might not be said that the spectacles of his reign were less brilliant than those of former emperors. If we except Tiberius—this crowned republican whose incurable misanthropy extended alike to plebeian and patrician—all the emperors vied with each other to enlarge the program of the traditional games, lengthening them sometimes till sunrise, and duplicating them with innumerable extra shows not in the calendar. Even the niggardly did not dare to shirk this expenditure. Under Claudius, who was economical, the Roman games cost 760,000 sesterces; and the Apollinarian games, which had cost their founder in his day 3,000 sesterces, ran to 380,000. Even under the upstart Vespasian, son of a clerk, whose reputation for economy is well established, the building of the Flavian amphitheatre began. The magnitude of its own dimensions even more than its proximity to the colossal statue of the sun earned it eventually the name of the "Colosseum." The wiser emperors vied with the worst in this debauchery of pleasure and squandering of money; and the most ostentatious, the most apparently foolish in the matter was perhaps Trajan, the model emperor . . . whose perfection was held to be worthy of Jupiter. In reality, as Fronto saw it, "his wisdom never failed to pay attention to the stars of the theatre, the circus, or the arena, for he well knew that the excellence of a government is shown no less in its care for the amusements of the people than in serious matters, and that although the distribution of corn and money may satisfy the individual, spectacles are necessary for the contentment of the masses." . . .

THE RACES. The games par excellence at Rome were those of

the circus (*circenses*). They cannot be considered apart from the building they took place in and drew their name from. The circuses were built expressly for them, and whatever their dimensions their plan was uniform, consisting of a long rectangle, rounded off at one end into a semicircle. The Circus Flaminius, built in 221 B.C. by the censor Flaminius Nepos on the site corresponding to the present Palazzo Caetani, was 400 metres by 260; the Circus Gai which Caligula built on the Vatican was 180 metres by 90; its central obelisk now adorns the Piazza San Pietro; the oldest and the largest of all was the Circus Maximus, which served as a model for the other two. . . . We must perhaps allow for some exaggeration in their estimate, but it is safe to pin our faith to the 255,000 seats which we can deduce from the testimony of the elder Pliny for the Flavian period, plus the additional 5,000 attributed to Trajan by Pliny the Younger.

Even with these allowances the figure is staggering. Like the Olympic Stadium at Berlin, the Circus Maximus when in use seemed a city in itself, ephemeral and monstrous, set down in the middle of the Eternal City. . . .

The truth is that the Roman crowd revelled in these spectacles where everything combined to quicken their curiosity and arouse their excitement: the swarming crowd in which each was carried off his feet by all, the almost incredible grandeur of the setting, the perfumes and gaily-coloured toilets, the sanctity of the ancient religious ceremonies, the presence of the august emperor, the obstacles to be overcome, the perils to be avoided, the prowess needed to win, the unforeseen vicissitudes of each of the contests which brought out the powerful beauty of the stallions, the richness of their accoutrements, the perfection of their training, and above all the agility and gallantry of drivers and riders. . . .

Excitement seized the public the moment dust began to fly beneath the chariot wheels, and until the last lap was ended the spectators panted with hope and fear, uncertainty and passion. What anguish at the slightest hitch, and thrills when the posts were turned without mishap! If the chariot hugged the turning post too closely, it ran the risk of crashing into it; if, on the other hand, it swung out too far, it either lost position or was run into by the chariot following and again ran the risk of being wrecked. The *agitator* was subjected to a double strain: looking ahead, he must encourage and guide his horses; looking behind, avoid the impact of the chariot which was trying to pass him. He could breathe freely again only when he had safely reached the goal, after having fourteen times steered clear of the turning posts, kept or improved his place, escaped the snares of the track, and outwitted the stratagems of his competitors. The inscriptions which commemorate his victories conceal none of the difficulties he had overcome in achieving them—he had kept the lead and won: *occupavit et vicit;* he had passed from second to first place and won: *successit et vicit;* he had been the "dark horse" whom no one expected to win and who in a supreme moment had triumphed: *crupit et vicit.* The winner was greeted with a storm of applause and the winning driver and his beasts were overwhelmed by the outburst of the crowd's enthusiasm. . . .

GLADIATORS, LIONS, AND CHRISTIANS. Revisiting the arenas of Rome after nearly two thousand years of Christianity, we feel as if we were descending into the Hades of antiquity. The amphitheatre demands more than reproach. It is beyond our understanding that the Roman people should have made the human sacrifice, the *munus,* a festival joyously celebrated by the whole city, or come to prefer above all other entertainment the slaughter of men armed to kill and be killed for their amusement. As early as 160 B.C. the public deserted the theatre where the *Hecyra* of Terence was being performed, for one of these gladiatorial combats. By the first century B.C. the populace had grown so greedy for the sights that candidates sought to win votes by inviting the people to witness spectacular scenes of carnage. In order to put an end to corrupt practices the Senate in 63 B.C. passed a law disqualifying for election any magistrate who had financed such shows for the two years preceding the voting. It was natural that aspirants for the imperial throne should play on the people's passion to promote their own ambitious aims. Pompey even sated his fellow-citizens with combats; Caesar freshened their attraction by the luxury with which he surrounded them. Finally the emperors, deliberately pandering to the murderous lust of the crowds, found in gladiatorial games the most sure, if also the most sinister, of their instruments of power. . . .

The *munera* usually lasted from dawn to dusk, although sometimes, as under Domitian, they were prolonged into the night. It was, therefore, all important to vary the fighting, and the gladiators were trained to fight on water in a *naumachia* as readily as on the firm arena of the amphitheatre. They were not, however, pitted against wild animals; such contests were reserved for the *bestiarii.*

Writers and inscriptions on monuments tell of several types of animal contests or hunts (*venationes*). There were some relatively innocent ones to break the monotony of massacre—tame animals doing incredible circus turns which surprised and amused Pliny the Elder and Martial: teams of panthers obediently drawing chariots; lions releasing from their jaws a live hare they had caught; tigers coming to lick the hand of the tamer who had just been lashing them; elephants gravely kneeling before the imperial box or tracing Latin phrases in the sand with their trunks. There were terrible spectacles, in which ferocious beasts fought duels to the death: bear against buffalo, buffalo against elephant, elephant against rhinoceros. There were disgusting ones in which the men, from the safe shelter of iron bars or from the height of the imperial box—like Commodus later—let fly their arrows at animals roaring with baffled rage, and flooded the arena with the blood of butchery. Some were given a touch of beauty by living greenery planted in the arena which ennobled the courage and the skill of the fighters. They risked their lives, it is true, in battle with bulls, panthers and lions, leopards and tigers; but they were always armed with hunting spears and glowing firebrands, with bows, lances and daggers, and often accompanied by a pack of Scotch hounds, so that they were exposing themselves no more than the emperor himself in the hunts, which were in those days a kind of minor war. They made it a point of honour to redouble the danger by their daring, stunning the bear with their fists instead of their weapons, or blinding the lion by flinging over his head the folds of their cloak; or they would quicken the spectators' pleasure by waving a red cloth in front of the bull, as the Spanish toreadors still do, or by eluding his charge with deft feints and skilful ruses. Sometimes to escape the beast's attack they would scale a wall or leap onto a pole, slip into one of the partitioned turnstiles... which had been prepared beforehand in the arena, or hastily disappear into a spherical basket fitted with spikes which gave it the forbidding appearance of a porcupine....

Some *venationes*, however, usually provided an added attraction to the main spectacle of gladiators. They were but a slight exaggeration of the stern reality of ancient hunting, and can hardly be a reproach to the amphitheatre, for the Praetorian cavalry sometimes took part in them as in military manoeuvres. What revolts us is the quantity of victims, the bath of animal blood: 5,000 beasts were killed in one day of the *munera* with which Titus inaugurated the Colosseum in 80 A.D.; 2,246 and 443 in two *munera* of Trajan....

*Hoplomachia* was the gladiatorial combat proper. The night before, a lavish banquet, which was destined to be the last meal of many, united the combatants of the morrow. The public was admitted to view this *cena libera*, and the curious circulated round the tables with unwholesome joy. Some of the guests brutalised or fatalistic, abandoned themselves to the pleasures of the moment and ate gluttonously. Others, anxious to increase their chances by taking thought for their health, resisted the temptations of the generous fare and ate with moderation. The most wretched, haunted by a presentiment of approaching death, their throats and bellies already paralysed by fear, gave way to lamentation, commended their families to the passers-by, and made their last will and testament.

On the following day the *munus* began with a parade. The gladiators
... alighted in front of the amphitheatre and marched round the arena
in military array, dressed in chlamys dyed purple and embroidered in
gold. They walked nonchalantly, their hands swinging freely, followed
by valets carrying their arms; and when they arrived opposite the imperial [couch] they turned toward the emperor, their right hands extended in sign of homage, and addressed to him the justifiably melancholy salutation: 'Hail, Emperor, those who are about to die salute thee!'
... When the parade was over, the arms were examined ... and blunt
swords weeded out, so that the fatal business might be expedited. Then
the weapons were distributed, and the duellists paired off by lot. Sometimes it was decided to pit against each other only gladiators of the
same category, while at other times gladiators were to oppose each
other with different arms ... or, to add spice to the spectacle, such
freak combinations as negro against negro, as in the *munus* with which
Nero honoured Tiridates, king of Armenia; or dwarf against woman, as
in Domitian's *munus* in 90 A.D.

Then at the order of the president the series of duels opened, to the
cacophonies of an orchestra, or rather a band, which combined flutes
with strident trumpets, and horns with a hydraulic organ. The first pair
of gladiators had scarcely come to grips before a fever, like that which
reigned at the races, seized the amphitheatre. As at the Circus Maximus
the spectators panted with anxiety or hope, some for the Blues, others
for the Greens, the spectators of the *munus* divided their prayers between the ... men armed with small shields ... whom Titus preferred,
or the ... men armed with large shields ... whom Domitian favored.
Bets or *sponsiones* were exchanged.... At every wound which the
gladiators inflicted on each other, the public—trembling for its stakes
—reacted with increasing excitement. If the opponent of their champion
happened to totter, the gamblers could not restrain their delight and
savagely counted the blows: "That's got him! (*habet*)"; "Now he's got
it! (*hoc habet*)"; and they thrilled with barbaric joy when he crumpled
under a mortal thrust.

At once the attendants, disguised either as Charon or as Hermes
Psychopompos, approached the prostrate form, assured themselves that
he was dead by striking his forehead with a mallet, and waved to their
assistants ... to carry him out of the arena on a stretcher, while they
themselves hastily turned over the blood-stained sand. Sometimes it
happened that the combatants were so well matched that there was no
decisive result; either the two duellists, equally skilful, equally robust,
fell simultaneously or both remained standing.... The match was
then declared a draw and the next pair was called. More often the loser,
stunned or wounded, had not been mortally hit, but feeling unequal to

continuing the struggle, laid down his arms, stretched himself on his back and raised his left arm in a mute appeal for quarter. In principle the right of granting this rested with the victor, and we can read the epitaph of a gladiator slain by an adversary whose life he had once spared in an earlier encounter. It professes to convey from the other world this fiercely practical advice to his successors: "Take warning by my fate. No quarter for the fallen, be he who he may!" ... But the victor renounced his claim in the presence of the emperor, who often consulted the crowd before exercising the right thus ceded to him. When the conquered man was thought to have defended himself bravely, the spectators waved their handkerchiefs, raised their thumbs, and cried: "*Mitte!* Let him go!" If the emperor sympathised with their wishes and like them lifted his thumb, the loser was pardoned and sent living from the arena.... If, on the other hand, the witnesses decided that the victim had by his weakness deserved defeat, they turned their thumbs down, crying: "*Iugula!* Slay him!" And the emperor calmly passed the death sentence with inverted thumb....

Then, too, there were moments in the normal full-day program at Rome when exceptional atrocities were committed. The *gladiatores meridiani*, whose account was squared at the noon pause, were recruited exclusively from robbers, murders, and incendiaries, whose crimes had earned them the death of the amphitheatre. ... Seneca has described this shameful procedure for us. The pitiable contingent of the doomed was driven into the arena. The first pair were brought forth, one man armed and one dressed simply in a tunic. The business of the first was to kill the second, which he never failed to do. After this feat he was disarmed and led out to confront a newcomer armed to the teeth, and so the inexorable butchery continued until the last head had rolled in the dust.

The morning massacre was even more hideous. Perhaps it was Augustus who unintentionally invented this spectacular punishment when he erected in the Forum a pillory which collapsed and dropped the victim, the bandit Selurus, into a cage of wild beasts. Later the idea was taken up and made general. Criminals of both sexes and all ages, who by reason of their villainy—real or supposed—and their humble status had been condemned *ad bestias*, were dragged at dawn into the arena to be mauled by the wild animals loosed from the basement below. This spectacle in which the victims were thrown defenseless to savage animals is graphically represented in a Tripolitan mosaic.

This was the kind of torture heroically undergone by the virgin Blandina in the amphitheatre at Lyons, by Perpetua and Felicita in Carthage, and in the Eternal City itself by so many Christians, anony-

mous or canonised, of the Roman Church. In memory of these martyrs
a cross now rises in the Colosseum in silent protest against the barbarism which cost so many of them their lives before the spirit of
Christianity succeeded in abolishing it. Today we cannot see this
emblem without a shudder.

# 7. The Roman Baths As Popular Recreation

## The Importance of the Roman Baths
✍️ Lawrence Wright

Wide-span roofs of the past tell us one important thing about the people who built them. The purpose that they thought deserved a great enclosed space, and the technical effort of roofing it, is likely to have been their main interest in life. Today it is the aircraft hangar, with an even greater span than the exhibition hall or the cinema. In the nineteenth century it was the railway station; in the eighteenth century the noble mansion; in the Middle Ages the cathedral. In Rome it was the public bath. Here was the focus of communal life. Bathing was a basic social duty. The highest architectural and constructional skills were devoted to its setting.

The colossal scale of these baths is difficult to grasp. The Baths of Caracalla covered a site about 1100 ft. square, more than six times the site area of St. Paul's Cathedral, and could take 1600 bathers at a time. The Baths of Diocletian are said to have had twice this capacity: the vestibule alone sufficed Michelangelo for conversion into the great church of S. *Maria degli Angeli*.

Rome was supplied with water by thirteen aqueducts of which the longest ran for about fourteen miles. Knowing tourists often point out that all this masonry was quite unnecessary, and that the silly Romans should have known that water finds its own level: a pipe run across the valley would have served. But the Romans were not so ignorant of hydraulic principles; they simply had no metal suitable to stand up to the pressure, such as bronze, in sufficient quantity to make such very large pipes. They well understood the relative costs of materials and labour.

61

The remaining overhead aqueducts have made such a dramatic impression on travellers, that it is not generally realised that the course of the Roman aqueducts was mainly underground. About A.D. 52 the total length of the eight main aqueducts was about 220 miles of which only about 30 miles ran above ground.

In the fourth century A.D., Rome had 11 public baths, 1352 public fountains and cisterns, and 856 private baths. Some private houses at Pompeii had as many as 30 taps. As well as private water-flushed latrines, there were plenty of public ones; Rome in A.D. 315 had 144; in Puteoli there was one for every 45 persons, and in Timgad one for every 28.

At the peak Rome supplied 300 gallons per head per day. In London today we use about 51 gallons per head per day, of which 34 are for domestic and 17 for trade use; they must have wasted more than we do, but even so must have used more, especially for bathing.

### The Baths and Bathers

⊷§ Jerôme Carcopino

The word for baths is Greek; but it represented a specifically Roman reality—the association for the first time of the sports of the *palaestra* which exercised the body and the *thermae* which cleansed it. The baths are one of the fairest creations of the Roman Empire. They not only benefited civilisation, after their fashion, but also served art, which has been permanently enriched by monuments whose spaciousness, proportions, and technical perfection command our profound admiration even in their decay. In building the *thermae* the emperors put personal hygiene on the daily agenda of Rome and within reach of the humblest; and the fabulous decoration lavished on the baths made the exercise and care of the body a pleasure for all, a refreshment accessible even to the very poor. . . .

The primary feature of these *thermae* was every type of bath that inguenity could devise: hot, cold, and hot-air baths, the swimming bath, and the tub bath. Externally the enormous quadrilateral was flanked by porticos full of shops and crowded with shopkeepers and their customers; inside it enclosed gardens and promenades, stadia and rest rooms, gymnasiums and rooms for massage, even libraries and museums. The baths in fact offered the Romans a microcosm of many of the things that make life attractive. . . .

This was not all: this imposing group of buildings was surrounded by an esplanade, cooled by shade and playing fountains, which gave space for playing grounds and was enclosed by a continuous covered promenade (the *xystus*). Behind the *xystus* curved the *exedrae* of the gymnasiums and the sitting-rooms, the libraries, and the exhibition halls. This was the truly original feature of the *thermae*. Here the alliance between physical culture and intellectual curiosity became thoroughly Romanised. Here it overcame the prejudice which the importation of sports in the Greek style had aroused. No doubt conservative opinion continued to look askance at athletics, as encouraging immorality by exhibitionism and diverting its devotees from the virile and serious apprenticeship required by the art of war, teaching them to think more of exciting admiration for their beauty than of developing the qualities of a good foot soldier. But opinion presently ceased to be offended at nudism in the baths, where it was obligatory, and admitted almost all athletic games to equal honour, as long as they were not practiced as a spectacle, but for their own sake and served the same salutary purpose as the baths themselves. Games prefaced and reinforced the tonic effect of the baths on bodily health and fitness. ... In vain Augustus, Nero, and Domitian had tried to effect a revolution in manners by transplanting to Rome a copy of the Olympic games. It was reserved to the *thermae* to succeed where the emperors had failed, for at the period of which we are writing the Roman people had contracted the habit of attending the baths daily and spending the greater part of their leisure there....

In the days of Martial and Juvenal, under Domitian, and still under Trajan, there was no formal prohibition of mixed bathing. Women who objected to this promiscuity could avoid the *thermae* and bathe in *balneae* provided for their exclusive use. But many women were attracted by the sports which preceded the bath in the *thermae*, and rather than renounce this pleasure preferred to compromise their reputation and bathe at the same time as the men. As the *thermae* grew in popularity, this custom produced an outcropping of scandals which could not leave the authorities undisturbed. To put an end to them, sometime between the years 117 and 138 Hadrian passed the decree mentioned in the *Historia Augusta* which separated the sexes in the baths ... by assigning different hours for the men's and women's baths.

The bath itself usually consisted of three parts. First, the bather, drenched in sweat [from his pre-bath athletic exertions], went off to undress—if he had not already done so—in one of the dressing-rooms or *apodyteria* of the baths. Then he entered one of the *sudatoria* [steam baths] which flanked the *caldarium* [warm water bath], and encouraged the sweating process in this hothouse atmosphere: this was "the dry bath." Next he proceeded to the *caldarium*, where the temperature was almost as warm and where he could sprinkle hot water from the large tub known as the *labrum* on his sweating body and scrape it with the strigil [scraper]. Cleansed and dried, he retraced his steps to the *tepidarium* [lukewarm bath] to cool off gradually, and finally he ran to take a plunge in the cold pool of the *frigidarium* [cold water bath]. . . .

It was in practice impossible for the bather to rub himself down properly with the strigil. An assistant of some sort was indispensable, and if he had not taken the precaution of bringing some slaves of his own with him, he discovered that such assistance was by no means furnished gratis. . . .

Hadrian's biographer relates that the emperor often bathed in the public baths with everyone else. One day he saw there an old soldier whom he had known in the army, busily rubbing himself against the marble with which the brick walls of the *caldarium* were faced, and asked why he was doing this. The old man replied that you had to have money to keep slaves, whereupon the princeps provided him with both slaves and money. Not unnaturally, the next day when the emperor's presence was announced a number of old men set to rubbing against the marble. Hadrian merely advised them to rub each other down.

We are safe in assuming that only the poor took the emperor's advice. Rich people could afford to have themselves served, rubbed, massaged, and perfumed as they would. . . .

It is impossible not to believe that the Romans, in the physical well-being and pleasant lassitude induced by exercise and bath, felt the beauty which surrounded them sink quietly into their souls.

It is true that the Romans themselves found evil to say about their *thermae*, and that many abuses flourished there. It is all too well established that there lurked under the stately porticoes vendors of food and drink and procurers of both sexes; that many congregated there to overeat and drink and indulge other disreputable tastes; that many heated themselves merely in order "to raise a thirst," and found bathing a stimulant for other excesses: "You will soon pay for it, my friend, if you take off your clothes, and with distended stomach carry your peacock into the bath undigested! This leads to death and an intestate old age!" Such overindulgence in bathing as Commodus practiced who took up to eight baths a day, could only soften the muscles and exasperate the nerves. We may fairly condemn abuses which the victims cynically acknowledged: "baths, wine, and women corrupt our bodies—but these things make life itself." . . .

Nevertheless I am convinced that the imperial baths brought immense benefit to the people. In their dazzling marble grandeur the *thermae* were not only the splendid "Palace of Roman Water," but above all the palace of the Roman people, such as our democracies

dream of today. In them the Romans learned to admire physical cleanliness, useful sports, and culture; and thus for many generations they
kept decadence at bay by returning to the ancient ideal which had
inspired their past greatness and which Juvenal still held before them
as a boon to pray for: "a healthy mind in a healthy body." . . .

# 8.  Roman Homes and Banquets

## The Houses in Rome
&§ Jerôme Carcopino

Now we must remember that the ancient Romans had no access to
the almost unlimited suburban space which overground and underground transport puts at the disposal of London, Paris, and New York.
... They were driven to compensate for this lack of room by two con-
tradictory expedients: narrow streets and tall houses. Imperial Rome
was continually forced to juxtapose her splendid monuments to an in-
coherent confusion of dwelling-houses at once pretentious and uncom-
fortable, fragile and inordinately large, separated by a network of
gloomy, narrow alleys....

   Even in the most luxurious Roman house, the lighting left much to
be desired: though the vast bay windows were capable of flooding it
at certain hours with the light and air we moderns prize, at other times
either both had to be excluded or the inhabitants were blinded and
chilled beyond endurance. Neither in the Via Biberatica nor in Trajan's market nor in the Casa dei Dipinti at Ostia do we find any traces
of mica or glass near the windows, therefore the windows in these
places cannot have been equipped with the fine transparent sheets of
*lapis specularis* with which rich families of the empire sometimes
screened the alcove of a bedroom, a bathroom or garden hothouse, or
even a sedan chair. Nor can they have been fitted with the thick,
opaque panes which are still found in place in the skylight windows
of the baths of Herculaneum and Pompeii, where they provided a
hermetic closure to maintain the heat without producing complete

66

darkness. The dwellers in a Roman house must have protected themselves, very inadequately, with hanging cloths or skins blown by wind or drenched by rain; or overwell by folding shutters of one or two leaves which, while keeping cold and rain, midsummer heat or winter wind at bay, also excluded every ray of light. In quarters armed with solid shutters of this sort the occupant, were he an ex-consul or as well known as the younger Pliny, was condemned either to freeze in daylight or to be sheltered in darkness. The proverb says that a door must be either open or shut. In the Roman *insula,* on the contrary, the tenant could be comfortable only when the windows were neither completely open nor completely shut; and it is certain that in spite of their size and number, the Romans' windows rendered them neither the service nor the pleasure that ours give us. . . .

To make matters worse, the [Roman house] was as ill supplied with water as with light and heat. I admit that the opposite opinion is generally held. People forget that the conveyance of water to the city at State expense was regarded as a purely public service from which private enterprise had been excluded from the first, and which continued to function under the empire for the benefit of the collective population with little regard for the needs of private individuals. According to Frontinus, a contemporary of Trajan, eight aqueducts brought 222,237,060 gallons of water a day to the city of Rome, but very little of this immense supply found its way to private houses. . . .

The Roman houses, moreover, caught fire as frequently as the houses of Stamboul under the Sultans. This was because, in the first place, they were unsubstantial; further, the weight of their floors involved the introduction of massive wooden beams, and the movable stoves which heated them, the candles, the smoky lamps, and the torches which lighted them at night involved perpetual risk of fire; and finally, . . . water was issued to the various stories with grudging hand. All these reasons combined to increase both the number of fires and the rapidity with which they spread. The wealthy Crassus in the last century of the republic devised a scheme for increasing his immense fortune by exploiting these catastrophes. On hearing the news of an outbreak, he would run to the scene of the disaster and offer profuse sympathy to the owner, plunged in despair by the sudden destruction of his property. Then he would offer to buy on the spot—at a sum far below its real value—the parcel of ground, now nothing but a mass of smouldering ruins. Thereupon, employing one of the teams of builders whose training he had himself superintended, he erected a brand new [house], the income from which amply rewarded him for his capital outlay.

## Country Villas
◁§ Samuel Dill

Great as were the attractions of the capital, its gay social circles with their multifarious engagements, its games and spectacles, and literary novelties, yet the most devoted "Ardelio," in the end, felt the strain and the monotony to be oppressive. Seneca and Pliny, Martial and Juvenal, from various points of view, lament or ridicule the inanity and the slavery of city life. Roman etiquette was perhaps the most imperious and exacting that ever existed. Morning receptions, punctilious attendance at the assumption of the toga, at betrothals, or the sealing of wills, or the reading of some tedious epic, advice or support in the law courts, congratulations to friends on every official success, these duties, and many others, left men, who had a large circle of acquaintance, hardly a moment of repose. Hence the rapture with which Pliny escapes to the stillness of the Laurentine pine woods, or the pure cold breezes that blew from the Apennines over his Tuscan seat. In these calm solitudes the weary advocate and man of letters became for a little while his own master, and forgot the din and crush of the streets, the paltry ambitions, the malevolent gossip and silly rumours of the great world, in some long-suspended literary task. There can be no doubt that an intense enjoyment was becoming more and more felt in country life. Its unbought, home-grown luxuries, its common sights and sounds, its antique simplicity, have a strange charm even for a hardened bohemian like Martial. But Pliny, besides this commoner form of enjoyment, has a keen and exquisite feeling for beauty of scenery. He loves the amphitheatre of hills, crowned with immemorial forest that looks down on rich pastoral slope, or vineyard or meadow, bright with the flowers of spring, and watered by the winding Tiber; he loves the scenery of Como, where you watch the fishermen at his toils from some retreat on the terraced banks. . . .

The literature of the Flavian age [late first and second centuries A.D.] has preserved for us many pictures of Roman villas. They occupied every variety of site. They were planted on rocks where the sea-foam flecked their walls, or on inland lakes and rivers, embowered in woods, or on the spurs of the Apennines, between the ancient forest and the wealthy plain. Some of these mansions were remote and secluded. But on the Bay of Naples, on the Laurentine shore or the banks of Lake Como, they clustered thickly.

It is possible that the great Roman country seat, in its vast extent, although not in the stateliness of its exterior, may have surpassed the corresponding mansions of our time. It was the expression in stone of the dominant passion of an enormously wealthy class, intoxicated with the splendour of imperial power, and ambitious to create monuments worthy of an imperial race. Moreover, the Roman's energy always exulted in triumphing over natural difficulties. Just as he drove his roads unswerving over mountain and swamp, so he took a pride in rearing his piles of masonry on the most obstinate and defiant sites, or even in the middle of the waves. But, in the extent of their parks, and the variety of floral display, the Romans of the most luxurious age seldom reached the modern English standard. The grounds of the villas which, in thick succession, lined the Laurentine or Campanian shore, cannot have been very extensive. Pliny has splendid views from his windows of forest, mountain, and meadow, but the scene lies plainly beyond the bounds of his demesne. The gardens and shrubberies are very artificial, arranged in terraces or labyrinths close to the house, or with hedges of box clipped into shapes of animals along an open colonnade. The hippodrome at his Tuscan seat, for riding exercise, is formed by lines of box and laurel and cypress and plane tree. The fig and mulberry form a garden at the Laurentine villa. The cultivated flowers are few, only roses and violets. But the Romans made up for variety by lavish profusion. In the Neronian orgies a fortune was sometimes spent on Egyptian roses for a single banquet.

## Roman Banquets

*Jerôme Carcopino*

To picture the *cenae* [evening meals] of the Romans as so many eating orgies would be like imagining an Arab's feast the measure of his usual fare, or supposing that the long, lavish, hospitable meal offered at a country wedding represented the peasant's normal standard of living. The truth is that in similar settings and with identical customs and etiquette, there was a great difference between one *cena* and another according to the circumstances, personal tastes, and moral standards of individuals. The Romans might make their one and only proper dinner a vulgar eating contest or a dignified meal of delicacy and distinction.

Apart from such historic monsters as Vitellius and Nero who sat down to table at noon, the hour of dinner was approximately the same for all; after the bath, that is to say, at the end of the eighth hour in winter and the ninth in summer. This was the usual time in Pliny the Younger's circle for their "elegant and frugal repast." It is the time suggested by Martial to his friend Iulius Cerialis whom he invites to meet him at the eighth hour at the baths of Stephanus, the nearest to his house, proposing to take him home for dinner afterwards. On the other hand the time the *cena* ended depended on whether it was an ordinary meal or banquet, on whether the host was temperate or a glutton. When Pliny the Elder rose from table it was still light in summer and in winter the first hour of the night was not yet past. Nero's *cena* lasted until midnight, and Trimalchio's till the small hours, the revelers to whom Juvenal addresses his reproaches "began their sleep with the rise of Lucifer, the morning star, at an hour when our generals of old would be moving their standards and their camps."

Whatever the length of the dinner, well-to-do people always served it in a special room of their house or flat, the *triclinium*, whose length was twice its breadth. The dining-room took its name from the couches with three reclining places each (*triclinia*) on which the guests reposed. This is an important detail of procedure to which we should have difficulty in adapting ourselves, and one nearer to the oriental custom of using cushions and divans, than to our practice. Nothing would have induced the Romans of the empire to eat otherwise. They considered the reclining position indispensable to their physical comfort, but also a mark of elegance and of social distinction. In the old days it was good enough for a woman to eat, seated at her husband's feet. But now that the Roman matron took her place beside the men on the *triclinia*, to eat sitting was suitable only for children, who sat on stools in front of their parents' couch, or for slaves, who received permission to recline like their masters only on holidays; for village rustics or provincials from distant Gaul, or the passing customers of inns or taverns. Whether or not they had donned for dinner the correct loose *synthesis* of light muslin which was suited to the warmth engendered by a ceremonial meal and was sometimes changed between the courses, the Romans would have thought it unseemly not to dine reclining, men and women side by side. Opinion approved the austerity of Cato of Utica who, in mourning the rout of the senatorial army, made on the eve of Pharsalus a vow which he kept to the day of his suicide: to eat seated as long as the tyranny of Julius Caesar should be triumphant.

Three sloping couches were ranked around a square table, one side of which was left free for the service. The slope of the couches was so contrived that the edges came slightly above the level of the table. Each couch, more or less luxurious in its equipment, was spread with a mattress and with coverings, while cushions divided the central place from the other two. The illbred host who was not minded to put himself out for his guests sometimes occupied the central couch alone, or tolerated only one companion beside or rather "below" him. For the places had a sort of hierarchic precedence, and their allotment was dictated by punctilious etiquette. The couch of honour was that op-

posite the empty side of the table ... ; and on it the most honourable
position was the right hand one, "the consular." ... Next in honour
came the couch to the left of the central one ... , and last that on the
right. ... On each of these couches the most privileged position was
that to the left nearest the fulcrum or head of the couch. The other
places were filled later. The guests reclined crosswise on the couches,
their left elbow resting on a cushion, their feet, which they had freed
from shoes or slippers and washed on entering, at the foot of the couch.
Not infrequently a round table was preferred to a square one, and the
three couches replaced by one ... forming an arc of a circle or, as the
phrase was, in the form of a *"lunar sigma."* The most important personages occupied the two ends of the [arch], on which nine people
could recline at a pinch, but which normally accommodated only seven
or eight. If more than nine persons were to dine, other [tables] had to
be brought ... into the dining-room, usually planned for thirty-six
guests around four tables or for twenty-seven around three.

An usher ... announced the guests and showed them to their couch and
place. Several waiters ... brought in the dishes and the bowls and placed
them on the tables. Since the time of Domitian it had been the fashion
to cover the table with a cloth ... ; before this it had been the custom
merely to wipe the marble or wooden table top after each course. The
guests were provided with knives and toothpicks and spoons of various
shapes ... , and a little pointed spoon ... with which eggs and shell-
fish were eaten. The Romans knew no more of forks than the Arabs
of today or the Europeans at the beginning of modern times. They
ate with their fingers and this entailed frequent hand washings—before
the meal began, and after each course. Slaves went round the couches
with ewers and poured fresh perfumed water over the diners' hands
wiping them with the towel they carried over their arm. Each guest
was provided with a napkin for his personal use, which he spread in
front of him so as not to stain the covering of the couch. A man had
no hesitation in bringing his own napkin with him, for good manners
permitted him to carry it away filled with titbits ... which he had not
had time to consume.

It would certainly have required a Gargantuan appetite to polish off
some of the menus recorded in literature. The full dress *cena* consisted
of at least seven courses or *fercula*—"which of our grandfathers dined
by himself off seven courses?" asks Juvenal, ... —the hors d'oeuvres or
*gustatio*, three entrées, two roasts, and the dessert. ... We see the procession of courses pass, with a supplementary roast thrown in, at Trimalchio's feast—a "ridiculous meal," not because of the excess of food,
which is scarcely more horrifying than the menu of certain official
banquets Macrobius records for us three centuries later, but for the

complacent folly of the master, his childish excitement over his inventions, and the pretentious eccentricities of his dishes.

> A donkey in Corinthian bronze stood on the sideboard with panniers holding olives, white in one side, black in the other. Two dishes hid the donkey; Trimalchio's name and their weight in silver was engraved on their edges. There were also dormice rolled in honey and poppy seed, and supported on little bridges soldered to the plate. Then there were hot sausages laid on a silver grill, and under the grill damsons and seeds of pomegranate.

The guests were still busy with the hors d'oeuvres "when a tray was brought in with a basket on it, in which there was a hen made of wood, spreading out her wings as they do when they are setting. . . . Two slaves came up and began to hunt in the straw. Peahen's eggs were pulled out and handed to the guests." Each egg was found to contain a "fat becafico rolled up in spiced yolk of egg." The second entrée arrived on a dish of monumental and puerile design.

> Its novelty drew every eye to it. There was a round plate with the twelve signs of the Zodiac set in order, and on each one the artist had laid some food fit and proper to the symbol; over the Ram, ram's head pease, a piece of beef on the Bull, kidneys over the Twins, over the Crab a crown, an African fig over the Lion, a barren sow's paunch over Virgo, over Libra a pair of scales with a muffin on one side and a cake on the other, over Scorpio a small sea fish, over Sagittarius a bull's eye, over Capricorn a lobster, over Aquarius a goose, over Pisces two mullets.

Underneath the top part of the dish "we saw in the well of it fat fowls and sows' bellies and in the middle a hare got up with wings to look like Pegasus," while at the corners of the dish "four figures of Marsyas also caught the eye; they let a spiced sauce run from their wine skins over the fishes which swam about in a miniature Euripus." After this the roasts came in, in corresponding style:

> A tray was brought in with a wild pig of the largest size upon it wearing a cap of freedom, with two little baskets woven of palm twigs hanging from its tusks, one full of dry dates, the other of fresh. Round it lay sucking pigs made of simnel cake with their mouths to the teats, thereby showing that we had a sow before us.

A bearded man came who drew a hunting knife which he plunged into the pig's side, whereupon "a number of thrushes flew out." Presently the slaves who were dressed up as Homeric heroes stood back

> to let a boiled calf on a presentation dish be brought in. There was a helmet on its head. Ajax followed and attacked it with his sword drawn as if he were mad; and after making passes with the edge and the flat he collected slices on the point, and divided the calf among the astonished company.

Finally came the dessert: "A Priapus made by the confectioner standing in the middle, holding up every kind of fruit and grapes in his wide apron." Between the *cena* proper and the ... dessert, the tables were taken away and replaced by others, and while the dining-room attendants were engaged on this task, others "sprinkled about sawdust coloured with saffron and vermilion and what I had never seen before— powdered talc."

It might have seemed that at this point the satiated guests would think of nothing but taking their leave and going home to bed. But just as the banquet seemed about to close, it began afresh. Trimalchio made his guests take a red-hot bath, and led them into a second dining-room where wine flowed in rivers, and where those weary of eating could at least continue to drink, ... the popular conclusion of such dinners.

A first libation inaugurated the meal. After the hors d'oeuvre a honey wine ... was served. Between the other courses the [waiters], while replenishing the guests' supply of little hot rolls, solicitously filled their drinking cups with every sort of wine, from those of Marseilles and the Vatican—not highly esteemed—up to the "immortal Falernian." Wine blent with resin and pine pitch was preserved in amphorae whose necks were sealed with stoppers of cork or clay and provided with a label ... stating the vintage. The amphorae were uncorked at the feast, and the contents poured through a funnel strainer into the mixing-bowl ... from which the drinking-bowls were filled. Anyone who drank these heavy wines neat was considered abnormal and vicious, a mark for contumely. It was in the [mixing-bowl] that the wine was mixed with water and either cooled with snow or in certain circumstances warmed. The proportion of water was rarely less than a third and might be as high as four-fifths. [Following] dinner was a sort of ceremonial drinking match in which the cups were emptied at one draught. It was the exclusive right of the master of ceremonies to prescribe the number of cups, imposed equally on all.... He also determined the style in which the ceremony should be performed: whether a round should be drunk beginning with the most distinguished person present . . . , whether each in turn should empty his cup and pass it to his neighbour with wishes for good luck, or whether each should drink the health of a selected guest in a number of cups corresponding to the number of letters in his *tria nomina* of Roman citizen.

We may well wonder how the sturdiest stomachs could stand such orgies of eating, how the steadiest heads could weather the abuses of the [ceremonial drinking matches].

Perhaps the number of victims was sometimes smaller than the number of invited guests. There were often, in fact, many called but few chosen at these ostentatious and riotous feasts. Out of vanity, the master of the house would invite as many as possible to dine; then from selfishness or miserliness he would treat his guests inhospitably. Pliny the Elder criticises some of his contemporaries who "serve their guests with other wines than those they drink themselves, or substitute inferior wine for better in the course of the repast." Pliny the Younger condemns severely a host at whose table "very elegant dishes were served up to himself and a few more of the company; while those placed before the rest were cheap and paltry. He had apportioned in small flagons three different sorts of wine," graduated according to the social status of his friends. Martial reproaches Lupus because his mistress "fattens, the adultress, on lewdly shaped loaves, while black meal feeds your guest. Wines of Setia are strained to inflame your lady's snow; we drink the black poison of a Corsican jar." . . .

The evils of gluttony were somewhat lessened also by the very leisureliness which characterised the long-drawn program of the elaborate *cena*. Many banquets lasted eight or ten hours, like Trimalchio's dinner. They were divided into acts, as it were: in the interval after the entrées a concert was accompanied by the gesticulations of a silver skeleton; after one roast there was an acrobatic turn and Fortunata danced the *cordex*; before dessert there were riddles, a lottery, and a surprise when the ceiling opened to let down an immense hoop to which little flasks of perfume were attached for immediate distribution. It was very generally felt that no dinner party was complete without the buffooneries of clowns, antic tricks of wantons around the tables, or lascivious dances to the clatter of castanets, for which Spanish maidens were as renowned in Rome as are the Aulad Nail among the Arabs of Algeria today. Pliny the Younger found nothing amusing in such entertainments: "I confess I admit nothing of this kind at my own house, however I bear with it in others." The Pantagruelian feast which such interruptions helped the diners to digest often ended in an orgy whose indecency was aggravated by the incredible lack of embarrassment displayed.

# 9. *The Diversions of the Legionaries*

## *The Off-Duty Roman Soldier*
~§ Ramsay MacMullen

Soldiers, even in the midst of war, are at grips with the enemy only a small part of the time, and as to a garrison—and frontier—force, such as the Roman, life within its routine was peaceful in the extreme. Many a recruit need never have struck a blow in anger, outside of a tavern. His unit, if it was the Third Augusta, Tenth Gemina, or the Second Adiutrix, remained fixed in the same camp over a period of centuries. In the conventional sense, he was a soldier only very occasionally, though he was always surrounded by the influences of his profession.

Had the Roman army been perpetually at war, those professional influences would have had an altogether negligible impact on the inner empire. Contact with civilians would have been infrequent, predatory, and abrupt; the largest social institution seen in ancient times (outside, or rather inside, of the Roman empire itself) would have stamped itself on history only through its victories and defeats; the study of the army would properly revert to the narrowest soldier. Since, however, the legionary was husband and father, local citizen and patron, a handicraftsman, tax collector, engineer, veterinarian, farmer, and plain idler —all in a military way—during most of most days, his mark on civilian life was profound, and its effects on him in turn were also profound, at least in the Empire's declining centuries. Only when he was not a soldier could he directly influence his fellows, only in his nonmilitary capacity could he militarize civilians; and only in the period after Septimius Severus did the gradual approximation of the two walks of life, military and civilian, become historically important. . . .

Separated from home and family by the act of his enlistment, cramped into very close sleeping quarters, and drifting from day to day in a routine strictly regulated, he grew restive. He rarely saw action, to provide excitement or a demonstration of the purpose of his career. . . . They might, for relief, lose their money at dice. They might even lose their lives. In the settlement outside the gate of the fort at Housesteads, one house was christened by the excavators "the gambler's rendezvous," and beneath the floor of another were found the bodies of two murdered people. It was safer to go hunting, or to fight lions and bears. The companies had men assigned to the chase, and their bear hunters, of whom one, a centurion at Xanten, thanked Diana, *merito*, for the capture of fifty bears in six months. He was perhaps supplying the troops of gladiators occasionally attached to the legions, pictures of which were popular at Dura. At Aquincum, the Second Adiutrix had an organist . . . troops in the Transjordanian desert were accompanied to their post by a lyre player; the men at Antioch, gathered for an eastern march, were said to "spend their time clapping actors"; while Dura had its own "play actors of the Fourth Scythian Legion." From the impressive, sometimes indeed monumental, amphitheaters regularly found near permanent camps, and at Dura built within the city, we would expect to learn even more of such delight in games and shows, but they were of course not advertised by commanders. They were a discreet concession to human nature.

At Dura, one last building deserves mention. It was a large house two blocks from the garrison, rented for nine months by a troupe of entertainers, operating out of Zeugma, and with a changing list of residents, some of whom in fact had to find rooms in other houses nearby. From a number of carefully displayed pictures we learn the names of sixty-three people. About two thirds were women. Men and women alike were identified by nicknames—mime, fool, hetaera—the women being mostly prostitutes without skills, the men being actors trained in special roles. . . .

City life demoralized troops, no doubt about it. The fact was a commonplace embroidered by literary men like Fronto, who point particularly to Syria, and revel in lurid details. Soldiers misbehaved in their billets; they brawled; and as the practice of lodging them in towns grew more common, in the later third and fourth centuries, criticism echoed from other places: Trapezus and Constantinople, as well as Antioch. One of the most common sources of trouble was the baths. Not only did the military authorities object to soldiers spending quite so much time in hot water, but local authorities complained about officers of terrifying importance demanding that town baths be heated up especially for them. Against such demands, a citizen had only the satisfaction of knowing that they were quite illegal. There was also the occasional scandal of soldiers hanging about the women's baths. . . .

In its relations with civilians, the army gained a very well-publicized notoriety, on which writers ancient and modern have concentrated their disapproval. The subject lends itself to full treatment: soldiers hanging about bars and brothels, women's baths and theaters; filching the very cooking pots from the poorest billets, or applying a kind of blackmail, "shakedown," or "protection racket" to their hosts, exactly like Prohibition gangsters; of greater historic significance, importing to peaceful centers the manners of an unreclaimed barbarism, in the later Empire. For all this there is at least some fragment of evidence, and sometimes a great amount. Against its implications may be set, especially in economic matters, equal evidence of stimulation from the presence of garrisons, evidence of the diffusion of Roman forms and (no less important) of good Roman silver. The army was a mixed blessing. The important thing to remember is not the good or bad in this relation but the fact, everywhere so manifest, that the relation existed at all; and a very close one it was.

# 10. Classical Religious Practices and Early Christianity

## The Eleusinian Mysteries

*⊷§ George Thomson*

The Great Mysteries of Eleusis were celebrated annually in the month of Boedromion, which coincided approximately with our September and immediately preceded the month in which the crops were sown for the ensuing year. . . .

The man or woman who wished to be admitted to the Great Mysteries had first of all to be initiated at the Little Mysteries of Agra, which were said to have been founded by Demeter for the benefit of Herakles. When Herakles was about to descend into Hades, he went to Eleusis and asked to be initiated, but was rejected on the ground that he was a stranger. Accordingly, he was adopted into the community by Demeter at Agra, and then his request was granted. The Little Mysteries were celebrated in the month of Anthesterion, corresponding to the latter part of February and the first part of March, when the last summer's wine matured. After participating in these Mysteries, the candidate was not initiated at Eleusis in the following autumn, but had to wait at least until the following year. This interval was evidently a period of probation. . . . We are also told that the cloak worn by the candidate during his initiation might not be changed, but had to be worn continuously until it fell off.

The candidates assembled at Athens in the presence of . . . the high priests of the Eumolpidai and the Kerykes, who issued a solemn proclamation in which they warned the unworthy to depart. Barbarians and unpurified homicides were explicitly disqualified.

Next followed purification. The candidate procured a pig, drove it down to the shore, and bathed with it in the sea. The pig was then slaughtered, and its blood spilt over the candidate, who sat on a low seat, his head veiled. On the analogy of primitive initiation, we may conjecture that the pig's blood was a substitute for the candidate's own, and the significance of the veil is explained when we find that it was worn by both parties at marriage, and that at death it was both placed over the head of the corpse and worn by the relatives as a sign of mourning. In the present instance it was perhaps associated with the myth of Demeter, who is described in the Homeric Hymn as sitting veiled in mourning for her daughter.

The next stage in the proceedings is obscure. It consisted apparently of a sacrifice and an intrusive element from the cult of Asklepios at Epidauros. The candidates are also described as "staying at home." Then ... singing and dancing through the fields, the great procession set out for Eleusis, escorting the image of Iakchos, which seems to be another intrusive element, derived from the cult of Dionysus. Various ceremonies were performed on the way, including the exchange of imprecations and obscene jests at the bridge over the Kephissos. This is a primitive fertility rite of world-wide distribution, but, not being specially connected with initiation, it need not detain us now. It appears that the procession included those who had only been initiated at Agra in the preceding spring as well as those whose probation was now completed; and consequently, on their arrival at Eleusis, the pilgrims fell into two grades—[those] who had to wait another year before proceeding further, and [those] who were admitted to the Hall of Initiation ..., where the secrets of Eleusis were revealed to them.

What precisely it was that was "seen and heard" on this occasion is a matter of conjecture. It seems clear, however, that there was a sacred marriage enacted by the high priest and priestess, and a ritual drama symbolising the journey of the soul to the judgment seat. One of the most striking features of the ceremony, which can be traced as far back as Æschylus, was the sudden blaze of torchlight which illuminated the darkness and transformed the sorrow of the onlookers into joy. It is also stated that an ear of corn was revealed to them as a sign of their salvation. The other features, deduced from the symbolism of the Homeric Hymn, are too uncertain to be relied on.

The initiates were under a vow to divulge nothing of what they had heard or seen, and the silence thus imposed on them was expressed in the mystical symbol of "the golden key on the tongue." Now, in the Egyptian ritual of the dead, after the body had been purified, the lips were touched by a sacred object called the *Pesesh-Kef*. This ceremony was called the Opening of the Mouth, and it ensured that the dead man would be born again in the Underworld. . . .

The main reason why our evidence for the actual content of the Eleusinian Mysteries is so slight is probably not that the secrets were so well kept, but that they were so well known. The habitual and casual familiarity with which such writers as Æschylus and Plato allude to these matters presupposes in their public a general and intimate knowledge, and shows that many of the mystical formulæ had passed into the common currency of everyday Attic speech. These half-veiled allusions, of which Greek literature is full, can be made to reveal, if not the ritual itself, at least the subjective attitude of the mystic, which is almost equally significant.

The Eleusinian initiate differed from other men in that he had "brighter hopes" of the future—the hope of a "better lot" in the life hereafter, when, "delivered from the evils" of mortality, he would obtain the crown of glory and live in the blessed company of the gods. . . .

We conclude that the sense in which the mystic had been "made perfect" by initiation was that he had been invested with a new *moîra* for the life after death. . . . The hope of the mystic was for a better lot, a better portion or *moîra*, in the other world. . . . Thus, the mystical doctrine reproduces the pattern of tribal initiation at every point. At the same time, the old pattern has been charged with an entirely new meaning. In the Mysteries, a ritual which had been designed as a preparation for life has been transformed into a preparation for death. There lies the essence of all mystical religions.

## Mithraic Practices

*❧ Franz Cumont*

In all the religions of classical antiquity there is one feature which, while formerly very conspicuous and perhaps the most important of all for the faithful, has today almost totally disappeared. It is their liturgy. The Mysteries of Mithra form no exception to this unfortunate rule. The sacred books which contain the prayers recited or chanted during the services, the ritual of the initiations, and the ceremonials of the feasts, have vanished and left scarce a trace behind. . . .

[The] ceremony of initiation appears to have borne the name of sacrament . . . , doubtless because of the oath which the neophyte took and which was compared to that made by the conscripts enrolled in the army. The candidate engaged above all things not to divulge the doctrines and the rites revealed to him, but other and more special vows were exacted of him. Thus, the mystic that aspired to the title of *Miles* was presented with a crown on a sword. He thrust it back with his hand and caused it to fall on his shoulder, saying that Mithra was his only crown. Thereafter, he never wore one neither at banquets nor when it was awarded to him as a military honor, replying to the person who conferred it: "It belongs to my god," that is to say, to the invincible god.

We are as poorly acquainted with the liturgy of the seven Mithraic sacraments as we are with the dogmatic instructions that accompanied them. We know, however, that conformably to the ancient Iranian rites, repeated ablutions were prescribed to neophytes as a kind of baptism designed to wash away their guilty stains. As with a certain class of Gnostics, this lustration doubtless had different effects at each stage of initiation, and it might consist according to circumstances either in a simple sprinkling of holy water, or in an actual immersion as in the cult of Isis. . . .

It must not be supposed that Mithraism exhibited nothing more than the benignant phantasmagoria of a species of ancient freemasonry. There had subsisted in its liturgic drama vestiges of its original barbarism, of the time when in the forests, in the depths of some dark cave, corybantes, enveloped in the skins of beasts, sprinkled the altars with their blood. In the Roman towns, the secluded caverns of the mountains were replaced by subterranean vaults . . . of far less imposing aspect. . . . But even in these artificial grottos the scenes of initiation were calculated to produce on the neophyte a profound impression. When, after having traversed the approaches of the temple, he descended the stairs of the crypt, he perceived before him in the brilliantly decorated and illuminated sanctuary the venerated image of the tauroctonous Mithra erected in the apse, then the monstrous statues of the leontocephalous Kronos, laden with attributes and mystic symbols, the meaning of which was still unknown to him. At the two sides, partly in the shadow, the assistants, kneeling on stone benches, were seen praying. Lamps ranged about the choir threw their bright rays on the images of the gods and the celebrants, who, robed in strange costumes, received the new convert. Fitful flashes of light skillfully manipulated impressed his eyes and his mind. The sacred emotion with which he was seized lent to images which were really puerile a most formidable appearance; the vain allurements with which he was confronted appeared to him serious dangers over which his courage triumphed. The fermented beverage which he imbibed excited his senses and disturbed his reason to the utmost pitch; he murmured his mystic formulas, and they evoked before his distracted imagination divine apparitions. In his ecstasy, he believed himself transported beyond the limits of the world, and having issued from his trance he repeated, as did the mystic of Apuleius: "I have transcended the boundaries of death, I have trodden the threshold of Proserpine, and having traversed all the elements I am returned to the earth. In the middle of the night I have seen the Sun scintillating with a pure light; I have approached the gods below and the gods above, and have worshipped them face to face." ...

The ... initiations kept alive in the heart of the neophyte the hopes of truth still more sublime, and the strange rites which accompanied them left in his ingenuous soul an ineffaceable impression. The converts believed they found, and, the suggestion being transformed into reality, actually did find, in the mystic ceremonies a stimulant and a consolation. They believed themselves purified of their guilt by the ritual ablutions, and this baptism lightened their conscience of the weight of their heavy responsibility. They came forth strengthened from these sacred banquets, which contained the promise of a better life, where the sufferings of this world would find their full compensation. The astonishing spread of Mithraism is due in large measure to these stupendous illusions, which would appear ludicrous were they not so profoundly and thoroughly human.

Nevertheless, in the competition between the rival churches that disputed under the Cæsars the empire of human souls, one cause of inferiority rendered the struggle unequal for the Persian sect. Whilst the majority of the Oriental cults accorded to women a considerable role in their churches, and sometimes even a preponderating one, finding in them ardent supporters of the faith, Mithra forbade their participation in his Mysteries and so deprived himself of the incalculable assistance of these propagandists. ... Among the hundreds of inscriptions that have come down to us, not one mentions either a priestess, a woman initiate, or even a donatress. But a religion which aspired to become universal could not deny a knowledge of divine things to one half of the [population].

## *Early Christian Practices*

ᴥᎦ *Louis Duchesne*

In spite of all the laws for its suppression, Christianity continued to spread. About the end of the reign of Marcus Aurelius, *i.e.*, about a century and a half after its birth, Christianity had taken root in the most remote provinces. There were Christian communities in Spain, Gaul, Germany, Africa, Egypt, and even beyond the Euphrates and the Roman frontier. Evangelization had begun with the Jewish communities and their proselytes, but it soon turned direct to the pagans. In this field, it quickly outstripped and absorbed the rival proselytizing movement of the Jews; it presented all the advantages of the religion of Israel, with the addition of more facility of adaptation. Greek, Roman, and Egyptian polytheism it met by the doctrine of One supreme God; idolatry, by spiritual worship; bloody sacrifices and riotous pageants, by devotional exercises of the utmost simplicity, prayers, readings, homilies, and common meals; and the dissolute libertinism, on which the ancient religions imposed no check, was encountered by an austere morality, maintained by the restraints of the life in common. The universal craving to know the origin of all things, and the final destiny of man, found satisfaction in teaching derived from ancient and venerable sacred books, which carried far greater weight than the fables of the poets. The doctrine of angels and more especially that of devils, solved many difficulties as to the origin and power of religious error. Satan and his host afforded an explanation of the problem of evil in general, and of particular ills, and thus formed a bulwark against the rival propaganda of the dualist Mithras worship.

The Jews had demonstrated the strength of all this before. The Christians imparted a new reality to it, by holding up to the love, the gratitude, and the adoration of men the person of their Founder, Jesus, Son of God, revealer and saviour, manifested in human form, seated now at the right hand of God the Father, and soon to appear as the supreme Judge and King of the elect. On Him, on His life portrayed in the new sacred books, and on His coming again—the end and aim of all their hopes—their hearts were continually set. Nay more. In some ways Jesus was present with them still. In the Eucharist, He lived in and amongst His own. And the marvellous charismata—prophecies, visions, ecstasies, and gifts of healing—were to them like a second point of contact with the unseen God. And thence there sprang, both in Christian communities and in individuals, a religious concentration and enthusiasm which proved a most efficacious and powerful means of conversion. Souls surrendered to the attraction of the divine.

And truly it was necessary that the attraction should be strong, for in those days, to aspire to Christianity was to aspire to martyrdom. No one could conceal from himself that by becoming a Christian, he became a sort of outlaw. Let but the authorities be on the alert, or the neighbours ill-disposed, and the heaviest penalties—usually death—ensued. But even martyrdom allured some souls; while for many it formed assuredly a very powerful incentive to belief. The fortitude of the confessor, the serenity with which he endured torture and met his death, the confidence of his upward gaze on the heavenly vision, all this was new, striking, and contagious. . . .

Nevertheless, its attractiveness did not touch the mass of mankind, for Christianity was far from being disseminated everywhere, and multitudes were hardly, if at all, aware of its existence. And many viewed it with profound horror. . . .

To become a Christian was a very momentous step. On many points it was necessary for a man to separate himself entirely from ordinary life. For instance, the theatres, and, speaking generally, the public games, were schools of immorality and foremost among the works of Satan which had to be renounced. So with sins of the flesh. The new Christian had of course to break with idolatry; but it was not always easy for him to avoid all contact with it, for the private life of the ancients was saturated with religion. Marriage, birth, seed-time, and harvest, the inauguration and functions of the magistracy, and family festivals—all were occasions requiring sacrifices, with oblations and incense and banquets. Paul permitted some concessions as to these last. He strictly forbade all participation in the religious feasts celebrated in the precincts of temples; but the fact that any particular piece of meat had formed part of a sacrificial victim was not, in his eyes, a reason for refusing it, provided nobody was scandalized. Here he showed himself more indulgent than they were at Jerusalem in 51 A.D., or than the synagogues were to their proselytes.

Separated as they were from paganism, it was necessary that the faithful should live together. Each Church formed in itself a complete society, the members of which, though they were bound, of course, by the fiscal or other laws of their city and the empire, were yet told to avoid carrying their differences before any other court than that of their own community. Christians intermarried with Christians. If one of the parties in a heathen marriage was converted, the marriage was only dissolved at the request of the one who remained a pagan. But, with this exception, divorce was absolutely forbidden. Absolute virginity was praised and even recommended, in view of the near approach of the Last Day; but it was in no way enforced. In ordinary life, the Christian was to be submissive to the authorities, as to his master if he were a slave; idleness was a disgrace; uprightness and modesty, courtesy in social intercourse the cheerfulness of a single heart, charity, and especially hospitality, were all strongly inculcated.

The religious life was very like that of the synagogue. The faithful met to pray, and to read the Scriptures, in which the great examples of righteous men of old were specially studied. The specifically Christian elements of this primitive worship were the Eucharist and the *charismata* or extraordinary gifts of the Holy Spirit. The Eucharist was celebrated in the evening, after a frugal meal . . . taken in common. The Lord's Supper on the eve of His Passion was thus repeated. As to the manifestations of the Holy Spirit, these appeared under various forms: sometimes there were miraculous cures or other wonderful manifestations; sometimes vision . . . ; sometimes an illumination of mind which manifested itself in a discourse on the mysteries of the Faith, or on the obligations of conscience. . . . The most remarkable of these manifestations were prophecy and glossolalia (the gift of tongues). Prophecy was the gift of knowing hidden things, especially "the secrets of the heart." . . . In like manner, the gift of tongues, which, on the Day of Pentecost enabled the apostles to make themselves understood by people of different nationalities, had nothing in common with this other gift of glossolalia, described by St Paul in his first Epistle to the Corinthians. Neither the speaker with tongues himself, nor those present understood what he said, communication could not be established between them (or rather, between those present and the Holy Spirit), except by means of an inspired interpreter. Yet, even if such an interpreter were not present, it was possible to distinguish in the strange sounds uttered by the speaker, the accents of prayer, praise, or thanksgiving.

Such spiritual phenomena were well calculated to arrest the minds and to sustain the enthusiasm of the first Christians. But abuses followed hard on the use of them, and the use itself might have its drawbacks, if not wisely regulated. The Church at Corinth had only existed four years, and already St Paul is obliged to intervene and to regulate the inspiration of his converts. Even in the celebration of the Eucharist, it was not long before abuses began to creep in. The common meal, which was the first part of it, had to be made as simple as possible. Later on it was separated from the liturgy, and finally it was more or less completely suppressed. . . . Visions, prophecies, and miraculous cures were not indeed destined to disappear entirely, but as they were not compatible with the regular order of the liturgical service, they soon dropped out of it.

No details of the rites of initiation into Christianity are found in the apostolic epistles, but nevertheless they very early assumed fixed and significant forms. For these ceremonies Paul relied on the practical help of his fellow-labourers. Some of the faithful, not content with being baptised themselves, tried to be baptised also for their dead relations and friends.

Among the charismata those should be especially noticed which pertained to the internal ministry of the community. St Paul speaks of those members of the society who worked for it, presiding and exhorting, and of the duties of the faithful towards them; he mentions the "gifts of governments, helps," etc. Soon the terms bishops, priests, and deacons make their appearance. But, in the beginning, the real or principal authority naturally remained in the hands of the missionaries, the founders. Their position was quite different from that of the neophytes who assisted them, at the moment in the practical details of the corporate life.

The meetings were held in private houses, chiefly in those large rooms on the upper storey, which have, at all times, been common in the East. In those countries people excel in the art of crowding themselves into a small space. The assemblies took place in the evening and often lasted till far into the night. And, alongside of the Jewish Sabbath, Sunday was early devoted to divine worship.

A question has often been raised as to whether the first Christian communities in Greek countries were modelled on the pagan religious associations. There are some analogies, as, for instance, in the method of obtaining converts. . . . But these analogies do not go very far. Even apart from the differences of faith and morals, and of worship—which latter amongst the Pagans always involved a temple, an idol, and a sacrifice—there exists a radical contrast in the conception and distribution of authority. The heads of the pagan associations were always temporary and generally elected annually, whilst the Christian priests and deacons held office for life. The pagan leaders derived their powers from the community which had nominated them, of which they were only the agents; the Christian priests, on the contrary, spoke, acted, and governed, in the name of God and the apostles, whose auxiliaries and representatives they were.

## The Success of Christian Fervor
*ᴇᴤ Edward Gibbon*

Our curiosity is naturally prompted to inquire by what means the Christian faith obtained so remarkable a victory over the established religions of the earth. To this inquiry, an obvious but satisfactory answer may be returned; that it was owing to the convincing evidence of the doctrine itself, and to the ruling providence of its great Author. But, as truth and reason seldom finds so favourable a reception in the world, and as the wisdom of Providence frequently condescends to use the passions of the human heart, and the general circumstances of mankind, as instruments to execute its purpose; we may still be permitted, though with becoming submission, to ask not indeed what were the first, but what were the secondary causes of the rapid growth of the Christian church. It will, perhaps, appear that it was most effectually favoured and assisted by the five following causes: I. The inflexible, and, if we may use the expression, the intolerant zeal of the Christians, derived, it is true, from the Jewish religion, but purified from the narrow and unsocial spirit which, instead of inviting, had deterred the

Gentiles from embracing the law of Moses. II. The doctrine of a future life, improved by every additional circumstance which could give weight and efficacy to that important truth. III. The miraculous powers ascribed to that primitive church. IV. The pure and austere morals of the Christians. V. The union and discipline of the Christian republic which gradually formed an independent and increasing state in the heart of the Roman empire. . . .

Whatever difference of opinion might subsist [among early Christian groups] . . . concerning the divinity or the obligation of the Mosaic law, they were all equally animated by the same exclusive zeal and by the same abhorrence for idolatry which had distinguished the Jews from the other nations of the ancient world. The philosopher, who considered the system of polytheism as a composition of human fraud and error, could disguise a smile of contempt under the mask of devotion, without apprehending that either the mockery or the compliance would expose him to the resentment of any invisible, or, as he conceived them, imaginary powers. But the established religions of Paganism were seen by the primitive Christians in a much more odious and formidable light. It was the universal sentiment both of the church and of heretics that the dæmons were the authors, the patrons, and the objects of idolatry. Those rebellious spirits who had been degraded from the rank of angels, and cast down into the infernal pit, were still permitted to roam upon earth, to torment the bodies, and to seduce the minds, of sinful men. The demons soon discovered and abused the natural propensity of the human heart towards devotion, and, artfully withdrawing the adoration of mankind from their Creator, they usurped the place and honours of the Supreme Deity. By the success of their malicious contrivances, they at once gratified their own vanity and revenge, and obtained the only comfort of which they were yet susceptible, the hope of involving the human species in the participation of their guilt and misery. It was confessed, or at least it was imagined, that they had distributed among themselves the most important characters of polytheism, one demon assuming the name and attributes of Jupiter, another of Æsculapius, a third of Venus, and a fourth perhaps of Apollo; and that, by the advantage of their long experience and aerial nature, they were enabled to execute, with sufficient skill and dignity, the parts which they had undertaken. They lurked in the temples, instituted festivals and sacrifices, invented fables, pronounced oracles and were frequently allowed to perform miracles. The Christians, who, by the interposition of evil spirits, could so readily explain every præternatural appearance, were disposed and even desirous to admit the most extravagant fictions of the Pagan mythology. But the belief of the Christian was accompanied with horror. The most trifling mark of respect to the national worship he considered as a direct homage yielded to the demon, and as an act of rebellion against the majesty of God.

In consequence of this opinion, it was the first but arduous duty of a Christian to preserve himself pure and undefiled by the practice of idolatry. The religion of the nations was not merely a speculative doctrine professed in the schools or preached in the temples. The innumerable deities and rites of polytheism were closely interwoven with every circumstance of business or pleasure, of public or of private life; and it seemed impossible to escape the observance of them, without, at the same time, renouncing the commerce of mankind and all the offices and amusements of society. The important transactions of peace and war were prepared or concluded by solemn sacrifices, in which the magistrate, the senator, and the soldier were obliged to preside or to participate. The public spectacles were an essential part of the cheerful devotion of the Pagans, and the gods were supposed to accept, as the most grateful offering, the games that the prince and people celebrated in honour of their peculiar festivals. The Christian, who with pious horror avoided the abomination of the circus or the theatre, found himself encompassed with infernal snares in every convivial entertainment, as often as his friends, invoking the hospitable deities, poured out libations to each other's happiness. When the bride, struggling with well-affected reluctance, was forced in hymenæal pomp over the threshold of her new habitation, or when the sad procession of the dead slowly moved towards the funeral pile; the Christian, on these interesting occasions, was compelled to desert the persons who were the dearest to him, rather than contract the guilt inherent to those impious ceremonies. Every art and every trade that was in the least concerned in the framing or adorning of idols was polluted by the stain of idolatry; a severe sentence, since it devoted to eternal misery the far greater part of the community, which is employed in the exercise of liberal or mechanic professions. If we cast our eyes over the numerous remains of antiquity, we shall perceive that, besides the immediate representations of the Gods and the holy instruments of their worship, the elegant forms and agreeable fictions, consecrated by the imagination of the Greeks, were introduced as the richest ornaments of the houses, the dress, and the furniture, of the Pagans. Even the arts of music and painting, of eloquence and poetry, flowed from the same impure origin. In the style of the fathers, Apollo and the Muses were the organs of the infernal spirit, Homer and Virgil were the most eminent of his servants, and the beautiful mythology which pervades and animates the compositions of their genius is destined to celebrate the glory of the dæmons. Even the common language of Greece and Rome abounded with familiar but impious expressions, which the imprudent Christian might too carelessly utter, or too patiently hear.

The dangerous temptations which on every side lurked in ambush to surprise the unguarded believer assailed him with redoubled violence on the days of solemn festivals. So artfully were they framed and disposed throughout the year that superstition always wore the appearance of pleasure, and often of virtue. Some of the most sacred festivals in the Roman ritual were destined to salute the new calends of January with vows of public and private felicity, to indulge the pious remembrance of the dead and living, to ascertain the inviolable bounds of property, to hail, on the return of spring, the genial powers of fecundity, to perpetuate the two memorable æras of Rome, the foundation of the city and that of the republic, and to restore, during the humane license of the Saturnalia, the primitive equality of mankind. Some idea may be conceived of the abhorrence of the Christians for such impious ceremonies, by the scrupulous delicacy which they displayed on a much less alarming occasion. On days of general festivity, it was the custom of the ancients to adorn their doors with lamps and with branches of laurel, and to crown their heads with a garland of flowers. This innocent and elegant practice might, perhaps, have been tolerated as a mere civil institution. But it most unluckily happened that the doors were under the protection of the household gods, that the laurel was sacred to the lover of Daphne, and that garlands of flowers, though frequently worn as a symbol either of joy or mourning, had been dedicated in their first origin to the service of superstition. The trembling Christians, who were persuaded in this instance to comply with the fashion of their country and the commands of the magistrate, laboured under the most gloomy apprehensions, from the reproaches of their own conscience, the censures of the church, and the denunciations of divine vengeance.

Such was the anxious diligence which was required to guard the chastity of the gospel from the infectious breath of idolatry. The superstitious observances of public or private rites were carelessly practised, from education and habit, by the followers of the established religion. But, as often as they occurred, they afforded the Christians an opportunity of declaring and confirming their zealous opposition. By these frequent protestations, their attachment to the faith was continually fortified, and, in proportion to the increase of zeal, they combated with the more ardour and success in the holy war which they had undertaken against the empire of the dæmons.

# Part Two. THE MEDIEVAL WORLD, 450 TO 1350

The dominant aspects of medieval popular culture involve religion, hierarchy, and combat, the three pervasive social realities of the era. Every facet of medieval life reflects one of these realities, and many reflect all of them.

The opening chapter of Part Two points up the fact that medieval man conceived of nature, himself, and time in such a way that these conceptions conditioned his responses to all existence. The chapter further indicates the tremendous transformation of social life after the breakdown of classical civilization. The second chapter describes the manners, home life, dress, and diversions of the Germanic peoples who introduced new cultural elements into European society after the dissolution of the Roman Empire. The primitive nature of their existence might be compared with the lavishness of Roman home life as described in Part One.

The long third chapter traces the manifold constituents of medieval religious life. Its concern is not with theology or dogma, but with the immediacy of religious practice in the lives of ordinary people. The seriousness of medieval religiosity can be measured by the fervor of the faithful, by their willingness to strive and sacrifice in order to enhance their spiritual lives, and by the multiplicity of social and intellectual trends and factors that contributed to religious devotion and ritual. These people were genuinely concerned about the salvation of their souls. In a relatively short span of time they devoted themselves to the creation and construction of the great Gothic cathedrals, at once the highest expression and best instrument for the implementations of their enormous faith. And the popular support for the crusades, discussed in the fourth chapter, demonstrates the breadth of medieval religiosity: peasants and children, as well as popes, warriors, and kings, set out to find salvation through crusading zeal.

The hierarchical nature of medieval society meant the development of class-oriented subcultures, each marked by somewhat different values, forms, and purposes. The chapter on the royal coronation shows that kings were not merely aristocrats writ large, but through the ritual and ceremony of their office fashioned for themselves an image and a place in society above all other secular figures. The subsequent chapter on aristocratic diversions indicates the dichotomy in the popular culture of the nobles, arising from the fact that aristocratic men were for the most part warriors, preoccupied with violence and the pursuit of glory, while the trappings of chivalry and courtly love were, at least in part, the fabrication of noblewomen attempting to convert a reality they found distasteful into one more satisfying. Eleanor of Aquitaine deserves a separate chapter because her life subsumed most of the significant elements of aristocratic and royal medieval life, and yet the result was virtually a subculture in itself. She, like the Gothic cathedral, was an expression and vehicle of medieval popular culture. At the other end of the social scale may be seen the life and amusements of the peasants. Their diversions depended almost entirely on those occasions in agricultural life which give the farmer and his family a chance to cease their round of toil and exhaustion for a brief moment. Births, marriages, deaths, the most basic and inescapable facets of existence, provided the peasants their moments of joy and release in a life otherwise dominated by the struggle to survive.

In the chapter on university life the modern reader will find much to ponder, especially when it is compared with similar chapters in later sections up to the contemporary era. Students in the middle ages were certainly able to find time for activities far removed from the ethereal and abstruse constructions of scholasticism.

The two final chapters touch on the romantic Arthurian legend and the impact of the Black Death. These chapters are complementary insofar as one is built upon emotional longings far removed from reality and the other involves the most crushing reality of the later middle ages—the death of vast numbers of Europe's population. This counterpoise between the spiritual and the mundane is a recurrent theme in medieval popular culture, and the final selection of the chapter, on the dancing manias following the plague, seems an expression of the violent tension between these two forces.

# 1. Nature, Man, and Time in the Middle Ages

## The Medieval World View
~§ Marc Bloch

The men of the [medieval era] were close to nature—much closer than we are; and nature as they knew it was much less tamed and softened than we see it today. The rural landscape, of which the waste formed so large a part, bore fewer traces of human influence. The wild animals that now only haunt our nursery tales—bears and, above all, wolves— prowled in every wilderness, and even amongst the cultivated fields. So much was this the case that the sport of hunting was indispensable for ordinary security, and almost equally so as a method of supplementing the food supply. People continued to pick wild fruit and to gather honey as in the first ages of mankind. In the construction of implements and tools, wood played a predominant part. The nights, owing to the wretched lighting, were darker; the cold, even in the living quarters of the castles, was more intense. In short, behind all social life there was a background of the primitive, of submission to uncontrollable forces, of unrelieved physical contrasts. There is no means of measuring the influence which such an environment was capable of exerting on the minds of men, but it could hardly have failed to contribute to their uncouthness.

A history more worthy of the name than the diffident speculations to which we are reduced by the paucity of our material would give space to the vicissitudes of the human organism. It is very naive to claim to understand men without knowing what sort of health they enjoyed. But in this field the state of evidence, and still more the inadequacy of our methods of research, are inhibitive. Infant mortality was undoubtedly very high in feudal Europe and tended to make people somewhat callous towards bereavements that were almost a normal occurrence. As to the life of adults, even apart from the hazards of war it was usually short by our standards, at least to judge from the records of princely personages which (inexact though they must often be) constitute our only source of information on this point. Robert the Pious died at about the age of 60; Henry I at 52; Philip I and Louis VI at 56. In Germany the first four emperors of the Saxon dynasty attained respectively the ages of 60 (or thereabouts), 28, 22 and 52. Old age seemed to begin very early, as early as mature adult life with us. This world, which, as we shall see, considered itself very old, was in fact governed by young men.

Among so many premature deaths, a large number were due to the great epidemics which descended frequently upon a humanity ill-equipped to combat them; among the poor another cause was famine. Added to the constant acts of violence these disasters gave life a quality of perpetual insecurity. This was probably one of the principal reasons for the emotional instability so characteristic of the feudal era, especially during its first age. A low standard of hygiene doubtless also contributed to this nervous sensibility. A great deal of effort has been expended, in our own day, in proving that baths were not unknown to seignorial society. It is rather puerile, for the sake of making this point, to overlook so many unhealthy conditions of life: notably under-nourishment among the poor and overeating among the rich. Finally, we must not leave out of account the effects of an astonishing sensibility to what were believed to be supernatural manifestations. It made people's minds constantly and almost morbidly attentive to all manner of signs, dreams, or hallucinations. This characteristic was especially marked in monastic circles where the influence of mortifications of the flesh and the repression of natural instincts was joined to that of a mental attitude vocationally centred on the problems of the unseen. No psychoanalyst has ever examined dreams more earnestly than the monks of the tenth or the eleventh century. Yet the laity also shared the emotionalism of a civilization in which moral or social convention did not yet require well-bred people to repress their tears and their raptures. The despairs, the rages, the impulsive acts, the sudden revulsions of feeling present great difficulties to historians, who are instinctively disposed to reconstruct the past in terms of the rational. But the irrational is an important element in all history and only a sort of false shame could allow its effects on the course of political events in feudal Europe to be passed over in silence.

These men, subjected both externally and internally to so many ungovernable forces, lived in a world in which the passage of time escaped their grasp all the more because they were so ill-equipped to measure it. Water-clocks, which were costly and cumbersome, were very rare. Hourglasses were little used. The inadequacy of sundials, especially under skies quickly clouded over, was notorious. This resulted in the use of curious devices. In his concern to regulate the course of a notably nomadic life, King Alfred had conceived the idea of carrying with him everywhere a supply of candles of equal length, which he had lit in turn, to mark the passing of the hours, but such concern for uniformity in the division of the day was exceptional in that age. Reckoning ordinarily—after the example of Antiquity—twelve hours of day and twelve of night, whatever the season, people of the highest education became used to seeing each of these fractions, taken one by one, grow and diminish incessantly, according to the annual revolution of the sun. This was to continue till the moment when—towards the beginning of the fourteenth century—counterpoise clocks brought with them at last, not only the mechanization of the instrument, but, so to speak, of time itself.

An anecdote related in a chronicle of Hainault illustrates admirably the sort of perpetual fluctuation of time in those days. At Mons a judicial duel is due to take place. Only one champion puts in an appearance—at dawn; at the ninth hour, which marks the end of the waiting period prescribed by custom, he requests that the failure of his adversary be placed on record. On the point of law, there is no doubt. But has the specified period really elapsed? The county judges deliberate, look at the sun, and question the clerics in whom the practice of the liturgy has induced a more exact knowledge of the rhythm of the hours than their own, and by whose bells it is measured, more or, less accurately, to the common benefit of men. Eventually the court pronounces firmly that the hour of 'none' is past. To us, accustomed to live with our eyes turning constantly to the clock, how remote from our civilization seems this society in which a court of law could not ascertain the time of day without discussion and inquiry!

Now the imperfection of hourly reckoning was but one of the symptoms, among many others, of a vast indifference to time. Nothing would have been easier or more useful than to keep an accurate record of such important legal dates as those of the births of rulers; yet in 1284 a full investigation was necessary to determine, as far as possible, the age of one of the greatest heiresses of the Capetian realm, the young countess of Champagne. In the tenth and eleventh centuries, innumerable charters and memoranda were undated, although their only purpose was to serve as records. There are exceptional documents which are better in this respect, yet the notary, who employed several systems of reference simultaneously, was often not successful in making his various calculations agree. What is more, it was not the notion of time only, it was the domain of number as a whole which suffered from this haziness. The extravagant figures of the chroniclers are not merely literary exaggeration; they are evidence of the lack of all awareness of statistical realities. Although William the Conqueror certainly did not establish in England more than 5,000 knights' fees, the historians of a somewhat later time, and even certain administrators (though it would certainly not have been very difficult for them to obtain the right information), did not hesitate to attribute to him the creation of from thirty-two to sixty thousand of these military tenements. The period had, especially from the end of the eleventh century, its mathematicians who groped their way courageously in the wake of the Greeks and Arabs; the architects and sculptors were capable of using a fairly simple geometry. But among the computations that have come down to us— and this was true till the end of the Middle Ages—there are scarcely any that do not reveal astonishing errors. The inconveniences of the Roman numerical system, ingeniously corrected as they were by the use of the abacus, do not suffice to explain these mistakes. The truth is that the regard for accuracy, with its firmest buttress, the respect for figures, remained profoundly alien to the minds even of the leading men of that age.

# 2. Germanic Life in the Early Middle Ages

## At Home with the Barbarians
*R. H. Hodgkin*

HOMES AND HOME LIFE. The first thing to strike our attention is that we find ourselves in an age of wood. The stone houses built in the great days of Roman rule are disused and falling into ruin. There is no new building in stone. The well-to-do, whether Saxon or British, are lucky if they now inhabit log houses. The humbler folk we shall find thankful for walls of wattle and daub, or mud and straw; but with them there is little change from Roman times....

'Heorot', the hall of the king of the Danes, described in *Beowulf*, is magnificent beyond any ordinary building. It was the poet's ideal, the kind of hall to make men stare and envy. From afar could be seen its gleaming roof, with its stag-horns placed on top of the gables. Outside the hall was a bench on which visitors could wait, and there was a place where they could leave their spears before they entered. Inside the hall the first thing to strike a new-comer would be the smell of wood-smoke, and then through the dim light he would see the open hearth running down the centre of the building between the pillars which bore the roof—a hearth with piled-up logs and crackling flames, from which the smoke rose eddying round the draughty room before it could find its way out through holes in the roof. Then the walls would be seen to be hung with arms, and, if it were a royal hall like Heorot, there would be also woven hangings, gold-embroidered.

Round the walls were the benches where the retainers sat through the long evenings, when they feasted and drank and listened to the minstrel, or themselves took their turns at the harp. On these benches they pledged one another, they compared the rings and the arms which had been given them by their lords in return for their services. The veterans, like petty officers, were separated on the benches from the young soldiers; but none the less an old warrior could egg on one of the young men to revive an ancient feud and slay a foreign prince, the guest of their lord. The retainers talked of the wonders of their lord's sword, of its magical powers, of the runic lettering on the blade, the gold of its handle, and its ringed pommel. Half-way down one side of the hall was the high-seat of the king or lord. In front of the king sat his spokesman. Along the opposite wall was the place next in honour to the high-seat. The queen or 'lady' sat by the side of her husband. The women, who had spent the day in housework or spinning, would come from their bower to attend in the hall during the earlier part of the evening's feast, and the 'lady' and her daughters would bear round the ale.

These feastings in the hall stood out in men's minds among the best things in life: the chink of a byrny when a well-armed warrior strode down the hall, the glint of the spears and swords hanging on the walls, cheered the spirits of the men as they drank at the tables. Their weapons were within easy reach; for who could feel sure that enemies, creeping up outside, might not attempt a surprise attack? Who could tell whether the heavy drinking inside might not end in blows?

So far we have been chiefly concerned with the hall of a great king, as it appears in *Beowulf*. It is the most splendid of its kind; but it may stand for the type, since there was no small similarity in the homes and in the customs of all men of the fighting class. Even a lesser thegn or a substantial ceorl might build himself a log house which reproduced the main features of the larger hall of the great man. As we descend in the social scale, we find the hall becoming smaller, the surrounding outhouses in the [village] becoming fewer, and the defences dwindling down to the mere hedge which protected the ceorl. Below these, however, in the lowest grades, we find small huts, miserable buildings crowded together in squalid conditions. . . .

We have been able to say something about the best and the worst dwellings of heathen England, about the halls of the great at the end of the heathen period and the huts of the poor made at the beginning of the settlement. The men and women who lived in these surroundings still escape us. Is it possible to raise the ghosts of these heathen forefathers of ours, the men who spent their days in hunting, fighting, and ploughing, and the women who spun and wove at home and directed their house-slaves? Can we picture even the clothes they wore? . . .

DRESS. The fighting-men have tunics which hang down to above the knee, much like kilts; garments like sleeved jackets; and cloaks or mantles fastened on the shoulder. Some of the men have clumsy puttees wound round their legs; others have their legs either bare or covered with hose. Altogether it is a custom not unlike that of the Highlander. Close-fitting breeches reaching down to the ankle . . . were also no doubt quite a normal mode of covering the legs throughout the Saxon period. The women . . . and the men when they are sedentary or men of dignity, wear long tunics reaching to the ankle or nearly to it, and longer mantles also—fine large sweeping garments, with hoods which can be drawn over the head.

With some exercise of imagination we may perhaps obtain a better idea of the appearance of these heathen men and women from their graves. We can picture the Anglian women with their sleeves caught together at the wrist with the small clasps which are so characteristic a feature of their graves, and their girdle-hangers, like a chatelaine, depending from their tunic-belt and jangling as they move; their menfolk also, long-haired, proud of their cruciform brooches, which become long and flat and increasingly vulgar as the heathen age draws to its close. The fashions of course changed with the changing decades or generations, if not like ours with the changing years.

# 3. *The Dimensions of Popular Religious Life*

## *Popular Aspects of Worship*
◄§ *J. A. Jungmann*

THE MEDIEVAL HUMANIZATION OF CHRIST. In the Middle Ages, the new spirit ruling religious life showed itself with special clarity in this very theme of the Passion. They desired to follow the course of the Passion-story in all its detail, and the favourite scenes were those calculated to evoke sympathy. . . .

The Passion theme was forced into the foreground of pictorial art at about the same time as in devotional life. Preference was now given to scenes, formerly neglected, which are specially capable of arousing feeling. The scourging appears for the first time in the 10th century. With ever increasing elaboration there now follow more pictures of the Way of the Cross, up to the taking down from the Cross. At first these are restrained, but realism slowly gains ground until we arrive at the naturalistic Passion pictures of Gothic art. The portrayals of the Resurrection and of the glorified Christ, which in many places were plentiful in the Byzantine art of the early Middle Ages, are not absent in this period and later, it is true; but they are no longer at the centre of interest. They form rather, the final scene in the Passion drama; and so, because of this and perhaps also because representatives of redeemed humanity are depicted as well, they have lost their historic-redemptive significance. They bear more the character of vanquished suffering than of the beginning of glory.

These manifestations we have just sketched, and which appear even more clearly and emphatically as the Middle Ages advance, are a sign of how the humanity of Christ has become the favourite subject of religious life, in contrast to primitive Christianity's emphasis on Christ's divinity. Devotion to the humanity of Christ was the great medieval innovation.... His earthly life, in the form of a servant, in that form which—contrasting with all that faith knows of divine transcendence—it can alone appeal to sense and arouse feelings of compassion, of amazement, of thanksgiving and repentance in the hearts of the faithful....

POPULAR INVOLVEMENT IN THE LITURGY. Everywhere, in town and country, the worship of God was carried out with great splendour on Sundays and feast days. Work ceased and rest from work was enforced by civil sanctions. As a Synod of Salzburg (1456) insisted afresh, the city gates must be closed on Sundays and feast days so that the peace be not disturbed by travellers with their carts. Feast days, which varied from state to state, were numerous—about fifty in all. Thus, besides Sunday, there was on average one holiday of obligation each week. The days of the apostles and of commemoration of famous saints and martyrs and virgin-martyrs were all observed by cessation of labour. Then there were many local holidays. People took time to worship God: inns were open as a rule not for profit, but for necessary provisions, and most of the free time was devoted to worship. The centre of liturgical life was, as of old, the cathedral church with its canons and clergy....

Setting aside the principle of worship on Sunday and feast days, the people shared in this wealth of liturgical life by the endowments with which they supported the clergy and built and furnished the churches. But the liturgy itself was a clerical liturgy. This was so not merely in conventual churches where the intention had always been to provide a liturgy only for the religious, as with the Cistercian whose churches had small naves reserved for the lay-brothers, but it was true also of churches where the people were meant to worship.

A more or less broad gulf separated clergy and laity. Characteristic of Church life in general, as the Middle Ages drew to a close, was the tension between the laity and the clergy—certainly the higher clergy....

But even at the end of the Middle Ages there remained a vestige of lay participation. There was the sermon; and towards the end of the Middle Ages the sermon enjoyed a certain increase in importance through the activity of the mendicant orders. The priest would at least relate some instruction, a few remarks about the meaning of the current feasts or the lives of the saints who were being commemorated, to the lessons from the liturgy of the Sunday and the days following. Congregation singing in the vernacular appeared first in association with the sermon as the sermon in song....

Another way in which the people took part was at the Offertory procession. This was still part of the liturgy on great festivals at the end of the Middle Ages. It was done chiefly at Christmas, Easter, Pentecost, often on the Assumption, on All Saints and the dedication of the Church. But it was at Nuptial and Requiem Masses that Offertory processions most frequently took place. The preachers of indulgences, too, made their financial gain chiefly through the Offertory procession. The people went up to the altar or walked round and paid their subscription. But we have to admit that an appreciation of the liturgical meaning of these processions was more and more being lost. It scarcely occurred to people, that through their offering they were sharing in the sacrifice of Christ; were expressing the surrender of their own hearts to God's will in the Spirit of Christ: their chief thought seems rather to have been that they could thus obtain a share in the fruits of the Mass on behalf of their deceased relatives or for some other intention. It is most significant that reception of Communion was very rare. Not through Communion but through a material gift did people seek to win a share in the fruits of the Mass.

There was another part of the Mass which people still appreciated at the end of the Middle Ages. That was the elevation of the Host at the *Consecration.* For the very reason that people did not want or did not dare to communicate—and the pastoral attitude put people off rather than encouraged them—they wanted all the more to look at the Host. By contemplating the sacred Host they hoped to gain a blessing on their earthly lives, and certainly profit for their eternal souls.... Benefits were said to attach to hearing Mass. While a man was hearing Mass he did not age; the holy souls in purgatory did not suffer while a Mass was being said for them; at each Mass one soul got out of purgatory; food taken after Mass was more nourishing, and so on.

And so the notion gained acceptance: you only have to be present at Mass—devoutly present, of course....

## Hysterical, Superstitious, and Apocalyptic Mass Religion
≈§ Norman Cohn

Journeymen and unskilled workers, peasants without land or with too little land to support them, beggars and vagabonds, the unemployed and those threatened with unemployment, the many who for one reason or another could find no assured and recognised place—such people, living in a state of chronic frustration and anxiety, formed the most impulsive and unstable elements in medieval society. Any disturbing, frightening or exciting event—any kind of revolt or revolution, a summons to a crusade, an interregnum, a plague or a famine, anything in fact which disrupted the normal routine of social life—acted on these people with peculiar sharpness and called forth reactions of peculiar violence. And the way in which they attempted to deal with their common plight was to form a salvationist group under the leadership of some man whom they regarded as extraordinarily holy.

In this they were following a very usual medieval practice, and one which obtained in the most diverse social strata; at least from the eleventh century down to the close of the Middle Ages the laity was constantly throwing up salvationist movements of one kind or another. To appreciate with what passionate fervour perfectly orthodox Catholics could throw themselves into such movements one has only to read the account given by the Norman abbot Aimo in the middle of the twelfth century. He describes how multitudes of both sexes and all ages, including some of noble birth and great wealth, helped in the building of a church. Having banded together in communities under the leadership either of a priest or of a layman noted for his piety, these people yoked themselves like oxen to wagons loaded with building-materials and dragged them across mountains and rivers to the site of the church. During halts the leaders, working themselves into a frenzy, called their followers to repentance; and the followers scourged themselves, weeping and crying to the Virgin for forgiveness of their sins. 'Hatreds were lulled to sleep, discord put away, debts forgiven, the union of minds restored. But if anyone refused to obey the priest and to put sin from him, his offering was thrown off the wagon as something unclean and he himself expelled with ignominy from the Holy People.' When the teams came to the mouth of a river, led by God they marched straight ahead and lo! the sea was held back for them as it had once been for the Children of Israel. And in their carts they carried sick and dumb and insane people, whom they cured by their prayers. A holy people indeed, chosen by God and endowed with superhuman, thaumaturgic powers. . . .

Tanchelm, the founder of a revolutionary movement which appeared in the north-eastern corner of the Empire about the year 1110, . . . seems to have started his career as a notary at the court of Robert II, Count of Flanders, who once even sent him on an important mission to the Holy See. It was a significant beginning, for the Count was a strong supporter of the policy of ecclesiastical reform which [Pope] Gregory had launched and which was being carried on by his successors. Later Tanchelm set up as a prophet; and found, like most prophets, that success had to be sought in lands other than his own. An attempt to establish himself at Bruges resulted merely in his expulsion from the

town, but outside Flanders—in the islands of Zeeland, in Brabant, in
the prince-bishopric of Utrecht and at Antwerp—he was extremely successful. These territories were going through a period of rapid social
change. Even in earlier centuries, when northern trade had almost died
out, it had always continued in the Rhine delta; and by the beginning
of the twelfth century a vigorous commercial revival was in progress.
At the same time the communal revolution was spreading. In the
episcopal city of Liége the burghers had recently triumphed and in the
episcopal city of Utrecht the rich and powerful merchants, who were
carrying on a lively trade along the Rhine, were becoming increasingly
restive. Despite mass emigrations to the colonial lands east of the Elbe
over-population had become chronic. The towns were filled with a
proletariat which was as unstable emotionally as it was economically
insecure.

Into this society Tanchelm erupted with a violent attack on the
clergy. Dressed as a monk, he began to preach in the open fields; we
are told that his eloquence was extraordinary and that multitudes
listened to him as to an Angel of the Lord. He appeared to be a holy
man—it was not for nothing that his mortal enemies, the Chapter
of Utrecht, complained that like his master the Devil he had all the
appearance of an Angel of Light. As it happened, the only priest in
Antwerp was living in open concubinage; and in his attacks on this
man Tanchelm spoke like any other ascetic reformer in the tradition
of Gregory VII. But soon he was striking out along lines of his own.
He taught not merely that sacraments were invalid if administered
by unworthy hands but that, things being as they were, sacraments
were no better than pollutions, churches no better than brothels. This
propaganda proved so effective that people soon stopped partaking of
the Eucharist and going to church. And in general, as the Chapter
ruefully remarked, things came to such a pass that the more one
despised the Church the holier one was held to be. At the same time
Tanchelm exploited a very material grievance; as the Chapter complained, 'he easily persuaded the populace to withhold tithes from the
ministers of the Church, for that is what they wanted to do'. Tithes
were indeed detested by medieval peasants, who bitterly resented having to surrender a tenth of all their produce from corn to the herbs
in their gardens and the down on their geese. It does not seem however
that Tanchelm's agitation brought any effective relief in this matter. A
priest who was his closest associate did take over a church in Utrecht,
having expelled its normal incumbent; but so far from abolishing the
tithes he merely appropriated them for himself and his master.

Tanchelm's followers formed a blindly devoted community in the
midst of which the heresiarch moved like a monarch. On his way to

deliver a sermon he would walk surrounded by an escort and preceded, not by a crucifix, but by his own sword and banner, borne like royal insignia. He dressed no longer in a monk's cowl but in gilded robes. he wore his hair bound in a triple golden band. Finally he proclaimed that he possessed the Holy Spirit in the same sense and in the same degree as Christ and that like Christ he was God; and all these claims were accepted by the people. He distributed his bath-water among them and some drank it as a substitute for the Eucharist, others treasured it as a holy relic. On one occasion he had a statue of the Virgin Mary brought to him and in the presence of a vast crowd solemnly betrothed himself to her. Coffers were placed on either side of the statue to receive wedding-gifts from male and female followers respectively. 'Now', said Tanchelm, 'I shall see which sex bears the greater love towards me and my bride.' The clergy who witnessed it record with horror how the people rushed to make their offerings, women threw in their ear-rings and necklaces and large sums were collected.

Soon Tanchelm's followers had become an organised movement. The inner circle of followers consisted of a fraternity of twelve men, in imitation of the Apostles, and a woman representing the Virgin Mary. The fraternity was headed by a smith and was called a 'guild'—a clear indication that the movement appealed primarily to artisans. A wider circle of followers was organised as an armed bodyguard and with these Tanchelm used to hold splendid banquets. Although contemporary estimates which put the strength of the bodyguard at 3000 are doubtless, like most medieval statistics, quite unreliable, it was certainly a formidable and fanatical force. These people claimed to be the only true church. We are told that it was unsafe for anyone, even the great princes of the neighbouring territories, to approach Tanchelm save as a follower and that those who did so were commonly killed by the bodyguard. At its height the power of the heresiarch was so great that no feudal lord in those parts could effectively oppose him. A striking tribute to his influence was provided by the Chapter of Utrecht on the occasion in 1112 when the Archbishop of Cologne succeeded in capturing and imprisoning Tanchelm and his right-hand-man the apostate priest. The Bishop of Utrecht had recently died and had not yet been replaced; and in a letter to the Archbishop the canons of the Chapter freely admitted their helplessness. Tanchelm, they insisted, had long been a danger to the church of Utrecht. If he were to be released and allowed to resume his work they would not be able to resist him and the diocese would be lost to the Church without hope of recovery.

Nevertheless Tanchelm did escape and it was only after he had caused 'many massacres'—as the chronicler puts it—that he was killed by a priest, in 1115. Even after that his personality continued to dominate Antwerp for another decade. A congregation of canons specially established for the purpose was unable to counteract his influence and in the end the task was entrusted to the future St Norbert. A great noble who had renounced a brilliant career at the Imperial Court to wander through the world in rags, Norbert was famed as a worker of miracles, a healer of the sick and insane, a tamer of wild beasts. Because of this he was able, though with difficulty, to win the allegiance of the common people away from the spirit of Tanchelm and recapture Antwerp for the Church.

Some thirty years later a similar movement formed around another layman, one Eudes de l'Étoile or Eudo de Stella. This heresiarch is known to have come from a noble family of Loudéac in Brittany; presumably he was one of the innumerable younger sons of noble families who, as primogeniture was gradually established, found themselves without a patrimony. Eudes was a man of dignified bearing and magnetic personality; those who had dealings with him were caught, we are told, 'like flies in a spider's web'. He instituted a church of his own, with archbishops and bishops whom he called by such names as Wisdom, Knowledge, Judgment, and by the names of the Apostles, while he himself assumed the name of Eon. Although these names suggest the influence of some Gnostic or Neo-Manichean tradition, all that is known of Eudes' doctrine is that, like Tanchelm, he declared himself to be the Son of God.

Eudes' movement was unusual in that it operated not in the great centres of commercial, industrial and urban civilization but in the wildest and loneliest regions of remote Brittany and Gascony. Where did the rank-and-file come from, those 'great multitudes of the rough populace' who followed Eudes as the 'King of Kings'? We do not know, although it is perhaps worth noting that the 1140's, when the movement was at its height, were a period of quite exceptional hardship. The winter of 1144 was a terrible one and was followed by two years of appalling famine, during which even the well-to-do found it difficult to meet the exorbitant price of bread. Multitudes of poor folk left lands which could no longer support them and migrated, even overseas. Brittany had been so utterly devastated by the Northmen some two hundred years before that in the twelfth century it still resembled a colonial territory, sparsely populated by free peasants, and much of it covered by dense forests. It was in these forests that Eudes and his followers had their base.

They were a restless and violent horde, moving from province to province with a speed so great that it was attributed to demonic assistance and that the armed bands sent against them were utterly confounded. They laid the land waste; wherever they passed many perished by the sword and many more died of starvation; above all they delighted in raiding and destroying churches, monasteries and hermits' cells. They themselves lived in luxury, magnificently dressed, never doing any manual labour, always in a state of 'perfect joy'. Like the followers of Tanchelm they formed a court over which their leader presided in state and with which he would hold splendid banquets. Contemporaries believed that these feasts were provided by demons and that anyone who partook of them forfeited his understanding and became one of the community forever. Eudes' influence extended far beyond his immediate followers. When the Papal Legate, with the support of the Archbishop of Rouen, undertook to preach against the heresy at Nantes the common people—whether from love or fear of the heresiarch—stayed away.

In 1148 Eudes was taken prisoner—his enemies noted that the capture was signalled by that familiar portent of great happenings, the sudden appearance of a comet. Brought before a synod which was held in Rheims Cathedral by Pope Eugenius III, he declared that he was the One who must come to judge the quick and the dead, and the world by fire. He also explained that a forked staff which he carried regulated the government of the universe: when the fork pointed upwards two-thirds of the world belonged to God and one to himself; when it pointed downwards the proportions were reversed. Though the synod laughed heartily at this it thought it best to commit this dangerous man to prison where, being fed on water and little else, he soon died. His principal disciples, who had been captured along with their master, steadfastly refused to deny him and bore proudly the titles he had given them. They were accordingly condemned to be burnt as impenitent heretics. They remained unshaken to the last. One of them threatened destruction to their executioners and as he was led to the stake cried out continuously: 'Earth, divide thyself!'

'Such', comments a chronicler, 'is the power of error when once it has taken hold of the heart.'

## Popular Vernacular Preaching
*⇌§ G. R. Owst*

"It is characteristic of the primitive mind that it finds a difficulty about universals and is most at home with particulars." ... "The Catholic peasant may find it easier to approach God through and in his special saint, or even a special local form of the Madonna. This is the inevitable corollary of the psychic level at which he lives; and to speak contemptuously of his 'superstition' is wholly beside the point." To some extent it is already true to say that the characteristic features of English medieval preaching ... exhibit this same desire to escape as far as possible from the abstract and the universal in religion, and to be "at home with particulars." ...

Illustrations of the breezy and forceful speech in which vernacular preachers could recount the more familiar Biblical narratives to their listeners need not detain us long. They will be found in sufficient number in the published edition of Myrc's *Festial*; as, for example in the accounts there given of Noah's Ark, the sacrifice of Abraham, Joseph in Egypt, or Adam and Eve in Paradise. It is enough to notice in passing that these same topics constitute favourite episodes of the miracle-plays. A point of greater interest to be observed is the way in which the homilists are often wont to "feudalize" scenes and characters of the sacred text. With a deft touch here and there they bring them "up to date," reclothing them, like ... the sacred figures in early painting, in garments of the period, giving them contemporary titles and ranks, thus making them vivid and familiar to common English folk of the Middle Ages. . . . These sermons bring home to us how living and real many incidents of Scripture must have seemed to ordinary folk in the Middle Ages, which now, through changed social conditions, have lost much of their force, and are clearly events of a dim past.

### The Impact of the Friars

&#x25c2;&sect; David Knowles

St Francis, in his latest Rule, supposed two forms of work as the employment of his friars: the manual work of a craft, or its equivalent in domestic duties, and the preaching of the gospel in its simplest form. The first of these two employments soon ceased to exist as an alternative to the second, especially in the transalpine provinces, where recruitment and training were from the first predominantly clerical. Eccleston, indeed, relates that one of the first friars in England practised a craft in accordance with the Rule, but his language shows that by the time he wrote the fact had become something of a curiosity. The early friars no doubt long continued to do the simple domestic and garden work for themselves, but very soon this, too, passed to the remaining lay brothers and even to servants.

With the disappearance of craft or garden work as a regular employment preaching, with its accompaniment, for those in priest's orders, of hearing confessions, remained alone in the field as work for the rank and file of the Friars Minor, and this was throughout the middle ages their distinctive employment, though in the case of many, during the heyday of scholastic theology, its place was taken by study and lecturing. Unfortunately, no contemporary document gives any detailed account of the preaching journeys and experiences of the first English friars. Eccleston, however, and other chroniclers give incidental anecdotes which show the brethren going about the country two by two, especially in the penitential seasons of Advent and Lent, under conditions of what was at first truly evangelical simplicity, their bare feet cut by the frozen ground and leaving a bloodstained impress on the snow of winter. . . .

The friars, and especially the Preachers, had been sent from Italy with a papal commission to preach, and had been welcomed and employed by many of the bishops. There had therefore at first been no question of any abstract right to preach or to confess; both tasks were no doubt usually executed in early years by mendicants engaged in specific missions or acting with the full cognizance of the bishop. The difficulties arose when the friars, established in all the large towns and no longer the immediate instruments of the diocesan, acquired a clientele among the well-to-do as well as among the poor, and attracted penitents by their more expert knowledge of theology and ethics, and by their more sympathetic attitude which, so their enemies alleged, sprang from easily comprehensible motives of self-interest. Many of their penitents wished to lie in death within the precinct of the friary, so as to share in the daily suffrage of the brethren; this inevitably deprived the parish clergy of the customary burial dues, as also of the normal accompaniment of legacies and foundations for Masses. The parish clergy put up a resistance, claiming the right of burying all parishioners, and to overcome this Innocent IV issued in 1250 the bull *Cum a nobis petitur*, which permitted the friars to bury in their own churches or cemeteries all who might ask this favour. . . .

The emergence of the friars as an official preaching and absolving body, . . . brought them into a collision with bishops and parish priests which issued often in mutual recrimination, sometimes in lawsuits, and occasionally in acts of physical violence. The forensic struggle had its counterpart in intellectual controversy, which as early as the middle of the thirteenth century rose to its height on two principal issues: the validity of the spiritual ideals of poverty and mendicancy, and the theological justice of the friars' claim to exercise the apostolic functions of preaching and administering the sacraments. . . .

At the first appearance of the friars, penniless, friendless, and with the glamour of Francis and Dominic about them, they met with a generous welcome. The monks of Christ Church gave hospitality to the first Minors and even Matthew Paris, who was later to become more bitter, devoted several pages to the stigmatized Francis and treated with unusual reverence the work of his companion, Brother William of England. At first, too, any beginnings of jealousy were forestalled by the humility of the Minors who, as at Reading, obeyed literally the directions of their founder by accepting an unenviable site for their house and by refusing to tie the hands of the owning abbey by any legal instrument.

The newcomers, however, could not long be treated with a tolerant charity. Their new fervour, as that of the Cistercians a century before, drew off from monks and canons several individuals of distinction, who made use of the canonical principle that transference to a stricter religious order was always permissible, besides attracting restless undesirables. Their ideal of poverty, however modestly and sincerely it might be preached and practised, involved at least a tacit comparison with the wealthy older orders which enthusiasm or indiscretion might easily make more explicit. Their presence in a monastic town, where the monks were acutely sensitive to trespass and dreaded a focus of opposition to their privileges, or on parishes where they might draw off some of the revenues appropriated to the monastery; the protection given them by the king or by magnates who had been none too favourable to the monks; their vindication of the common rights they had at first been ready to waive; their novel privileges and ready access to the popes, who issued bull after bull in their favour: all these gave cause for suspicion and friction. These, in early days at least, would seem to have been needlessly fostered by many of the monks and canons, both black and white, who yielded to the irrational, if not unnatural, resentment felt by an old concern in face of a competition claiming to make use of improved methods; they were aggravated by the language held by some of the friars who, like the Cistercians a hundred years before, criticized the older orders where they were most vulnerable and sensitive.

## The Gothic Cathedral As an Instrument and Expression of Popular Religion
◄§ Allan Temko

In the single century from 1170 to 1270 the medieval French built some eighty cathedrals and five hundred large churches of the cathedral class. The Cathedral of Paris, geographically and chronologically, was at the heart of this movement.

Notre-Dame was built by a superb common effort in which the entire community took part, the manual laborer as well as the master artist, the serf and villein as well as the merchant and prince. From their collective energy and enthusiasm the Cathedral emerged as the crowning structure of the walled city of the Middle Age. Paris then crowded about the church with inexpressible love. Hundreds of simple dwellings clustered beneath its walls, hiding the base of the monument; and from their midst the shape of the cross jutted in an astonishing display of mass and power. The size and scale of Notre-Dame, which not even the fortified palace of the king could challenge, were an absolute indication of its unique place in the lives of the people. The Cathedral was not isolated, as was the inhuman pyramid of Cheops. It was the organic heart of Paris, and from it flowed hope, confidence, joy, and exaltation, in which the working people had a full share.

By modern definition, the medieval community was of course a slave society. Scholarship such as Coulton's has made it impossible to romanticize feudalism. The serf, in spite of theoretical obligations owed him by his lord, was usually exploited in practice. Nor did a day pass when bones were not smashed on the wheel or eyes blinded in prisons. But this is not the entire story. A paradox distinguished the Middle Age from the Money Age which succeeded it, and which is not yet ended. The paradox lay in the medieval Church, which was one Church and all Churches. . . . All belonged to the Church, and the Church belonged to all. Its gods and demigods watched over every human creation. Feudal politics, the feudal economy, and feudal art became inseparable from the magical rule of the priests.

It is important to realize what this magic meant in practical results. The magic worked, as penicillin works today, although the ordinary man had as little real knowledge of its secrets. He knew its main principle, which is all that mattered. Medieval Christianity carried with it the ideal of the New Testament, with its promise of reward in Heaven or penalty in Hell; and however far reality may have wandered from it, the ideal was never lost. On the contrary, it frequently emerged in splendor, thrusting above medieval society in the profile of a church. When, in the construction of a cathedral, the loose feudal economy for a moment grew cohesive and society collectively endeavored to be worthy of its Christian abstractions, medieval France could match its achievements against those of any state, including the Athens of Pericles. . . .

"I know that my Redeemer liveth," Maurice de Sully spoke out on his deathbed in 1196, "and that He shall stand at the latter day upon the earth." But when, precisely? When would the trumpet sound and the graves fly open? "Ye know neither the day nor the hour," replied the Lord through Saint Matthew. Not even the angels of heaven knew, but the Middle Age thought the day might come very soon.

Predictions varied. Saint Hildegarde foresaw Domesday as imminent after 1180; the year 1200 seemed more likely to the Abbot Joachim of Calabria, a Cistercian monk whose prophecies elevated him to Dante's *Paradiso*. When the Day of Wrath failed to arrive at the turn of the thirteenth century, new prophecies fixed the end in 1300.

There were signs. The four horsemen of the Apocalypse were riding in the West. Kingdom had risen against kingdom, and there was bloody war on the earth as Philip the Conqueror battled first with Coeur-de-Lion and then with King John. Plague erupted, and was called "sacred fire"—*ignis sacer,* or, more properly, *ignis infernalis.* Famine struck France repeatedly at the end of the twelfth century: the starvation of 1195–1199 was hideous. Men ate wine dregs for bread and devoured beasts dead of disease. They chewed on roots; there were cases of cannibalism. In 1197, according to the Chronicle of Reims, innumerable persons died of hunger.... Hungry nobles rode out of their donjons, like minions of the Anti-Christ, and sacked such rich abbeys as Saint-Loup of Troyes in 1184. Such men did not spare the barns of the poor.

All this provides a correction for the idyl of agricultural plenty depicted in the portals of the cathedrals. The twelve Months of Notre-Dame are pictures of *ideal* conditions and must be understood as such. Often, they were irresponsibly wrong. The Church itself could be a cruel exploiter of its serfs; and during Saint Louis' first Crusade, when Queen Blanche governed the kingdom, she personally came with soldiers and liberated a crowd of prisoners from a jail of the Cathedral of Paris; the serfs and villeins of several suburban villages had refused to pay a tithe, whereupon the Chapter of Notre-Dame had arrested men, women, and children and jammed them in cells, where "several died of heat."

Beyond widespread human misery, there were other warnings of Apocalypse. Heresy had grown out of hand during the twelfth century, especially in the charming and articulate South. The whole of Languedoc lay in the passionate error of Catharism, and would soon be put to the sword by Simon de Montfort, in the name of the Church Militant, but to the profit of the Capets. The Albigensian Crusade destroyed more than the fine cities Béziers and Narbonne; it eradicated an independent civilization that had produced the troubadors and such churches as Saint-Sernin of Toulouse....

There were false prophets even in Paris. In 1210 there was a heretic hunt in the capital, and the body of Amaury of Chartres, an intellectual who during his lifetime had the bad judgment to read Averroës, was ejected from the cemetery of the Holy Innocents. Some ten of Amaury's students were burned at the stake; others were sentenced to life imprisonment. The writings of Amaury's disciple, David of Dinant, who had the good fortune to flee, were publicly consumed by fire. The Church Council responsible for these condemnations also decreed that to study the natural philosophy of Aristotle, or Averroës's commentary on it, was an offense punishable by burning. A generation later Aquinas and Albert the Great would make Aristotle the foundation of their theology—Amaury, like Abélard, had simply been ahead of his time. Finally the Council declared a heretic any man in whose home either the *Credo* or the *Pater Noster* was found translated into French. These prohibitions were renewed five years later in Paris by the papal legate; at the same time the Lateran Council of 1215 was establishing the Inquisition at Rome.

In this atmosphere of heresy, sin, and disaster upon the earth there were natural calamities and accidents that added to the general fear of the unknown. Fire was a constant danger. From 1200 to 1225 the city of Rouen burned five times. In the single year of 1188, not only Rouen, but Troyes, Beauvais, Provins, Arras, Poitiers, and Moissac were virtually destroyed by flame. There were also floods, shakings of the earth, and landslides, like that which inspired Dante's steep descent between the sixth and seventh circles of Hell.

Every sign indicated that Judgment was near and the Church insisted—by force, if necessary—that the world be ready. This urgency was intensified by phenomena in the heavens. Comets passed overhead in irregular flight; there were showers of stars and eclipses of the sun and the moon—any of which could have meant that the Day of Wrath was at hand. Heavy bursts of thunder were signals that the Archangel Michael—who had replaced Mercury as the god of hilltops and storms and the guide of the dead—was about to begin his wide voyage over the earth. . . .

Here, at Notre-Dame, about the year 1210, is the Son of Man come to judge! Meet His glance, if you are able. Against a background of golden glory, of which bright traces remain, Christ sits enthroned in His human image: a half-naked God of suffering, showing His wounded hands, and the wound in His side. Angels hold the instruments of torture that became symbols of triumph: the nails, the spear, the cross. As they did at Golgotha, the Virgin and Saint John have fallen to their knees at either side and pray.

"But behold," cried Saint Paul to the Corinthians, "I shall show you a mystery":

> . . . and we shall all be changed, in a moment, in the twinkling of an eye: for the trumpet shall sound, and the dead shall be raised incorruptible. . . .

And the dead have awakened! blinded by the light of eternity, deafened by the ivory trumpets of the angels. On the lower lintel they rise startled from their tombs, fully dressed, distinguished from one another by sex and age and by social rank. In the upper lintel a little naked soul has already hopped into the scales of Saint Michael and outweighs his evil deeds, which take the form of an imp. In the wink of an eye . . . the Elect have started off to Heaven, overcome with joy, crowned as queens and kings, attired in celestial robes; on the left hand of Christ, the Damned, weeping and swearing, pushed by devils, are led in chains to Hell.

This tremendous scene of Judgment, spilling over into the Heaven and Hell of the voussoirs, has ramifications throughout the central portal [at] Notre-Dame. . . .

Leave all hope, ye that enter. The cauldron is directly beneath, and its flames have already mingled with the hair of the descending victim. Two devils stand ready with hooks and forks and drag and push another sinner into the frothing pot. The devils' skin is flame; the mouth of a beast opens on their lewd bellies; their faces are snouts or horrible masks. The fire rises hot about the cauldron, and monstrous toads bite at the hands of the Damned, which search even here for a grasp.

In the next voussoir a pale horse, with a pale blindfolded woman rider, her ghastly breasts flapping on her ribs, springs out of the Book of Revelation and rides over a fourth part of the earth. Death kills with the sharp daggers she holds in either hand; and Hell follows her: an eviscerated sinner with his entrails pouring out and bleeding, his arm lopped and falling behind, his hair spreading backward in the dust, his legs yanked forward by the momentum of the ride, crossing the vile legs of the old woman riding nakedly before him, her arms flying outward about the neck of the whinnying horse, her daggers striking.

More Hell follows. Bodies and parts of bodies twist and struggle but cannot escape. And another Horseman of the Apocalypse gallops past on a frantically neighing steed, whipping his mount savagely over the ears.

And more Hell: Carnal Pleasure is a satiric queen, sporting a shattered crown. . . . Her sharp claw-feet dig into the shoulders of a bishop, whose chest is crammed against the back of a king. Below are flames.

Hell, deeper and crueler. A horned demon points to the text of the Avenging Christ who had ordained these hot tortures. Below, other devils have a woman upside down and prepare to devour her loins. Toads and serpents bite away her breasts, while another devil hooks at her belly. This is the end: the Damned have begun to torture the

Damned; and a male figure reaches up out of the lower flames and drags her downward with him.

Hell is an allegory, explained Saint Thomas; but the medieval man, when he was presented with this burning vision of the underworld, must have believed, like Shakespeare's Horatio, at least in part. Jesuits in Ireland could believe—with amazing visual imagination—as recently as the young manhood of James Joyce. Hell is easy to understand. The Middle Age knew as well as Sartre that "Hell is other people"; and knew better than any Existentialist that there is no exit once Hell is entered. For the medieval man was perhaps as aware as any Frenchman who endured the Occupation that Hell is possible on earth. The Gestapo did not invent torture chambers; the jailers of Philip Augustus were expert in chaining men to great timbers, blinding them, and cutting off their hands and ears; smearing their bodies with grease before a roasting fire; hanging them up by the hands; breaking their limbs with iron bars; immersing their heads in water. Eventually, when the Inquisition was in full force, the jailers of the Church, too, would accomplish so thorough a job on prisoners that there was nothing left for the secular arm to burn.

Heaven, as it seemed to the Fabian Bernard Shaw, may very possibly be boring. . . . Yet Heaven has a subtle delight of its own, which is visible to him who will see and which may be heard by him who will listen. Dante's Heaven is music and golden space: the backdrop of a Giotto. And at Notre-Dame the same Heaven shows hundreds of varied attitudes and joys, such as the happy little winged cherubs who lean over their celestial balustrades to have a view of the Lord, smiling, sighing, closing their eyes, lifting their hands, touching their breasts, flying forward over the railing to Christ. Heaven takes all the room it can claim in the façade, lifting slowly in the air until the apex of its triangle touches the Gallery of Kings, almost to the rose. Neither of the other doors has this majestic field of sanctity, which in the thirteenth century was painted with gold.

On the benevolent right hand of Christ the Elect go to Paradise with quiet smiles, as a tall angel shows them to their places, like a celestial usher. They are crowned as queens and kings, since the only rank in Heaven is royal; and all seem uniformly young. From the battlements of the True Jerusalem they look down serenely at Paris, done with cares and filled with wordless joy at the thought of the future. One holds a sovereign's orb, as if it were a ball, in anticipation of a game.

In the midst of the Elect, Abraham, Isaac, and Jacob are surrounded by flowers and haloed. Abraham holds three lately arrived souls in a scarf, cradling them to his bosom. Above, the circles of Paradise wheel upward, in liturgical precedence: Moses and the other patriarchs and prophets are nearest Christ; then a college of confessors, holding books opened to some illuminated page, or with the gemmed covers closed; next, a host of beardless martyrs, so mild that they scarcely gesture with their palms of triumph; and finally, the great outer choir of virgins, also carrying palms, and chanting Dante's music.

Heaven, then, was attainable. The Church showed the Way, which was Christ—Christ Teacher—who holds the book at the Door and with his feet tramples the aspic and basilisk of ignorance. The original central Christ of this portal was not only the model for the Beau-Christ of Amiens, which was in turn copied in the restoration, but the very image of intellectual Christianity as it attained its encyclopedic triumph in the West. The Teacher was mounted on a pedestal of the liberal arts and surrounded by his teaching apostles, who may be imagined as the apostles of Amiens, but in a graver mood, which the Paris atelier gave all its creations. They composed the faculty of the University of Christ, whose one essential textbook was the Evangel. A single lesson, in fact, properly learned from Saint Matthew, would provide the whole education. The parable of the ten virgins has been restored on either side of the entrance: above the five who were wise, the door is open; above those who were foolish, the door is shut.

## POPULAR PREPARATION FOR SALVATION

### The Cult of the Virgin
&ξ G. G. Coulton

The cult of the Virgin was fully systematized, we may say, by the beginning of the thirteenth century; in all churches of the first rank, and in many of the second or third, special chapels were built for her, often with an elaboration of ornament beyond all the rest of the church. The greatest monastic reforms had boasted her special patronage; it is interesting to note how the Cistercian, the Franciscan, the Dominican and the Carmelite claim, each for himself, her peculiar favours. . . .

Mary of the Middle Ages . . . is very feminine and very much the *noble dame*; not only does her mercy temper the strictness of divine justice, but her moods and caprices redeem the formalities of classical patristic theology. The multitude has always hated not only dragooning order, which we all hate, but also the milder order which is generally necessary to progress. . . . Official theology, taken literally, was very ruthless; upon its fundamental doctrine of original sin an inexorably logical system was built which no serious mind could contemplate without horror, even though it were a holy horror. Not only was there that wholesale perdition of the unbaptized; not only the almost certainty of purgatory at the very best; but, even so, it was the merest fraction of baptized Christians that could hope to see final salvation, however the preachers might encourage each man to hope that he might be among those few. The cult of the saints, and of Mary in especial, offered relief from this intolerable nexus of fate: the Franciscan Pelbart, in his *Pomerium Sermonum de Beata Virgine*, has a whole section entitled: *Profit No. 10.—That the blessed Mary frees men from damnation*. In support of this he recites in full five of her most popular miracles; first, before the Judgement-Seat, she saved "a cleric given up to lechery, in whom however there was this one good thing, that he was wont to say the Hours of the Blessed Virgin with devotion." Her protection was similarly given, and for the same reason, to a notorious robber, to a woman with a sin on her conscience which she dared confess to no priest, to a youth who had, by his mother's curse, been predestined to hell from his very conception, and to Theophilus, who had made a pact with Satan and executed a charter formally renouncing his Christian profession. "From which examples," adds Pelbart, "it is manifest that this very Mother of Mercy doth not suffer sinners to perish, but that she will mercifully free from damnation those who turn unto her." ...

Mary, then, perhaps more than all the other saints put together, brought relief from that intolerable logic of the law in matters of salvation or damnation: "Let us go secretly to the Queen and promise a present!" Women felt this even more than men; women had most reason to rebel against that priestly rigorism which condemned the dance, and all elaboration of dress, and light unstudied speech; and which, even in natural beauty itself, often saw one of Satan's deadliest snares. ...

## Relic Worship
⊰ G. G. Coulton

Medieval relic-worship had not grown up quite unopposed. Apart from ridicule from without the Church, it was attacked from within by Vigilantius [410], whose treatise we know only from St Jerome's angry reply: this sacrilegious fellow "opens his fetid mouth and spits filth against the relics of the holy martyrs, calling us dustmen for treasuring them, and idolaters because we venerate the bones of the dead." St Jerome evidently represented the sense of the great majority; for the practice, so far from suffering a check, grew to enormous proportions. . . .

The collection and worship of relics naturally became one of the busiest occupations of the Middle Ages. For instance, the Emperor Frederick I (Barbarossa) was a most munificent patron of Cologne: he even purposed, if he had lived longer, to build a stone bridge over the mighty stream; "but posterity reckoned it as his greatest achievement that he had brought to 'Holy Cologne', rich in relics and greedy of relics, one which increased the glory of the city and attracted thousands of pilgrims—the bones of the Holy Three Kings." St Louis is said to have offered the Count of Fondi 15,000 florins for the bones of St Thomas Aquinas, but in vain. It was natural, therefore, that each great abbey should have possessed a veritable thaumaturgic museum; each vied with its fellows in the rarity and curiosity of its specimens. The monks of Durham, for instance, had griffins' eggs and claws—*i.e.* ostrich-eggs and ibex-horns. They boasted not only the coals of St Lawrence, reminiscent of Boccaccio, but also one of his joints, still bearing traces of the sacrilegious fire. They had portions of Moses's rod, of John Baptist's raiment, and the charger which had held his head; the Virgin Mary's shirt, and rock marked with spots of her milk; of the tree under which the three angels sat with Abraham, and of the Tree of Paradise; of the flesh and fat of St Thomas Becket; a tooth of St Gengulphus, sovereign for the falling sickness; of the twelve thrones of the Apostles. . . . The long list of St Albans' relics . . . is almost as ludicrous: there is perhaps no surviving list of monastic relics which might not palliate, if not justify, the irreverence of Henry VIII's Visitors. But it is very significant to compare the inventories, when more than one has survived from the same house, and to note how many of these relics had disappeared in the later generations of the Middle Ages, when faith had lost much of its naïveté and sometimes the gold or silver settings had tempted financial reformers or thieves. Abundant evidence could be adduced for the slow decay of this or that relic, as memory faded or popular taste changed.

## *Piers Plowman: The Quest for Perfection*
&§ *Morton W. Bloomfield*

*Piers Plowman* [written in the fourteenth century] ends, as it begins, with a quest. At the conclusion of the poem, the seeker is Conscience, who, unlike the questing Will at the beginning, knows what and whom he is seeking. Whether or not he finds Piers Plowman, the reader is not told, but he may at least assume that Piers can, and some day will, be found. As a good Christian, the author certainly must have believed this. He has shown that Piers in the later part of the poem is the human manifestation of Christ—either as Jesus or as an ideal head of the Church, His continuing vicar—for it is only through Him that perfection may be found. Conscience and Will are in search of spiritual knowledge that will transform society and the self. The poem deals with the search not the finding; and although the quest has not been in vain, the goal is yet to be attained. More is known at the end than at the beginning—that there is a guide and principles to follow, that there are forces within men and within history working for Christian perfection—but the journey is not yet complete. *Piers* is a work whose artistic and moral claims on the reader reinforce each other. What is sought is a way to seek. . . .

Christian perfection is a well-known subject of Christian thought and endeavor, and it normally presupposes the existence of grades or levels. Salvation is an all or nothing proposition; but the poem is, as the section on the three Do's shows, closely concerned with levels of Christian living and with moral distinctions and subtleties. In every way, then, *Piers Plowman* is fundamentally concerned with the problem of Christian perfection.

The poem is divided into four major sections—the Visio and the Lives of Do-wel, Do-bet, and Do-best, the last three being known as the Vita. The whole Visio (from the Prologue to Passus VII) may be regarded as an introduction in which the dreamer remains the observer. He locates himself and defines his self-image—a hermit and possibly a monk seeking after Christian perfection. He describes his contemporary world, which is full of sin and yet in a confused way longs to be free of sin. In this introduction, Langland also shows how men fail in their attempt to find salvation and perfection because they are fooled by Meed (cupidity) and because, even if cleansed of sin, they cannot find the way to the Saviour and fall into sin again. Their leaders betray them. The guide, Piers, who appears in the last few passus of the Visio, seems to be misled by a false pardon, and all ends in wrangling and despair. New complexities have opened up, and new distinctions must be made. Now the dreamer himself must undertake a pilgrimage and become active instead of passive, a seeker instead of an observer.

The Vita (Passus VIII–XX) consists of three parts, corresponding to three grades of perfection. Do-wel is concerned with the ordering of self to the natural world in terms of Christianity and raises questions about such topics as predestination, the value of learning, and the meaning of nature, natural man, and natural law. The quest in the

first part of Do-wel (VIII–XII) is in general concerned with a burning fourteenth-century problem—that of authority. The movement of
Will from one authority to another here dramatizes the problem of
the relative authority of learning, reason, the Bible, and the Church.
... Do-wel [is] the best way to lead the Christian life in the world, the
lowest but by no means unworthy way of Christian perfection, which,
perforce, must embrace the vast majority of Christians. . . .

Do-bet is concerned with the ordering of the self to Christ. The
part centers on a discussion of the theological virtues, especially love,
and culminates in a vision of the Harrowing of Hell. Do-best, coming
back again, as in the Visio, to society and history, is concerned with
the ordering of self to the Kingdom of God and to the regenerated
society, centered in the cardinal virtues. The true Church is in the
throes of "a time of troubles" and is being assailed by Antichrist at a
time of crisis. Tribulation and persecution are the fate of the elect
throughout the history of the world, and the betrayal of the ideals and
doctrines of the Church by its adherents and leaders is the clearest
sign of a coming renewal and of a further step towards the Kingdom
of God.

How must a Christian live in order to attain as much perfection as
possible within the limits of his human nature? What is the meaning
of Christian perfection in general, and how can it be applied in Langland's own time? These are the basic questions of the poem and are
closely related to the whole crisis of late medieval thought. . . .

The very subject of the poem, Christian perfection, in its social
form, bespeaks apocalypticism. Social thinking on the subject of perfection, above all in the fourteenth century, had to be apocalyptic. The
transcendence of society to a new level was thought by many to be the
only way out of the crushing dilemmas. The sad state of the contemporary Church could be explained only on these grounds. God was
planning, if not a new age, at least a renewal of the good and the just.
The evil was the result of the birth throes of the good. What was
hidden "in the womb of time" would be revealed at the proper moment; and as Antichrists assailed the true Church, Unitas, a new life
and renewal was being prepared, soon to manifest itself. The true
Church would reassert itself, and the false Church would be overcome.

In recent years there has been a tendency to find in *Piers* the odyssey
of a mystic towards God, and perhaps in one sense this is true. But
*Piers* is first of all socially oriented—that is, apocalyptic in its view
of perfection. History and society must come first, and the last parts of
the poem show this very clearly. The journey of the individual soul to
God is perhaps also implied, but it is not central. It is Piers, not Will,
who, starting as a simple peasant, becomes the human aspect of Christ

and in effect passes through the three grades of perfection to become Christ as man....

Piers Plowman is an eschatological figure—both the way and the goal of Christian perfection. He is both the model and the norm of human existence for Christians, and he can lead them into the transformed society—the Kingdom of God, which may also be an age of the Holy Ghost. He will lead them back so that they may go forward to their proper destiny.

# 4. Popular Support for the Crusades

## The Penetration of the Crusading Ideal

ᴥ§ *Steven Runciman*

POPE URBAN II PREACHES THE FIRST CRUSADE. Pope Urban arrived in France in the late summer of 1095. On 5 August he was at Valence and on 11 August he reached Le Puy. From there he sent letters to the bishops of France and the neighbouring lands, requesting them to meet him at Clermont in November.... It was announced that on Tuesday, 27 November, he would hold a public session, to make a great announcement. The crowds, clerical and lay, that assembled were too huge to be contained within the cathedral, where hitherto the Council had met. The Papal throne was set up on a platform in an open field outside the eastern gate of the city; and there, when the multitudes were gathered, Urban rose to his feet to address them.... It seems that he began his speech by telling his hearers of the necessity for aiding their brethren in the East. Eastern Christendom had appealed for help; for the Turks were advancing into the heart of Christian lands, maltreating the inhabitants and desecrating their shrines. But it was not only of Romania (which is Byzantium) that he spoke. He stressed the special holiness of Jerusalem and described the sufferings of the pilgrims that journeyed there. Having painted the sombre picture, he made his great appeal. Let western Christendom march to the rescue of the East. Rich and poor alike should go. They should leave off slaying each other and fight instead a righteous war, doing the work of God; and God would lead them. For those that died in battle there would be absolution and the remission of sins. Life was miserable and evil here, with men wearing themselves out to the ruin of their bodies and their souls. Here they were poor and unhappy; there they would be joyful and prosperous and true friends of God. There must be no delay. Let them be ready to set out when the summer had come, with God to be their guide.

Urban spoke with fervour and with all the art of a great orator. The response was immediate and tremendous. Cries of 'Deus le volt!'—'God wills it!'—interrupted the speech. Scarcely had the Pope ended his words before the Bishop of Le Puy rose from his seat and, kneeling before the throne, begged permission to join in the holy expedition. Hundreds crowded up to follow his example. Then the Cardinal Gregory fell on his knees and loudly repeated the *Confiteor* [prayer of confession]; and all the vast audience echoed it after him. When the prayer was over Urban rose once more and pronounced the absolution and bade his hearers go home.

The enthusiasm was greater than Urban had expected. His plans for its direction were not yet fully made. No great lay lord had been present at Clermont. The recruits were all humbler men. It would be necessary to secure more solid secular support. In the meantime Urban reassembled his bishops for further consultation. The Council had probably already at his request passed a general decree giving remission from temporal penalties for the sins of all that took part with pious intentions in the holy war. It was now added that the worldly belongings of the participants should be placed under the protection of the Church during their absence at the war. The local bishop should be responsible for their safekeeping and should return them intact when the warrior came home. Each member of the expedition was to wear the sign of the Cross, as a symbol of his dedication; a cross of red material should be sewn on to the shoulder of his surcoat. Anyone that took the Cross should vow to go to Jerusalem. If he turned back too soon or failed to set out, he would suffer excommunication. Clerics and monks were not to take the Cross without the permission of their bishop or abbot. The elderly and infirm must be discouraged from attempting the expedition; and no one at all should go without consulting his spiritual adviser. It was not to be a war of mere conquest. In all towns conquered from the infidel the churches of the East were to have all their rights and possessions restored to them. Everyone should be ready to leave his home by the Feast of the Assumption (15 August) next year, when the harvests should have been gathered; and the armies should assemble at Constantinople. . . .

By the time that Urban was back in Italy he was assured of the success of his scheme. His summons was eagerly obeyed. From as far afield as Scotland, Denmark and Spain, men hastened to make their vows. Some raised money for the journey by pawning their possessions and their lands. Others, expecting never to return, gave everything over to the Church. A sufficient number of great nobles had adhered to the Crusade to give it a formidable military backing. Besides Raymond of Toulouse and Hugh of Vermandois, Robert II of Flanders, Robert, Duke of Normandy, and the latter's brother-in-law Stephen, Count of Blois, were making preparations to set out. More remarkable was the adherence of men devoted to the emperor Henry IV. Chief amongst these was Godfrey of Bouillon, Duke of Lower Lorraine, who took the Cross with his brothers, Eustace, Count of Boulogne, and Baldwin. Grouped round these leaders were many of the lesser nobility and a few eminent ecclesiastics, such as the Bishop of Bayeux.

In Italy Urban found similar enthusiasm. In September 1096 he wrote to the city of Bologna to thank its citizens for their zeal and to caution them not to leave for the East without their priests' permission. Nor should newly married husbands leave without their wives' consent. Meanwhile news of the project had reached southern Italy and was warmly welcomed by many of the Normans there, who were always ready to start on a new adventure. The princes at first held back, but Guiscard's son Bohemond, now prince of Taranto but thwarted in his ambitions in Italy by his brother Roger Borsa and his uncle Roger of Sicily, soon realized the possibilities that the Crusade would open out for him. Together with many of his family and his friends, he took the Cross. Their participation brought to the movement many of the most experienced and enterprising soldiers in Europe. When Urban returned to Rome in time for Christmas 1096, he could feel assured that the Crusade was truly launched.

He had in fact launched a movement greater than he knew. It might have been better if fewer great lords had answered his appeal. For, though with all of them except Bohemond genuine religious fervour was the strongest motive, soon their terrestrial schemes and rivalries would create troubles far beyond the papal legate's control. Still more uncontrollable was the response shown by humble folk throughout France and Flanders and the Rhineland.

THE PEASANTS' CRUSADE: PETER THE HERMIT'S FOLLOWERS. The Pope had asked his bishops to preach the Crusade; but far more effective preaching was done by poorer men, by evangelicals such as Robert of Arbrissel, founder of the Order of Fontevrault, and still more by an itinerant monk called Peter. Peter was an oldish man, born somewhere near Amiens. He had probably tried to make the pilgrimage to Jerusalem a few years previously, but had been maltreated by the Turks and forced to turn back. His contemporaries knew him as Little Peter, ... but later the hermit's cape that he habitually wore brought him the surname of 'the Hermit', by which he is better known to history. He was a man of short stature, swarthy and with a long, lean face, horribly like the donkey that he always rode and which was revered almost as much as himself. He went barefoot; and his clothes were filthy. He ate neither bread nor meat, but fish, and drank wine. Despite his lowly appearance he had the power to move men. There was an air of strange authority about him. 'Whatever he said or did', Guibert of Nogent, who knew him personally, tells us, 'it seemed like something half-divine.'

Peter probably had not assisted at the Council of Clermont; but before the year 1095 was out he was already preaching the Crusade. He began his tour in Berry, then moved during February and March through Orléannais and Champagne into Lorraine, and thence past the cities of the Meuse and Aachen to Cologne, where he spent Easter. He gathered disciples whom he sent to the districts that he could not himself visit. Among them were the Frenchmen Walter Sans-Avoir, Rainald of Breis, Geoffrey Burel and Walter of Breteuil, and the Germans Orel and Gottschalk. Wherever he or his lieutenants went, men and women left their homes to follow him. By the time that he reached Cologne his train was estimated at about 15,000 persons; and many more joined him in Germany.

The extraordinary success of his preaching was due to many causes. Life of a peasant in north-western Europe was grim and insecure. Much land had gone out of cultivation during the barbarian invasions and the raids of the Norsemen. Dykes had been broken, and the sea and rivers had encroached on to the fields. The lords often opposed the clearing of the forests in which they hunted for their game. A village unprotected by a lord's castle was liable to be robbed or burnt by outlaws or by soldiers fighting petty civil wars. The Church sought to protect the poor peasants and to establish *bourgs* in empty lands; but its help was fitful and often unavailing. Greater lords might encourage the growth of towns, but lesser barons opposed it. The organization of the demesne was breaking down, but no orderly system was taking its place. Though actual serfdom had vanished, men were tied to the land by obligations that they could not easily escape. Meanwhile the population was increasing, and holdings in a village could not be subdivided beyond a certain limit. 'In this land', said Urban at Clermont, according to Robert the Monk, 'you can scarcely feed the inhabitants. That is why you use up its goods and excite endless wars amongst yourselves.' Recent years had been especially difficult. Floods and pestilence in 1094 had been followed by drought and a famine in 1095. It was a moment when emigration seemed very attractive. Already in April 1095 a shower of meteorites had presaged a great movement of peoples.

Apocalyptic teaching added to the economic inducement. It was an age of visions; and Peter was thought to be a visionary. Medieval man

was convinced that the Second Coming was at hand. He must repent
while yet there was time and must go out to do good. The Church
taught that sin could be expiated by pilgrimage and prophecies declared
that the Holy Land must be recovered for the faith before Christ could
come again. Further, to ignorant minds the distinction between Jerusalem and the New Jerusalem was not very clearly defined. Many of
Peter's hearers believed that he was promising to lead them out of
their present miseries to the land flowing with milk and honey of which
the scriptures spoke. The journey would be hard; there were the legions
of Antichrist to be overcome. But the goal was Jerusalem the golden....

Peter the Hermit arrived with his followers at Cologne on Holy
Saturday, 12 April 1096. There he began to realize the difficulties that
beset the leader of a popular expedition. The vast motley collection of
enthusiasts that he had gathered together consisted of men from many
districts and of many types. Some brought their women with them,
some even their children. Most of them were peasants, but there were
townsfolk among them, there were junior members of knightly families,
there were former brigands and criminals. Their only link was the
fervour of their faith....

THE CHILDREN'S CRUSADE. One day in May 1212 there
appeared at Saint-Denis, where King Philip of France was holding his
court, a shepherd-boy of about twelve years old called Stephen, from
the small town of Cloyes in the Orléannais. He brought with him a
letter for the King, which, he said, had been given to him by Christ in
person, who had appeared to him as he was tending his sheep and who
had bidden him go and preach the Crusade. King Philip was not impressed by the child and told him to go home. But Stephen, whose
enthusiasm had been fired by his mysterious visitor, saw himself now
as an inspired leader who would succeed where his elders had failed.
For the past fifteen years preachers had been going round the countryside urging a Crusade against the Moslems of the East or of Spain or
against the heretics of Languedoc. It was easy for an hysterical boy to
be infected with the idea that he too could be a preacher and could
emulate Peter the Hermit, whose prowess had during the past century
reached a legendary grandeur. Undismayed by the King's indifference,
he began to preach at the very entrance to the abbey of Saint-Denis
and to announce that he would lead a band of children to the rescue
of Christendom. The seas would dry up before them, and they would
pass, like Moses through the Red Sea, safe to the Holy Land. He was
gifted with an extraordinary eloquence. Older folk were impressed, and
children came flocking to his call. After his first success he set out to
journey round France summoning the children; and many of his converts went further afield to work on his behalf. They were all to meet

together at Vendôme in about a month's time and start out from there to the East.

Towards the end of June the children massed at Vendôme. Awed contemporaries spoke of thirty thousand, not one over twelve years of age. There were certainly several thousand of them, collected from all parts of the country, some of them simple peasants, whose parents in many cases had willingly let them go on their great mission. But there were also boys of noble birth who had slipped away from home to join Stephen and his following of 'minor prophets' as the chroniclers called them. There were also girls amongst them, a few young priests, and a few older pilgrims, some drawn by piety, others, perhaps, from pity, and others, certainly, to share in the gifts that were showered upon them all. The bands came crowding into the town, each with a leader carrying a copy of the Oriflamme, which Stephen took as the device of the Crusade. The town could not contain them all, and they encamped in the fields outside.

When the blessing of friendly priests had been given, and when the last sorrowing parents had been pushed aside, the expedition started out southward. Nearly all of them went on foot. But Stephen, as befitted the leader, insisted on having a gaily decorated cart for himself, with a canopy to shade him from the sun. At his side rode boys of noble birth, each rich enough to possess a horse. No one resented the inspired prophet travelling in comfort. On the contrary, he was treated as a saint, and locks of his hair and pieces of his garments were collected as precious relics. They took the road past Tours and Lyons, making for Marseilles. It was a painful journey. The summer was unusually hot. They depended on charity for their food, and the drought left little to spare in the country, and water was scarce. Many of the children died by the wayside. Others dropped out and tried to wander home. But at last the little Crusade reached Marseilles.

The citizens of Marseilles greeted the children kindly. Many found houses in which to lodge. Others encamped in the streets. Next morning the whole expedition rushed down to the harbour to see the sea divide before them. When the miracle did not take place, there was bitter disappointment. Some of the children turned against Stephen, crying that he had betrayed them, and began to retrace their steps. But most of them stayed on by the sea-side, expecting each morning that God would relent. After a few days two merchants of Marseilles, called, according to tradition, Hugh the Iron and William the Pig, offered to put ships at their disposal and to carry them free of charge, for the glory of God, to Palestine. Stephen eagerly accepted the kindly offer. Seven vessels were hired by the merchants, and the children were taken abroad and set out to sea. Eighteen years passed before there was any further news of them.

Meanwhile tales of Stephen's preaching had reached the Rhineland. Children of Germany were not to be outdone. A few weeks after Stephen had started on his mission, a boy called Nicholas, from a Rhineland village, began to preach the same message before the shrine of the Three Kings at Cologne. Like Stephen, he declared that children could do better than grown men, and that the sea would open to give them a path. But, while the French children were to conquer the Holy Land by force, the Germans were to achieve their aim by the conversion of the infidel. Nicholas, like Peter, had a natural eloquence and was able to find eloquent disciples to carry his preaching further, up and down the Rhineland. Within a few weeks an army of children had gathered at Cologne, ready to start out for Italy and the sea. It seems that the Germans were on the average slightly older than the French and that there were more girls with them. There was also a larger contingent of boys of the nobility, and a number of disreputable vagabonds and prostitutes.

The expedition split into two parties. The first, numbering according to the chroniclers, twenty thousand, was led by Nicholas himself. It set out up the Rhine to Basle and through western Switzerland, past Geneva, to cross the Alps by the Mont Cenis pass. It was an arduous journey for the children, and their losses were heavy. Less than a third of the company that left Cologne appeared before the walls of Genoa, at the end of August, and demanded a night's shelter within its walls. The Genoese authorities were ready at first to welcome the pilgrims, but on second thoughts they suspected a German plot. They would allow them to stay for one night only; but any who wished to settle permanently in Genoa were invited to do so. The children, expecting the sea to divide before them next morning, were content. But next morning the sea was as impervious to their prayers as it had been to the French at Marseilles. In their disillusion many of the children at once accepted the Genoese offer and became Genoese citizens, forgetting their pilgrimage. Several great families of Genoa later claimed to be descended from this alien immigration. But Nicholas and the greater number moved on. The sea would open for them elsewhere. A few days later they reached Pisa. There two ships bound for Palestine agreed to take several of the children, who embarked and who perhaps reached Palestine; but nothing is known of their fate. Nicholas, however, still awaited a miracle, and trudged on with his faithful followers to Rome. At Rome Pope Innocent received them. He was moved by their piety but embarrassed by their folly. With kindly firmness he told them that they must now go home. When they grew up they should then fulfil their vows and go to fight for the Cross.

Little is known of the return journey. Many of the children especially the girls, could not face again the ardours of the road and stayed behind in some Italian town or village. Only a few stragglers found their way back next spring to the Rhineland. Nicholas was probably not amongst them. But the angry parents whose children had perished insisted on the arrest of his father, who had, it seems, encouraged the boy out of vainglory. He was taken and hanged.

The second company of German pilgrims was no more fortunate. It had travelled to Italy through central Switzerland and over the Saint Gotthard and after great hardships reached the sea at Ancona. When the sea failed to divide for them they moved slowly down the east coast as far as Brindisi. There a few of them found ships sailing to Palestine and were given passages; but the others returned and began to wander slowly back again. Only a tiny number returned at last to their homes.

Despite their miseries, they were perhaps luckier than the French. In the year 1230 a priest arrived in France from the East with a curious tale to tell. He had been, he said, one of the young priests who had accompanied Stephen to Marseilles and had embarked with them on the ships provided by the merchants. A few days out they had run into bad weather, and two of the ships were wrecked on the island of San Pietro, off the south-west corner of Sardinia, and all the passengers were drowned. The five ships that survived the storm found themselves soon afterwards surrounded by a Saracen squadron from Africa; and the passengers learned that they had been brought there by arrangement, to be sold into captivity. They were all taken to Bougie, on the Algerian coast. Many of them were bought on their arrival and spent the rest of their lives in captivity there. Others, the young priest among them, were shipped on to Egypt, where Frankish slaves fetched a better price. When they arrived at Alexandria the greater part of the consignment was bought by the governor, to work on his estates. According to the priest there were still about seven hundred of them living. A small company was taken to the slave-markets of Baghdad; and there eighteen of them were martyred for refusing to accept Islam. . . .

THE FEROCITY OF THE SACK OF CHRISTIAN CONSTANTINOPLE. There was little fighting in the streets as the invaders forced their way through the city. By next morning the Doge and the leading Crusaders [on what is called the Fourth Crusade, 1202–1204] were established in the Great Palace, and their soldiers were told that they might spend the next three days in pillage.

The sack of Constantinople is unparalleled in history. For nine centuries the great city had been the capital of Christian civilization.

It was filled with works of art that had survived from ancient Greece and with the masterpieces of its own exquisite craftsmen. The Venetians indeed knew the value of such things. Wherever they could they seized treasures and carried them off to adorn the squares and churches and palaces of their town. But the Frenchmen and Flèmings were filled with a lust for destruction. They rushed in a howling mob down the streets and through the houses, snatching up everything that glittered and destroying whatever they could not carry, pausing only to murder or to rape, or to break open the wine-cellars for their refreshment. Neither monasteries nor churches nor libraries were spared. In St Sophia itself drunken soldiers could be seen tearing down the silken hangings and pulling the great silver iconostasis to pieces, while sacred books and icons were trampled under foot. While they drank merrily from the altar-vessels a prostitute set herself on the Patriarch's throne and began to sing a ribald French song. Nuns were ravished in their convents. Palaces and hovels alike were entered and wrecked. Wounded women and children lay dying in the streets. For three days the ghastly scenes of pillage and bloodshed continued, till the huge and beautiful city was a shambles. Even the Saracens would have been more merciful, cried the historian Nicetas, and with truth.

# 5. The Royal Coronation As Grand Spectacle

## Coronation Ritual and Festivities

◄§ Percy E. Schramm

Ever since coronation had become a Christian observance it had been a brilliant affair, and its splendour extended to those occasions upon which the King appeared wearing his crown. Formerly, when the crown had been a golden helmet, he could put it on himself just as he put on his helmet before going into battle. But gradually a change came about in this practice. As far back as the tenth century it was the custom in Germany that the King should fast before wearing his crown, and a similar custom prevailed elsewhere. Therefore the number of days on which the King wore his crown became strictly limited; but they became increasingly important when the theory came also to be held that only an ecclesiastic might put the crown on the King's head. A ritual derived from the inaugural coronation was adopted for these 'crown-wearings'—*coronamenta* was the term adopted for them in France. This shows that they were not viewed merely as a splendid pageant. They were an ecclesiastico-legal act which bestowed no new status on the King, but did exhibit him anew, in the language of symbolism then understood, as the manifest ruler of his people....

Consider the framework of secular festivities within which the solemn act of coronation was by now inseparably fixed....

Throughout the Middle Ages this side of the coronation was continually growing. Indeed, this showy husk threatened to conceal entirely the original kernel of Christian consecration and constitutional investiture. Herein England was not peculiar, for other Western countries saw their coronation ceremonies expand on similar lines....

The age of chivalry excelled in pageantry which displayed itself in splendour of clothing, arms, horses, all paraded before spectators at tournament and banquet in festal attire. Yet it had its educative side, for all persons who took part, whether as ideal King or knight or lady had to pass muster in deportment. This kind of refinement in a festival had been foreign to early Teutonic custom; the Church alone had an old tradition which enabled expression to be given in outward forms and ceremonies to all the passions of the human soul, from deepest dejection to the most intense happiness. And with what ability did the medieval Church develop its power of making its holidays the more emotional by bringing into its service the arts of architecture and music! Under the lofty vaults of her cathedrals, filled with incense and melody, the clergy moved in the solemn manner prescribed by tradition and regulated down to the minutest detail during the era of the canonists and the schoolmen. Nor was this all. Both within the churches and outside them, opportunity was found for the production of mystery-plays in which the Middle Ages created the drama best suited to their own ideas.

The men of the later Middle Ages were brought up on courtly and knightly festivities no less than on ecclesiastical, for, there being no antithesis between the two, they were complementary to one another and encouraged each other. Now begins the period when spiritual plays reach their fullest, perhaps even an excessive, development, but when secular plays also begin to divert both actors and spectators. This period, which witnessed the invention of fire-arms, saw a change in the spirit of the tournament. Hitherto, under the guise of a festivity, it had reflected the serious side of life; now it became merely a living representation of the past. Another outcome of these late medieval plays is to be seen in the festal processions and cavalcades, in the art of which not only princes and court society, but cities, with their councillors, merchants, and artisans, were supreme. . . .

In this way the ethical evolution of the age of chivalry was overshadowed by the idea of festivity prevalent in the later Middle Ages. It was as though the world, which saw the old rules of class and morality growing slack and the *bourgeois* element asserting itself more and more strongly, had invented these festivities in order to check this unbridled licence in human behaviour. Processions and banquets, therefore, are the occasion for once more making the rungs of the social ladder clearly distinct. One man may wear this costume or that chain, while another may not. This man has his place in the procession or at table; that man must be content with a more modest position. Every man's line of conduct is prescribed by a carefully regulated etiquette. Of all this the chief example in the fifteenth century was the Burgundian court. In the sixteenth it was the Spanish that took the lead in all such matters. . . .

The festivities began two nights earlier, at the Tower, when the King conferred knighthoods. Other countries also linked the bestowal of honours on the nobles with a coronation. Here in England it was the creations of Knights of the Bath. Their order, a rival to that of the Garter, was one of the many foundations which were the fashion in the courts of the later Middle Ages. Thus in the fourteenth century the King of France had founded the order of the Star, and, after that, every prince was ambitious to become the head of a similar order; so we have the orders of the Porcupine in Orleans, the Golden Fleece in Burgundy, and many others. All these creations, following the fashion of the day and the whim of princes, enabled men a little longer to play at chivalry, which by now had outlived its purpose. These knights were to live according to a rule and come forward as champions of Christian principles, but we must not be deceived by such a profession as this. Chivalry was in reality dead and these 'knights' were in fact calculating statesmen, adroit courtiers, and scions of eminent houses, whose descent secured their admission to the order.

Of course, the members of the orders created by the King of England had a special claim to appear prominently at the coronation. Four Knights of the Garter had the right of holding a canopy over the King at the anointing, and, on the evening but one before the coronation, the honour of knighthood in the order of the Bath was conferred on certain persons at the Tower. Henry V created no less than fifty in this way. Inasmuch as the King also took a ceremonial bath on that same evening, a close connexion was thereby established between the King and his new knights, for it was from that bath, in which they prepared themselves for being dubbed, that they obtained their name.

On the next day there followed the procession from the Tower to Westminster Hall. It had lost all trace of what was originally a semi-ecclesiastical character, and had become a triumphal progress in which the King's majesty was shown to the people. Brilliant splendour surrounded him: was it not a matter of political prestige that the King of England yielded place to no other monarch? The memoranda for the coronation of Henry VII have survived, and the expenses for new robes for king and court, down even to the bodyguard, are entered in a register. One on the top of the other come items of expenditure for silk, purple, cloth of gold, buttons, ribands, saddles, flags, and coats of arms, and an expert in the royal accounts might well reflect how large a proportion of the year's revenue must have been squandered on this one day. An extravagance, yet not an extravagance, for the records of contemporaries reveal clearly the deep impression made on every occasion by this ride from the Tower to Westminster. It is first described in 1377; it took place for the last time at the coronation of Charles II.

In this royal progress we never miss anything that we should expect at this period. Thus, for example, we learn that, on the occasion of Richard II's progress, it passed by a great erection in Cheapside made of coloured linen, from the turrets of which four beautiful 'damosels' threw pieces of gold in the King's path. High above this structure rose a central tower, on which a golden angel stretched out a crown towards the King. At the coronation of Charles II there stood near the same place a triumphal arch 'representing the Temple of Concord, where three personated Concord, Love, and Truth'. At another arch along the route there waited 'one representing the River Thames', while other arches represented Plenty, Rebellion, and Monarchy. The author remarks that it would be 'the Worke of many sheets to discribe them'. But in spite of his brevity we can well picture to ourselves these temporary structures with their allegorical figures, for hundreds and hundreds of similar cases have made them familiar to us. The taste of the Middle Ages appreciated them. Here they are again, decked out in the attire of the baroque period, but essentially the same figures— half monument, half spectacle.

Finally, it is worth while to glance at the 'herauldes of Arms, Sergeauntes of Arms, trumpettes, mynstrells, and all the other officers' enumerated in the progress of Henry VII, for they, too, incarnate the later Middle Ages, with their love of pomp, their graduations of rank, and their delight in pseudo-chivalry with heralds, banners, coats of arms, and trumpets.

From these examples it is clear that modern times have introduced no break in the secular side of the festivities at a coronation. Fashions and taste come and go; the external setting may be dictated by the taste of the Renaissance or by baroque fashion, but this yearning for brilliance is a constant feature.

# 6.  Aristocratic Diversions and Entertainments

---

## Chivalry and Courtly Love

&s§ *Sydney Painter*

NOBLEWOMEN AND MINSTRELS FASHION THE IM-
AGE. While the clergy was bombarding the noblemen with the
precepts of religious chivalry, the ladies of France were carrying on a
more effective campaign of propaganda in favor of their conception
of the ideal knight. Few ladies could write, but all could dispense good
dinners, fine clothes, and rich gifts to the wandering minstrels who
supplied the feudal caste with its literary entertainment. Hence the
nobles were continually exposed to the ideas of courtly love which came
to them neatly concealed among the tales of battles and tourneys which
were the delight of their long evenings. This creation of the ladies and
their allies the minstrels is in at least one respect the most interesting
of the three sets of chivalric ideas. Feudal chivalry was simply the
spontaneous development of the immemorial warrior virtues under the
influence of mediaeval conditions. Religious chivalry grew naturally
out of St. Augustine's conception of the Christian soldier. As complete
concepts both were products of mediaeval life, yet their component
ideas were not new. Courtly love, on the other hand, was essentially
novel. The romantic aura which has always surrounded the relations
between men and women, waxing and waning in accord with contemporary conditions, was given a new form by the courtly writers. To
them love was neither the god-sent madness that caused the siege of
Troy and dogged the footsteps of Odysseus and Aeneas nor the highly
cultivated appetite which gave so much pleasure to the Hellenistic
lyric poets and their Roman successors. Courtly love was to its adher-

*135*

ents the most vital element of noble life—the source of all noble virtues. Love and lust are as old as the human race, but *fin amour* was essentially a product of the Middle Ages. . . .

The ideas of courtly love first appeared in the lyric poetry composed by the troubadours of southern France. One day toward the middle of the eleventh century a very hungry minstrel who was wandering about the duchy of Aquitaine came to a castle where he hoped that his tales of battles, broad stories, and tumbling tricks would earn him a good dinner. Unfortunately he found the lord absent and the lady heartily tired of hearing about endless battles. Then it occurred to the minstrel that if he composed a song in praise of the lady's beauty and virtue and described their effect on him in glowing terms, he might get the dinner after all. The experiment was successful, and soon the minstrel was recommending the same course to his colleagues. It was not long before the baronial halls of southern France were ringing with songs in praise of ladies who were able to dispense lavish hospitality. If a lady did not have a minstrel singing her virtues, she felt definitely out of fashion. Then one day a great and lusty lord, William IX, count of Poitou and duke of Aquitaine, heard one of the songs and decided to turn his hand to composing love lyrics. He had no need to sing for his dinner. His purpose seems to have been to furnish a pleasant ac-companiment to his numerous triumphs over feminine virtue and then to regale his boon companions with songs recounting his amorous victories. The poetic activities of this mighty feudal prince, the suzerain of a third of France, soon set the fashion. A baron of the south felt that his prestige demanded that he sing songs in praise of a lady. If this was completely beyond his talents, he could at least patronize poor poets. Thus the singing of love lyrics became a fad. Barons and knights sang because it was pleasant and fashionable, poor minstrels because they had to live.

The fundamental idea which formed the basis for the lyric poetry of the troubadours was their conception of love. To them love was the emotion produced by unrestrained adoration of a lady. Love might be rewarded by smiles, kisses, or still higher favors, but their presence or absence had no essential effect on love itself. All the benefits and tor-ments which came to the lover grew out of simple worship of a lovely and worthy woman. This love was caused by the lady's good qualities— her beauty, charm, wit and character. "The great beauty, the good manners, the shining worth, the high reputation, the courteous speech, and the fresh complexion which you possess, good lady of worth, inspire me with the desire and the ability to sing." Once aroused this emotion had tremendous effects on the lover. "My heart is so full of joy that everything in nature seems changed. I see in the winter only white, red and yellow flowers; the wind and rain do nothing but add to my happiness; my skill waxes and my song grows better. I have in my heart so much love, joy, and pleasure that ice seems to me flowers and snow green grass. I can go out without clothes, naked in my shirt: my passion protects me from the iciest wind." "When I see her, when I consider her eyes, her face, her complexion, I tremble with fear like a leaf in the wind; a child has more sense than I retain in the violence of my transports." The true lover never slept, but tossed and turned in his bed. His thoughts were so centered on his lady that nothing else interested him. But the effects of love were not purely emotional and physical—it improved a man in every way. "Behold again the good things which love gives: it makes a vile creature into a distinguished man, a fool into a man of agreeable conversation, a miser into a spend-thrift, and it transforms a rascal into a man of honor. By it insane men become sages, the gauche become polished and the haughty are changed into gentle and humble men." "For the ladies always make valiant the most cowardly and wickedest felons: for however free and gracious a man is, if he did not love a lady, he would be disagreeable to everyone." To this let us add a sentence from Pons de Chapteuil's lament for his dead lady "The most valiant counts, dukes, and barons were more *preux* because of her." The term *preux* implied the possession of the chief virtue of feudal chivalry and was the most honorable appellation that could be applied to a knight. Thus in Pons' opinion the chivalric qualities were strengthened by the worship of a lady. A man would be a better knight if he loved—in fact it was doubtful whether a man who did not adore a lady could be a true knight.

By developing this idea that a noble could not be a perfect knight unless he loved a lady the troubadours laid the foundation of courtly chivalry. If the doctrine was accepted by the noblemen, it would be bound to elevate woman's position in society. Although she could not fight herself, she could make men more *preux*. The troubadours did not, however, carry this theory to its logical conclusion—that a good knight should possess qualities pleasing to ladies. The ladies of troubadour poetry were passive goddesses who were adored whether they wished to be or not. Hence the troubadours laid little emphasis on the qualities which might make a lover acceptable. While it is true that the knight was expected to serve his adored one, this service consisted merely of fidelity and continuous worship. In short troubadour love was not mutual. The knight loved. The lady might or might not reward him, but she apparently never felt any great passion. Only when sexual intercourse became an integral and necessary part of the conception of love did the knight who wished to perfect himself by being in love feel called upon to make himself more attractive to ladies. This

important step was the work of writers of northern France who took
over the ideas of the troubadours and modified them to suit themselves
and their patronesses. . . .

THE NOBLEMAN'S TRUE IDEAL. The feudal male was
chiefly absorbed in war and the chase. His wife bore him sons, his
mistress satisfied his momentary lusts. Beyond this women had no place
in his life, and he had no interest in them. They were freely beaten
and treated in general with callous brutality. The *chansons de geste*
show very clearly the attitude of the twelfth-century knight toward
women. As these works were obviously composed with a male audience
chiefly in mind, they emphasized what the nobleman liked. For the
most part they dealt with war and feudal intrigue, but occasionally a
woman slipped into the story. Some were noble and virtuous wives and
mothers. They appeared nursing their children, mourning their slain
husbands, and exhorting their sons to brave and often cruel deeds.
They were the victims of savage indignities. If a wife opposed her husband, his usual reply was to hit her on the nose so that it bled. The
emperor calmly told the wife of one of his rebellious barons that if she
did not accept a different husband at his command he would turn her
over to his varlets for their amusement. But on the whole little space
was devoted to these worthy ladies—they simply did not interest the
knightly listeners. The only women who received any great amount
of attention were beautiful and sensual young girls of exalted rank,
usually Christian or Moslem princesses. Apparently the favorite diversion of the former was to slip into the beds of unsuspecting and often
not very receptive male guests. The Moslem princesses invariably removed the handsome Christian captives from their fathers' dungeons
and entertained them luxuriously and lasciviously in their own apartments. From the point of view of the composers of the *chansons* the
great advantage of using Moslem ladies lay in the fact that eventually
they could be converted. The baptism of a fair Saracen gave scope to
their best lyrical efforts. The lady could be undressed and her charms
and their effect on the knightly onlookers described in great detail all
with the pious and worthy object of recounting a solemn religious
ceremony. These entertaining but shameless girls profoundly shocked
Léon Gautier, the historian of chivalry as portrayed in the *chansons*.
As Gautier was firmly convinced that these songs gave an accurate
picture of feudal life, he was faced with the conclusion that young
noblewomen actually behaved that way. He finally extricated himself
by saying that while the authors of the *chansons* knew all about
knights, they had very little knowledge of young girls. Obviously no
such dubious hypothesis is needed to protect the reputation of the
maidens of mediaeval France. The girls of the *chansons* did not neces-

sarily represent young noblewomen as they were but as the males would have liked them to be. As a matter of fact these minxes rarely married the knights on which they lavished their favors. They were either calmly deserted or passed off on secondary characters in the story. The composer of the songs dealt with what the knights of the day were interested in—war, feudal intrigue, and light women. A high-born virgin burning with desire to climb into his bed has probably always been a favorite subject for man's daydreams....

THE NOBLEWOMAN'S DESIRE. A lady wished her knight to have a military reputation that would do her honor, but she was far more intimately interested in his possession of the qualities appropriate to the boudoir. The courtly knight should be handsome, should keep his teeth and nails clean, should wear neat and rich clothes. He was expected to be gay, witty, and amusing. He must be courteous to everyone. He should be careful not to quarrel or brawl in the presence of ladies. The noble's fierce arrogance and proclivity for boasting must be curbed if he wished to arouse his lady's love. Above all the courtly knight must be able and willing to please the feminine taste. Perhaps few noblemen could compose songs in honor of their ladies, but they could at least learn to sing those written by others and to accompany themselves on a musical instrument. They could also master the intricate patter of courtly love and be prepared to take part in the endless debates which delighted its devotees. In short the ladies expected their lovers to be both warrior and *cavaliere servente*. In one of his *jeux-partis* the trouvère Perrot de Beaumarchais asked a lady whether she preferred a good knight full of prowess but lacking courteous qualities or a handsome blond youth who was good company and a master of the lover's art. The lady unhesitatingly chose the man of prowess. He could learn courtesy in her arms.

When the courtly knight had won his lady's affection he was expected to demonstrate his love by serving her. The troubadours thought it sufficient if he was loyal and composed songs in her honor, but later writers were more exacting. In the fanciful romances like those of the Arthurian cycle the knights served their ladies by killing dragons and subduing bandits whose castles were always filled with lovely captive maidens. The more realistic tales simply demanded that the lover honor his lady by performing deeds of prowess. The castellan of Coucy bore his lady's badge into as many tournaments as possible. The courtly knight must not only serve his lady but he must also be scrupulously careful of her honor. He must keep his love a close secret lest the lady's fame should suffer. Obviously even in the literature this was usually pure pretense. The ladies gloried in the knights who served them and had no desire to hide their love except perhaps from their husbands.

The most that this injunction to secrecy meant was that a lover who had enjoyed his lady's favors should be discreet about his success. Finally the true knight would respect all ladies and defend their fame. Many a hero of courtly romance was characterized as one who would never listen to evil about ladies and would chastise anyone who defamed them. Such in brief was the conception of the qualities and behavior suitable to a courtly knight as it was expressed in contemporary literature.

## The Profit and Glory of Tournaments

 Sydney Painter

William Marshal was of knightly birth. Two vigorous generations had raised his family to a place within the pale of the nobility. The feudal aristocracy never really accepted anyone who had been born outside its ranks. No matter how capable or how successful an upstart might be he was always hampered by the contempt, dislike, and distrust of the dominant class. But within this charmed circle the distinctions, great as they were, were economic rather than social. While the heir of an earl who was lord of two hundred knightly vassals inherited a position which one less fortunate could scarcely hope to attain, he was perfectly willing to accept as a peer any man of knightly birth who might acquire equal feudal power. One well-worn path—the service of the crown—had led many a landless English noble into the ranks of the baronage. If a member of the feudal aristocracy could not assure his son of a position in society by leaving him a fief, he could lay open before him the road to ultimate success by endowing him with the royal favor and the abilities required to turn it to account. In this latter respect the father of William Marshal was eminently successful. . . .

During the period between his twenty-fifth and fortieth years William devoted himself to chivalry—not the chivalry of Launcelot or Galahad, but one which was purely military and feudal. He sought fame and fortune through knightly exploits. The romantic service of God and fair ladies was . . . unimportant in his mind. . . . For this decade and a half William's biography seldom touches the course of history. It follows the adventurous career of a knight-errant whose only connection with the political events of the day arose from the fact that the lord whom he served happened to be Henry Plantagenet, eldest son of Henry II and heir to the Angevin domains. . . .

The comparatively quiet life in England soon palled upon young Henry and his household, and their adventurous spirits longed for the land of knightly deeds. It occurred to the prince that a pilgrimage to the shrine of St. James of Compostella along the route made famous by the legends of Charlemagne and his paladins might furnish amusement and excitement. King Henry did not approve of so extended an expedition, but he gave his son leave to cross to the continent. Landing in Normandy in May 1176, Prince Henry and his knights plunged into the chivalric life of northern France in which they were soon to become central figures.

As a debutante seeks the support of an established social leader, so young Henry, desiring an auspicious introduction into the chivalric world, turned to his cousin, Philip of Alsace, count of Flanders, who was generally recognized as the age's foremost patron of chivalry. Count Philip received his royal cousin most hospitably and took him on a grand tour through his extensive domains. One day word came to Prince Henry of a tourney to be held between Gournay and Ressons in the county of Clermont. The young king and his mesnie wanted to go, but for some unexplained reason they lacked arms and war horses. This misfortune gave Philip of Flanders a splendid opportunity to display his generosity. When his guests arrived at the scene of the tournament, they were so richly equipped that a spectator could hardly have estimated the value of their accoutrements. Thus young Henry and his suite were introduced to the chivalric world by one of the foremost knights of the day and served as shining examples of his *largesse*.

This was but the first of a number of tourneys attended by Prince Henry and his knights during the course of 1176. William continued to serve his master as guardian and tutor. In the press of the combat he stayed near the prince and beat off with mighty blows anyone who might try to capture the heir to the Angevin lands. But William was more than a mere bodyguard, he was a strategist as well. It appears that Count Philip of Flanders, the flower of chivalry, took an extremely practical view of tournaments. He was accustomed to hold aloof from the combat until the contestants were thoroughly exhausted. He could then charge into the mêlée at the head of his mesnie and take many valuable prisoners at small risk to his own men. After the young king and his followers had suffered several times from these tactics, William decided to beat the count at his own game. At the next tournament Prince Henry pretended that he would take no part in the contest, but at the opportune time, he and his knights rode into the field and attacked the count's household. So successful was this stratagem, that young Henry and his men used it in many other tourneys. William served his master with a clear head as well as with a strong arm.

Shortly after their visit to Flanders, Prince Henry and his mesnie attended a tournament between Anet and Sorel-Moussel in the valley of the Eure to the north of Dreux. The knights of the Angevin lands were so encouraged by the presence of their king that they drove the French from the field with their first charge. In the confusion of the pursuit William and his master became separated from their men. While riding through a street in Anet, they were suddenly confronted by three hundred foot serjeants under Simon de Neauphle, a French baron, who was apparently covering the retreat of his compatriots. Not to be disturbed by a few wretched infantrymen, William, closely followed by the prince, rode straight towards their line. The serjeants gave way before the two knights, and as he rode through their ranks, William, seizing Simon's horse by the bridle, forced the unwilling baron to accompany him. As they rode on through the town, a low-hanging water drain swept Simon from his horse. The young king, who was riding behind, saw the accident but kept it to himself. When they finally arrived at their camp William, who still led the riderless horse, proudly ordered his squire to take charge of the captured knight. Great was William's merriment when he learned how he had lost his prisoner.

Early in the spring of 1177 word came to young Henry's court of a tournament which was to be held at Pleurs near Épernay in the valley of the Marne. The prince decided that it was too long a journey for him to undertake with all the baggage required by his household, but he readily gave William, who was unwilling to miss any opportunity to acquire glory, leave to go with a single companion. At Pleurs they found a splendid assembly of the chivalry of France, Flanders, and the adjacent Imperial provinces. Hugh, duke of Burgundy, Count Philip of Flanders, Count Theobald of Blois and Chartres, the counts of Clermont and Beaumont, and the valorous William des Barres were at hand to take part in the contest. The valley swarmed with knights who hoped to gain honor and profit. There one could see fine horses from Spain, Lombardy, and Sicily put through their paces. The accoutrements of the knights were so rich as to beggar description. In the tourney William gained the admiration of all by his valor and his skill in the use of arms. When the contest was over, the knights gathered together to discuss the events of the day. Some sought news of friends or relatives who had been captured, others were trying to raise money for their ransoms or to find pledges who would guarantee their payment. A lady of high rank, possibly that famous patroness of chivalry and courtly love the Countess Marie of Champagne in whose husband's fief the tourney was held, presented to the duke of Burgundy a very fine pike. Wishing to "double the honor to the lady" the duke sent the gift to Count Philip of Flanders who in turn passed it on to the count of Clermont. The latter, not to fall behind his peers in courtesy, sent it to Count Theobald of Blois. As the proceeding was becoming rather ridiculous, Count Philip suggested that they give the pike to the knight who had borne himself most worthily in the tournament. As everyone acclaimed this idea, the count was asked to name his candidate. He replied that the hero of the day was a knight of the young king's household—William Marshal. Two knights were deputed to make the presentation of this strange prize. Preceded by a squire bearing the pike, they set out for William's lodgings. There they were informed that he could be found at the blacksmith's shop. In the smithy they discovered William kneeling with his head on the anvil while the smith labored with hammer and tongs to draw off his helmet which had been beaten out of shape and driven down on his head by the force of the blows received in the tournament. When the helmet had finally yielded to the smith's efforts, the two knights presented the prize to William who received it with becoming modesty. The barons, learning from their emissaries the strange situation in which they had found the hero of the tourney, were greatly impressed and felt that they had shown excellent judgment in awarding the prize to so hardy a warrior.

Apparently not even so enthusiastic a patron of chivalry as Prince Henry could attend enough tournaments to satisfy William's craving for glory and profit. In the spring of 1177 Roger de Gaugi, a fellow member of young Henry's mesnie, asked William to join him in a systematic tour of all the tournaments that might be held. William agreed, and the two knights entered into partnership for the full exploitation of their military abilities. For two years they journeyed from tourney to tourney in search of honor and gain. In its commercial aspects at least their venture was a great success. According to a list kept by Wigain, the young king's clerk, the partners captured in the course of ten months one hundred and three knights.

One day William and his partner went to a tourney at Joigni which lay in the Seine valley south of Sens. The party to which they attached themselves armed in the castle and reached the field before their opponents. There they found the countess of Joigni and her ladies who had come to watch the sport. To while away the time the knights and ladies danced to a song sung by William. When he had finished, a young minstrel who had just been made a herald gave a piece of his own composition of which the refrain was "Marshal, give me a good horse." Just at that moment the first knight of the opposing party arrived on the field. William calmly left the dancing throng, mounted his charger, dismounted the newly arrived knight, and gave his horse to the minstrel. It was a nice exploit—a combination of the two knightly virtues of generosity and prowess. Scarcely less entrancing is the picture of knights dancing in full armor. As for William, the sight of the fair ladies so raised his spirit that he carried all before him.

In the course of the year 1179 William dissolved his partnership with Roger de Gaugi and returned to Prince Henry's court. The continual round of tournaments did not cease, but once more William attended them as commander of young Henry's mesnie rather than as a knight-errant. Soon after he rejoined his master, a series of three tourneys drew all good knights to the region of Dreux and Chartres. The largest of these took place in the valley of the Eure between Anet and Sorel-Moussel, the scene of a former tourney attended by William. This time Prince Henry did not go, but he sent his mesnie under William's command. When William and his companions reached the field, they found that the combat had already begun and that the French were getting the best of it. The arrival of the young king's mesnie turned the tide in favor of the knights of the Angevin lands, and their opponents were put to rout. Some of the fugitives took refuge on a mound surrounded by a palisade and moat. So great was their haste that they did not stop to take their horses inside the enclosure but simply tethered them to the outside of the palisade. William, who had as usual lost his companions in the heat of the pursuit, chanced to ride by the mound and realized that here was a splendid opportunity. Leaving his mount in charge of the squire who was his sole attendant, he jumped into the moat, climbed the mound, seized two of the horses, and led them back the way he had come. As he was coaxing them up the bank of the moat, two French knights rode by. Seeing that William was dismounted and helpless, they bore down upon him and relieved him of the two horses. William realized that he was at a hopeless disadvantage and made little attempt to protect his booty. As he knew the names of the two knights, he could settle with them later.

Remounting his charger, William rode on until he came to a group of farm buildings in which fifteen French knights were being besieged by a greatly superior force. When William arrived on the scene, the hard-pressed defenders offered to surrender to him rather than to the besieging party. The latter were naturally annoyed at seeing fifteen good prisoners slip from their grasp, but as none of them cared to fight William over the matter, they were forced to withdraw. When he had escorted his prisoners to safety, William let them go and declined to accept any ransom. Considering that the besieging party must have formed part of William's own side in the tournament, this whole proceeding seems rather high-handed, but it undoubtedly earned him the friendship of the French knights and added to his reputation for generosity.

William rode back to his lodgings thoroughly satisfied with his day's work. There he disarmed and prepared to set out in search of the two horses which had been taken from him. To the modern mind it seems eminently proper that the horses he had captured should in turn be taken from him, but it was, apparently, against the laws of chivalry. Mounting his palfrey, William rode to the quarters of William des Barres who was the uncle of one of the young knights who had taken the horses. William des Barres was greatly shocked at his nephew's conduct. Had the story come from any less trustworthy man he would not have believed it. As it was he ordered the youth either to restore the horse or to leave his household. Someone suggested that William show his knightly generosity by giving the young man half the horse and then throwing dice with him to see who should have the whole animal. Accepting the suggestion, William promptly threw an eleven against his opponent's nine and won the horse. William des Barres urged William to stay, but he insisted on going after the other horse. The knight who had taken it was a member of the mesnie of a French baron. When the latter heard William's story, he commanded his vassal to return the stolen charger. Again it was suggested that he give the young knight half the horse. William agreed and asked the youth to estimate the value of the animal. Supposing William had no money with him and realizing that he could put a low valuation on the horse, pay his half at once, and get the animal very cheaply, the young man valued the charger at only fourteen pounds though it was worth thirty or forty. Much to his surprise, William threw seven pounds on the table and went off with the horse. The young knight had been caught in his own trap. William had in each case sustained his reputation for generosity and still gained his object.

# 7. Eleanor of Aquitaine: Europe's First Jet-Setter

### *I Wonder What the Queen Is Doing Tonight*
⋙ *Amy Kelly*

THE RICHEST HEIRESS.  The Duchess Eleanor was a prize to draw the covetous attention of ambitious nobles, for the patrimony she inherited from her forbears was one of the goodliest of the feudal world. It spread from the river Loire to the foothills of the Pyrenees, from the central heights of Auvergne to the western ocean. It was wider and fairer than that of her overlord, the King of France himself; ampler and more gracious than the counties which the Dukes of Normandy held north of the Loire; richer and more genial than the island of Britain, where Stephen of Blois wore the crown of the Norman conquerors. The fief of the duchess was rich and desirable in itself; but its special importance was that its addition, through the marriage of its heiress to any other domain in western Europe, would raise that domain to preëminence over all the others. . . .

The duchess herself was no liability to her rich dower. She was no simple marriage prize to be gathered in by the Capets for her weight in gold. She claimed descent from Charlemagne, whose effigy was still borne on the coins of Poitou, and knew herself the heiress of a great tradition, who could acquire no incomparable luster from the marriage decreed for her by circumstance. . . .

That the young heiress was fair enough to content any king appears from subsequent accounts. "Charming," "welcoming" and "lively" (*avenante, vaillante, courtoise*) are the words used by the chroniclers to portray her. While the Prince of France had been indentured to canons and abbés to learn his destined role as archbishop, Eleanor had made another use of time. What the magnates of the prince's escort noted especially when they met her in Bordeaux was her maturity of mind. She had grown in the enlightened traditions of her family. Her education had not of course furnished her with the orderly intellectual baggage fit for an abbess. Though doubtless, like all the heirs of her race, she had had her tutors, her real school had been a varied experience. Movement with the itinerant ducal family from castle to castle had afforded that training in taste and judgment that comes from frequent contrast of persons, places, things. Though but fifteen, and therefore the prince's junior by two years, in practical experience, in that decisiveness gained from instant appraisals, she far outdistanced him. Her education had taught her especially to be intolerant of ennui.

As a girl she must have traveled much with the peripatetic household from the foothills of the Pyrenees to the Loire on those long *chevauchées* made necessary by the ducal business of overlooking intriguing vassals and presumptuous clergy, and carrying law and justice to the remoter corners of creation. She knew a land of mellow harvests, where grain shocks bent like humble homagers; of forests dark at noon; of scraped heights where the baronial strongholds loomed with their clustering mud hamlets; the vast agglomerations of the abbeys, their mills, salt marshes, vineyards, wine and olive presses, their fantastic dovecotes and apiaries spread along garden walls. She knew the aspect of the red-roofed towns, and the traffic of each one, here a fair, there a market; here a lazar house, there a hostel thronging with pilgrims returning from Saint James or the shrines of the pious Limousin. Familiar were the domes of Saint Jean d'Angély showing from afar as the road wound in; familiar the church of Saint Eutrope of Saintes, its dark Romanesque nave cut across with swords of sunlight, the great collegials of Limoges. Melle she knew where there was a mint, and Blaye, where, in the glow of forges, armorers repaired their traveling gear; and Maillezais, where her aunt, the Abbess Agnes, never failed to halt the ducal progress for a largess. At the end of *chevauchée* she found herself in motley assemblies of castellans, bishops, abbots, merchant princes, poets, travelers, and all the entertainers and hangers-on that gave an outward air of careless wealth and gaiety to a solid program of feudal business. . . .

THE QUEEN OF FRANCE'S PIOUS KING. In 1145 the king and queen assembled their barons for their Christmas court again in Bourges. On the crossroad between France and Poitou, the court was the grand gathering of the year, an assembly in which to grasp and direct the driving currents of the feudal will. When the Capets had received the homage of their vassals in the palatine city, Louis addressed the concourse gathered from the far corners of Gaul on the matter he had so much at heart. The fall of Edessa had stirred the

West; but there was obvious consternation at the king's proposal of
a new holy war to redress that grievance. The barons of France, and
especially those of the queen's provinces, had been made circumspect
by the costly and inconclusive character of former expeditions to the
Orient....

Abbé Suger surveyed with distinct alarm his sovereigns and his wards
in the high mood that possessed them in Bourges. He perceived somewhat belatedly that Louis's education, his indoctrination first with the
ideology of a bishop and then with that of a king, had produced a
strange confusion in his brain. Louis's ideas of himself were mixed,
his decisions clouded with conflict. The issue seemed likely to be folly. It
was certain that the queen meant to accompany the expedition.
Whether her going were to be preferred to her abiding at home was
an important question; but it was a vain one. Who could detain her
or circumvent her resolution? Could the king, or the Pope, or Abbé
Bernard? She could muster more soldiers for the succor of Jerusalem
than her lord, and the revenues of her duchy were indispensable. Her
spirit fanned the king's aspirations. With *élan* she moved among the
barons of Aquitaine who remembered Raymond of Antioch—the sieurs
of Rancon and Lusignan, of Limoges and Angoulême, of Thouars and
Poitiers. Speaking as one of them in the amiable *langue d'oc*, she exhorted
the hesitant, jibed at poltroons, fired the ambitious, called upon the ardors
of the old Limousin, invoked its saints. Who could say that her motives
were less pure than the king's? While the momentous decision was still
in the balance, Abbé Suger gave his support to the hesitation of the
vassalage. With the courage that challenges martyrdom, he raised his
solitary voice against the royal plans, urging reflection and delay. But
how could even the Abbé of Saint Denis oppose the Pope, the Abbé of
Clairvaux [St. Bernard], his king and queen? ...

OFF TO THE SECOND CRUSADE. When Louis had taken his
cross [the sign that he would go on the crusade], Eleanor knelt before
the abbé and offered her thousands of vassals from Poitou and Aquitaine. It was a wonder to see the young dynasts, who less than a year
before had been so rash and arrogant, upon their knees receiving the
symbol of their dedication from the humblest of all their subjects, the
poor little brother of Clairvaux. With the queen came "many other
ladies of quality," Sybille, Countess of Flanders, whose half brother
was King of Jerusalem, Mamille of Roucy, Florine of Bourgogne,
Torqueri of Bouillon, Faydide of Toulouse, and scores of others whom
the chroniclers could not afford the parchment to enumerate.

Whatever may have been said secretly behind the palm of the hand,
no one appears to have asked publicly what these female warriors were
to inflict upon the Saracens. The historians do not well explain why

hordes of women took the cross. However, the chronicler Newburgh suspects that in the case of Queen Eleanor, Louis was overborne; she had doubtless, he says, so bedazzled her young spouse with her excellent beauty that, fearing out of jealousy to leave her behind, he decided to take her with him to the wars. The annalist deplores the fact that the queen's example made other ladies intractable, and the policy led in the end to the infiltration of a good many women who had no business to be included in the army ... markets for forage. And there beyond the floods of the Danube rose glorious Byzantium on the Bosporus and beyond Byzantium the fabulous bazaars of Antioch and Tripoli, the incomparable shrines of Jerusalem.

At Vézelay the crosses gave out and still the crowd bore down upon the saintly abbé. The token! The token! A legend tells us that the queen and her ladies disappeared and presently reappeared on white horses in the guise of Amazons, in gilded buskins, plumed, and with banners: that like Penthesilea and her warriors, the queen and her cavalcade galloped over the hillside of Vézelay, rallying laggard knights, tossing distaffs to faint-hearted cavaliers. The tale is in character, and later allusions to Amazons en route, found in Greek historians, give some substance to it. This dazzling dramatization of the story of the Amazons, popular in every castle, must have made a sensation and stimulated the recruiting notably. Even the foot soldiers called for the sign that should keep them safe. Other supplies failing, the abbé's white wool cassock was snipped into little crosses, and these he sowed rather than distributed with his blessing among the crowd. As at Clermont fifty years before, the cry rose to heaven in all the dialects of Gaul, "It is God's will." ...

The vast movement of the pilgrim soldiers over central Europe was a prodigy. They kept a pace of ten to twenty miles a day by river and by road, for they were but three summer months from Metz to the Bosporus, and they found their forage by the way. The great barons, turn by turn, led the van, and Louis, like a good shepherd, brought up the rear. Having been taught that the crusade of the troubadour Count of Poitou fifty years before had been rejected by heaven and come to nought by reason of the godlessness of the rabble that followed in his train, Louis maintained a rigorous discipline among the malefactors in his host. He put down pillagers and ravishers with severity and made an example of recreants by cutting off their noses and their ears. But to the needy he showed a liberal compassion. Even in the utmost stress, he began every day with mass and undertook no movement without the guidance of his bodyguard. Odo of Duilio, who slept beside the royal tent, vouches for the blameless purity of all the king's designs.

Eleanor was by some oversight less carefully protected from the impact of the world. The very arrangements for keeping Louis safe were in their nature destined to deprive the queen of the soundest influence and leave her somewhat to the devices of her own heart. Though she doubtless had her chaplain and said her prayers, her entourage was on the whole distinctly secular. She appears to have kept en route to her role of Penthesilea, which, as it is said, had been such a success and inspiration at Vézelay. The Greek historian Nicetas, who writes of the crusade, remarks that "there were in the army women dressed as men, mounted on horses and armed with lance and battle axe. They kept a martial mien, bold as Amazons. At the head of these was one in particular, richly dressed, that went by the name of the 'lady of the golden boot.' The elegance of her bearing and the freedom of her movements recalled the celebrated leader of the Amazons."

In the course of the expedition Penthesilea, as mistress of the forces of Poitou and Aquitaine, was of necessity thrown much among the barons of her own provinces, old friends and relatives, who naturally made much of her. There were Geoffrey de Rancon the Poitevin, Hugh of Lusignan, and Geoffrey of Thouars, and many another, friends and kinsmen of Raymond of Antioch, all dreaming of glorious and profitable careers in the Orient. These knights were not sustained by the ideology that kept Louis upright. They were "younger sons of younger brothers," emigrating from the unemployment and the profitless ennui of the old counties south of the Loire, with whom Eleanor could express herself in her native dialect. It is said that, in spite of the bull of Vézelay [forbidding them], there were troubadours among them who, singing of love and beauty, accustomed the queen to moods of grandeur and elation, as the crusaders traversed the plains of Hungary or floated on the bosom of the Danube in the soft summer weather and the moonlit nights, on their way to the holy city of Jerusalem. . . .

The queen, upon her arrival in [Antioch], was weary after the three-weeks' confinement in the foul little sailing bark from Satalia and vexed by the melancholy allusions of her fellow passengers to that horrible February night in Asia Minor. She was moreover certainly tired of movement, of mountain scenery, of ruined apostolic cities, of stinking boats and drafty tents, of snow and rain, roast mutton, sour cheese, and reveille. She was infinitely relieved to find in the palace of the Prince of Antioch shelter from the censure of the Franks, from the surveillance of the king's chaplain with his recording eye, and from the aggrieved stares of those remnants of the Amazons who had lost too many relatives near Laodicea to be any longer boon traveling companions. But when in the delicious sunshine of the East her native vitality returned, she showed herself to her relatives and the expatriates from her provinces a loyal Poitevin and a radiant Queen of France. She was of so much consequence in Antioch that Louis, who continued, in spite of all his trials, to cherish her with an unreasoning love, appears to have felt almost repaid for the hardship and expense of bringing her out three thousand miles from Paris.

A sympathy at once sprang up between the Prince of Antioch and his niece the queen. Raymond's clear Poitevin eye at once divined that the fortunes of Antioch rested not with Louis, his diminished forces and his monkish counselors, but with Eleanor and her Provençaux. The queen and the prince, who had now to compensate for their ten years' separation, conversed long hours together in their native dialect, whose racy idiom was perhaps not quite intelligible to the Franks. After having caught up with each other on the vital history of that decade, so full of incident to them both, it is probable that they found themselves in accord not only on the proper objectives of the crusade, but also on the character of the idealists who had come from the West for the rescue of Jerusalem. Since these visionaries from Gaul lacked a clear-cut policy, the Poitevin genius aspired to maneuver them one by one into action on behalf of Antioch. This strategy was tried. Raymond ransacked his bazaars and his princely treasure for the spoils of the East; he called ceremoniously upon the most noble of the Frankish barons where they lodged in his villas and palaces, and plied them with strange and splendid gifts. He was a liberal and a persuasive man, and he employed all the seductions of his riches and his eloquence to prevail upon his guests. At his expense they tasted wines cooled with mountain snows, the fruits and spices of the Orient; they were enriched with jewels, amulets, and the most precious relics of the Holy Land. But these costly overtures evoked from the Franks no evidence of gratitude of a strictly practical quality. . . .

It was in the course of [their] intimacies that Raymond learned about the queen's attacks of *accidia*, which, beginning with moderate onsets in Paris, had swollen to a first-rate malady between Metz and Antioch. He was not surprised to find she was discontented with her role as Queen of France and that her mind had strayed to alternatives. The bishops and abbés and chaplains assigned to hedge Louis from dangerous influences in the course of his pilgrimage had thwarted her native gifts for creating a milieu of her own that might have given a little luster to the enterprise of kings and nobles even on the dusty way to Palestine. The vigils of Odo of Duilio outside the king's chamber, and the grip of Thierry Galeran upon the coffers of the expedition, had deprived her of her lawful influence in the counsels of her lord, an influence to which not only her station as queen, but her contribution to the resources of crusade, seemed to entitle her.

There was a touch of chagrin too in her malaise. Louis's counsel of wise men found some fault with her and armed him and themselves against her with concerted disapproval. Abbé Bernard had discovered in her the evil genius of the king in his wretched wars with Thibault of Champagne; in ten years of marriage she had given the Franks no prince. . . .

THE BREAK WITH KING LOUIS. Louis, alive now to the snares of Satan, was in the midst of the intricate and perplexing business of marshaling his hosts and getting his harness together when the queen demanded and obtained an audience. At this critical moment she brought him face to face with what proved in the long run the major incident of the holy war. In short, she let him know that she had taken a resolution to separate herself then and there from the Capetian dynasty, to go with him no further on crusade, to lay aside her crown adorned with the lilies of France, to resume her status as Duchess of Aquitaine, to fix her pilgrim staff in Antioch and remain with Raymond in his high place on Mount Silpius. . . .

The council, to which Louis repaired in this crisis, was more alive to Raymond's role in the affair than to the novel and capricious ideas of the queen. Queen or no queen, syllogism or no syllogism, Eleanor was Louis's vassal and his lawful marriage prize, the most valuable piece on the chessboard of feudal Europe. In case of her separation from the king, she could not long remain at large as Duchess of Aquitaine. On whom then did the treasonous Raymond intend to bestow the king's ward in order to butress his own estates? On himself? On a vassal? On one of the Pullani? On some merchant prince of Amalfi or Genoa? On some emir of the Saracens, with whom he seemed to be so privy? The council fell into a panic. How was Louis, the Pope's emissary, the most Christian King of the Franks, to appear in Jerusalem for the conference on the holy war with King Baldwin and his barons, with the Templars, the Patriarch, the Holy Roman Emperor, if, after all his losses from Metz to Antioch, he were to lose besides, within the very limits of the Latin Kingdom, his queen and all her provinces? What story would this be for Abbé Bernard, for Abbé Suger, for the Pope?

The sound vigorous counsels of Thierry Galeran to keep the queen in custody at any cost prevailed. A signal was given to the French army in the night. The queen was seized and fetched, in what state of woe and anguish or downright Poitevin rage we can only guess, to Saint Paul's gate. Before the prayer call sounded from the minarets or Raymond's sleepy watch awoke upon the towers of Mount Silpius, the Frankish hosts for the rescue of *Dame-Dieu outre-mer* had shaken the dust of the city from their feet and taken the road past the fortress of

Margab for Tripoli. The midnight exit of the King of the Franks from Antioch with his captive queen, observes William of Tyre, was by no means suitable to the dignity of the foremost king of Christendom, nor by any means comparable to his entrance a few weeks before with flying banners, the pomp of instruments, and the psalmody of choirs.

However, in spite of the discretions of the high council, the "resentment" of which the abbé wrote could not be "concealed" from the profane ranks of the crusading pilgrims. The custody of Eleanor made it very apparent that something dreadful had occurred in Antioch to warrant such proceedings. Only some shocking misbehavior on her part seemed adequate to account for the breach between the Franks and the Poitevins that threatened once more to dissipate the forces for crusade. In consequence, a variety of stories arose among the Franks to explain the anomaly and to preserve Louis and the high command from blame for the situation. William of Tyre charges the queen with indiscretions and with conduct both in Antioch and later unworthy of her royal dignity and disregardful of her marriage bond; but his sources were certainly the French high command. John of Salisbury accuses her of too great familiarity with the Prince of Antioch. The Minstrel of Reims, most of whose other yarns are preposterous, details the queen's effort to escape with her jewels from Tyre in a galley supplied by Saladin (a potentate at the time about ten or twelve years of age), and he relates that Louis himself frustrated her flight by setting his foot on the landing stage, just as the craft was ready to slip its moorings, and convoying her back under the shelter of midnight to the palace where she had been lodged. The stories are all suspect in view of their Frankish source and of the Frankish interest in giving a proper color to the grievous incident. Gervase of Canterbury recommends silence for rumors current in regard to Eleanor's conduct in the Orient. But whether or not there was in any of them an element of fact, they became, in spite of efforts to stifle them, a stock in trade, revived from time to time, of scandalmongers and balladeers, and so pursued the Duchess of Aquitaine to the end of her days and farther down the corridors of history. . . .

QUEEN OF ENGLAND. Eleanor was enchanted by [the] rich and rising young Duke of Normandy and desired a marriage with him on mere grounds of compatibility. What seems clear is that Eleanor at this time grasped at some tangible prospect the Angevins offered her of freedom from the Capetian yoke.

Henry, already a belted knight, who had entered upon a vast and goodly portion of his heritage, was for his part casting about for a solid alliance and one that should offer him every possible advantage in dealing with his overlord, the King of France, with whom he was certain to have conclusions to try. Of course, whatever the theories of women

might be, the property value of great heiresses made it impractical for
feudal lords to be carried away by regard for temperament in choosing
wives. But in this case, though Henry was a born and bred feudal bar-
gainer, he could see the queen was no liability to her dower. Newburgh,
writing of this time, speaks of Eleanor's charms of person and her lively
mind. As arbiter of the *haut monde* in the île, she was mistress of her
queen's role, and Henry expected to have uses for a proper queen. She
had seen the world at its very best, its notables in all the citadels of
Christendom. Her knowledge of places and personages, of affairs, of
gossip and intrigue, made her a helpmate nonpareil for an ascendant
king. That she was the proud victim of calumny, enkindled by unmas-
tered emotions, merely enhanced her with an air of melancholy sophistication. Youth, "the fast-withering flower," still bloomed triumphant
in her mien. The queen was nearly thirty, Henry but eighteen; but
such disparate marriages were not uncommon where great fiefs were at
stake. Henry's own mother, the Empress Matilda, was fifteen years
older than Geoffrey the Fair. Eleanor was unquestionably a prize with
a dower meet for any king. With the acquisition of her fiefs, there
would be new stores of men and treasure for the vindication of Henry's
claim to England, and England the Angevins were determined shortly
to wrest from the house of Blois. . . .

The queen was to poets, as one of her apologists has said, "what
dawn is to birds." They sang for her. It would require a textbook to
catalogue the dedications and rededications and other literary saluta-
tions addressed to Eleanor herself. Wace had offered his redaction of
Geoffrey of Monmouth's *History of the Kings of Britain*—that bubbling
spring of Arthurian lore—to her while she was still only Duchess of
Normandy; and she is commonly identified as the "riche dame de riche
rei" of Benoît de Sainte-Maure in his romance of *Troie*.

> *For my presumption shall I be chid*
> *By her whose kindness knows no bounds?*
> *Highborn lady, excellent and valiant,*
> *True, understanding, noble,*
> *Ruled by right and justice,*
> *Queen of beauty and largess,*
> *By whose example many ladies*
> *Are upheld in emulous right-doing;*
> *In whom all learning lodges,*
> *Whose equal in no peer is found,*
> *Rich lady of the wealthy king*
> *No ill, no ire, no sadness*
> *Mars thy goodly reign.*
> *May all thy days be joy.*

Even old things were brought from the closet and refurbished with an eye to Plantagenet munificence. Philippe de Thaün revived interest in the bestiary which he had formerly dedicated to Henry I's queen, Adelaide of Louvain, with a few offertory words to the Countess of Poitou.

> God save lady Alianor,
> Queen who art the arbiter
> Of honor, wit, and beauty,
> Of largess and loyalty.
> Lady, born wert thou in a happy hour
> And wed to Henry King.

The queen's fame was spread far beyond the precincts of the court along the pilgrim routes by minnesingers and balladeers.

> Were the lands all mine
> From the Elbe to the Rhine,
> I'd count them little case
> If the Queen of England
> Lay in my embrace.

The new literature brought with it a cult of manners. Under court discipline the careless male learned that to present himself before the queen's assize with hair unkempt, "like an ill-dressed shock of barley," was to be effaced from the presence of majesty. John of Salisbury and Walter Map, who must often have seen what they describe, report that the aesthetic movement of their time was producing an effeminate effect upon the ways of hearty England. From the civilizing influence of dress, it was only a step to the ritual of flattery which these critics found so depressing. Barons renounced their native dignity and addressed each other in meaching phrases as "best of men, mirror of wisdom, my refuge, my sun, my life." John declared that the foolish dawdling and love-making of rustics, once reckoned depraved by serious men, was affected by gallants of the court, a statement that suggests that the mortifying ritual of the courts of love was somewhat understood in London, even as it had been in Poitou and the Limousin. This particular branch of art, dramatized so especially by Ventadour and other troubadours in the queen's provinces, seems never to have had the thoroughgoing success in England that it enjoyed on the Continent; yet something it must have accomplished, for, when the innovations were well under way, the cynical Map exclaims, "There is now in London no Lucretia, no Penelope, no Sabine woman. Fear all the sex." . . .

In the intervals of her cultural activities, Eleanor, crossing and recrossing the Channel at any season of the year, and making the rounds from castle to castle in England and abroad, shared Henry's confidence and the labors of his government. Sometimes in his absence, herself holding a royal court, she sat with the king's justiciars on matters of importance and set her own seal to writs of royal exigence. She drew her own revenues and kept oversight of a lively domestic household, as is shown by her expenditures for rushes, plate, and linen. And in the meantime, with a perversity to confound the Franks, she secured the future of the Angevin empire and supplied the instruments of a diplomacy which, no less than force of arms, was to solidify the whole.

Her first son, Guillaume, born on the Continent before Henry's accession, died in 1156; but in the meantime she had given birth to Prince Henry (February 1155) and to a princess named for the Empress Matilda (June 1156). In September 1157 the future Coeur-de-Lion was born in the palace of Oxford and designated in Guillaume's stead as the queen's special heir to the County of Poitou and Duchy of Aquitaine. In 1158 a fourth son, born at the moment of Henry's absorption of lower Brittany, was named for the king's brother Geoffrey, and subsequently designated as the Count of Brittany. In September 1161 the queen gave birth in Domfront in Normandy to a second daughter, who was baptized by the cardinal legate with her own name; in October 1165 the Princess Joanna was born in Angers; and in Oxford in December 1166, John "Lackland," the last of the "eaglets." The names make a roster of famous kings and queens.

# 8. Peasant Life and Amusements

## Village Pleasures

ᴥ§ H. S. Bennett

We shall be making a rough guess at the medieval peasant's condition if we observe the present circumstances of the small peasant-proprietor in France, Germany or Austria. Tens of thousands of French "small-holders" are facing the daily struggle now that their forbears endured many generations ago. They are freed of week-works and boon-works, they no longer are subject to certain "customs of the country" which exact tallage or chevage, or the like, nor are they forced to grind here nor sell there. But the land is always there: harsh, exacting, insatiate, and rapidly overcoming the puny efforts man can put into it unless he is constantly fighting. And the fight is unending—the harvest is but the signal for the autumn ploughing; and the autumn ploughing for the sowing, and so on. Season follows season: the rhythmic passage of the year drags in its wake the rural society. And this society, now as then, is a unit, a little world of its own. Necessarily the great world affects it, and the fair once a year or the weekly markets take the villager some miles out of his own fields just as they did in the Middle Ages. But otherwise, the village is the unit, and there in the main life goes on as it always has and (seemingly, to the peasant at least) always will. There are a few days or hours of happiness, but on the morrow the old routine reasserts itself. Always, as the day wears on to evening, in the falling dusk the horses and oxen are put into their stalls for the night. The cows are milked and bedded down. Lights move about the farm outbuildings as the tired men assure themselves that everything is well for the night. Meanwhile, the housewife, busied at her fire, tends the soup and makes all ready for the men's return. When at last they come and gather round the table, set out with its rude and meagre cutlery and

platters, the evening meal begins—bread, soup, cheese, beer—the same
meal eaten by peasants since the beginning of time as it seems. There
they talk or jest or argue as the occasion serves; and, after the meal,
perhaps sit awhile by the dying embers before fatigue calls them to
sleep, only in order to begin yet another day.

That is the background: and in that endless routine most of their
life is spent, and so it was with their ancestors six centuries ago. There
are, however, a few days now and then given over to festivity, and a
few hours snatched from this grim travail with the soil. It is to these
that we must now turn, in order to see yet another side of medieval
peasant life.

We may well start with John Stow's translation of the famous account by Fitzstephen of the manner in which the Londoner of the
twelfth century refreshed himself when work was put on one side.

> Every yeare also at Shrovetuesday, (that we may begin with
> childrens sports, seeing we al have beene children,) the schoole
> boyes do bring Cockes of the game to their Master, and all the
> forenoon delight themselves in Cockfighting: after dinner all the
> youthes go into the fields to play at bal. The schollers of every
> schoole have their ball, or [staff], in their hands: the auncient
> and wealthy men of the Citie come foorth on horse-backe to
> see the sport of the yong men, and to take part of the pleasure
> in beholding their agilitie. Every Friday in Lent a fresh company
> of young men comes into the field on horse-backe, and the best
> horsman conducteth the rest. Then march forth the citizens
> sons, and other yong men with disarmed launces and shields,
> and there practise feates of warre.... In Easter holy dayes they
> fight battailes on the water. A shield is hanged on a pole, fixed
> in the midst of the stream; a boat is prepared without oares to
> bee caried by the violence of the water, and in the fore part
> thereof standeth a yong man readie to give charge upon the
> shield with his launce; if so be hee breaketh his launce against
> the shield, and doth not fall, he is thought to have performed a
> worthy deed. If so be without breaking his launce he runneth
> strongly against the shield, downe he falleth into the water, for
> the boat is violently forced with the tide; but on each side stand
> great numbers to see, and laugh therat. In the holy dayes all the
> Somer the youths are exercised in leaping, dancing, shooting,
> wrastling, casting the stone, and practising their shields: the
> Maidens trip in their Timbrels, and daunce as long as they can
> well see. In Winter, every holy day before dinner, the Boares

prepared for brawne are set to fight, or else Buls and Beares are bayted.

When the great fenne or Moore, which watreth the wals of the Citie on the Northside, is frozen, many yong men play upon the yce; some, striding as wide as they may, do slide swiftly . . . some tie bones to their feete, and under their heeles, and shoving themselves by a little picked staffe, doe slide as swiftly as a bird flieth in the ayre, or an arrow out of a Crossebow . . . thus farre Fitzstephen of Sportes. [Stow continues] Now for sportes and pastimes yearely used. First, in the feaste of Christmas, . . . every mans house, as also their parish churches, were decked with holme, Ivie, Bayes, and whatsoever the season of the yeare afforded to be greene. . . . In the moneth of May, namely on May day in the morning, every man, except impediment, would walke into the sweete meadows and greene woods, there to rejoyce their spirites with the beauty and savour of sweete flowers, and with the harmony of birds praysing God in their kind.

We must discount something for the romantic glow cast over the past by Stow's eager imagination, and make other necessary allowances, but when all is done, does not this passage suggest to us innumerable happy hours spent on water or in the fields, not only by the Londoners, but by the peasants of the days of Fitzstephen and for centuries afterwards? In the countryside, even if the opportunities for merriment were more limited, the great Church festivals of Christmas and Easter, or the more popular festivals associated with the harvests, gave considerable opportunities for enjoyment. At Christmas, for example, work ceased altogether for some fourteen or fifteen days, and often a feast was provided for the peasantry by the lord. . . .

To while away the long winter nights popular amusements were everywhere to be found. They were essentially of the folk, although they had been much affected by Christian elements, so that it was a strange mixture of pagan and Christian that had evolved by the twelfth and thirteenth centuries. All this is admirably dealt with in Sir E. K. Chambers' fascinating volume, *The Medieval Stage*, where the development of the various elements which went to the making of the medieval play are analysed and discussed. To the lord and his dependents, however, the strange history behind the Christmas festivities or the setting of the Midsummer watch were mysteries of which they knew or suspected nothing. Christmas, to them, was a brief respite in the yearly cycle of events, bringing its central and heavenly message, but also bringing much that was of the earth earthy. The villager, gaping admiringly at the pranks and buffoonery of the mummers' play, or join-

ing in the choruses of the songs, or taking part in the dispute between
the holly and the ivy, in which the young men and women of the village all took sides, forgot for a while the fatigues of the autumn and
the ardours of the coming spring. . . .

So from time to time throughout the year the great religious festivals
gave the peasant a few hours of pleasure making: the ceremonies connected with Easter would enthral him with such dramatic incidents as
crawling to the Cross on the Good Friday, or the rending of the veil
which had hidden the sanctuary throughout Lent; or perhaps, if he
were near some great Abbey church, he might behold the elaborate
miming which portrayed to the congregation the rising of Christ and
His absence from the tomb. Then again at the Corpus Christi feast he
would take part in the processions, and enjoy such rough dramatic representations of the events of the Scriptures as the wandering players,
or the nearby town gilds could perform. Less closely associated with the
Church were the great popular festivals of May Day, or of Midsummer Day, when the whole village gave itself up to mirth and dance.
"From a very early period in England the summer festivals were celebrated elaborately with dance and song and games, and there are many
references to them in the fourteenth century", and these references
make no suggestion that the games are new. On the contrary they tacitly
assume their antiquity, and "somour games" may be looked on as one
of the oldest elements of English social life.

As well as these ceremonies which were part of the communal life of
the whole village we must also notice the way in which the great occasions of life in the individual families were celebrated. Birth, marriage
and death were all eagerly seized upon by the peasant as a welcome
relaxation from his daily cares. Marriage, indeed, was so scandalously
made an occasion of immoderate mirth that we have a constant series
of episcopal pronouncements against the lax behaviour of those attending the marriage ceremony. Bishop Poore, about 1223, ordered that
marriages "be celebrated reverently and with honour, not with laughter
or sport, or in taverns or at public potations or feasts". A number of
similar injunctions during the next hundred years show how difficult it
was to keep these "bride ales" (as they were often called) within reasonable limits. After the church ceremony the party would adjourn to
a private house, or to the village ale-house, and there drink heavily of
the ale which had been brewed for the occasion, and the profits of
which went to the new bride. These "bride ales" attracted such characters as Perkin, the prentice of *The Cokes Tale*, and the Wife of
Bath herself.

Funeral ceremonies were also the occasion of much rude merriment.
The vigil or wake had its serious moments, but it also had much about

it that caused moralists to link "wakes" and taverns together as leading to sin. In 1342, a church council denounced wakes as giving opportunities for fornication and theft, while a century earlier bishops had prohibited singing, games and choruses during the time the dead person still lay in the house. Although we have little direct evidence for our period the constant series of prohibitions from Anglo-Saxon times onwards against pastimes at vigils for the dead, together with the abundant evidence from the sixteenth century onwards, makes us certain that throughout the Middle Ages elaborate meals and drinkings, accompanied by boisterous behaviour, were an inseparable part of funeral ceremonies. The rich, as we should expect, made much of these occasions, and rich and poor were summoned to pay their last respects to the dead, and were lavishly entertained during and after the ceremonies. The death of Maurice, the fourth Lord Berkeley, on 8 June 1368, was the signal for the reeve on his manor of Hinton to start fatting up one hundred geese for his funeral, "and divers other Reeves of other Manors the like, in geese, duckes, and other pultry". These were but a small part of what was provided, as may be seen from more detailed accounts of some fifteenth-century funeral arrangements. And there, it will be noticed, the presence of "poor men" is constantly mentioned, and we may feel sure that the funeral of the lord of the manor, no less than the funeral of a neighbour, was a day of mixed sorrowing and feasting for the medieval peasant. Sidney's famous phrase "Hornpipes and funerals" is but another way of indicating the frame of mind which was capable of turning "the house of mourning and prayer into a house of laughter and excess".

Mention of the "bride ales" and "wake ales" recalls one of the most popular forms of medieval festivity. Scot ale, church ale, play ale, lamb ale, Whitsun ale, hock ale, and the like: we are constantly meeting with such terms in medieval documents. Each of these ales was the excuse for much heavy drinking, together with dance and games. They were frowned upon by the Church (as we have seen in speaking of the "bride ales" and "wake ales") and with good reason, for they undoubtedly encouraged licence. Yet, all the efforts of the Church could not suppress them, and little by little we find the Church forced to recognise the church ales in an endeavour to exercise some control over their more extravagant phases.

But even though the church ales gradually came under ecclesiastical control, many other ales remained. The main function of many of these was undoubtedly to provide money for the lord or his bailiff or the forester who held them, and in consequence they were not always welcomed by those who were invited. They were, in fact, a kind of bazaar, which all had to attend and at which all had to buy. . . .

The village ale-house must have its place in any account of village life. It is true that many families brewed their own ale, but there was room for some houses (perhaps a little larger than most villagers' cots) where "bride ales", or convivial meetings could be held. We have only to turn the pages of the preachers and didactic writers to see what an evil reputation they had. "The devil's chapel" was well known to the medieval moralist, and Dr Owst in his learned *Literature and Pulpit in Medieval England* devotes several pages to the outbursts of Bromyard, Rypon and other English preachers, who season their discourses with "details of the scene, such as the rude pot-house songs, snatches of lewd conversation from the bench of cronies, the low tricks played amongst this fellowship of Satan".

# 9. Popular Participation in Medieval Common Law

## Instant Justice

⊷§ Frederick Pollock and Frederick W. Maitland

When a felony is committed, the hue and cry...should be raised. If, for example, a man comes upon a dead body and omits to raise the hue, he commits an amerciable offence [one subject to a penalty set at the court's discretion], besides laying himself open to ugly suspicions. Possibly the proper cry is 'Out! Out!'...The neighbours should turn out with the bows, arrows, knives, that they are bound to keep and, besides much shouting, there will be horn-blowing; the 'hue' will be 'horned' from vill to vill.

Now if a man is overtaken by hue and cry while he has still about him the signs of his crime, he will have short shrift. Should he make any resistance, he will be cut down. But even if he submits to capture, his fate is already decided. He will be bound, and, if we suppose him a thief, the stolen goods will be bound on his back. He will be brought before some court (like enough it is a court hurriedly summoned for the purpose), and without being allowed to say one word in self-defence, he will be promptly hanged, beheaded or precipitated from a cliff, and the owner of the stolen goods will perhaps act as an amateur executioner.

In the thirteenth century this barbaric justice is being brought under control. We can see that the royal judges do not much like it, though, truth to tell, it is ridding England of more malefactors than the king's court can hang. The old rule held good that if by hue and cry a man was captured when he was still in seisin of his crime—if he was still holding the gory knife or driving away the stolen beasts—and he was brought before a court which was competent to deal with such cases, there was no need for any accusation against him, for any appeal or any indictment, and, what is more, he could not be heard to say that he was innocent, he could not claim any sort or form of trial. Even royal judges, if such a case is brought before them, act upon this rule. It is not confined to cases of murder and theft. A litigant who in a civil suit produces a forged writ is hanged out of hand in a summary way without appeal or indictment, and the only chance of exculpation given him is that of naming a warrantor. Even in much later days if a man was [caught redhanded], though he was suffered and compelled to submit the question of his guilt or innocence to the verdict of a jury, he could be put on his trial without any appeal or any indictment.

# 10. University Life

## Reading, Writing, and Rioting
*◄§ Hastings Rashdall*

ENTERING THE UNIVERSITY. In the first place, it is natural to ask the age at which a boy usually went up to Paris and probably most other universities. Twenty was the minimum age for the mastership, and the full course in arts lasted seven years. Fourteen might, therefore, be considered the normal minimum age for admission; but the Paris statute, which requires the 'determining bachelor' to be at least fourteen, distinctly implies that some went up much earlier than this. Many would naturally have been older. On the whole it appears that the age of admission varied much more considerably than is now the case; but as a rule the freshman would be between thirteen and sixteen. . . .

When we have grasped the fact that the medieval student in arts was usually much younger than the modern undergraduate, we are very apt to fall into the mistake of seeing him merely the modern public-school boy, taught Aristotle instead of Cicero, and disputing sophisms instead of writing Latin verse. Such a view would, however, involve a complete misconception of his status. When we remember the youth of the medieval freshman, the unfettered liberty—not to say licence—which he originally enjoyed, is certainly one of the most astonishing facts about him. In some cases we do, indeed, hear of his being escorted from home by a 'fetcher', 'caryer', or 'brynger', but the roads were dangerous, and protection of some kind was necessary even for men, while travelling in a carrier's cart was of course cheaper than riding. The proclamations against bearing arms often contain exceptions in favour of students travelling to or from the university. On arrival at Oxford or Paris our student had full liberty (unless his parents had made some provision for him, which would have been an impossibility for all but the rich) to choose the master to whose lectures he would go, and the hall or *hospicium* to which he would attach himself.

While temporarily established at an inn before finding permanent quarters for himself, he would very probably be visited by some touting master or one of his students (who no doubt expected a commission on any business which he might introduce), anxious to secure the new-comer for his own hall or lecture-room. In the matter of lectures, indeed, a trial was respectfully solicited with all the accommodating obsequiousness of a modern tradesman. The pseudo-Boethius of the thirteenth century represents a scholar as advising freshmen not to com-mit themselves to a regent before they had attended his lectures for three days experimentally; and the statutes of some universities pro-vide that fees shall not become payable till after the expiration of that or some longer interval. With regard to residence, indeed, it was in the earlier period not necessary or even customary for the student, how-ever young, to live under the nominal supervision of a master; he might seek out his own lodgings in the town or join a party of students in hiring a hall. . . .

Badgering or 'hazing' (as the American students call it) of the *bejaunus* . . . gradually assumed a stereotyped form. The raw youth from the country is supposed to be a wild beast who has got to lay aside his horns before he can be received into the refined society of his new home. By this time the actual ceremony of 'depositio' has become a solemn university function, patronized though not actually conducted by the university authorities. The student is first represented as con-versing with his new master, whom he asks to arrange for his 'depositio', and entreats to let the expenses be as moderate as possible. Then, after returning from matriculation before the rector, he is visited in his room by two of the students. They pretend to be investigating the source of an abominable odour which has reached their nostrils. At last they dis-cover the cause; it is the new-comer, whom they take to be a wild boar. A closer inspection reveals that it is a 'beanus', a creature that they have heard of but never seen. Then follows much chaff about the wild glare in his eye, the length of his ears, the ferocious aspect of his tusks, and so on. Then with mock sympathy it is suggested that the horns and other excrescences may be removed by an operation—the so-called 'dep-osition'. The ceremony is apparently rehearsed in rough horse-play. The victim's face is smeared with soap or something of the kind by way of ointment; his ears are clipped; his beard cut; the tusks removed with a saw; and so on. Finally, they are afraid that the operation will be fatal: the patient must be shriven without delay. One of them feigns him-self a priest, and puts his ear to his mouth. His confession is repeated, word for word by the confessor. The boy is made to accuse himself of all sorts of enormities: as a penance for which he is enjoined to provide a sumptuous banquet for his new masters and comrades....

STUDENT AMUSEMENTS. A very striking feature of medieval university life (at least in English eyes) is the almost total absence of authorized or respectable amusements. The statutes of the college founder or university disciplinarian on such matters are often more severe than they are in the repression of crime or vice. It is difficult to find in our records any allusion to recognized amusements except some vague mention of playing at ball out of doors, and within doors of singing or playing on the lute. But here again we are simply encountering one of the characteristics, not of the universities in particular, but of the age in general. The upper class of feudal society was an essentially military class: its amusements consisted in jousts and tournaments, hunting and hawking. Such recreations were not unnaturally considered too unclerkly and too distracting as well as too expensive for the university student, and were consequently forbidden in medieval statutes. Contempt of the body was too deeply rooted a sentiment of the religious mind for a pious college founder to recognize the necessity of bodily exercise and a free vent for animal spirits. Even 'playing with a ball or a bat'—the nearest approach to 'athletics' which we encounter —is at times forbidden among other 'insolent' games. A sixteenth-century statute includes the machinery of tennis or fives among the 'indecent instruments' the introduction of which would generate scandal against the college; though it charitably allows playing with a soft ball in the college court. Though gambling was not so strong a passion in the north as in the south of Europe, a good many statutes are directed against it even in northern universities. The sterner college founders forbade games of chance and playing for money altogether: the more indulgent contented themselves with limiting the stakes to eatables or drinkables and confining the games to festivals. Chess is a pastime which might seem severe enough to propitiate the most morose disciplinarian, but it seems to have enjoyed a curiously bad reputation with the medieval moralist, and is forbidden by many academical legislators. At Heidelberg, for instance, visits to the public chess-tables are forbidden 'especially on legible days'; at New College the stern Bishop of Winchester includes chess among the 'noxious, inordinate, and unhonest games' which are forbidden to his scholars.

College statutes are not unnaturally full of prohibitions directed against musical or other noises calculated to disturb the studies of others. Some few German statutes condescend so far to human infirmity as to permit at seasonable hours musical instruments, 'provided they are musical'. As to the keeping of dogs, hawks, ferrets, 'unclean beasts or birds', the practice was viewed by the college disciplinarian with a traditional horror which (as regards dogs) still lingers in the breasts of the deans and porters of Oxford and Cambridge. As the grim sixteenth century is reached, the prohibitions against all 'profane games, immodest runnings, and horrid shoutings', become increasingly sweeping.

The institution of a sort of public university ball for the express purpose, it would seem, of introducing the students to the 'most honourable, and elegant daughters of magnates, senators, and citizens', deserves to be mentioned as a rather exceptional peculiarity of sixteenth-century Leipzig. Much more frequently we encounter stern denunciations of dancing in any form whatever. But we may infer that the amusement was a favourite one with the students from the fact that, even in a college jealously guarded against female intrusion, William of Wykeham [in the fourteenth century] found it necessary for the protection of the sculpture in the chapel reredos to make a statute against dancing and jumping in the chapel or adjoining hall [of New College, Oxford]. His language is suggestive of that untranslatable amusement now known as 'ragging', which has no doubt formed a large part of the relaxation of students—at least of English students— in all ages. At the same college there is a comprehensive prohibition of all 'struggling, chorus-singing, dancing, leaping, singing, shouting, tumult and inordinate noise, pouring forth of water, beer, and all other liquids and tumultuous games' in the hall, on the ground that they were likely to disturb the occupants of the chaplain's chamber below. A moderate indulgence in some of the more harmless of these pastimes in other places seems to be permitted.

The ideal student of the Middle Ages probably amused himself little or not at all. The only relaxation which the university system provided for was the frequent interruption of the regular routine for the whole or part of a day in honour of the greater holidays of the Church, or of the festivals of the patrons of a particular nation, or province, or faculty. For the faculty of arts the great days were the feasts of S. Scholastica and S. Nicholas. Some statutes contain severe prohibition of carnival-tide licence, but in Scotland two or three days' holiday was expressly allowed for cock-fighting at this season. In all medieval universities—but especially at Paris—the student enjoyed an abundance of what may be called ecclesiastical dissipation. For the masters at Paris there were national vespers and a national mass once a week, as well as on many festivals. These functions were followed by a distribution of money or a dinner. . . . For master and scholars alike there were frequent processions, university masses, and university sermons, which at least afforded a welcome relief from morning lecture. The afternoons of holidays supplied the chief opportunity for country walks or recreation in the Pré-aux-clercs. In the German universities we find, however, a growing tendency to abridge even this scant liberty by providing afternoon lectures on festivals. Mathematics are sometimes introduced as a light study specially appropriate for such times, it being alleged that half-holidays were usually spent in the tavern. In the evenings of festivals even the sternest of college disciplinarians relaxed so far as to allow story-telling or carol-singing, or the reading of 'poems, chronicles of the realm, or wonders of the world' round the fire in the college hall. This was probably regarded as a harmless substitute for the entertainments of strolling jesters or actors or mountebanks largely patronized by the student when free from collegiate restraints. Only on Twelfth-night were mummers allowed within the sacred precincts of the college.

By some universities we find even Sunday utilized for lectures or disputations, and there are traces of the same institution in the early days of the Italian law-schools; but this would appear to have been the exception rather than the rule. In general, the Sunday was free for worship and rest, and seems to have been rarely abused by the outrages or disturbances so common on other festivals.

The comedies which began to be acted in the halls or colleges towards the end of the fifteenth century form almost the only amusement of an intellectual character which relieved the stern monotony of academic life. But these are not heard of till the first breath of the Renaissance spirit had reached even Paris and Oxford: these comedies represent the first contact of the stream of academic culture with the now fuller and more vigorous current of popular literature, and exercised an important influence over the development of the modern drama both in France and England. It is needless to say that the innovation was looked upon with considerable suspicion, though not altogether prohibited, by the university disciplinarians.

Alike in the universities and out of them the asceticism of the medieval ideal provoked and fostered the wildest indulgence in actual life. If we want to realize what were the probable amusements of the un-ideal student we must turn to the things which laws and statutes prohibit rather than to those which they permit. For the bolder spirits there were sporting excursions into the country. Poaching in the king's forests at Shotover or Woodstock was a favourite pastime of the Oxford scholar. The University of S. Andrews with unwonted liberality actually allowed its students to go a-hawking, provided they went in their own clothes and not in 'dissolute habiliments borrowed from lay cavaliers'. On the roads round the university towns were even to be met parties of scholars—many of them expelled or banished for previous transgressions—who had turned highwaymen and now waylaid the more peaceful student approaching the university with his purse equipped for a nine months' residence.

The proportion of idle men was perhaps not larger than in most modern universities, but for the idle, as for the average student in his lighter moods, there were hardly any amusements except drinking, gambling, and singing at taverns, roaming the streets in large gangs under a 'captain' or otherwise, singing, shouting, dancing, throwing stones, breaking doors or heads, and fighting or quarrelling with towns-folk or students of a hostile 'nation'. Various forms of practical joking of the more violent order enjoyed a high degree of popularity. Among the archives of the University of Leipzig is a 'libellus formularis' or collection of forms for rectorial proclamations against the various kinds of disorder which were wont to break out periodically in a medieval university like the recurrent epidemics of pea-shooting, catapulting, and the like at a modern school. Among these is a form of proclamation against destroying trees and crops in the adjoining country, against 'wandering with arms after the town-hall bell', against throwing water out of the window upon passers-by, against wandering at night and beating the watch, against 'horrible shoutings and noisy and unwonted songs', against wearing disguises, masks, and 'rustic garments' at carni-val-tide, against interfering with the hangman ... in the execution of his duty, ... against attending exhibitions of tilting, wrestling, boxing, and the like, against 'insolences' or practical jokes in general....

To return to the subject of drinking customs—no important events of life could be got through without drinking. We have already spoken of the mode of celebrating 'jocund advents', determinations and incep-tions; and many of the minor steps in the career of a university man were celebrated by feasts and drinking-parties given by the successful and elated candidate. And it was not only after a university exercise but during its progress that the need of refreshment was apt to be felt. Wine was provided for the distinguished visitors to the schools at determinations. Many statutes allude—some by way of prohibition, but not always—to the custom of providing refreshment of the same kind for the examiners by the examinees, whether before, during, or after an examination.

# 11. The Arthurian Legend As Popular Romance

## Arthur Lives!
ьⱨ R. S. Loomis

The belief in Arthur's survival ... prevailed among the Cornish and Bretons as early as 1113. We have at least two testimonies from the same century to the existence of this belief among the Welsh....

During the next centuries we continue to get echoes of the tradition from English writers. The chronicle attributed to Robert of Gloucester (*c.* 1300) mentions the Cornish as sharing the hope with the Bretons. Peter de Langtoft and his redactor, Robert Mannyng (1338), also mention it; the first author is noncommittal, the second calls it 'the Bretons' lie'. In the *Fall of Princes* (1431–8) Lydgate ascribes to them the belief that Arthur 'shall resorte as lord and sovereyne Out of fayrye and regne in Breteyne'. According to Malory (*c.* 1469), 'some men say in many parts of England that King Arthur is not dead, but had by the will of our Lord Jesu into another place; and men say that he shall come again, and he shall win the Holy Cross'. Malory continues, with great caution: 'Yet I will not say that it shall be so, but rather I would say: here in this world he changed his life.' One of the most extraordinary stories which was in circulation, though after our period, was reported by Julian del Castillo in 1582. According to common talk, King Arthur had been enchanted in England into the form of a crow, and some said that Philip II swore (evidently at the time of his marriage to Mary Tudor in 1554) that he would resign the kingdom if Arthur should return!

The vague belief in Arthur's survival took on certain specific forms. ... Giraldus Cambrensis attributed to the 'fabulosi Britones' the story that the king had been borne to Avalon by Morgan; so also did Gervase

of Tilbury. Geoffrey of Monmouth in his *Vita Merlini* (*c.* 1150) and
Guillaume de Rennes in *Gesta Regum Britanniae* (*c.* 1235) give
elaborate and independent descriptions of this blissful isle, of its ever
green vegetation, of its long-lived denizens, and of its mistress who was
to heal Arthur's wounds....

[For some reason] Avalon came to be identified with Glastonbury.
...It has often been assumed that Henry II, wishing to stifle the
hope of Arthur's return, induced the monks to do some excavating in
their cemetery, with the result that, after Henry's death, certain large
bones were discovered, together with those of a woman; above was a
leaden cross with an inscription, variously reported, identifying these
remains as those of Arthur and his queen....

Nevertheless, the discovery did not put a quietus on the widespread
belief that Arthur still lived on in a winterless isle. The author of
*Floriant et Florete* (*c.* 1250) identified it with Sicily, for he informs
us that the chief fortress of Morgain was Mongibel, that is, Etna, and
that Arthur was destined to be brought there....

The tradition of Arthur's sojourn in Sicily was blended by Gervase
of Tilbury (*c.* 1211) with the belief that he dwelt in the cavernous
depths of a mountain. A groom of the Bishop of Catania, in pursuit
of a runaway palfrey, entered the side of Mount Etna through a narrow path, emerged on a delightful plain, and discovered Arthur lying
on a regal couch in a marvelous palace. Here the king had lain since
the battle with Modred, his wounds annually breaking out afresh....

The legend of Arthur in the hollow mountain took other forms. The
thirteenth-century *Wartburgkrieg* makes allusion to Arthur as dwell-
ing 'in dem berge' with the Sibyl's child and with hundreds of knights
whom he had brought from Britain; there they live in delight, supplied
with food, drink, arms, and horses. An English poem, *A Dispute between a Christian and a Jew* (*c.* 1375), describes a vision of Arthur
and the knights of the Round Table in a magnificent manor, reached
by a path under a hill. Stories akin to the Welsh cave legends of
Arthur and his sleeping men, awaiting their destined hour to sally
forth, were reported in the last century from Richmond castle and
Sewingshields in northern England, and quite recently from Alderley
Edge, south of Manchester. The country folk in the neighbourhood of
Cadbury Castle, an earthwork in Somerset, firmly believed that Arthur
lived on under the hill, and a party of antiquaries who visited this spot
in the last century were approached by an old man with the question,
'Have you come to take the king out?' It surely makes one reflect on
the fallibility of rational expectations that the belief in Arthur's survival
was still flourishing at a place within sight of Glastonbury, where 800

years before his bones had been officially discovered and where his tomb had been displayed for centuries for all and sundry to behold.

Here at Cadbury there survived also the concept of Arthur as leader of the Wild Hunt, the phantom chase known to the peasantry throughout much of Europe; for an old track near the camp was called King Arthur's Lane, and on rough winter nights the king and his hounds were heard going along it. In many parts of France likewise the phenomenon was called 'la Chasse Artu,' and this goes back to at least the twelfth century. Gervase of Tilbury and the *Didot Perceval* record the belief early in the thirteenth, and about 1260 Étienne de Bourbon tells how on a moonlight night a woodcutter met near the Mont du Chat in Savoy a large hunting-party, who declared that they were of King Arthur's household and that his court was near by. He followed them into a most noble palace, filled with knights and ladies, dancing and feasting. As directed, he lay down in a bed beside a beautiful lady, went to sleep, only to find himself the next morning ignominiously reposing on a bundle of faggots. This story combines three themes: 'la Chasse Artu,' the voluptuous fay, and the common folk-tale ending of the visit to the fairy palace.

A related story is told about Peter des Roches, Bishop of Winchester, in the *Lanercost Chronicle* under the date 1216. The worldly prelate was hunting when he saw with astonishment a splendid mansion. Servants invited him to dine with their master and ushered him into the presence of a king who confessed himself to be Arthur. In order that the bishop might convince sceptics that he had actually seen the ancient lord of Britain, Arthur endowed him with the miraculous power of producing a butterfly whenever he wished by opening his closed fist.

We have a unique version of Arthur's survival alluded to by Godfrey of Viterbo, secretary to Frederick Barbarossa, about 1190. Merlin prophesies that though the king will perish from wounds, he will not perish wholly but will be preserved in the depths of the sea and will reign for ever as before.

This array of diverse traditions about the survival of the British hero calls for three remarks. First, they embody an interesting variety of Celtic concepts of the Other World and its inhabitants. The concept of a sleeping deity surrounded by his attendants was attached by Plutarch to an island near Britain, where Cronus was imprisoned, with Briareus keeping guard over him as he slept; round him were many deities, his henchmen. The concept given us by Geoffrey of Monmouth, of an isle of nine enchantresses, endowed with gifts of prophecy and shape-shifting, who cured the ills of those who sought them, was attached by Pomponius Mela to Sein, an island off the coast of Brittany. The island paradise is familiar to readers of the Voyage of Bran, the island of amorous women, to readers of the Voyage of Maelduin. The subterranean world of noble dwarfs was reported by Giraldus Cambrensis to have been visited by a boy of Swansea. The Wild Huntsman was identified by the Welsh with Gwyn ap Nudd, a king of the Other World. . . .

Secondly, it must be obvious that the spread and elaboration of these beliefs in Arthur's survival were almost entirely oral. . . .

Thirdly, there is a sort of corollary in the fact that these legends were largely ignored by the romancers who dealt with Arthur and his times, except for the references by Malory and the authors of the Didot Perceval and Floriant. Most literary men seem to have felt that they could not compromise their own credibility by taking such ridiculous notions seriously. Nevertheless, as we have seen, the legends cropped up in the most unexpected places, they resisted the attacks of scepticism, they outlasted the marble tomb of Arthur itself. It is an astounding phenomenon that belief in Arthur's survival was still living 1,300 years after his death.

ARTHURIAN INFLUENCE ON SPORT AND SPECTACLE. Oscar Wilde's paradox that 'Life merely holds the mirror up to art' has seldom been better exemplified than in the reflections of Arthurian literature in the practices and pageantries, as well as the plays, of our medieval ancestors. Kings presided at Round Tables and founded orders modelled on Arthur's fellowship; great lords adopted the names, the blazons, and the roles of Gawain, Lancelot, and Palamedes; young merchants caught the same fever, and in south Germany apprentices enacted Shrovetide plays, burlesquing Arthur's court. These mimicries of the Matter of Britain are recorded from Acre in the East (1286) to Dublin in the West (1498), and from Valencia (1269) to Prague (1319). . . .

The first recorded evidence for the imitation of Arthurian figures comes from Cyprus under the date 1223. When the lord of Beirut celebrated the knighting of his eldest sons, 'there was much giving and spending; there were bohorts [tourneys with precautions against serious injury], the adventures of Britain and the Round Table were enacted . . . ., and there were many other amusements . . .'. A continuation of the same chronicle tells how in 1286, when Henry II of Cyprus was crowned King of Jerusalem at Acre, there was a splendid festival, including bohorts, imitations of the Round Table, and impersonations . . . of Lancelot, Tristan, and Palamedes.

From 1223 far into the fourteenth century a similar combination of jousting, feasting, dancing, known as a Round Table, was one of the most fashionable diversions of Christendom. Instances are attested in

Britain for the years 1252, 1259, 1279, 1281, 1284, 1302, 1328, and 1345. That of 1284 was held at Nevin to celebrate Edward I's conquest of Wales, and the last was the consequence of Edward III's vows in 1344 to found an order of 300 knights in imitation of King Arthur. This order later turned into the Order of the Garter, and for some unknown reason all Arthurian associations were dropped. Across the Channel Round Tables were held at Hesdin in 1235; at Bar-sur-Aube in 1294, when Duke John of Brabant was fatally wounded; at Bruges in 1300, attended by the King and Queen of France; and at Paris in 1332. *Tables rondes* are mentioned in Adam de la Halle's *Jeu de la Feuillée* (1262) and in the *Livre du Chevalier de la Tour Landry* (1372). When Edward I arranged for the marriage of his daughter to Alfonso III of Aragon at Oloron in Gascony in 1287, there were Round Tables and dancing.

Such celebrations were at this time peculiarly favoured by the kings of Aragon, for we read of them in Muntaner's chronicle as being held at Valencia, probably in 1269, at Saragossa in 1286, at Barcelona in 1290, and at Calatayud in 1291. On the last occasion the great Catalan admiral, Roger Luria, had a wooden castle built at the end of the lists, which served as his station. When he was challenged by a knight from Murcia, umpires brought the two combatants two pointless shafts, the challenger took his choice, and Luria the other. In the encounter Luria's shaft struck his opponent's helm, crushed his nose, and covered his face with blood. The Round Table was then halted for fear of quarrels.

While on the one hand Edward III . . . founded a short-lived Arthurian order, and while John of France in rivalry set up another to attract knights to his banner, other kings forbade tournaments and King Henry III specifically banned Round Tables in 1232 and in 1251. Popes and prelates thundered against these costly, dangerous, and sometimes licentious frivolities, and denied Christian burial to those who took part. But even the threat of hell fire does not seem to have deterred Western chivalry from breaking their bones and risking their lives in a pastime which enjoyed the prestige of King Arthur's patronage.

Though many notices of these passages of arms provide little detail, others provide too much for more than brief summary. Ulrich von Lichtenstein, a forerunner of Don Quixote, tells in his *Frauendienst* how he set out in 1240, assuming the role of King Arthur, challenging all knights whom he met to a joust, and admitting those who broke three spears on him without missing into the order of the Round Table. The knights whom he met were given names such as Lanzilet, Ywan, and Segremors, and some of them joined his train. The Prince of Austria sent him a messenger, thanking him for coming from Paradise to his land—a reference to the Breton belief—and soon after brought a number of knights to swell the company. Near Neustadt a Round Table was held, tents were pitched, banners set up, and to the music of flutes, pipes, and sackbuts there were individual encounters which lasted for five days. On the sixth there was a general *mêlée* between two sides, broken off by the prince's order. The only damage mentioned, it is pleasant to relate, was a dislocated thumb.

The *bourgeoisie* were caught by the craze. In 1281 a burgher of Magdeburg sent invitations to the merchants of Goslar, Brunswick, &c., to come and try their knightly prowess, and he who excelled the rest was to receive as a prize a woman called Dame Feie. Troops of young men came to Magdeburg and were met by two 'constables' with spears outside the town. A 'gral', consisting of tents and a tree hung with the shields of the local champions, was arranged in a marsh. To touch one of these shields with a spear was a challenge to its owner. Somewhat inexplicably an old merchant from Goslar won Dame Feie, and magnanimously gave her so much money that she was able to leave her wild life for a respectable husband. Similarly in 1330 the burghers of Tournai formed a society of the Round Table and sent out invitations for the next year to Valenciennes, Bruges, Paris, &c. The members of the society took the names of kings, such as Gallehos, Pellez du Castel Périlleux. There was the usual procession of combatants, and the jousts took place in the market square. The prize was a golden vulture.

One of the most famous of these passages of arms was that of St. Ingelvert, described by Froissart. The Maréchal de Boucicaut and two other French knights sent out in 1390 a challenge to all comers from England, Spain, and Germany to meet them in the plain near Calais. Any foreign knight who wished to joust would approach a large elm on which each of the challengers had hung two shields, blow a horn, touch either the shield of peace or the shield of war, and the combat would accordingly take place with either pointed or blunt spears. A large pavilion was provided for the visitors to arm or repose in, and there was an abundant supply of wines and food for their entertainment. Among the English knights who came to the jousting were the half-brother of Richard II, John Holland, and the future Henry IV. Somewhat similar in character was the Pas de la Belle Pélerine held between Calais and St. Omer in 1449. It was so called for the alleged reason that a fair lady had set out with her company on a pilgrimage to Rome, had been attacked by robbers, and delivered by a knight, who promised to escort her to the Holy City as soon as he had fulfilled his vow to guard a pass at the Croix de la Pélerine. This knight was Jean de Luxembourg, lord of Haubourdin, who presented all who accepted his challenge with a pilgrim's staff . . . of gold set with a ruby, in allusion to the lady's pious vow and his own title. The accounts vary widely as to what happened, but it appears that Jean assumed the role of Lancelot, his shield blazoned with the charge of that hero, argent a bend gules, and that the Duke of Burgundy presided.

King René of Anjou in 1446 organized near Saumur jousts according to the terms established by the knights of the Round Table, had a wooden castle called 'Joyeuse Garde' constructed; and introduced into the pageantry lions, tigers, and unicorns (?) from the royal menagerie. There were kings of arms, judges of the field, a dwarf dressed like a Turk, bearing the royal shield, and a lovely damsel leading the king's horse. This like other jousts was stopped because of a fatal injury. René caused a painting to be made of the jousts and in 1451–2 composed his *Livre des Tournois*.

One of the latest and most elaborate of the festivals which followed Arthurian precedent, held in 1493 at the castle of Sandricourt, near Pontoise, was described by the Herald of Orléans. There were on successive days combats on foot at the Barrière Périlleuse, a general tourney at the Carrefour Ténébreux, individual jousts at the Champs de l'Espine. The climax of the last day was the Adventures of the Forest Desvoyable. The participating knights rode out of the castle accompanied by their ladies, and were presented with lances and swords at the Pin Vert, where knights of the Round Table had formerly resorted in search of adventure. Proceeding separately along the forest paths, they would couch their spears when they met and batter each other. Servants were on hand to provide wine and refreshments for the weary. At eve the knights repaired to the castle to banquet and to relate their adventures on oath. Followed dances and farces lasting till two in the morning. Orléans estimated that nearly 2,000 persons including armourers, saddlers, and leeches were entertained at the castle for eight days, and declared that never since the time of Arthur and his order, which comprised Lancelot, Gawain, Tristan, and Palamedes, had there been a *Pas d'Armes* which approximated more closely the deeds of the knights of the Round Table.

As we have seen, impersonation of Arthurian characters had been a recurring feature of these festivals from the very beginning, and there were occasional efforts to adopt their heraldic charges and to emulate their deeds of arms. We have records of two occasions when the imitation of the romances went farther in the direction of drama, both from the last quarter of the thirteenth century when the vogue of Round Tables was at its height. The first is elaborately described by Sarrasin in his *Roman du Hem* and probably took place at Hem-Monacu, near Péronne, in the year 1278. The principal role of the

Chevalier au Lion was taken by Robert II, Count of Artois and patron
of the dramatist Adam de la Halle; while the part of Guenièvre was
played by the sister of Aubert de Bazentin, one of the organizers of the
tournament.

Apparently the entertainment began with Guenièvre seated at supper with her court, when Soredamors rode in on a hackney led by a
dwarf, to demand succour for her imprisoned lover. Keu remarked that
any knight who imperilled himself for her sake ought to be tonsured.
When, however, all the knights present asked the queen for the privilege, Keu claimed it as his right, and on the arrival of the knight who
kept Soredamors's lover in prison arranged to meet him the next mom-
ing in the field. It would seem that immediately thereafter seven
knights, taken captive by the Chevalier au Lion, presented themselves,
accompanied by a lion which made itself at home by resting its muzzle on the table. Keu once more indulged in his mockery, but the queen
accepted the surrendering knights into her service, and dancing followed. The next day Keu, while waiting for his opponent, was unmerci-
fully teased by the ladies and finally retorted with a wish that a flame
would burn their tongues. The joust which followed left both combatants unhurt. The Knight of the Lion arrived with several rescued
damsels, and a dark-complexioned handmaiden who announced their
coming elicited some ironic compliments from Keu, which caused the
queen to remark that it was futile to teach an old cat. The rest of the
day was occupied with a series of jousts, the arrival of another distressed
maiden, more comedy furnished by the lion and Keu, and with supper.
The influence of Chrétien's work on the proceedings is obvious, and
one wonders whether Adam de la Halle may have had something to
do with a dramatic performance in which his patron played the chief
heroic role.

A somewhat similar affair seems to have celebrated the marriage of
Margaret, daughter of Marie de Brabant, to the sixty-year-old Edward
I of England in 1299. It is described by the Brabançon priest, Lodewijk
van Velthem, and though he mistakenly assigns it to the occasion of
Edward's first marriage to the Spanish princess Eleanor, it is fairly
clear that it consisted of a tournament and three interludes recalling
Edward's triumphs over the Welsh, the Scots, and the barons. At sunrise the Round Table began with a *mêlée* in which the knights who
had taken Arthurian names had the best of their opponents, except
Keye, whose saddle-girths had been cut—in fun of course—and whose
consequent tumble evoked roars of laughter. When the company
adjourned to the banquet hall, after the first course a page disguised as
a squire rode in, spattered with blood, and called for vengeance on
the Welsh, which the knights of the Round Table promised to wreak.

After the second course and a pause a second squire rode in on a sumpter, his hands and feet tied, and after being released by Lancelot delivered a challenge to him from the King of Irlant—doubtless an error for Scotland. The third course was followed by the entrance of the Loathly Damsel on a bony nag, charmingly made up with a nose a foot long, a goitre on her neck, and teeth projecting a finger's length from her wry mouth. She called on Perchevael to win the castle of Leicester from its lord (Simon de Montfort), and bade Walewein ride to Cornuaelge (doubtless a corruption of Kenilworth, a stronghold of the rebel barons) to end the strife between commons and lords. While the squire who impersonated the Loathly Damsel slipped out to remove his make-up, a date was set for the campaigns which had been undertaken. It will be noted, that, together with the Round Tables of 1279, 1284, 1287, and 1392, this makes the fifth such festival which Edward attended, and, according to Lodewijk, he was personally active in the arrangements.

In 1336 and at intervals thereafter, the Nine Worthies, the supreme warriors of pagan, Jewish, and Christian history, were represented in pageants, displaying their heraldic shields, and boasting of their exploits, Arthur, Charlemagne, and Godfrey de Bouillon formed the Christian trio, and several versions of Arthur's speech have come down to us.

The only dramatic pieces which may be called medieval and of which the texts have survived are far removed in tone and in the circumstances of their performance from any of the spectacular displays thus far noted. They are three South German farces of the second half of the fifteenth century, which were presented at Shrovetide by groups of apprentices who went from house to house collecting money and enjoying refreshments. All three deal with the theme of the chastity test at Arthur's court, of which the earliest literary form is Robert Biket's *Lai du Cor* of the twelfth century and one of the latest is the ballad of *The Boy and the Mantle*. The immediate sources of these *Fastnachtspiele* were the *Meisterlieder*. In one play the discriminating talisman is a drinking horn, in the second a mantle, and in the third we have an innovation, a crown which when donned by a cuckold causes antlers to sprout on his head. All were calculated to provoke ribald guffaws at the expense of female virtue, deceived husbands, and the idealistic chivalry of King Arthur's day.

# 12.  The Impact of the Black Death

## The Plague Conquers Europe

ဗၖ Hans Zinsser

THE COMING OF THE PLAGUE RAT. The first rat to arrive in Europe was *Mus rattus*—the black rat, house rat, or ship rat. It may have wandered in between 400 and 1100 A.D., with the hordes that swept into Europe from the East in that period of great unrest—the *Völkerwanderung*. It may not have arrived until somewhat later, when the first Crusaders returned. It is not mentioned in the Epinal Glossary of 700 A.D., but may have been meant by the word "raet" in the English Archbishop Ælfric's Vocabulary of 1000 A.D. But the authorities from whom we cite this call attention to the fact that the word "rata" was the Procençal for the domestic mouse of that time, and the word may have been introduced into England. Hamilton and Hinton say that the first clear differentiation between rats and mice is found in the writings of Giraldus Cambrensis (1147–1223). After that date, it is referred to frequently.

As to the Eastern origin of the black rat, there seems to be no difference of opinion among authorities, though there is much uncertainty about the exact part of the Orient from which it came. De L'Isle believes that the *Mus alexandrinus* represents the source stock of the European *Mus rattus*. This—the Alexandrine rat—did not, according to him, become parasitic on human society until the seventh century —living before this time a wild existence, possibly in the Arabian deserts, a fact which would account for its failure to migrate into classical Europe with trade, and, in the early Middle Ages, with Saracen invasions. By the time of the Crusaders, it had begun to domesticate and consequently to follow human travel. Being a climber and therefore a ship rat, it spread rapidly to Mediterranean ports....

The Genoese mistook it for a mole, calling it "Salpa," another point of evidence that it may have been new to them.

From the time of its arrival, the rat spread across Europe with a speed superior even to that of the white man in the Americas. Before the end of the thirteenth century, it had become a pest. The legend of the *Rattenfänger von Hameln*, who piped the children into the hollow Koppenberg because the town refused his pay for piping the rats into the Weser, is placed at or about 1284. By this time, the rat had penetrated into England. It had reached Ireland some time before this, where it was the "foreign" or "French" mouse, "ean francach." Our authorities tell us that in Ireland, even until very recent times, everything foreign was called "francach," or French. A little later, the rat was in Denmark, Norway, and the adjacent islands. By Shakespeare's time, the black rat was so formidable a nuisance that days of prayer for protection against its ravages were set aside, and rat catchers (see *Romeo and Juliet*, Act III) were important officials, probably calling themselves, as they would to-day, scientists or artists (or "rattors" —cf. "realtors" and "morticians").

For twice as long as the Vandals had their day in North Africa, or the Saracens in Spain, or the Normans in Italy, the black rats had their own way in Europe. Their reign covered the periods of the devastating epidemics of plague that swept through the battle areas of the Thirty Years' War and the later ones of the seventeenth century. And during the centuries of its supremacy there occurred the most destructive typhus epidemics, accompanying wars and famines, that have occurred up to our own time. Whether the black rats of mediæval Europe played a rôle in these remains uncertain. That they played the leading part in the plague epidemics of this time seems beyond question.

But just as the established civilizations of Northern Europe were swept aside by the mass invasions of barbarians from the East, so the established hegemony of the black rat was eventually wiped out with the incursion of the hordes of the brown rat, or *Mus decumanus*—the ferocious, short-nosed, and short-tailed Asiatic that swept across the Continent in the early eighteenth century; until at the present time, the slender-nosed, long-tailed, climbing *Mus rattus* has been all but exterminated in its former strongholds, and continues to thrive only in relatively small groups along the littoral, in seaports, on islands, or in countries like South America and other tropical regions where it is not confined to parasitic life in competition with its larger and more barbaric rival, or where the brown *conquistadores* have not yet arrived. It maintains its former superiority only on ships, where, because of its greater ability in climbing, it can still hold its own....

THE PLAGUE'S TOLL. The Black Death, which was mainly

bubonic plague, is one of the major calamities of history, not exclud-
ing wars, earthquakes, floods, barbarian invasions, the Crusades, and the
last war. It is estimated by Hecker that about one quarter of the entire
population of Europe was destroyed by the disease—that is, at least
25,000,000. It carried in its wake moral, religious, and political disintegration. This epidemic is an excellent example of the biological phenomena which accompany the process of what the Germans call
*Durchseuchung*, which ... means thorough saturation of a population
with an infection. There were, of course, ... formidable plague epidemics in Europe before the fourteenth century, but these—as far as
we can tell from the records—did not reach Central and Northern
areas within the centuries immediately preceding the Black Death.
Resistance to infectious disease, an acquired characteristic, is not
hereditary—except in the evolutionary sense of the selective survival
of the more resistant. And such increase of resistance by natural selection is not noticeably active, unless the infection continues uninter-
ruptedly throughout centuries and is of such an order that a majority of
the infected survive. The Black Death, spreading in Europe, therefore,
found an entirely susceptible population, which accounts for its terrific
ravages. When its first sweep across the Continent was exhausted for
want of victims, it remained endemic, smouldering until relighted by
the accumulation of new fuel; and thus it broke out again in 1361,
1371, and 1382. These successive calamities, covering only thirty-four
years, illustrate the manner in which an epidemic disease can become
progressively less fatal, when it occurs repeatedly in populations that
have been thoroughly saturated in immediately preceding years. Statistics are of course incomplete, but the records left behind by Chalin
de Vinario, whom we cite from Haeser, are particularly instructive in
this regard. In 1348, two thirds of the population were afflicted, and
almost all died; in 1361, half the population contracted the disease,
and very few survived; in 1371, only one tenth were sick, and many
survived; while in 1382, only one twentieth of the population became
sick, and almost all of these survived. Had the disease continued,
constantly present, and attacking a large proportion of the new generations as they appeared, it might gradually have assumed an endemic,
sporadic form, with relatively low mortality. As it is, plague appeared
throughout the fifteenth century in Europe, but relatively localized and
in incomparably milder form, gradually diminishing until it again
broke out in the last European pandemic from 1663 to 1668, reached
London in 1664, and was so vividly described by Defoe and—in some
of its episodes—by Pepys.

There was an outbreak in Turkey in 1661, which spread first to the
coast of Greece and the Greek Islands, then traveled rapidly westward

and, more slowly, in an eastward direction. In 1663, it reached Amsterdam, where it killed 10,000 out of a total population of less than 200,000. In the following year it gained velocity, killing about 24,000 in Amsterdam, spread to Brussels and Flanders, and thence to London. In the first week of December, 1664, two Frenchmen died in a house in Drury Lane. No other cases occurred for six weeks. On the twentieth of February, 1665, there was another case; than a pause until April. By the middle of May, the epidemic was in full swing. It was reported by Pepys:—

> This day (June 7th, 1665), much against my will, I did in Drury Lane see two or three houses marked with a red cross upon the doors and "Lord have mercy upon us" writ there; which was a sad sight to me, being the first of the kind that, to my remembrance, I ever saw. It put me into an ill conception of myself and my smell, so that I was forced to buy some roll-tobacco to smell and to chaw, which took away my apprehension.

King Charles, rejoicing in the victory over the Dutch fleet, saw more and more houses marked with the terrifying cross, and removed the court from town. Two thirds of the inhabitants fled London, carrying the disease first to other cities along the Thames, and finally throughout England.

The epidemic remained several years in Flanders, passed thence to Westphalia, down the Rhine, into Normandy, Switzerland, and Austria, which it reached in 1668. Throughout the remainder of the seventeenth century, trailers of the disease continued, and lasted well into the eighteenth century. There were localized epidemics in Hungary, Silesia, Prussia, the Baltic Provinces, and Scandinavia. In 1711, 215,000 people died of the disease in Brandenburg; 300,000 in Austria. Another wave spread from Marseilles across Provence in 1720 and 1721. After that, the disease, in severe but localized outbreaks, continued through the second half of the eighteenth century, but was gradually pushed eastward, so that the considerable epidemic which occurred in Russia and the Balkans between 1770 and 1772 failed to make headway in a westerly direction. Russia and the Caucasus continued to suffer up to 1820, but since that time no great plague epidemic has swept beyond Russia, and no widespread outbreaks have occurred anywhere in what is spoken of as the Western World.

This disappearance of epidemic plague from Europe presents one of the unsolved mysteries of epidemiology. The disease has been introduced into various parts of Europe and America again and again dur-

ing intervening years, but has never shown any tendency to spread
in epidemic form. . . .

THE DANCING MANIAS. In searching the literature for an-
cestral forms of infectious diseases of the nervous system, one cannot
overlook a curious chapter of human affliction—namely, that dealing
with the dancing manias spoken of in mediæval accounts variously as
"St. John's dance," "St. Vitus's dance," and "Tarantism." These
strange seizures, though not unheard of in earlier times, became common during and immediately after the dreadful miseries of the Black
Death. For the most part, the dancing manias present none of the
characteristics which we associate with epidemic infectious diseases of
the nervous system. They seem, rather, like mass hysterias, brought on
by terror and despair, in populations oppressed, famished, and wretched
to a degree almost unimaginable to-day. To the miseries of constant
war, political and social disintegration, there was added the dreadful
affliction of inescapable, mysterious, and deadly disease. Mankind stood
helpless as though trapped in a world of terror and peril against which
there was no defense. God and the devil were living conceptions to
the men of those days who cowered under afflictions which they believed imposed by supernatural forces. For those who broke down
under the strain there was no road of escape except to the inward
refuge of mental derangement which, under the circumstances of the
times, took the direction of religious fanaticism. In the earlier days
of the Black Death mass aberrations became apparent in the sect of
the flagellants, who joined in brotherhoods and wandered by thousands
from city to city. Later, for a time, it took the form of persecution of
the Jews, who were held guilty of the spread of disease. The criminal
proceedings instituted against the Jews of Chillon were followed by a
degree of barbarism throughout Central Europe that can only be
regarded as a part of the mass insanity of which the dancing manias
were a manifestation. These manias are, in many respects, analogues of
some of the political and economic crowd hysterias which have upset
the balance of the civilized world in modern times. In some parts of
Europe the World War was followed by famine, disease, and hopeless-
ness not incomparable to the conditions which prevailed in the Middle Ages. For obvious reasons, in the reactions of our own day, economic and political hysterias are substituted for the religious ones of
earlier times. Jew baiting alone seems common to both.

Although it is likely that the overwhelming majority of these outbreaks were purely functional nervous derangements, a certain number
of them may have represented early traceable beginnings of the group
of epidemic infectious diseases of the nervous system, in which we now
include infantile paralysis and the various forms of encephalitis.

In 1027, in the German village of Kolbig, there was an outbreak among peasants which began with maniacal quarreling, dancing, and hilariousness, but went on to stupor and in many cases to death, and, in the survivors, left behind permanent tremors, possibly not unlike the "Parkinsonian syndrome" which follows encephalitis lethargica. Hecker has given a detailed account of most of the reliable historical records. In Erfurt, in 1237, over one hundred children were taken with a dancing and raving disease which, again, in many cases led to death and permanent tremors in the survivors. The most severe dancing mania began in 1374, in the wake of the Black Death, at first at Aix-la-Chapelle, soon in the Netherlands, at Liége, Utrecht, Tongres, and Cologne. Men, women, and children lost all control, joined hands, and danced in the streets for hours until complete exhaustion caused them to fall to the ground. They shrieked, saw visions, and called upon God. The movement spread widely, and undoubtedly the numbers of the truly afflicted were enhanced by multitudes of the easily excited, in a manner not unlike that observed in modern camp meetings and evangelistic gatherings. Yet there must have been a physical disease in many of the cases, because throughout the accounts there is frequent reference to abdominal swelling and pain, for which the dancers bound their bellies with bandages. Many suffered from nausea, vomiting, and prolonged stupor. The condition was sufficiently widespread and important to warrant a long dissertation by Paracelsus, who tried to classify the malady into three subdivisions by a system not of sufficient modern importance to warrant review.

The tarantism of Italy, supposed by many of its chroniclers to have been caused by the bite of the tarantula, belongs to the same category. It probably had little relationship to spider bite. The descriptions left behind by Perotte, in the middle of the fifteenth century, and by Matthiolo and Ferdinando in the sixteenth and seventeenth centuries, are quite clear in indicating that many of the cases of tarantism represented a nervous disease of probably infectious origin. Some of them have much resemblance with hydrophobia. Melancholy and depression, followed by maniacal excitement and motor activity, ended in death, or less fatally in semiconsciousness, with alternating laughter and weeping. Ferdinando's descriptions add sleeplessness, swollen abdomens, diarrhœa, vomiting, gradual loss of strength, and jaundice. By the middle of the seventeenth century, the disease as an epidemic menace had practically disappeared. Schenck von Graffenberg, writing in 1643, says that St. Vitus's dance attacked chiefly sedentary people—tailors and artisans. When it came upon them, they rushed about aimlessly, and many dashed out their brains or drowned themselves. In others, renewed attacks followed periods of exhaustion. Many never recovered completely.

Hecker's account, which is the source of most of the facts here cited, includes extensive abstracts of the mediæval literature which indicate that, in the dancing manias, many things were involved. In great part, no doubt, the outbreaks were hysterical reactions of a terror-stricken and wretched population, which had broken down under the stress of almost incredible hardship and danger. But it seems likely that associated with these were nervous diseases of infectious origin which followed the great epidemics of plague, smallpox, and so forth, in the same manner in which neurotropic virus diseases have followed the widespread and severe epidemics which accompanied the [First World War].

# Part Three. THE EARLY MODERN ERA, 1350 TO 1700

The early modern era is the cultural way station between the medieval and industrial worlds. Much of the popular culture of the period represents survivals of the medieval era; the first chapter of this part deals with three manifestations of this perpetuation of medieval culture.

And yet the preponderant proportion of early modern culture was created by new circumstances, new developments, and new attitudes. Certainly, the single most important historical occurrence in the period was the religious, political, social, and cultural struggle arising from the Protestant Reformation and the Catholic Counter-Reformation. The religious zeal and penchant for violence which had marked the medieval epoch reappears in the early modern era, supported and amplified by improved military technology and made more threatening by the existence of two opposing and highly influential ideologies. The second chapter describes two aspects of this development.

The third and fourth chapters discuss the two major poles of political and social power in the early modern period: the royal court and the aristocratic establishment. European court life reached its highest expression during these years, the French court being the model for all others. The selections show the changes in court life, from the rather coarse, late-Renaissance court of Louis XIII's childhood to the mannered life of Louis XIV's grand establishment. The extracts describing aristocratic life center on the involvement of the nobles with their land and their people, which was often close and cordial despite the vast gulf separating the classes socially and economically.

Although the era was dominated politically and socially by the great kings and nobles, it also witnessed the increasing involvement in public life of other social groups. Florentine and Elizabethan politics, discussed in the fifth chapter, were in effect popular diversions for a considerable segment of the well-to-do population, and such people brought to these areas of popular life a zest and drive often lacking in the aristocratic classes. The chapter on the rich bourgeois centers on the efforts of an emergent class to adjust itself to the social and cultural expectations of the leaders of society.

The other side of the picture of wealth and elegance depicted in the first six chapters is presented in the seventh, which describes the terrible poverty and insecurity experienced by the poor and allows us to appreciate the enormous determination of men to make a life for themselves even in the face of overwhelming difficulties. The next chapter, on army life, similarly shows how men drawn into a seemingly single-minded pursuit can convert and adapt their activities to suit their need for diversion and release.

The final chapter is significant because it deals with the remarkable enrichment of popular culture which resulted from the development of printing, the discovery of the New World, and the advent of Humanism. It was in response to these innovations that popular culture expanded to include experiences that were intellectually fulfilling and exciting for more people. Furthermore, it now became apparent that separate and distinct subcultures were growing up to appeal to different audiences, to impinge upon one another, and to produce cadres of professional artists, musicians, scholars, and writers. In the next part this broadening of popular culture and professionalization of creativity will be seen in the growth of the opera and the coming of the novel, and the process reaches fruition in the more modern eras when men devote themselves to very specialized cultural pursuits for the edification of very particular audiences.

# 1.  The Survival of Medieval Attitudes

## Fascination with the Dance of Death
৶§ Johann Huizinga

At the close of the Middle Ages the whole vision of death may be summed up in the word *macabre*, in its modern meaning. Of course, this meaning is the outcome of a long process. But the sentiment it embodies, of something gruesome and dismal, is precisely the conception of death which arose during the last centuries of the Middle Ages. . . .

Towards 1400 the conception of death in art and literature took a spectral and fantastic shape. A new and vivid shudder was added to the great primitive horror of death. The macabre vision arose from deep psychological strata of fear; religious thought at once reduced it to a means of moral exhortation. As such it was a great cultural idea, till in its turn it went out of fashion, lingering on in epitaphs and symbols in village cemeteries.

The idea of the death-dance is the central point of a whole group of connected conceptions. The priority belongs to the motif of the three dead and three living men, which is found in French literature from the thirteenth century onward. Three young noblemen suddenly meet three hideous dead men, who tell them of their past grandeur and warn them of their own near end. Art soon took hold of this suggestive theme. We can see it still in the striking frescoes of the *Campo santo* of Pisa. The sculpture of the portal of the church of the Innocents at Paris, which the duke of Berry had carved in 1408, but which has not been preserved, represented the same subject. Miniature painting and woodcuts spread it broadcast.

The theme of the three dead and three living men connects the horrible motif of putrefaction with that of the death-dance. . . .

The Dance of the Dead has been acted as well as painted and engraved. The duke of Burgundy had it performed in his mansion at Bruges in 1449. If we could form an idea of the effect produced by such a dance, with vague lights and shadows gliding over the moving figures, we should no doubt be better able to understand the horror inspired by the subject, than we are by the aid of the pictures of Guyot Marchant or Holbein.

The woodcuts with which the Parisian printer, Guyot Marchant, ornamented the first edition of the *Danse Macabré* in 1485 were, very probably, imitated from the most celebrated of these painted death-dances, namely, that which, since 1424, covered the walls of the cloister of the churchyard of the Innocents at Paris. The stanzas printed by Marchant were those written under these mural paintings.... The woodcuts of 1485 can give but a feeble impression of the paintings of the Innocents, of which they are not exact copies, as the costumes prove. To have a notion of the effect of these frescoes, one should rather look at the mural paintings of the church of La Chaise-Dieu, where the unfinished condition of the work heightens the spectral effect.

The dancing person whom we see coming back forty times to lead away the living, originally does not represent Death itself, but a corpse: the living man such as he will presently be. In the stanzas the dancer is called "the dead man" or "the dead woman." It is a dance of the dead and not of Death; the researches of Monsieur Gédéon Huet have made it probable that the primitive subject was a roundabout dance of dead people, come forth from their graves, a theme which Goethe revived in his *Totentanz*. The indefatigable dancer is the living man himself in his future shape, a frightful double of his person. "It is yourself," said the horrible vision to each of the spectators. It is only towards the end of the century that the figure of the great dancer, of a corpse with hollow and fleshless body, becomes a skeleton, as Holbein depicts it. Death in person has then replaced the individual dead man.

While it reminded the spectators of the frailty and the vanity of earthly things, the death-dance at the same time preached social equality as the Middle Ages understood it, Death levelling the various ranks and professions. At first only men appeared in the picture. The success of his publication, however, suggested to Guyot the idea of a dance macabre of women. Martial d'Auvergne wrote the poetry; an unknown artist, without equalling his model, completed the pictures by a series of feminine figures dragged along by a corpse. Now it was impossible to enumerate forty dignities and professions of women. After the queen, the abbess, the nun, the saleswoman, the nurse, and a few others, it was necessary to fall back on the different states of feminine life: the virgin, the beloved, the bride, the woman newly married, the woman with child. And here the sensual note reappears, to which we referred above. In lamenting the frailty of the lives of women, it is still the briefness of joy that is deplored, and with the grave tone of the *memento mori* is mixed the regret for lost beauty.

Nothing betrays more clearly the excessive fear of death felt in the Middle Ages than the popular belief, then widely spread, according to which Lazarus, after his resurrection, lived in continual misery and horror at the thought that he should have again to pass through the gate of death. If the just had so much to fear, how could the sinner soothe himself? And then what motif was more poignant than the calling up of the agony of death? It appeared under two traditional forms: the *Ars moriendi* and the *Quator hominum novissima*, that is, the four last experiences awaiting man, of which death was the first. These two subjects were largely propagated in the fifteenth century by the printing-press and by engravings. The Art of Dying, as well as the Last Four Things, comprised a description of the agony of death, in which it is easy to recognize a model supplied by the ecclesiastical literature of former centuries. . . .

Nowhere else were all the images tending to evoke the horror of death assembled so strikingly as in the churchyard of the Innocents at Paris. There the medieval soul, fond of a religious shudder, could take its fill of the horrible. Above all other saints, the remembrance of the saints of that spot, and of their bloody and pitiful martyrdom, was fitted to awake the crude compassion which was dear to the epoch. The fifteenth century honoured the Holy Innocents with special veneration. Louis XI presented to the church "a whole Innocent," encased in a crystal shrine. The cemetery was preferred to every other place of burial. A bishop of Paris had a little of the earth of the churchyard of the Innocents put into his grave, as he could not be laid there. The poor and the rich were interred without distinction. They did not rest there long, for the cemetery was used so much, twenty parishes having a right of burial there, that it was necessary, in order to make room, to dig up the bones and sell the tombstones after a very short time. It was believed that in this earth a human body was decomposed to the bone in nine days. Skulls and bones were heaped up in charnel-houses along the cloisters enclosing the ground on three sides, and lay there open to the eye by thousands, preaching to all the lesson of equality. The noble Boucicaut, among others, had contributed to the construction of these "fine charnel-houses." Under the cloisters the death-dance exhibited its images and its stanzas. No place was better suited to the simian figure of grinning death, dragging along pope and emperor, monk and fool. The duke of Berry, who wished to be buried there, had the history of the three dead and the three living men carved at the portal of the church. A century later, this exhibition of funeral symbols was completed by a large statue of Death, now in the Louvre, and the only remnant of it all.

Such was the place which the Parisians of the fifteenth century frequented as a sort of lugubrious counterpart of the Palais Royal of 1789. Day after day, crowds of people walked under the cloisters, looking at the figures and reading the simple verses, which reminded them of the approaching end. In spite of the incessant burials and exhumations going on there, it was a public lounge and a rendezvous. Shops were established before the charnel-houses and prostitutes strolled under the cloisters. A female recluse was immured on one of the sides of the church. Friars came to preach and processions were drawn up there. A procession of children only (12,500 strong, thinks the Burgher of Paris) assembled there, with tapers in their hands, to carry an Innocent to Notre Dame and back to the churchyard. Even feasts were given there. To such an extent had the horrible become familiar.

## The Heyday of Witchcraft

⋙ Aldous Huxley

In mediaeval and early modern Christendom the situation of sorcerers and their clients was almost precisely analogous to that of Jews under Hitler, capitalists under Stalin, Communists and fellow travellers in the United States. They were regarded as the agents of a Foreign Power, unpatriotic at the best, and, at the worst, traitors, heretics, enemies of the people. Death was the penalty meted out to these metaphysical Quislings of the past and, in most parts of the contemporary world, death is the penalty which awaits the political and secular devil-worshippers known here as Reds, there as Reactionaries. In the briefly liberal nineteenth century men like Michelet found it difficult not merely to forgive, but even to understand the savagery with which sorcerers had once been treated. Too hard on the past, they were at the same time too complacent about their present and far too optimistic in regard to the future—to us! They were rationalists who fondly imagined that the decay of traditional religion would put an end to such devilries as the persecution of heretics, the torture and burning of witches. . . . But looking back and up, from our vantage point on the descending road of modern history, we now see that all the evils of religion can flourish without any belief in the supernatural, that convinced materialists are ready to worship their own jerry-built creations as though they were the Absolute, and that self-styled humanists will persecute their adversaries with all the zeal of Inquisitors exterminating the devotees of a personal and transcendent Satan. Such behaviour-patterns antedate and outlive the beliefs which, at any given moment, seem to motivate them. Few people now believe in the devil; but very many enjoy behaving as their ancestors behaved when the Fiend was a reality as unquestionable as his Opposite Number. In order to justify their behaviour, they turn their theories into dogmas, their by-laws into First Principles, their political bosses into Gods and all those who disagree with them into incarnate devils. This idolatrous transformation of the relative into the Absolute and the all too human into the Divine, makes it possible for them to indulge their ugliest passions with a clear conscience and in the certainty that they are working for the Highest Good. And when the current beliefs come, in their turn, to look silly, a new set will be invented, so that the immemorial madness may continue to wear its customary mask of legality, idealism and true religion.

In principle ... the law relating to witchcraft was exceedingly simple. Anyone who deliberately had dealings with the devil was guilty of a capital crime. To describe how this law was administered in practice would require much more space than can here be given. Suffice it to say that, while some judges were manifestly prejudiced, many did their best to give the accused a fair trial. But even a fair trial was, by our present Western standards, a monstrous caricature of Justice. "The laws," we read in *Malleus Maleficarum* [*The Hammer of Witches*, (1484)] "allow that any witness whatever is to be admitted in evidence against them." And not only were all and sundry, including children, and the mortal enemies of the accused, admitted as witnesses; all kinds of evidence were also admitted—gossip, hearsay, inferences, remembered dreams, statements made by demoniacs. Always in order, torture was frequently (though by no means invariably) employed to extort confessions. And along with torture went false promises in regard to the final sentence. . . .

To contemporary Western eyes, the most absurd, as well as the most iniquitous feature of a mediaeval or early-modern witch trial was the fact that almost any of the odd and untoward events of daily life might legitimately be treated as the effects of diabolic intervention brought about by the magic arts of a sorcerer. Here, for example, is a part of the evidence on which one of the two witches tried in 1664, at Bury St. Edmunds, before the future Lord Chief Justice, Sir Matthew Hale, was condemned to be hanged. In the course of a quarrel, the accused had cursed and threatened one of her neighbours. After this, the man testified, "so soon as his sows pigged, the pigs would leap and caper, and immediately fall down dead." Nor was this all. A little later he was "vexed with a number of lice of extraordinary bigness." Against such supernatural vermin, the current methods of disinfection

were unavailing and the witness had no alternative but to consign two
of his best suits to the flames. Sir Matthew Hale was a just judge, a
lover of moderation, a man of wide learning, scientific as well as literary
and legal. That he should have taken this kind of evidence seriously
seems now almost incredible. But the fact remains that he did take it
seriously. The reason is to be sought, presumably, in the fact that, as
well as all the rest, Hale was exceedingly pious. But in a fundamentalist
age piety involved belief in a personal devil and the duty to extirpate the
witches who were his servants. Moreover, granted the truth of everything
contained in the Judaeo-Christian tradition, there was an antecedent
probability that, if preceded by an old woman's curse, the death of pig-
lets and the multiplication of lice were supernatural events, due to the
intervention of Satan on behalf of one of his votaries.

Into the Biblical lore of devils and witches had been incorporated
a number of popular superstitions which came at last to be treated with
the same veneration as was accorded to revealed truths of Scripture. For
example, until late in the seventeenth century, all inquisitors and most
civil magistrates accepted without question the validity of what may be
called the physical tests of witchcraft. Did the body of the accused
exhibit unusual marks? Could you find in it any spots insensitive to
the prick of a needle? Were there, above all, any of these "little teats,"
or supernumerary nipples, at which some familiar—toad or cat—might
suck and fatten? If so, your suspect was undoubtedly a witch; for tradition affirmed that these were the brands and seals with which the devil
marked his own. (Since nine per cent of all males and a little under
five per cent of all females are born with supernumerary nipples, there
was never any shortage of predestined victims. Nature punctually did
her part; the judges, with their unexamined postulates and first principles, did the rest.)

Of the other popular superstitions which had crystallized into axioms
there are three which, because of the enormous miseries entailed by
their general acceptance, deserve at least a brief mention. These are the
beliefs that, by invoking the devil's aid, witches can cause
tempests, diseases and sexual impotence. In the *Malleus* Kramer
and Sprenger treat these notions as self-evident truths, established not
merely by common sense but also by the authority of the greatest doctors. "St. Thomas, in his commentary on Job, says as follows: It must
be confessed that, with God's permission, the devils can disturb the
air, raise up winds and make the fire fall from heaven. For, although in
the matter of taking various shapes, corporeal nature is not at the
command of any Angel, either good or bad, but only at that of God
the Creator, yet, in the matter of local motion, corporeal nature has to
obey the spiritual nature. . . . But winds and rain and other similar

disturbances of the air can be caused by the mere movement of vapours released from the earth or the water; therefore the natural powers of devils is sufficient to cause such things. So says St. Thomas."

As for diseases, "there is no infirmity, not even leprosy or epilepsy, which cannot be caused by witches, with God's permission. And this is proved by the fact that no sort of infirmity is excluded by the doctors."

The authority of the doctors is confirmed by our authors' personal observations. "For we have often found that certain people have been visited with epilepsy or the falling sickness by means of eggs which have been buried with dead bodies, especially the dead bodies of witches . . . particularly when these eggs have been given to a person either in food or drink."

In regard to impotence, our authors draw a sharp distinction between the natural variety and the supernatural. Natural impotence is the incapacity to have sexual relations with any member of the opposite sex. Supernatural impotence, caused by magic spells and devils, is incapacity in relation to one person only (especially a wife or husband), potency being unimpaired in regard to all other members of the opposite sex. It should be noted, say the authors, that God permits more bewitchments to be performed in relation to the generative powers than in any other department of human life, the reason being that, since the Fall, there exists in everything that pertains to sex "a greater corruption than in the case of other human actions."

Devastating storms are not uncommon, selective impotence affects most men at some time or another, and disease is never absent. In a world where law, theology and popular superstition were all agreed in holding witches responsible for these everyday occurrences, the occasions for spying and the opportunities for delation and persecution were innumerable. At the height of the sixteenth century witch-hunts, social life in certain parts of Germany must have been very like social life under the Nazis, or in a country newly subjected to Communist domination.

Under torture, or moved by a sense of duty or some hysterical compulsion, a man would denounce his wife, a woman her best friends, a child its parents, a servant his master. And these were not the only evils to be met with in a devil-haunted society. On many individuals the incessant suggestions of bewitchment, the daily warnings against the devil, had a disastrous effect. Some of the more timorous were driven out of their minds, some actually killed by the ever-present fear. On the ambitious and the resentful this harping on supernatural dangers had quite another effect. In order to win the prizes they so frantically coveted, men like Bothwell, women like Mme. de Montespan, were ready to exploit the resources of black magic to their criminal limit. And if one felt oneself oppressed and frustrated, if one bore a grudge against society at large and one's neighbours in particular, what more natural than that one should appeal to those who, according to St. Thomas and the rest, were capable of doing such enormous mischiefs? By paying so much attention to the devil and by treating witchcraft as the most heinous of crimes, the theologians and the inquisitors actually spread the beliefs and fostered the practices which they were trying so hard to repress. By the beginning of the eighteenth century witchcraft had ceased to be a serious social problem. It died out, among other reasons, because almost nobody now bothered to repress it. For the less it was persecuted, the less it was propagandized. Attention had shifted from the supernatural to the natural. From about 1700 to the present day all persecutions in the West have been secular and, one might say, humanistic. For us, Radical Evil has ceased to be something metaphysical and has become political or economic. And that Radical Evil now incarnates itself, not in sorcerers and magicians (for we like to think of ourselves as positivists), but in the representatives of some hated class or nation. The springs of action and the rationalizations have undergone a certain change; but the hatreds motivated and the ferocities justified are all too familiar.

## *The Persistence of Hierarchy and Authority*
~§ Peter Laslett

In this society, subordination and politics were founded on tradition. Therefore critical examination of the reasons why some men were better placed than others was unlikely to come about. This submissive cast of mind is almost universal in the statement made by the men about themselves. 'There is degree above degree, As reason is ...' 'Take but degree away, Untune that string, And hark what discord follows.' It would seem that once a man in the traditional world got himself into a position where he could catch a glimpse of his society as a whole, he immediately felt that degree, order, was its essential feature. Without degree, unquestioning subordination, and some men being privileged while all the others obeyed, anarchy and destruction were inevitable. Any threat to the established order was a danger to everyone's personality.

There are two reasons why this is what might be expected to have been the almost universal attitude. One is implied by the word traditional itself, which meant that the set of standards used to make judgements about society and varying positions within it stayed constant for almost all people at all times. Put into more technical language, it must be presumed that neither peasant, pauper nor craftsman nor even gentleman in the pre-industrial world ever changed his reference group in such a way as to feel aware of what is called relative deprivation. Directly this assumption is recorded, it raises questions about those occasions on which change of reference group did come about in seventeenth-century English society. It could be argued, for example, that the disturbances caused by the Civil War and especially those connected with the recruitment and activities of the parliamentary army, did bring humble people into contact for the first time with those who were better off and had a more aspiring outlook. Indeed the isolation of individuals from their counterparts in other village communities was so marked a feature of ... society ... that the very fact of bringing them together to share a common, vital purpose for months and years together might be expected to have some crystallizing effect on their attitudes to their social position and political rights.

If for example the literature of the Levellers of Cromwell's army and of the city of London could be shown to have arisen to any extent from such circumstances as these, it would provide a fascinating parallel with events in our own century. National war, conscription and disbandment are now commonly assumed to be associated with intense feelings of relative deprivation and revolutionism. Social mobility in industrial society is also known to have the expected effect on reference groups. Once the opportunity of rising in society is envisaged, and once its actual fulfillment begins to look possible, then men do become aware that they are being deprived of what their superiors enjoy, and may well begin to question the rationale of the established social order. Now that we have reason to believe that social mobility was present in pre-industrial society as well, we must suppose that some discontent and criticism was engendered in traditional societies for similar reasons. Social quiescence, therefore, should not be regarded as quite fully descriptive of England or of Europe three hundred years ago, especially of the kingdom which Oliver Cromwell found himself responsible for.

Interesting as these possibilities are, they can hardly have been of much importance. The second reason why the society we are so hastily describing must be presumed to have been nearly always socially quiescent is that the phrase stable poverty does on the whole seem to be a fair description of most of its area. It is a commonplace of social observation that stable poverty means resignation to the situation as it is. ...

Nevertheless it is generally supposed that a society in such a situation will have its share of desperate men, and that the downtrodden pauper if ever he does find an opportunity will express his resentment of the

hardships he is forced to suffer. [There is some] evidence of the awareness of contemporary observers that the deprived in their society might
be expected on occasion to break out into violence. Quite apart from
those in extreme situations, some rationale must have been present
to settle the doubts of those who were disposed for any reason to question the rightness of arrangements as they were and the duty of submission and obedience. Social superiority and political authority did to
some small extent depend for their maintenance on outside sanctions.

The outside support for authority in the traditional world was religious, though 'outside' scarcely expresses its relationship with the
social system. We can gain a little somewhat unexpected insight into
the way in which attitudes of obedience were inculcated into every
personality in the formative years. The stated duty of each parish priest
was to teach the children of his flock the catechism. After matins on
Sundays in every one of the 10,000 parishes of England there gathered
or should have gathered, the group of adolescents from the houses of
the gentry and the yeomen, the husbandmen, the tradesmen, the
labourers and even the paupers to learn from the priest what it meant
to be a Christian. This is what they all had to repeat after him: every
single one of them had to get to know it by heart:

> *My duty towards my neighbour is to love him as myself, and to
> do to all men as I would they should do unto me: to love,
> honour and succour my father and mother: to submit myself to
> all my governors, teachers, spiritual pastors and masters; to order
> myself lowly and reverently to all my betters; to hurt nobody
> by word nor deed: to be true and just in all my dealings; to bear
> no malice nor hatred in my heart: to keep my hands from pick-
> ing and stealing, and my tongue from evil-speaking, lying and
> slandering: to keep my body in temperance, soberness and chas-
> tity: not to covet nor desire other men's goods: but to learn and
> labour truly to get my own living, and to do my duty in that
> state of life unto which it shall please God to call me.*

These words are still familiar and evocative because they come from
the catechism of the Church of England, originally composed in 1549
and still in use. Some effort of the historical imagination has to be
made to recognize how important they were at the time when every
living person in England was both a believing, fearing Christian and
also by compulsion a member of the national church. 'We hold,' said
Richard Hooker, the official spokesman of the established order, 'that
there is not any man of the Church of England but the same man is
also a member of the Commonwealth. Nor any man a member of the

Commonwealth which is not also a member of the Church of England.

What is more this was the only thing that young people were ever told about obedience, authority, and the social and political order. It was solemnly inculcated on one of those few public occasions when, as we have seen, they left the circle of the household and the authority of its master, to find themselves in the church under the authority of the priest. Many of these youths and maidens, moreover, had no means of confirming or revising what the grave minister had to tell them, for they could not read. He had to teach them by word of mouth what they would have to say before the formidable figure of the Lord Bishop when it came to their service of Confirmation.

Lest it should be thought that only the orthodox had this formal lesson so firmly impressed upon them, here are the words adopted for the *Shorter Catechism* in the year 1644, when the Puritan clergy were taking control of the Church of England at the height of the war between King and Parliament.

> *Question 64:* What is required in the fifth commandment?
> *Answer: The fifth commandment requireth the preserving the honour and performing the duties, belonging to every one in their several places and relations, as Superiors, Inferiors or Equals.*
> *Question 65:* What is forbidden in the fifth commandment?
> *Answer: The fifth commandment forbiddeth the neglecting of or doing anything against the duty which belongeth to every one in their several places and relations.*

In this case the English presbyterians were overtly stating the position universally adopted in the traditional interpretation of the Bible, by separatists and sectarians as well as by the hierarchies, that the duty of Christian obedience rested on the commandment *Honour thy Father and thy Mother*. It was a nonconformist minister who wrote the exhortation to the husbandman which we quoted in our first chapter, reminding him that obedience was due to his landlord because of the fifth commandment. What more familiar sentiment for the beneficed rector or the itinerant preacher to appeal to when the children of the village community were being instructed in their Christian duties? Submission to the powers that be went very well with the habit of obedience to the head of the patriarchal family, and it had the extremely effective sanction of the universal fear of damnation to the defiant 'Short life,' so the doctrine went, 'was the punishment of disobedient children.'

Of course the tenant obeyed his landlord for what may be thought

were much more tangible reasons than his early training and his care
for the salvation of his soul. He might be evicted if he showed insufficient respect, especially in what was his clear political duty when,
providing that he had got a vote, it came to exercise the franchise. His
landlord was also very likely to be a justice of the peace, with all the
forces of the established order on his side. As for those below the
landholders, there was the relationship of menial service, past, present
and to come, which was described when we talked of the village commu-
ity. A labourer, or a craftsman, a cottager or even a lowly husbandman
could very well have been a servant in one of the larger houses in the
locality, and his sons and daughters might in fact be in that position
at the time. Each of them might well have to look to those same
substantial householders for a day's work all his life.

There is no need to labour the point about the familial basis of
society and submissiveness further than this. It may begin to look
strange that any one was ever bold enough to escape at all, impossible
that ideas of individual rights, of the accountability of superiors, of contract as the basis of government could ever have occurred to the men
of seventeenth-century England.

# 2. Reformation and Counter-Reformation Zeal

## The Impact of the Puritan Preachers
⌐§ William Haller

The disagreements that rendered Puritans into presbyterians, independents, separatists and baptists were in the long run not so significant as the qualities of character, of mind and of imagination, which kept them all alike Puritan. Coming revolutions commonly thrust forward a numerous vanguard of pioneers, rebels, cranks, martyrs, saints and heroes. Some of these organize parties, sects and juntas. Some publish programs and manifestoes, or start demonstrations, parades, riots and secessions. They are the devoted band who would save the world without delay and build Jerusalem in their own time. The activity of not a few of the early Puritan leaders and factions was of this description. We do not detract from the honor due them when we suggest that perhaps they were less the authors than the symptoms of a disturbance that at its own pace under the impulsion of more patient men, aided by circumstance, was slowly but surely breaking up the ancient pattern of English life. The force of revolutionary movements most truly shows itself in the gradual transformation of the imaginative ideals, of the habits of thought and expression, of the moral outlook and modes of behavior of whole classes of people. Puritanism was such a movement. It was, then, more than an affair of church government, more than the logomachy of churchmen and schismatics. It was a new way of life, overrunning all the divisions which from time to time seamed its surface and threatening in each of its manifestations to disrupt the existing society. Eventually it was to subdue English civilization to an attitude of mind, a code of conduct, a psychology, a manner of expression, the vitality of which far outran the particular forms of religious life which sprang up from time to time in the course of its irresistible advance.

The preachers were the true authors of that advance, and among the preachers those were far from being the least influential who mainly devoted themselves to setting forth the Puritan way of life by precept, image and example in pulpit and press rather than to agitation against the existing government or to the effort to erect separate churches in defiance of law. They and not the doctrinaire controversialists or the martyrs of persecution were the men who did most in the long run to prepare the temper of the Long Parliament and to spread among their countrymen the characteristic Puritan version of the age-old epic of man's spiritual striving. . . . [And] inevitably the Puritan preachers exercised an incalculable influence on the development of popular literary taste and expression, an influence no less great for having been ignored by critics and historians. . . .

The difference between the preaching of the Anglicans and that of the Puritans, between witty and spiritual preaching so-called, between 'the Wisdom of Words' and 'the Word of Wisdom,' was not merely one of style. As a matter of conviction and of convention, the Puritans professed to disapprove the citation of human authors and to depend solely upon scripture. They even held up a perfectly arid and schematic dialectic as the ideal mode of discourse—knowing better, it must be said, than to practice it upon every occasion. The truth was that from the beginning they shared fully the Elizabethan love of witty phrase and poetic image, and far from abandoning such devices developed them in their own way, sometimes to extravagant lengths. Literary allusions, conscious Euphuism, far-fetched metaphysical metaphors, these they laid aside in favor of homely similes, parables, exempla, moral emblems and the like. The result was a modified but not less imaginative style arising naturally out of medieval and Elizabethan practices in response to the needs and tastes of the audience upon which the preachers depended for personal support as well as for the eventual triumph of their cause. The preachers, if they wished to survive, had to find means to stir imaginations, induce emotional excitement, wring the hearts of sinners, win souls to the Lord, in other words make themselves understood and felt. The necessity determined the nature of their stylistic method. They would not have been the children of their age had they not supplied theological science appropriate to their ends, telling themselves that, when all the godly were gathered in and the ungodly controverted and confounded, nothing but syllogisms would be needed. But until that glorious time should come they granted to the limitations of carnal minds the most unblushing exploitation of the dramatic images of temptation, struggle and triumph which the newly popularized Bible put into their hands.

Scrutiny of the lists of English printed books from the close of the sixteenth century to the outbreak of the [English] revolution shows that it was the Puritan writers who probably did more than any others of the time to keep the printers and booksellers busy and the common public supplied with reading matter. . . .

These writers were called practical because they taught men what to believe and how to act. They were called affectionate because they appealed through the imagination to men's emotions. They were all primarily preachers who with few exceptions wrote popular sermons or works of edification directly derived from sermons. Their aim was to arouse every man to ask and then to answer for himself the ancient question which the keeper of the prison asked of Paul and Silas, 'Sirs, what must I do to be saved?' Their method of attaining this end was to make every man see himself under the eternal images of the pilgrim and the warrior. For at least a century such was a chief mode of stimulating popular imagination, and we must therefore fix attention upon the men who so freely used it if we are to understand the rise of the Puritan epic and of the way of life it did so much to promote. The earliest names mentioned by Baxter are Richard Greenham, John Dod, Arthur Hildersam, Henry Smith and Richard Rogers. Dod and Hildersam were destined to live far into the next century and to take so important a place in the subsequent development of Puritan preaching that they may be more fittingly discussed at a later point. They were, however, like the other men just mentioned, except Henry Smith, among the friends and sympathizers of Cartwright at Cambridge in 1570. Greenham was one of the signers of two petitions sent to Cecil in 1570 in the reformer's behalf. But, though they favored Cartwright's views of church government, they did not, after his expulsion from Cambridge, follow him into the paths of ecclesiastical agitation and public controversy. They proceeded instead by the usual academic courses to ordination and the cure of souls. At the same time, they endeavored to conduct their lives and spiritual ministrations according to what they considered a purer and more godly plan. They proposed, that is, within the church and under the conditions of the society around them, to try the experiment of living according to a self-imposed discipline which they derived from Paul, Augustine and John Calvin. The attempt in each case flowered in a book which, accompanied as it was by popular legend about the author, became in the next generation a classic of Puritan edification. Of no less importance was the fact that there also grew up about these men something like a school and a succession of preachers and writers devoted to following their example. . . .

It is not difficult to believe that in that age of perplexing change many men and women, many of lowly position and simple understanding but also not a few neither simple nor humble, were racked by anxiety for their future here and hereafter. It was a period of storm and stress seldom equalled and probably never surpassed. Consequently the 'spirituall weepers' who, in the words of William Whately, required cheering up seemed well-nigh numberless. There was little comfort for such in the dialectical rustlings of controversialists or in the stylistic fireworks of literary pulpiteers, and this lack the spiritual preachers of the type of Greenham set themselves to supply. It would be a mistake to suppose that they were inferior in education or in literary scholarship to their rivals. They merely made a point of laying their learning aside in order to win, or at least to make a show of seeking, the ear and the confidence of all men in order the better to address themselves with whatever gifts of mind they might possess and with whatever knowledge of the human heart their science gave them to the sympathetic treatment of the troubles, call them spiritual or psychological, by which men in their time were actually beset. Their function was to probe the conscience of the downhearted sinner, to name and cure the malady of his soul, and then to send him out strengthened and emboldened for the continuance of his lifelong battle with the world and the devil. . . .

It was the people's tastes, their state of mind and spiritual condition, by which the Puritan lecturer dependent upon their favor was governed when he stood up to preach before them. Edward Topsell, whose exhortations were an excellent example of clerical railing in the older manner, asked a pertinent question in his *Times Lamentations* of 1599. He was inveighing—a favorite theme with men of his cloth—against popular neglect of moral instructions. 'Must our gallant youthes,' he exclaims, 'and proper servingmen, whose heads are hanged with haire, as if they would fright away both Christ and his ministers . . . come from the taverns, from gaming-houses, from the play-houses, from the Ale-houses, from the whoore-houses . . . to be ratled up for their follies by preaching, & forsake their fashions of the world to be new fashioned in their minds?' Obviously the preacher thought they should, but the fact was that the gallant youths and proper servingmen were not likely to come and have their minds new-fashioned unless what was offered to them in church were made equally as exciting as what they were hearing in the haunts of sin. The grocers, locksmiths and other virile illiterates, also the persons of quality, who flocked to St. Clement's to hear Smith, were, we must remember, the very men for whose attention

Marlowe and Shakespeare were competing. The preachers no less than the playwrights had to give the Elizabethan and Jacobean public something approaching what it wanted. That public, as the rapid developments of the marvellous decade of 1590 in the theatre testify, was more than ready to drop old conventions and abstractions and to thrill to the poetic and dramatic representation of individual human character and experience. This was what the preachers, like the playwrights, were now to discover. They were to discover that their listeners, still keeping undiminished their zest for wit and rhetoric, took a livelier interest in sin itself than in its categories, in the psychology of spiritual struggle than in the abstract analysis of moral behavior or even the satirical exposure of vice and folly. Who that saw Tamburlane, Faustus and Richard on the boards was more concerned with edifying identification of the sin of pride than with the proud souls of Tamburlane, Faustus and Richard? Who that could enjoy the two-hour traffic of the stage with such figures, though he no doubt had his own private fears for the welfare of his soul, could be any longer inclined to see his own moral life adequately reflected in the seven deadly sins of medieval moral science? Men knew what it was to be sinners. They longed to know what they must do to be saved. The opportunity that presented itself to the preachers was to minister to troubled minds and cleanse stuffed bosoms. So they set out to describe the warfare of the spirit, to portray the drama of the inner life, to expound the psychology of sin and redemption. This, they found, was what the people would come to hear, and more actively they responded to ever-increasing audiences the more they gave up abstractions in order to mirror the individual consciousness of spiritual stress, to convince the individual of sin in order to persuade him of grace, to make him feel worse in order to make him feel better, to inspire pity and fear in order to purge him of those passions. No longer content to be analysts, moralists, satirists and stylists, they would make themselves physicians to the soul.

## *St. Bartholomew's Day Massacre*
*⤳ O. I. A. Roche*

When the alert sounded at four o'clock on the morning of St. Bartholomew's Day [August 24, 1572], municipal official Claude Marcel began the chores outlined for him by Catherine [de Medici, the Queen Mother] and added, as a Guisard [Catholic extremist], his own fateful touches. Throughout the city his fanatic partisans went about their tasks, forming into mobs which skilled agitators, many of them foreign professionals, whipped into frenzy. They roamed the night seeking out and killing Huguenot leaders; but the selected slaughter almost at once turned into mass slaughter. The mobs grew as by infection; kindly men and fond mothers underwent curious mental transformations and raged like beasts through the filthy streets of Paris, burning the houses of supposed heretics, looting shops and mills, running suspects down as they fled, sometimes tearing them apart with their bare hands. All the suppressed resentment of Parisians against endless corruption, poverty, disease, class privilege, tyranny and hunger burst out against the target so long held before their eyes by the clergy of the Established Church, the only institution which offered to those masses even a glimmer of hope or a gloss of understanding.

As a group, the Huguenots were too easy to identify. They were literate, clean in body and mind, disciplined in their personal habits—and prosperous amid poverty. For example, they owned most of the great French weaving enterprises. They were among the biggest employers of free labor. They ran many of the small shops. For the ragged, disenfranchised mass of Parisians, they bulked large as a target.

The Huguenots had the characteristics of the classical scapegoat always sought by corrupt politicians for their own cynical purposes. The Spanish Moors and Sephardim Jews, killed, tortured and exiled in hundreds of thousands by Philip II, had offered a similar means of directing the anger of hungry people away from their corrupt feudal oligarchy. And the Guises not only took money from Philip; they learned from him and obeyed his orders. They modeled their anti-Huguenot crusade on Philip's example. The Spanish monarch's slogan, "Death to Heretics!" began to resound in France louder than ever before, from Flanders to the Mediterranean....

The streets of Paris smelled of death. Bodies of Huguenots by the hundreds lay in piles or were already floating down the Seine. So great was the Terror, the number of the foe so overwhelming, that few Huguenots even tried to fight back....

When the supply of Huguenot leaders was exhausted, the Guise-guided mobs turned on all suspects. A bookbinder named Niquet was roasted with his seven children in a bonfire made of his books. Two babies who cried forlornly when their parents were murdered were picked up by a matronly woman and hurled into the Seine. Cackling men undressed a tiny girl and rolled her in the blood of her murdered mother. Teen-age choir-boys giggled as they dragged through the streets the body of a girl child dressed in once-white linen.

The naked bodies of dead Huguenot nobles were carted to the Square before Louvre Palace and laid out in long rows. Between the rows walked simpering courtesans of the Palace, observing the corpses of those whom, a few nights before, they had danced and possibly

slept with. They looked intently at the body of a certain baron renowned even at the Court for his puritan morals, and wondered if it
was true that the basis of his morality was sexual incapacity. Jacques
Auguste de Thou verified the curiosity of these women. "They looked
at the body intently," Thou wrote, "pour voir si elles y trouveroient
quelque cause ou quelque marque de l'impuissance qu 'on lui
reprochoit."

The massacre enabled many to blackmail erstwhile friends, to loot
with impunity and to vent jealousies. The Duke of Anjou cynically
took 150,000 crowns worth of jewelry from Baduère, jeweler to the King,
then killed him anyway. Albert Gondi, Duke of Retz, King's Councilor
whose family included Jérôme Gondi, Philip II's spy, took over
Versailles after promising its Huguenot owner, Martial Loménie, his
life; thereupon he had him killed. Gondi eventually sold Versailles to
Louis XIII. Jesuit-influenced "intellectuals" took advantage of the
occasion to eliminate Huguenot luminaries. Pierre de la Ramée, or
"Ramus," was one of these victims. His mortal enemy on a pseudo-
intellectual plane was Jacques Charpentier, who, as an article of faith,
believed in the primitive gropings of Aristotle, which Ramée ridiculed.
Charpentier got a job as militia captain during the massacre, attacked
the College of Presles, founded by Ramée and become a center of
European learning, had the professor killed and his body thrown to the
street below. There, still not satisfied, he oversaw its decapitation.

Michieli, Ambassador of Venice and [extremist Holy] League representative, reported enviously that his friends had shaken down
Huguenots for at least two million gold livres. Small vendors also
thrived. At each Roman Catholic church in Paris, they sold medals inscribed with "Jesus-Mary." These were supposed to protect wearers,
miraculously, against being mistaken for heretics. The vendors made
predictable fortunes, though Guisards murdered Roman Catholics
with or without medals if they had goods to steal or were personal
enemies. A canon of Notre-Dame, staunch supporter of the papal wing,
was killed, as was Pedro Salcede, a Spaniard who may have been in
Philip II's employ. It began to appear that the "holy" massacre of
Huguenots was a business enterprise. . . .

By September 1 the same Parisians who the previous week had
reveled in slaughter had become peaceful citizens, solicitous of their
neighbors and assiduous attendants at early mass. Only a few highly
organized bands of assassins continued to operate in the capital, though
the gallows and their fruit were left standing at every crossroads.

But as Paris quieted, the bloody flood inundated the provinces. When
news of the massacre in the capital reached Lyons, the clergy there
called on the faithful to go and do likewise. Lyons Governor Mandelot

tried to hold the mobs back, then ordered all Huguenots into "protective custody"—of the monasteries—and proceeded to confiscate
their homes and goods. A Huguenot overflow of about seven hundred
persons was placed in less protective custody in the Lyons prisons.
Sunday night, August 31, the faithful, fresh from priestly incitement,
broke down the prison doors and cut the throats of everyone inside,
from the aged to babes in arms. Frightened of consequences, Mandelot
ordered his own men to kill all surviving Huguenots so tales of the
massacre could not be carried elsewhere. That night more than a
thousand bodies were thrown into the Saône and Rhône rivers. A few
who had been held in the Roanne Prison in Lyons and some in the
Célestins prison escaped by fervently professing their belief in any
Roman Catholic doctrine mentioned....

At Meaux, once a Huguenot center and later a favorite spot of
Catherine's, Police Chief Louis Cosset arrested some two hundred
heretics, put them in prison, then had them called one by one to the
gate, where their throats were cut. The faithful of the Established
Church took advantage of the occasion to cut the throat of a Meaux
tax collector of their own faith.

At Tours, Beaupréau, Blois, Angers and Saumur several thousand
Huguenots were slaughtered. At Rouen, where they were especially
numerous, Governor Carrouges imitated Mandelot's techniques at
Lyon. He arrested about six hundred, put them in "protective" custody,
then left town. Aroused parishioners of the Established Church cut
the throats of the entire group. At Troyes, where the same technique
was used, a fanatic named Caclot boasted of killing personally thirty
men and women. At La Charité, once a fortified Huguenot town, the
Royal Governor [and] the inhabitants, used to Huguenots, were remiss
in murdering their fellow townsmen. Gonzague, possibly fearing that
the Guises might be suspicious of him, brought in a crew of Italian
assassins to do the job. At Toulouse, four hundred Huguenots were
caught and jailed. The townspeople, who had seen years of mutual
slaughter, left them alone. A merchant named Delpech, eager to get a
share of Huguenot goods, recruited a band of one hundred professional
killers, smashed in the jail and killed them all. After incitement by two
Jesuits, Father Auger and Father Emond, Governor Montferrand of
Bordeaux organized the slaughter of seven hundred heretics....

The rivers of France were so filled with corpses that for many months
no fish were eaten by Frenchmen. In the valley of the Loire, wolves
came down from the hills to feed upon the decaying bodies of
Huguenots. The list of massacres was as endless as the list of the dead.

Even so, all was not barbarism.... Throughout France, thousands
of the common people sheltered Huguenot friends against the Terror.

There were even cases of hangmen who refused to place nooses around the necks of "the innocents"—so risking their own.

Maximilien de Béthune, Duke of Sully, who lived through the massacre to become Minister of Henry IV, estimated the dead, on the basis of documents he then obtained access to, at about 60,000, in Paris and the provinces. The Archbishop of Paris, Hardouin Beaumont of Péréfixe, reckoned the total at 100,000. The careful Thou figured only 40,000 were killed. There is no way to check even approximately at this date. The municipal records of Paris indicate that about 2,000 bodies were thrown into the Seine as part of a street-cleaning operation. Ditch-diggers who were hired to clear the river at various points outside Paris where bodies had clogged it collected for 1,900 corpses at twenty livres a thousand. From the provinces no records at all are trustworthy, and estimates hover around 25,000 to 30,000. An apologist for King Charles, Jean-Papyre Masson, claimed that no more than 13,000 were killed in all France. Thou's figures may approximate the truth....

If every people has the government it deserves—it being understood that otherwise they would not put up with it—then it was the people of France in the final analysis who bore the blame for the blackest day in their country's history. It may have been their realization of this, and their shame through the slow generations, which led to the French Revolution—when the only royal statue left unsmashed by the avenging, anticlerical mobs was that of the Huguenot, Henry of Navarre.

# 3. The Coarseness and Splendor of Court Life

## The Ribald Childhood of Louis XIII

⊷§ *Philippe Ariès*

Henri IV's physician, Heroard, recorded the details of the young Louis XIII's life....

Louis XIII was not yet one year old: 'He laughed uproariously when his nanny waggled his cock with her fingers.' An amusing trick which the child soon copied. Calling a page, 'he shouted "Hey, there!" and pulled up his robe, showing him his cock.'

He was one year old: 'In high spirits,' notes Heroard, 'he made everybody kiss his cock.' This amused them all. Similarly everyone considered his behaviour towards two visitors, a certain de Bonières and his daughter, highly amusing: 'He laughed at him, lifted up his robe and showed him his cock, but even more so to his daughter, for then, holding it and giving his little laugh, he shook the whole of his body up and down.' They thought this so funny that the child took care to repeat a gesture which had been such a success; in the presence of a 'little lady', 'he lifted up his coat, and showed her his cock with such fervour that he was quite beside himself. He lay on his back to show it to her.'

When he was just over a year old he was engaged to the Infanta of Spain; his attendants explained to him what this meant, and he understood them fairly well. 'They asked him: "Where is the Infanta's darling?" He put his hand on his cock.'

During his first three years nobody showed any reluctance or saw any harm in jokingly touching the child's sexual parts. 'The Marquise [de Verneuil] often put her hand under his coat; he got his nanny to

210

lay him on her bed where she played with him, putting her hand under his coat.' 'Mme de Verneuil wanted to play with him and took hold of his nipples; he pushed her away, saying: "Let go, let go, go away." He would not allow the Marquise to touch his nipples, because his nanny had told him: "Monsieur, never let anybody touch your nipples, or your cock, or they will cut it off." He remembered this.' Again: 'When he got up, he would not take his shirt and said: "Not my shirt, I want to give you all some milk from my cock." We held out our hands, and he pretended to give us all some milk, saying: "Pss, pss," and only then agreeing to take his shirt.'

It was a common joke, repeated time and again, to say to him: 'Monsieur, you haven't got a cock.' Then 'he replied: "Hey, here it is!" —laughing and lifting it up with one finger.' These jokes were not limited to the servants, or to brainless youths, or to women of easy virtue such as the King's mistress. The Queen, his mother, made the same sort of joke: 'The Queen, touching his cock, said: "Son, I am holding your spout." ' Even more astonishing is this passage: 'He was undressed and Madame too [his sister], and they were placed naked in bed with the King, where they kissed and twittered and gave great amusement to the King. The King asked him: "Son, where is the Infanta's bundle?" He showed it to him, saying: "There is no bone in it, Papa." Then, as it was slightly distended, he added: "There is now, there is sometimes." '

The Court was amused, in fact, to see his first erections: 'Waking up at eight o'clock, he called Mlle Bethouzay and said to her: "Zezai, my cock is like a drawbridge; see how it goes up and down." And he raised it and lowered it.'

By the age of four, 'he was taken to the Queen's apartments, where Mme de Guise showed him the Queen's bed and said to him: "Monsieur, this is where you were made." He replied: "With Mamma?" ' 'He asked his nanny's husband: "What is that?" "That," came the reply, "is one of my silk stockings." "And those?" [after the manner of parlour-game questions] "Those are my breeches." "What are they made of?" "Velvet." "And that?" "That is a cod-piece." "What is inside?" "I don't know, Monsieur." "Why, a cock. Who is it for?" "I don't know, Monsieur." "Why, for Madame Doundoun [his nanny]." '

'He stood between the legs of Mme de Montglat [his governess, a very dignified, highly respectable woman, who however did not seem to be put out—any more than Heroard was—by all these jokes which we would consider insufferable today]. The King said: "Look at Madame de Montglat's son: she has just given birth." He went straight away and stood between the Queen's legs.'

When he was between five and six, people stopped talking about his sexual parts, while he started talking more about other people's. Mlle Mercier, one of his chambermaids who had stayed up late the night before, was still in bed one morning, next to his bed (his servants, who were sometimes married, slept in his bedroom and do not appear to have allowed his presence to embarrass them). 'He played with her, toyed with her toes and the upper part of her legs, and told his nanny to go and get some birch twigs so that he could beat her, which he did. . . His nanny asked him: "What have you seen of Mercier's?" He replied calmly: "I have seen her arse." "What else have you seen?" He replied calmly and without laughing that he had seen her private.' On another occasion, 'after playing with Mlle Mercier, he called me [Heroard] and told me that Mercier had a private as big as that (showing me his two fists] and that there was water inside.'

After 1608 this kind of joke disappeared: he had become a little man—attaining the fateful age of seven—and at this age he had to be taught decency in language and behaviour. When he was asked how children were born, he would reply, like Molière's Agnès, 'through the ear.' Mme de Montglat scolded him when he 'showed his cock to the little Ventelet girl.' And if, when he awoke in the morning, he was still put in Mme de Montglat's bed between her and her husband, Heroard waxed indignant and noted in the margin of his diary: *insignis impudentia*. The boy of ten was forced to behave with a modesty which nobody had thought of expecting of the boy of five. Education scarcely began before the age of seven; moreover, these tardy scruples of decency are to be attributed to the beginning of a reformation of manners, a sign of the religious and moral restoration which took place in the seventeenth century. It was as if education was held to be of no value before the approach of manhood.

By the time he was fourteen, however, Louis XIII had nothing more to learn, for it was at the age of fourteen years two months that he was put almost by force into his wife's bed. After the ceremony he 'retired and had supper in bed at a quarter to seven. M. de Gramont and a few young lords told him some broad stories to encourage him. He asked for his slippers and put on his robe and went to the Queen's bedchamber at eight o'clock, where he was put to bed beside the Queen his wife, in the presence of the Queen his mother; at a quarter past ten he returned after sleeping for about an hour and performing twice, according to what he told us; he arrived with his cock all red.'

## THE GRANDEUR OF THE FRENCH COURT

### The World of the Sun King
**⋘ Frantz Funck-Brentano**

Under the Ancien Régime the Royal Court had reached an importance such as no Court of our times can ever realize again. The motley and ill-regulated crowd of noblemen, gentlemen, intimates, favourites and courtiers within the circle, played an active part in the direction of the State as successors of the *curia regis*, which at the time of the early feudal Kings had consisted of the relations and closely united vassals of the Princes—the *familia regis*—and had formed the Government. The Marquis d'Argenson, Minister of Foreign Affairs, writes in this connection: "The Court has become the Senate of the nation," and "the chamber-women have a share in the government." This would surprise us more, and seem wellnigh incomprehensible, did we not constantly bear in mind the permanent facts of our history down to the Revolution, and that the institutions, ways of thinking, customs and usages of ancient France had their *raison d'être* and explanation which may be summed up in these three words—family, patronage, and tradition; nay more, in one single word—the family, for patronage proceeds from the family as it enlarges its action, and tradition is the essential law of the family as continued from one generation to another.

It was not the action of the Kings themselves which in successive ages welded together the elements constituting their greatness and power, and created their renown. The dazzling monarchy of the seventeenth century, at which posterity is still bewildered, and which is sometimes held up to criticism by the foreigner through envy, and because he has nothing like it to show, was built up little by little, by unceasing alluvial deposits of the national stream.

Picture to yourself the Court of Honour at the Château of Versailles in the time of Louis XIV, a swarming mass of liveries, uniforms, costumes and retinues of a thousand brilliant and varied colours; it might almost be likened to an immense cloak of Scotch tartan in perpetual motion, or a picturesque piece of Indian cashmere, the colours mingling in multiple designs.

And watch the Court issuing from the château in attendance on the King, and spreading down the avenues. "It is a fine sight," writes Primi Visconti, the Italian, "to see Louis XIV going forth escorted by his lifeguards, coaches, horses, courtiers, valets and a whole multi-

tude of people all running about in a confused mass amid a noisy
clatter. It reminds me of the queen bee flying over the fields accompanied by her swarm."

In the numberless and vast *salons* of Versailles on the days of the
receptions—Mondays, Wednesdays and Thursdays of each week—the
throng was so great that it was only possible to talk to the two or
three people close to where one was standing. One was literally
hemmed in, and only with great difficulty and patience managed to
pass from one room to another. Persons of the highest rank, the King's
own brother and sister-in-law, were [often] pinned in a corner....

Rank, dignities, renown of birth or public service—all were blended
together there. "I was stupefied with amazement," writes Visconti,
"to see Cardinal de Bouillon, Cardinals de Retz, Bonzi and other
ecclesiastical dignitaries, who hold such lofty rank in Rome, jostled
about in the crowd here. It was explained to me that there were too
many persons of distinction at the Court to stand on ceremony."
There was a block in the stream of the time-honoured crowd which
from every point in a great country had ceaselessly pushed forward in
the same direction. For the great personages in the kingdom, whether
of the nobility or clergy, the ever present concern came to be to live
under the eyes of the King....

THE COURTIERS. "Whoso will consider the fact that the
King's countenance constitutes the entire happiness of the courtier,"
says La Bruyère, "and that he occupies and fills his whole life in regarding him, will understand in some measure how God constitutes all
the glory and felicity of the saints."

"The passion evinced by men at Court to be noticed by the King,"
writes Primi Visconti, "is incredible; when he deigns to cast a glance
at certain of them, the one who receives it thinks that his fortune is
made, and boasts of it to the others, saying:

" 'The King looked at me!'

"You may take it that the King is fairly acute," adds the Italian,
"how many people does he not thus repay with a look!"

This life in common, which was lived in such close promiscuity, had
consequences which Taine has clearly pointed out:

"The Court of Louis XIV was the place in the world where men
best learned the art of living together. They reduced it to maxims, and
drew up its guiding principles. They made it the subject of reflections,
matter for discussion, the end and purpose of education, the outward
sign of merit, and the employment of life."

On the other hand, this constant close contact of so many people,
often divided by conflicting interests, ambition, or vanity, gave to

people of that time a singular skill in studying character: whence sprang that admirable literature which portrayed the human soul and its passions like none other in the world: Mme. de la Fayette, La Rochefoucauld, La Bruyère, Molière, Racine and Bourdaloue. It still has its influence even in our times.

It was a bustling, moving, buzzing crowd, agitating round the monarch from morning to night, "an appalling crowd," writes the Duchesse d'Osnabrück, "that makes a most fatiguing racket." Visconti calls it "a fair of nobility," and adds, "I wish you could see the Court; it is a real bear-garden of men and women." Voltaire emphasizes it as "the crowded life of a great town house, a kind of huge caravanserai which concealed underneath it many miseries and had not even the advantage of being comfortable."

The highest nobility were attached to Versailles like an oyster to its bed.

The Maréchal de Noailles had gone to bed and was going to sleep. Drawing the curtains round him, his valet asked:

"At what o'clock does Monseigneur wish me to call him?"

"At ten, if no one dies during the night."

The oldest courtiers who had reached the most advanced age—and these the best of them—had passed the greater part of their existence in the royal ante-chamber, like herons standing motionless in the muddy marsh. One of them remarked to a young débutant in this noble career:

"You have only to do three things: say nice things to everybody; solicit every post that is likely to become vacant, and sit down when you can."

"What is a nobleman?" asks de Mesmes; to which he replies, "a pillar of the ante-chamber."

This appalling rôle—and one may as well say here, this basest of rôles—imposed thus miserably upon so many men adorned by the greatest names in France, proud of their lineage, and of the glory shed forth by the standard they bore, resulted in deforming the character of even the best of them. Read the Memoirs of the Duc de Croÿ, a fine and upright man.

Who to-day would not prefer to sweep the gutters in the town rather than drag along the existence of an everlasting beggar, more often rebuffed than favourably received, not only at the hands of the Prince whom no one could dare to approach freely, but at the hands of his mistresses and favourites, of Ministers and their clerks? The Duc de Croÿ took his son to Versailles: "I showed him the doors where I had so constantly waited."

In his book on *Le Gouvernement et les Mœurs* Senac de Meilhan quotes these lines of Montesquieu:

"Ambition in idleness, meanness accompanied by pride, the desire to grow rich without working, an aversion for truth, contempt for the duties of a citizen, apprehension from the virtue of the Prince, and hope from his weaknesses—such was the character of the greater proportion of the courtiers."

But let us not judge with too great severity those unfortunate beings in Court dress—a poverty-stricken nobility pushed on into an *impasse*. It was a class of society which had fulfilled its task, and, taken all in all, had fulfilled it magnificently; there was no further reason for them to remain at home on their lands, on which, moreover, it was becoming difficult for them to live. As a social class at least, it should have disappeared, but to renounce its rank, privileges and precedence, and become a commercial, trading, financial and industrial class, this it could not do. Humanity does not free itself by a mere turn of the wrist of the stamp with which it is imprinted in its inmost recesses.

Do not compare our aristocracy under the Ancien Régime with the English nobility, as is too often done. The latter was by heredity and tradition the product of quite a different formation, just as the English monarchy in its origin and development was fundamentally other than the French monarchy. Let us mention only one fact, a very important one it is true, among many others that might be cited: by its rôle in Parliament the English nobility and gentry continued to be the directing power in the country; the French nobility no longer directed anything. Listen to the furious cries of Saint Simon, who, moreover, would have been more incapable than anyone else of directing anything.

> "All those people were lodged in Versailles," writes Gustave Geffroy in his fine book on the Palace of the Great King, "Versailles was pulsating with the animation and ambitions of ten thousand persons. One or two narrow rooms, partitioned off from the large apartments, which temporary makeshift lasted for years, formed the only lodgings of these privileged ones."

We see the Duc de Saint Simon giving up the regiment of which he was Colonel to shut himself up at Versailles in "a hole in the entresol" without any air or light, so as to be near to the rays of the sun. In the end the Duchesse de Saint Simon was appointed to be a lady-in-waiting to the Duchesse de Berry, and the noble Duke was then able to lodge in the château in an apartment containing five rooms.

"Huddled one against the other in this way," proceeds Geffroy, "outwardly satisfied, and feverish when behind their closed doors, inwardly filled with the tumult of their conflicting interests and passions, and maintaining with difficulty on their pinched countenances the marks of an amiable impenetrability, the seigneurs came and went, descending from their miserable garrets in the roof, the honour of occupying which they had persistently solicited, and assisted at the daily ceremonies attaching to Court life, *le grand lever*, and *le petit lever*, the royal repasts, and the morning Mass. More than one would groan over the new conditions attaching to life, more than one would curse that immense palace which absorbed the activities of the kingdom, wherein were accumulated the Ministries, the public services, the services of the Court, those of the chapel, of the King's bedchamber, of his private office, of the King's table, of the most trifling amusements, of the King's stables and military household."

A few rare individuals had the strength to resist this fatal attraction, like the Marquis de Mirabeau, so closely resembling Saint Simon in the piquancy and colour of his style, and so far above him in intelligence and character: "Inasmuch as the nobles at Court make a profession of dabbling in the mire of intrigue, I have never wanted to go to Versailles, I, a wild bird nesting between his four towers . . ."

Consuming anxieties and feverish preoccupations pursued their course in undertones beneath the brilliant play of colour of those most wonderfully arranged *fêtes*. "The beauty of things and the virtue of art are powerless to discipline the ebb and flow of the passions" (Geffroy).

Under Louis XIII the amusements of the Court assumed a popular guise; there was dancing to airs of the Auvergne, going so far as clog dances and beating together of heels as at village weddings. The ladies and gentlemen danced in circles, holding each other by the hand; distant reserve was effaced, the ladies engaging the gentlemen by offering them bouquets; the King himself would take part in them just like any private individual, and the first-comer could invite him to dance.

This was no longer the fashion at the Court balls under Louis XIV and Louis XV. The *pavane* was replaced by *la courante*, and that in its turn gave way to the *passe-pied*, which enjoyed a long run of favour; it was a nimble, light-footed dance, the special feature of which was the movement of the left foot advancing along the floor like the paw of a kitten. The ladies did not dance after reaching the age of twenty-five.

The balls given on State occasions were called *bals parés*, and

etiquette ensured that they should be magnificent rather than agreeable. The ladies could only appear *en grande toilette* with enormous
*paniers*; the weight of the heavy material on their shoulders was so
great that they could hardly lift their arms; they wore narrow pointed
shoes with high heels; their dresses were immensely long, made of a
thick rich material embroidered with gold, or of brocaded silk; the
hair was arranged in a very high *coiffure* loaded with precious stones.
Heavy clusters of diamonds, hanging from their ears, completed their
costume, in which it was very difficult for them to dance with any
lightness. The men wore richly ornamented coats, embroidered down
all the seams, and a sash; in the time of Louis XIV they also wore an
ample wig, but later on they had their hair pressed down and plaited.

At ordinary Court balls—called *bals de le reine*—the ladies were in
*dominos* with long folds falling behind, from the neck to the heels.
These *dominos*, which were made entirely of white taffeta, were worn
with small *paniers*, floating sleeves and short trains. The ladies were
therefore all in white, while the gentlemen were decorated with multi-
coloured and brilliant embroideries.

As regards paint, if fashion no longer required the men to cover
their faces with it, as in the time of the Médicis Queens, it was nevertheless *de rigueur* for the ladies. It was not a question of painting themselves so as to resemble nature, or of giving to their lips and cheeks
the radiance of springtime beauty. "This rouge which seemingly wished
to be natural is truly ridiculous," the Comtesse says in Mme. de Staal's
*La Mode*. A rouge was required "which told you something," and of
these there were different kinds according to the rank and position of
the lady using it. In this way the kind of rouge used would announce
the person appearing in it, as was remarked by the Goncourts: "The
rouge worn by the lady of quality was not the same as that of the lady
at Court; the rouge of the woman of the *bourgeois* was merely a
suspicion of rouge—a mere hint of it."

The Princesses, on the contrary, wore it very much accentuated and
of a very pronounced colour, and they wished the ladies of the Court
to be no less pronounced.

"Nevertheless, the startling rouge used in the time of the Regency,
colouring Nattier's portraits with purple—and due no doubt to the
use of Portuguese rouge, thickly applied—gradually lost favour under
Louis XV, and was only seen on the cheeks of actresses, on which it
marked that vivid patch which the artists of the time made a point
of showing in their paintings of opera costumes."

And beneath all this outward splendour and superficial varnish,
under all this beauty of form which has never since been attained,
what an oppressive gloom and boredom brooded! The Duchess of

Osnabruck emphasizes the trouble they gave themselves at the French Court to be amused. "I see many *fêtes* at the French Court," Madame Palatine writes, "but no gaiety of heart." Even Mme. de Sévigné's letters, despite her efforts to write in a light, lively, and smart strain, draw some depressing pictures when speaking of the Court. It clung to frivolities and vanities which even a market woman would despise, so as to work them up into occasions for joy and pleasure. Boredom at the Court affected even those seemingly the most favoured, even Mme. de Maintenon, who, from a most humble condition, had reached the pinnacle of fortune. This she confided to her friend, Mme. de Maisonfort: "How impossible it is for me to tell you what I go through, or to make you realize the boredom which consumes the great, or the difficulty they have in filling the day! Do you not see that I am dying with depression in circumstances it would be difficult to imagine?" To her brother d'Aubigné she said: " I can stand it no longer; I wish I were dead!" To which he replied jokingly: "*Vous avez donc parole, ma sœur, d'épouser Dieu le père!*"

Poor uprooted nobility! "We get our meals in all kinds of different places," writes Visconti, "and we are always on the move, like Bohemians. . . . In Paris there are twenty thousand gentlemen who exist haphazard."

The Duchess of Osnabruck writes to her brother: "The position of the French nobility created by the royal predominance has deprived them of their dignity. The life the courtiers lead would not suit me; necessity reduces them to slaves."

"One day I heard someone say about Louis XIV," writes Visconti, "that with one glance he sees everybody, whether he be in his study, in the chapel or in the country, and facts show him to have been right. On one occasion when he was on horseback at Versailles he was the only one to notice a thief putting his hand into the pocket of young Villars Orondate."

Thus vanished the fine independence of the country nobility of earlier days, when Montaigne still spoke of them with enthusiasm.

Louis XIV made it an essential point that all his nobles should be seen around him. Saint Simon tells us: "It was accounted to be failing in all that was most distinguished for a man not to make his usual sojourn at Court, for others to come there only rarely, and certain disgrace never, or almost never, to go there." And the *Grand Roi*, with his eye ever on the watch, made a daily inspection of the crowd surrounding him.

"In short," concludes Visconti, "the great men of the land live under the King to-day like so many novices under a father director."

And in what a wonderful degree did this aristocracy—which the Monarchy by removing its foundations had commited to unavoidable destruction—dazzled by the Fate that was sweeping it away, remain faithful to the Prince who was ruining it, burning to serve him with most generous devotion in the army, and ready to sacrifice both life and fortune for his sake.

## Court Etiquette
🖛§ W. H. Lewis

Court etiquette was a life study. Who for instance could guess that at Versailles it was the height of bad manners to knock at a door? You must scatch it with the little finger of the left hand, growing the finger nail long for that purpose. Or could know that you must not *tutoyer* an intimate friend in any place where the King was present? That if the lackey of a social superior brought you a message, you had to receive him standing, and bareheaded? You have mastered the fact that you must not knock on a door, so when you go to make your first round of calls in the great houses in the town, you scratch: wrong again, you should have knocked. Next time you rattle the knocker, and a passing exquisite asks you contemptuously if you are so ignorant as not to know that you give one blow of the knocker on the door of a lady of quality? Who could guess that if you encounter the royal dinner on its way from the kitchens to the table, you must bow as to the King himself, sweep the ground with the plume of your hat, and say in a low, reverent, but distinct voice, *La viande du Roi?* Many times must the apprentice courtier have echoed the psalmist's lament, "Who can tell how oft he offendeth?" And it behoved you not to offend, for the King had an eye like a hawk, or shall we say, like a school prefect, for any breach of etiquette, and not even the most exalted were safe from his reproof. One night at supper his chatterbox of a brother put his hand in a dish before Louis had helped himself: "I perceive," said the King icily, "that you are no better able to control your hands than your tongue." Once at Marly, Mme. de Torcy, wife of a minister, took a seat above a duchess at supper. Louis, to her extreme discomfort, regarded her steadfastly throughout the meal, and when he reached Mme. de Maintenon's room, the storm broke; he had, he said, witnessed a piece of insolence so intolerable that the sight of it had prevented him from eating: a piece of presumption which would have been unendurable in a woman of quality. It took the combined efforts of Mme. de Maintenon and the Duchess of Burgundy the rest of the evening to pacify him. Decidedly not a king with whom to take liberties, or even make mistakes. This is Louis, or one side of Louis, at the height of his arrogance and prosperity: the *Grand Monarque* of the middle 'eighties, now forty-five or so, and in reluctant transition from Prince Charming to the impenetrably dignified King who struck Visconti as having the *gravité d'un roi de Théâtre*. Louis and Louis' Court had both been very different twenty years earlier, when the King's ambition had been to be the smartest of the smart set, *homme à bonnes fortunes* in his own right, owing his successes not to his crown but to his own graces. The King who climbed about the roofs of the Louvre at night to find an unbarred window in the quarters of the Maids-of-Honour was a very different man from the King who married Mme. de Maintenon; and for old courtiers it must have been difficult to realize that the new Louis was the same man who, when pinched *a tergo* by a pretty girl in full Court, sprang upwards with a shout of "Damn the bitch!" Villeroi was perhaps the only man left who could venture to remind the King of those old days, in this new Court in which a freezing but superficial decorum and a rigid etiquette had become the rule.

# 4. *The Mode of Aristocratic Life*

---

## *The French Château*

### ᴈȘ *Frantz Funck-Brentano*

[The country seigneur's] home was the manor, a half-way house between the feudal castle with its towers and keep, and the peasant's home. It was made up of an agglomeration of buildings, with a principal house where the owner lived, and outhouses for the purposes of the farm. It was provided with courtyards and orchards, and was surrounded by gardens and walls, for if the manor no longer had the important defensive surroundings of a fortified castle it was not devoid of the means to repel a band of pillagers.

After the pacification of the kingdom in the sixteenth century, the manor underwent still further changes; it shed its defensive characteristics; the outer walls were pierced to make windows, and the moats were transformed into terraces or made into fishponds; there was no longer any tower to be seen, save that for the pigeons, and the thick walls were used principally for training espaliers of fruit trees. The manor houses then assumed the name of "*gentilhommières*" and "*noblesses.*"

The interior arrangements were almost always the same. There was an avenue leading to the entrance gate, and a large courtyard the origin of which went back to remote antiquity; within the courtyard (*curtis*) were Gallo-Roman living-quarters; at the far end was the seigneur's house; to left and right, backing on to the outside walls, were the servants' quarters, and behind the seigneur's house were the cattle sheds, stables and garden.

In the time of Henri IV the custom was introduced of building the barns and stables at a certain distance from the seigneur's house. Possibly some of our *gentilshommes champêtres* began to find the smells

222

therefrom a little strong, but Olivier de Serres considered this new custom a regrettable one:

"To move the barns, stables, and sheds for the cattle away from the house is a sorry matter, for when the quarters for the animals are put farther back the seigneur is unable conveniently to keep a watch over his stock and manage it in a fitting manner."

The most important room in these manors was the kitchen. It was the largest room of all and the best furnished. Placed, in the best houses, on the first storey, it gave on the one side on to the *salle*—we should call it to-day the *salon*—and on the other, on the *chambre* or sleeping quarters.

"Your kitchen," says Olivier de Serres, "should be situated on the first storey of the house, near your living room and bedroom. In this wise those in the kitchen are able to be controlled by access from the *salle* and the *chambre*, where one often happens to be, and the idleness, clamour and blasphemy of the servants can thus be reprimanded."

In the kitchen both the master and servants had their own customs. The seigneur took his meals there with his household, and if any peasant, a tenant in the neighbourhood, happened to come when they were at table the diners would squeeze up to make a place for him.

The meals were of patriarchal simplicity. There would be a huge dish piled up with beef, mutton, veal and bacon, and a large bowl filled with broth made of cooked herbs, like a vegetable soup. Each one helped himself as he wished in accordance with his appetite. "Everything proceeded good-naturedly and with no formality," observes Noel du Fail. Before sitting down to table they would go and wash their hands at the well and sharpen their knives "in order the better to cut off long broad slices of the fat ham, or the huge and quivering piece of salt beef, and spread them on the good brown bread."

In his *gentilhommière* of Mesnil-au-Val, the Sire of Gouberville dined and supped in the kitchen where he passed his evenings, made up his accounts and wrote his letters. This room was called the "*chauffoir*" in more than one province—which appellation we have already met with when treating of the peasant communities; the furniture too of these manorial "*chauffoirs*" was very like what we have described in the *maisons de village*—the great chimney, table, sideboard and huge cooking pot, also the beds similarly ranged against the wall, and two or three chairs with backs to them, generally of wood, like those reserved for the old people in the rural communities.

As regards ornaments there were pewter or earthenware dishes on the dresser or on the ledge of the projecting hood of the chimney, and there would be family portraits on the wall. Seated by this huge chimney, where faggots of broom or vine crackled under the iron or shining

copper cauldron, the seigneur and his wife would pass the winter evenings surrounded by their servants. It was very comfortable in the
*"chauffoir"* seated there with the household, everyone at their ease and
conversation interspersed with old songs—those good wholesome songs
of the land of France in which each province would echo its customs,
traditions, and rustic Christmas glees. And then there would be different games, or one of the party would start telling some pretty legend
or fairy tale from which the son of Charles Perrault drew his immortal
little stories—stories of brigands and family legends the entrancing
veracity of which no one doubted; the seigneur would recount his
military exploits under the King's standard, and sometimes he would
read aloud to his people to rest them after their rough toil on the
farm. "That day my people were in the fields, but the rain drove them
in," notes Gouberville in an entry dated 6th February, 1555, "and
throughout the whole evening we read aloud *Amadis in Gaul* and how
he overcame Dardan."

In the course of the sixteenth century the good old custom of French
seigneurs taking their meals in the kitchen together with their household was tending to die out. Olivier de Serres notes this with regret,
also the Constable de Montmorency whose statue now stands on the
terrace at Chantilly. The latter remarks: "A gentleman who has arrived at an income of 500 *livres* no longer knows how to observe good
cheer because in his desire to cut a great figure he now dines in his
*salle*, subject to his cook's inclinations, whereas formerly, when he took
his meals in the kitchen, he had himself served to his own liking."
Nevertheless the old custom continued in many respects right down to
the end of the Ancien Régime. Retif de la Bretonne was yet to show us
the country gentleman eating in the same room with his household.
He took his seat at a round table with his wife, his three daughters and
four sons. Hung on the wall in a conspicuous position was the portrait
of an ancestor; close by there was another very long rectangular table
over which hung the portrait of the seigneur's father. At this second
table the servants took their places, farm hands and day labourers on
the one side, the women on the other; there were six plough boys,
eight vine-dressers, the cow-hand, the shepherd, the goat-herd and
swine-herd. The women servants and farm girls sat opposite the men,
occupying the same side as the mistress of the household at her round
table. One of them served the meal.

The *salle*, as compared with the *chauffoir* and bed-chamber, was a
state-room. It was a chamber of honour containing a bedstead with
columns and canopy, and served as a dining-room where the tables were
spread for guests of high descent; it was the chamber where animated
conversation took place when everyone was dressed in their Sunday

best in honour of select company. High up on the wall was a stag's head used for hanging up bonnets and hats, hunting horns and leads for the hounds. A collection of picturesque arms reminded those present of old tradition, and showed the tastes of the seigneur. There were bows and quivers of arrows, haquebuts or arquebuses, and ash-stemmed lances measuring no less than seven yards long, inherited from the tourneys of their ancestors; huge formidable-looking swords, halberds and cross-bows with their strings and wooden finger pieces fastened through the cord. Shirts or coats of mail were kept in chests filled with bran. At a little distance off on the wall might be seen large hawking nets, hunting implements, and the shining armour worn by the horses on ceremonial occasions. Standing on the shelves of a primitive bookcase were the Bible, and a few books for amusement, such as *Les Quatres Fils Aymon, Ogier le Danois, Mélusine, Le Calendrier des Bergers, Le Roman de la Rose* and the beautiful stories in the *Légende Dorée.*

You need not expect to find in this chamber any soft, rich bright-coloured carpets, but herbs would be scattered on the floor and these were often renewed giving an agreeable scent to the room. It was the *jonchée* of the old manors, for it often consisted of rushes (*joncs*); at the foot of the long benches and chests, which latter also served as seats ranged round the walls, was a layer of straw which kept the feet warm in winter and was used to wipe them on at all seasons of the year. It also provided litter for the dogs, "for they are all the better and more vigorous when they hear and scent their masters near them," as Noel du Fail remarks. In the fire-place "great big green logs, with one or two dry faggots, gave a fire which lasted a long time." The chests along the walls continued to serve as seats just as in the Middle Ages, hence the expression *"piquer le coffre"* when one has a long wait. With what care did the mistress of the house lay her well-arranged linen therein, perfuming it with lavender for her daughters, and the baron's apparel! The chests closed down with huge wrought iron locks, and what a collection of things issued therefrom when it was unpacked— *Tournois écus* and *livres,* jewels, rare weapons, bed-warmers, crockery and harness! In a coffer painted with flowers lay the trousseau for the bride to be. It sometimes happened that the bride was not very beautiful "Elle est belle au coffre" (she has gold in her coffers), would murmur the friends of the bridegroom. Enormous beds, sometimes several in the same room, would be arranged end to end, in which several people would sleep; the girls were in one room and the boys in the other, for it was a well-known custom in the old days for several people to sleep in the same bed, often with complete strangers at inns. . . .

[The ideal] country nobility [possessed] at least three great qualities:

It was rooted to the soil, like the homes they had themselves built; it assured the defence of the country; it was careful to afford protection to its tenants, among whom it strove to maintain order and mutual understanding.

This nobility lived on familiar terms alike with their vassals and the humblest. With wife and children they took part in *fêtes* of the people at which the seigneur, his wife and daughters danced with the peasants. At *fêtes* commemorated by a general banquet, held on the green sward under the great elms in the village square, the seigneur would sit at table with his tenants, bringing with him wine, game and sweet-meats to brighten up the *ménu*.

The seigneur would play bowls and skittles with the young lads and clink glasses with them; he would intervene in their quarrels and smooth out differences in a friendly manner; he preserved them from blood-sucking lawyers and all their gibberish. Even at the taverns he would not mind putting his own legs under the same white wooden table with his vassals.

Our country gentlemen made the country safe against marauders and vagabonds. As at the best period of the Middle Ages their castles served as a safe shelter in the event of danger.

## *The English Country House*
ᴈ§ Mary Coate

In the Middle Ages, men built their houses primarily for defence, but under the Stuarts the desire for beauty, which had led the Elizabethans to lighten their rooms with stately windows, and to carry off the smoke of their fires in tall and ornamental chimneys, was developing. Gilded leather, Eastern embroideries, French tapestries, marble mantelpieces, and silver and china of rare beauty, all these had a growing attraction for the country squire, while the patronage given by Charles I to Van Dyck set the fashion for family portraits. Beds, too, were elaborate. The bed built for James I, by the Earl of Dorset, at Knole, cost £8,000; and Celia Fiennes, in her "Rides through England on a Side-Saddle," frequently mentions the heavy canopies of gold and silver embroidery, while more formidable was that great black bed of the Verneys, which toured the country when a death in the family was imminent.

As a rule, these houses stood in their own parks. "Every gentleman of five hundred or a thousand pounds rent by the year," says Fynes Moryson in 1617, "hath a park for Deer enclosed with pales of wood for 2 or 3 miles compasse." But more recent was the interest in the garden or "pleasance" immediately around the house, and it was largely due to French and Italian influence.

When Henrietta Maria became Queen of England [in 1625], she found it almost impossible to procure in England the shrubs and flowers she had loved in France, while at his Restoration one of Charles II's first actions was to send for French gardeners for Whitehall and Hampton Court. John Evelyn, who had seen rare gardens in France and Italy, was an authority on horticulture; he translated into English, "Le Jardinier français," in his "Sylva" he laid down the principles of forestry, and his diary is full of allusions to gardens. For instance, he notes that Beddington "is famous for the first orange-garden in England, being now overgrown trees . . . secured in winter with a wooden tabernacle and stove."

In the literature and memoirs of the period, the garden figures largely. "God Almighty first planted a garden," said Bacon, "and indeed it is the purest of human pleasures," and so he planned with loving detail and the zest of the born gardener, an ideal garden with rosemary and lavender, "roses of all kinds," and in spring "the yellow daffodil and the almond-tree in blossom."

Marvell's garden, with "its green thought in a green shade," has an exquisite simplicity; but much more elaborate are the gardens seen by Celia Fiennes in 1689, with their formal grottoes and cascades, which were now the fashion since Louis XIV's gardener "Le Notre" had visited the English Court.

Beyond the park lay the demesne and the farms and villages on the estate, and in the relations between the squire and his tenantry, much that was feudal still persisted. Sir Bevill Grenville, whose tenants loved him so much that they followed him devotedly in war, yet insisted that they should grind at his mill, while the language of Sir Simonds D'Ewes, at a Court leet of his tenants at Lavenham, is almost mediæval; he reminds them that their relation to him is a "three fold" tie, the "sacramental" one of loyalty, the "servile" one of traditional services due to him, and the "redital," or the payment of the rent into which many of these old obligations had been commuted.

# 5. *Political Activity As Popular Diversion*

---

## *Popular Involvement in Florentine Politics*
⊷ Gene A. Brucker

Deeply ingrained in the Florentine political mentality was a fundamental precept of republicanism: the formulation of policy through group consultation. The right of free and untrammeled discussion was considered one of the bulwarks of independence, and it was thus stated in the preamble to one provision: "For the conservation of liberty and welfare and for the direction of public affairs, nothing appears to be more advantageous than a free spirit (*animus liber*) in discussion." The policy debates in the *Consulte e Pratiche* protocols have a double value. Besides their substantive importance, they reveal clearly how decisions were arrived at through the sieve of intensive public debate and consultation. These deliberations were advisory only, and technically the Signoria could ignore the views of these councils. But rarely, if ever, did the priors flout the consensus of opinion expressed in these consultative assemblies. This procedure became part of the unwritten code of the city's political life.

The Florentine commitment to the solution of problems and issues through the channel of group discussion is seen even more clearly in a nonpolitical context: the deliberations of reconstruction of the cathedral church of S. Reparata. The records of the officials (*operarii*) in charge of this project indicate that every aspect of this work was the subject of intense discussion. In December 1364 the *operarii* decreed, "In order that the work of the church should proceed in future, every month a council will be convened with masters and other citizens." In accordance with this policy, the consuls of the druggists' guild were invited to send "the best and most proficient sculptors, goldsmiths

and painters in their guild to consult with them concerning the construction of the church." Although the *operarii* relied heavily upon the
counsel of the artisans, with their special knowledge of building problems, they also summoned other citizens, both lay and cleric, to these
meetings. A council of October 1367 included several merchants and
industrialists, three magnates, a judge, a priest, an innkeeper, and a
wine vendor. The atmosphere of these meetings was remarkably egali-
tarian, as citizens from all classes expressed their candid opinions on
the plans for the cathedral.

Another sentiment shared by citizens of all classes was the desire
to attain high communal office. Only the most dedicated merchant
shunned participation in communal affairs, as did Francesco Datini,
on the grounds that it was detrimental to business. Membership in
the Signoria was not only a symbol of political influence; it was also
a mark of social distinction. An indication of the high prestige value
of the Signoria was the popularity of the *prioriste*, the catalogues listing
the dates of each family's representation in the supreme executive. In
the view of some observers, the thirst for office was so intense that it
constituted a grave danger to the commune and was a principal cause
of the government's instability. The fact that some citizens resorted
to bribery to insure their inclusion among the list of eligible candidates
for the Signoria indicates that the passion for office occasionally passed
legitimate bounds. . . .

Among the motives, altruistic and egoistic, which induced citizens to
compete for office, none was more potent than self-interest. . . . Political
power was an essential prerequisite for securing private advantage. Half
the legislative proposals submitted to the councils did not pertain to
public affairs; they were petitions submitted by individuals requesting
tax exemptions, judicial dispensations, or monetary reimbursement.
Whether these petitions were accepted or rejected often depended less
on the merits of the case than on the influence which the petitioner
wielded among the council members. Men of all classes—magnate,
merchant, artisan—engaged in this quest for special benefits and favors.

## *The Excitement of an Elizabethan Election*
&§ J. E. Neale

Our . . . story concerns the Montgomeryshire election of 1588, which led
to a Star Chamber suit by the unsuccessful candidate, Arthur Price
of Vaynor, against the Sheriff, Jenkin Lloyd of Berthlloid. Hitherto,
the electoral history of this county had been peaceful. It was dominated
by one person, Edward Herbert, whose principal house was Blackhall,

just outside the borough of Montgomery. He was High Steward and Constable of Montgomery Castle, Deputy-Lieutenant to his powerful relative, the Earl of Pembroke, Justice of the Peace, and *Custos Rotulorum*. The famous Lord Herbert of Cherbury, his grandson, wrote of him in his *Autobiography*: 'My grandfather's power was so great in the country that divers ancestors of the better families now in Montgomeryshire were his servants, and raised by him. He delighted also much in hospitality; as having a very long table twice covered every meal with the best meats that could be gotten, and a very great family. It was an ordinary saying in the country at that time, when they saw any fowl rise, "Fly where thou wilt, thou wilt light at Blackhall"; which was a low building, but of great capacity, my grandfather erected in his age.' As our Star Chamber documents describe him in 1588, he was an 'ancient, grave gentleman' of seventy-five, 'a man of great wealth', 'reputed to be the best man of living and government in the shire.'

For forty years past, say these documents, he had at all times carried the voices of the freeholders in the county for himself or for such others as he thought convenient. No less complete was his control of the borough seat. He himself had sat for the county in every parliament from March 1553 to 1571, while the members in 1572, 1584, and 1586, one of whom was his son, had been elected on his nomination or at least with his approval. And so it continued with the Herbert family. With the exception of 1593, the year in which Edward Herbert died, a Herbert sat for the county until the Long Parliament.

The other Deputy-Lieutenant was John Price of Newtown, elder brother of Arthur Price, one of the candidates in 1588, and his right-hand man in that election. The family were second only to the Herberts, and in the important Hundred [political district] of Newtown were all-powerful. They, if anyone, might have broken the electoral peace of the county. But their sister, Elizabeth Price, was married to Edward Herbert, and both John and Arthur Price took their turns in parliament with the goodwill of their brother-in-law. The former represented the borough of Montgomery in 1563 and the county in 1572, while the latter sat for the borough in 1571.

So long as Elizabeth Price lived there was peace, but her death in 1588, and Herbert's old age, seem to have allowed minor factions to effect a breach between the two great families of the county. There is a degree of mystery about the initial events of the 1588 election. It looks as if at the outset Edward Herbert had no intention of standing. Had John Price coveted the seat, he could have secured it without opposition; for, if a Herbert was not available, who more inevitable than the head of the Price family? But it was quite a different matter for a younger brother to aim at representing the county. Though Arthur Price's first wife was a Bourchier, daughter of the second Earl of Bath, and though he had his elder brother's backing, in the opinion of his opponents he was 'not so fit' to be knight of the shire. It was this weakness in his candidature that gave the enemies of the Price family their chance.

When talk of an election first began, it seems that a certain Roland Pugh, who belonged to a hostile group of gentry, intended to stand in opposition. Certainly Price began his electoral campaign with this story, and appears to have had no inkling that Edward Herbert, who was an old man, a very old man by Elizabethan standards, might wish to stand. After all, he had not sat in parliament since 1571. Consequently, Price's friends and servants canvassed Herbert's kinsmen and followers, telling them that Price had secured the goodwill of the Herbert clan—of Sir Edward Herbert, lord of Powis, of Edward Herbert himself, and of his son, Richard; and many of these people promised him their voices. Indeed, when the day of election arrived, some felt so constrained by their promise, that they actually voted against their natural allegiance.

Then, suddenly, the prospect changed. Roland Pugh was obviously no match for the marshalled might of the Price family. Realizing this, their enemies, led by the Sheriff, Jenkin Lloyd, gathered to themselves all the Herbert forces by the simple and sure device of persuading the aged and perhaps senile Edward Herbert to stand himself. Jenkin Lloyd was Herbert's son-in-law, and, with Elizabeth Price dead, was probably able to make the old man his tool. The ineffective Pugh offered no difficulty. He was induced to efface himself by the gift of the borough seat, the nomination to which belonged to Herbert.

Once Edward Herbert entered the contest, its whole nature was transformed. Play fair, play foul, in Montgomeryshire a Herbert had to win. On the one side, Price was too far involved to withdraw with dignity, while on the other, the unchallenged primacy of the Herberts was at stake. This explains the tricks and ill humour of the election. It also explains—if the charge be true—Herbert's promise to save the Sheriff from all troubles and harms that might follow his behaviour.

The Sheriff made no pretence of neutrality, and took open part in the canvassing of the electorate. This was carried out in an elaborate and methodical manner. Both sides prepared careful lists, Hundred by Hundred, of the freeholders whose promises they secured. Morgan Glynn of Glynn, cousin-german to the Sheriff, a rather muddle-headed, garrulous, and therefore useful witness, told how he, together with Richard Herbert of Park and others, prepared such a list for the Hundred of Llanidlos. Sir Edward Herbert, lord of Powis, lent his support by ordering the bailiffs of his manors to canvass their freeholders. On Price's side, Oliver Lloyd of Leighton, through his servants, canvassed the most part of three hundred and eighty freeholders in three Hundreds, while a second supporter secured ninety freeholders in one of these Hundreds and one hundred and twenty in another.

They may have gone further, anticipating a notorious eighteenth-century practice by the creation of forty-shilling freeholders to swell their numbers. At any rate, one of the Sheriff's witnesses in our Star Chamber case named four voters living in his Hundred who, so far as he knew, did not possess forty-shilling freeholds, 'saving that he heard it reported that some of them had leases of John Vaughan esquire, for term of lives, colourably the day next before the election.' As we shall see, this was not the only election when such an allegation was made; but the practice was not general, nor ever on a large scale. It was a striking curiosity; little more.

The county court was to be held at Montgomery on October 26th; and as the day drew near, tension grew. Hearing of armed preparations by the other side, the Sheriff took the advice of two lawyers on the expediency of going armed to the election. He probably also consulted them about the devices open to him to secure a victory for his side. Certainly, he was prepared to resort to tricks. Several of Price's witnesses testified to hearing servants and followers of Herbert—one, for example, who wore a 'mandilion' or loose coat bestowed on him by his patron as livery—prophesy that their master would carry the election, whatever his votes and whatever the cost. If Price had a majority of a thousand, said a brother-in-law of Herbert's still Herbert would be returned; and Herbert himself was overheard reassuring a servant who told him that his freeholders were outnumbered. Some of Price's followers, on their way to the election were bade 'get them home like fools, seeing that they should not carry the knightship of the shire'; a deposition which the witness or his examiner thought too homely and forthright, for in the manuscript 'fools' is crossed out and 'unwise men' inserted in its place!

Such reports put Price on his guard. Evidently he feared that the Sheriff might try to overreach him by holding the county court at the Castle of Montgomery instead of the Shire Hall, or alternatively might seize the Shire Hall, exclude opponents, and carry the election by the acclamation of the voters within the Hall, ignoring those without. He took precautions against both possibilities. As the Sheriff and his party rode into Montgomery along the Newtown road on the eve of the election, they saw about a hundred 'light and desperate persons,' armed with swords, bucklers, forest-bills, long staves, and glaives. They were under the leadership of a captain and other officers, and paid by

Price, and were stationed between the road and the Castle. There they remained all night and part of the next day, and broke down the bridge leading to the Castle in order to prevent access to it. In the town itself another group, armed with 'divers kinds of monstrous weapons,' guarded the Shire Hall all night, ready, so an opponent said, to quarrel with any of Herbert's followers who passed amongst them.

Morgan Glynn described how that night he and the Sheriff went to bed together. He rose before daylight, and, leaving the Sheriff in his lodging in company with Richard Herbert and other gentlemen, repaired to Edward Herbert's house, Blackhall. There he found Herbert and other friends, who, accompanied by the main body of their supporters, moved off towards the Booth or Shire Hall. As they were coming down from the churchyard, they met the Sheriff's party by the Market House and halted while he made a proclamation for keeping the peace. He had just made a similar proclamation by the Shire Hall where Price and his followers were. During the halt, Richard Herbert of Llyssen, one of Edward Herbert's supporters, took a 'view' of the rival companies and reported that, although there were some three to four hundred of their men among Price's supporters at the Shire Hall, yet the company gathered round Edward Herbert was greater than that at the Hall. It so happened that at this very time one of Price's men was also taking a preliminary 'view.' He arrived at the opposite conclusion; and we may let one optimist cancel out the other.

The Sheriff returned to a hasty breakfast, after which he came to the Shire Hall, and, finding some of Price's followers standing guard over the door, armed with weapons, bade them begone and allow free entrance. He then entered the Hall, went to the bench, and caused the county court to be set and proclaimed. There were about two thousand persons present, overflowing into the streets on all sides. After certain actions had been called, the Sheriff's clerk read the election writ, whereupon the Sheriff declared its effect in English and required the freeholders to nominate and choose a knight. Some shouted 'Herbert!', others 'Price!'; and the cries were taken up by those without. Men knocked and beat the Hall with their feet, and there was such confusion, contention, and hurly-burly that the people were in great uproar and tumult. Some light and unruly persons, says Glynn, imagining that the company within had fallen to violence, rushed upon the doors, while others began to quarrel and brawl, being desperately bent and more desirous of brabblement and contention than of any civil government.

Price's side claimed that in this 'general election'—their own phrase —they easily had a preponderance of voices. They 'did in a manner clean drown the voices that cried "Herbert! Herbert!" ' Price himself put his majority at between five and six hundred. Nevertheless, the Sheriff, because, as he told the Star Chamber, the number of people was great, and being dispersedly placed, some above the Shire Hall, some below, and some on each side thereof, together with the sounding of their voices all at or about an instant, bred such confusion that he could not judge; for this reason, and because many were not forty-shilling freeholders and many were from foreign counties, he decided upon a poll. 'Gentlemen,' he said, 'I do take these voices to be equal or indifferent, and therefore I will make trial by the polls, and the readiest way I think to be thus (and so I am advised by counsel); to call the Hundreds of the shire in order, and so to make trial of the greater number.'

He can scarcely be blamed. On each side there were many unqualified persons, who for good will, as one witness put it, did cry or make voice with their friends. According to one of Price's followers, there were forty such men in Herbert's company from the parish of Montgomery alone, while a witness actually named fifty-four on Price's side from a single parish in the Hundred of Newtown, and it was implicitly admitted that there were sixty—though no more—from this Hundred. Richard Herbert of Park put the grand total of 'insufficient freeholders' and 'foreigners' present for Price at two or three hundred—an exaggeration, no doubt.

Price does not seem to have objected seriously, if at all, to a poll. For a time, owing to the disturbance outside the Hall, it was doubtful whether the election would proceed. From one of the windows the Sheriff made a proclamation for keeping the peace, and sent certain Justices out to quell the brawl. But it increased rather than diminished, and order was only restored when the most eminent men from each side went out.

Now came the arrangements for taking the poll. The Hall was cleared of all but twelve to sixteen chosen on each side to see fair play. Two gentlemen, John Price and Roland Pugh, the latter acting for Herbert, were assigned to keep the outer door of the Hall at the stair-foot, and two others, Lewis Blayney and Morgan Glynn, to keep the door at the top of the stair. Another four, chosen two from each side, with the Sheriff's clerks acting for Herbert were appointed to register the names of the voters and compile duplicate lists. The freeholders themselves were called one at a time on the instruction of the Sheriff, their names being taken from lists prepared by each candidate and handed to the Sheriff. Each Hundred had its separate list, drawn up during the canvassing and checked on the election day; each also had its party manager or managers, and it was no doubt through them that the gentlemen at the door worked. They saw that the men were forthcoming when their names were called. The voters were merely 'perused' by the Sheriff and their names registered, unless the other side challenged their qualifications, when they were sworn on the Holy Evangelist touching the yearly value of their freehold in the county, and a note set against their names to show that they had been put to the oath.

The order of calling the freeholders was a crucial question. Several suggestions were made on Price's side. One old gentleman of seventy-six, Thomas Williams of Great Wollaston in Shropshire, who had been a Justice of the Peace and High Sheriff in the county of Montgomery and had stood for parliament there, urged the Sheriff to divide the voters into two companies and so peruse and examine them by the polls—presumably taking one from each side alternately or, possibly, conducting a simultaneous, double scrutiny as was done in Wiltshire in 1559. This course he had seen used at divisions in Shropshire. Price and his leading supporters, no doubt with the idea of saving the time and trouble of a poll, offered to deduct three hundred from their number, take their company aside, and if it were still not greater than Herbert's then to pay him one hundred pounds. On the other hand, if there was to be a poll, they suggested that the Sheriff should call the electors from the Hundreds of Machynlleth and Newtown, one from each Hundred alternately; and so on throughout the county, balancing a 'Price' Hundred against a 'Herbert' Hundred. The Sheriff rejected all their proposals. It was his court, he declared, and he would proceed as pleased himself, but would do justice or else the law was open to take remedy against him.

The Sheriff justified his refusal to divide the electors into two rival companies by asserting that it would have been dangerous. Whether he entertained any such fear, is in fact quite irrelevant. His intentions, or rather, his tactics, were already decided: he was determined to call the Hundred of Machynlleth first. For excuse, he maintained that, being the furthest Hundred from the town of Montgomery, it was customary when county courts were held at that town to call actions from there first. Maybe it was; though the custom was not such common knowledge that all his own witnesses could confirm it. But parliamentary elections were not the same as legal actions. His motive was only too manifest. Machynlleth was Herbert country, where Herbert himself dwelt, and where his greatest strength in voters lay. Price's strong suit was the Hundred of Newtown. The principle of selection adopted by the Sheriff enabled him to postpone calling the Newtown freeholders until, as we shall see, he gave up calling at all.

The Sheriff's intention was first to call all the freeholders on Herbert's side from Machynlleth, and then, for anything we know to the contrary, to call Price's supporters in the same Hundred. But Price by now was in a state of revolt. Naturally, he wanted to play his best card against his opponent's; and therefore, after the first of Herbert's voters had been perused and a second called, John Price at the outer door let in a man from Newtown, whose name the clerks for his party proceeded to record. This he continued to do, letting in one from Newtown for every one from Machynlleth, until, on complaint being made, the Sheriff demanded to know what warrant Price's clerks had to keep a court there while he kept another where he sat. He ordered them to cease. For a time they persisted, but after arguments and cross-speeches the Sheriff promised to peruse Price's supporters in Machynlleth immediately after Herbert's, before going on to another Hundred; and to this Price at last yielded.

After all the names had been registered for Machynlleth, another attempt was made to have the Hundred of Newtown called; but the Sheriff insisted on calling the two adjoining Hundreds of Mathravall and Llanvilling. In one of these, Mathravall, Edward Herbert's son, Richard, lived. In the other, says Price, the number voting for him exceeded the number for Herbert by sixty. The tide was turning.

But it was now four or five o'clock on the Sunday morning, and the Sheriff had continued in the Hall, without meat, sleep, or rest, since before nine o'clock the previous morning. He had already decided to finish after the third Hundred. Seeing the day approached, he says, and being wearied by his long toil and disappointed in what he had believed to be the best course, he thought out another way of deciding the election. His 'other way' was a purely arbitrary verdict. John Price tried to dissuade him. If there were not a majority of three hundred sufficient freeholders on their side, he and all his friends, he said, would give their voices with Herbert. And when the Sheriff finished, he made a last offer, suggesting that he choose any one from five of the six remaining Hundreds, and this Hundred should end the election. The Sheriff would not yield.

A great demonstration followed. The men of Newtown, waiting with many others in the lower part of the Hall, shouted the name of their candidate, and others in the town, hearing the cry, assembled round the Hall and called out for Price. The voices for Herbert, said old Thomas Williams, were scarcely heard at all; and Price, his mortification playing havoc with his numbers, declared that there were at least fourteen hundred of his supporters there from the uncalled Hundreds, among them the greatest number of gentlemen and people of substance and valour. To these, it was a bitter humiliation that the mountain people of Machynlleth and the other two Hundreds should have such privilege and they be utterly rejected. Asked to make an indenture for

Price's election, the Sheriff refused. In the Hall—'in court and at the bar'—were a group of gentlemen and others belonging to both parties, with divers weapons, such as swords, bucklers, halberts, etc., ready, as it seemed, 'to fall by the ears and to do mischief.' There were cross-speeches and provocations. Making proclamation that every man should put away his weapons and depart, the Sheriff adjourned the court. Later he returned Herbert as knight of the shire. Price, perhaps, would have been prepared to swallow his pride and forgo his remedy at law, but the best gentlemen among his followers told him that if he took this wrong quietly at the Sheriff's hands, they, the freeholders, would never again vote for him.

# 6. The Life of the Rich Bourgeois in an Aristocratic Society

## Keeping Up with the Nobles

*ᴖ̌ Lawrence Stone*

The major business preoccupation of [Horatio Palavicino's] father Tobias in the 1560's and 70's had been the handling of the great papal monopoly of alum, that involved leasing both the mines at Tolfa and the distribution rights in north-west Europe from the principal commerical centre at Antwerp. It is as head of the Antwerp branch of this international business that Horatio Palavicino first enters into recorded history, when in 1578 he carried out a deal which was to be the cornerstone of his career. He and his associates sold their huge stock of alum to the Dutch rebels against Spain, in return for the granting of an import monopoly that would exclude the future farmers of the papal alum mines. The Dutch did not pay cash for these stocks, but bound themselves to repay the money within a few years. But since their credit was low and it was of the highest political importance for England to keep their revolt alive, it was Queen Elizabeth who actually underwrote the loan so far as the Pallavicini were concerned. The consequences of this deal were to throw Horatio Palavicino openly on to the side of England in the ensuing European struggle, to introduce him into court circles at London, and to link his financial position with the solvency of the English Crown.

As it happened, Horatio could have chosen no more favorable moment in which to offer his services to the English Government. For over a quarter of a century the great London merchant Sir Thomas Gresham had handled the complex ramifications of the Government's loan dealings, exchange juggling, and economic diplomacy. When he died in 1579 there was no other English merchant who could fill the void. London possessed men of wealth and ability, but none of the international stature and experience that was required. Palavicino saw his chance, exploited it to the full, and in a few years had stepped into the responsible position of the Government's financial agent in its continental dealings. . . . In the year 1600 Sir Horatio died, probably about sixty years of age, by now one of the richest commoners in England and rumoured to be worth £100,000. . . .

Horatio was born into a society for which there was no parallel in England. Here the pressure of social conventions had always been so strong that a merchant and a gentleman were terms universally held to be mutually incompatible. In consequence the ambition of every commercial magnate was to retire from business, purchase land, and become absorbed into the class of landed gentry who set the tone to the whole society. In Italy the situation was altogether different, and it would be highly misleading to imagine that Horatio was brought up in an atmosphere of bourgeois mediocrity. Although a merchant, Tobias was by heredity armigerous and by wealth and position a member of the refined and educated upper class. All his son's letters and actions show him to have been a man of taste and breeding. This fact is of great importance, both in providing an explanation of Horatio's extraordinarily successful career and in dispelling any illusion about a vulgar, pushful *nouveau riche* thrusting himself up into a higher stratum of society. Thus Queen Elizabeth—who was far from indifferent to the claims of birth and status—referred to Horatio in 1579, in an official letter to Cardinal Galli, as *nobilis Genuensis*. It was because of this semi-aristocratic background that Horatio was able to step naturally and without strain into the society of princes, courtiers, and ambassadors, upon his intimate relations with whom he contrived to build his fortune. Alone of the great financiers of the age, with the exception of old Anton Fugger, he was the friend as well as the servant of the kings and magnates upon whose financial necessities he preyed. Another consequence of his inherited social position was the manner in which he spent the money he acquired. He avoided both the squalid Volpone miserliness of his Cambridgeshire neighbour Thomas Sutton, and the vulgar ostentation of the London magnate Sir John Spencer. He enjoyed to the full all the luxuries that money could buy, but he never indulged in the cheap pleasure of showing off. Thus though frequently hated, he was never despised or ridiculed. . . .

Palavicino . . . held a position of some considerable political and social prominence, deeply engaged in affairs of state of the highest responsibility and secrecy, and partaking in some of the obligations of court life which were the privilege of few save the hereditary aristocracy and personal favourites of the queen. In the eyes of his con-

temporaries he was no mere merchant financier, but a courtier, a gentleman, and a member of the governing class.

Palavicino's personal friendships and domestic life go some way
to confirm this estimate of his status. For the greater part of his life
he remained unmarried, and we know nothing of his private affairs
during this period, except that in about 1578 he became the acknowledged father of an illegitimate son, Edward, who appears to have been
educated under his care, and perhaps under his roof. If he had any close
friends during this period of the 70's and 80's, no trace of their correspondence has survived, and such personal relationships as have
left their mark are with fellow Italians. He appears to have been
genuinely devoted to his brother Fabritio, and he claimed that another
Genoese gentleman, Prospero Spinola, was a very close friend. It is
noticeable, moreover, that at least two of his servants in his London
house were Italians. His relations with Englishmen appear mainly on
the official level, and only Sir Edward Stafford, the English ambassador
in Paris, speaks of him with any genuine warmth and affection. But in
1591, while in Germany on his second diplomatic mission, Horatio
made a decision of fundamental importance: on 27 April Lord Burghley carefully noted in his diary: 'Sir Horatio Pallavicino marryed at
Frankford.' . . .

The sober reasons which impelled Horatio to marry are not very
hard to find. He was by now a man of great wealth and had begun to
build up an estate in the country by means of judicious land purchases.
A legitimate heir was essential if this fortune was to be preserved and
handed down intact. Secondly the attraction of the dowry that went
with the bride was probably not without its appeal. There were, moreover, more intimate reasons for marriage. He was by now suffering severely
from gout and arthritis, and no doubt felt himself in need of the care
and devotion of a woman. More intimate still, his doctor a few months
before had pointed out to him the well-known fact that sexual intercourse was a most useful prophylactic against those pains of arthritis
from which he was suffering, an argument which Horatio—unlike
Falstaff—used as a reason for matrimony. All these were surely arguments the cogency of which even the queen would be obliged to admit.
The only two possible objections that could be raised against the match
were the wide disparity of age between bride and groom and the fact
that Horatio was marrying below him into a family of *nouveaux riches*.
For Horatio's bride was unfortunately not a Fugger, though rumor was
correct in saying that she was the daughter of a wealthy merchant
prince. Her name was Anna Hooftman and her father was a rich
burgher of Antwerp, Gielis van Eychelberg, *alias* Giles Hooftman. . . .

Anna's life with Horatio cannot have been a very happy one. When she accepted Horatio in 1591 he was still a courtier, and no doubt she had looked forward to a gay social life in London. Cut off from her family and friends, isolated in an alien country-side in the wet lands round Cambridge, involved in Horatio's unpopularity with many of the neighbouring gentry, and burdened with an elderly and crippled husband to nurse and comfort, it is not surprising if as early as 1593 she was a prey to melancholia and was suffering from insomnia and loss of appetite. Nor can she be blamed if at the earliest possible moment after Horatio's death she should have married again, this time to a gay, extravagant young spark who could give her all those things of which she had hitherto been deprived.

The household that established itself in the early 90's in the newly purchased manor at Babraham near Cambridge was a highly cosmopolitan one. There, keeping up a style of living 'fit for the greatest state in England' dwelt the aged Italian financier, now crippled with gout and arthritis, his young Dutch wife, and numbers of servants, some of whom were Italians. Indeed this retention of alien trappings is highly characteristic of Palavicino. Though a highly skilled and fluent linguist, he never learnt to write anything but Italian, or at a pinch French. This lack of mastery of writing the language was of little importance when dealing with the old school of cultured statesmen. Walsingham, Burghley, or the queen were perfectly at home in most European languages. Robert Cecil, on the other hand, had difficulty, particularly as his Italian tutor, whom Horatio had thoughtfully provided for him, found the lessons interrupted during the Armada crisis of 1588 and consequently departed. And so for the benefit of the less well-educated younger generation like the Earl of Essex, Horatio took the trouble to write French, while on one occasion at least 'for better comprehension' he tried his hand at English, being careful to add: 'I beg you to pay no attention to the mistakes but only to the substance.' As for Anna, the recipients of her correspondence in her most ungrammatical French must have found her lack of grasp of languages a real problem.

But if the household was alien in one sense, in all others it conformed strictly to the type of that of the English country gentleman. For all this cosmopolitan air, the family partook of the local gatherings, such as weddings and christenings, they busied themselves with the rustic pleasures of sheepshearing, they baptized their three children Henry, Toby, and Baptina in the little church in the park beside the house. Only in his rather strict views on education did Horatio differ noticeably from his country neighbours. When offered a schoolmaster, he replied that he wanted to know more about the man: 'his age, his habilitye to teach the Accidence & the grammer ... for singinge and playinge I will have no use at all, but of the wrightinge I wilbe carefull.' . . .

His intellectual qualities were never called into question. Friend and enemy alike, from the Pope and Philip II to Burghley and Queen Elizabeth, were agreed upon his quick perception, his shrewd judgement, and his tactical skill. In commerce, finance, and diplomacy he was equally outstanding. His estimates of personality were on the whole extremely sound—witness his opinion of the worth of Sir Edward Stafford, the ambassador in Paris, or his character sketches of the German princes. Nor were his interests exclusively confined to material affairs. He possessed, so a panegyrist relates, command of six languages —presumably Latin, Italian, French, Dutch, German, and English— and from his cosmopolitan education, wide travels, and extensive acquaintance he was more a citizen of Europe than that of any one country.

# 7. Poverty and Insecurity in Town and Country

## Town Life
ی M. St. Clare Byrne

THE LONDON SLUMS. Overcrowding had already begun to create slums. Nothing creates a slum quarter more quickly than old houses that have come down in the world. The palace that was originally designed for some nobleman and his enormous establishment becomes first the tenement house and then the rabbit-warren, the plague spot, crowded from garret to cellar with dirty, poverty-stricken wretches. The tide of fashion, ebbing westwards, had left stranded many such city houses. Elizabeth tried to enforce the rule of "one house one family," but not even a Tudor could arrest this inevitable process, whilst others of her measures literally forced such cohabitation upon the poorest section of the community. Elizabeth, and James after her, feared the natural growth of London, feared the growth of the City's power; and their legislation forbade the erection of new buildings upon hitherto unoccupied sites in the City, and also within a three mile radius beyond the gates. A letter written in 1602 really gives the whole situation in a nutshell: "The Council have lately spied a great inconvenience, of the increase of housing within and without London, by building over stables, in gardens, and other odd corners; whereupon they have taken order to have them pulled down; and this week they have begun almost in every parish to light on the unluckiest, here and there one, *which, God knows, is far from removing the mischief."*

Gardens and open spaces admittedly there were throughout the length and breadth of Elizabethan London. They helped to sweeten the air in slum localities, but, as the letter just quoted admits, they

were being encroached upon, so that the bad condition of the streets
of the town intensified the evils resulting from the bad housing conditions. Except for its two or three main thoroughfares London was
a network of narrow, badly paved lanes, half darkened by the over-
hanging fronts of the houses, and rendered wholly unsavoury by the
unpleasant habit which prevailed of depositing all the garbage in the
kennel or in front of one's door. Some of these lanes were not even
paved; the Strand, for example, not until Elizabeth's time. In such
parts the pedestrian picked his way along a trodden, rutted soil,
"soaked," says one modern sanitary authority, "with the filth of centuries." When one of the plague's many visitations occurred the city
authorities would bestir themselves and order every citizen to make a
bonfire in front of his house and burn his own rubbish three times a
week at seven o'clock in the evening. In 1563 the Mayor and Council
even asserted themselves so far as to order that "the filthy dunghill
lying in the highway near unto Finsbury Court be removed and carried
away"; they further instructed the inhabitants that their monstrous
garbage heap was not to be renewed. Even so, in spite of these spas-
modic efforts, the filth and mud of these lanes in wet weather and their
stench in the summer was indescribable. The very names of some of
them are horribly suggestive: Chick Lane near Smithfield, Stow notes,
was popularly known as Stinking Lane.

At nightfall each householder was supposed to hang up a lantern
for the benefit of the passers-by; but even when this ordinance was
strictly observed these very primitive affairs, with their thick, dis-
coloured horn panes and their guttering candles, did little to reveal
either the condition of the path underfoot or the lurking assailant,
crouching in the deep shadow, and as willing to cut a throat as a purse.
A prudent body preferred not to go unaccompanied after dark, and the
habit of hiring link-boys or of equipping servants with torches to light
the way was general. Gallants who had spent a convivial evening at
the tavern would hire one of the drawers to carry a lantern and light
them home. . . .

NIGHTLIFE. The literature of the day abounds in sketches of
town life and character. From the gallant to the water carrier the Londoners jostle their way through the pamphlets, the comedies, the
ballads and the broadsides; the realistic impulse in letters was not slow
to make use of the motley crowd of them. Naturally the result was by
no means always literature; this impulse turned first and foremost, as
it generally does, to the exploitation of the sordid and the sensational.
But the picture, if crudely limned, is nevertheless a vivid one. If we
know Paul's Walk, the theatres, and the taverns, we need have no
diffculty in peopling them. Individual after individual steps forth,

naïvely assertive and self-confident—brave or sorry, each cuts a figure and challenges our attention. Just so must they have challenged the gaze of many an honest countryman, setting foot in the city for the first time. If in imagination we may follow such a one as he wanders from street to street, seeing "the sights" of London, we shall find ourselves rubbing shoulders with them all, may watch them intent upon their lawful—and unlawful—occasions. . . .

The noise of the town which has surrounded him all day seemed to be lessening. The sun was getting low; every one seemed to have gone indoors. There was a creaking above his head; he looked up and saw another swinging tavern sign; he pushed open the door and went in for his supper.

Inside all was bustle and confusion. From upstairs came the noise of a roystering party in one of the private rooms, and in the large parlour that he had entered men were supping or drinking in small groups, while busy drawers ran to and fro with glasses and tankards, wine and ale, responding invariably to impatient customers' calls with their "Anon! Anon, sir!" In one corner a company of some half-dozen men were listening to a tall fellow who was reading a play aloud. He sat down at the table nearest to them, watching them as they commented gravely or boisterously on the matter and the manner and made suggestions to the reader. Each had a cup of wine before him, but their meeting was obviously a business one, and the drink did not circulate freely. Listening to their discussion he realized that they were players, and that they were considering a new play. Parts were being apportioned by the tall man as he read, and details of stage business were being discussed. The countryman ate his supper, and listened hard as their voices rose and fell; he was surprised at their quietness and at the small amount of wine consumed. He had believed that these players were troublesome rogues, but this little group was the most serious in the room, and the man who was reading might well, by his clothing and his general sobriety of demeanour, have been taken in any assembly for a prosperous merchant; evidently, however, he was the chief actor in the company, and when the little group finally dispersed, the countryman noticed that it was he who paid the reckoning, two shillings in all.

When the players had gone he turned his attention to another table, where two smartly dressed fellows, who were plying their companion with more than his fair share of the drink, had just summoned one of the drawers to fetch them dice and "a pair of cards." He watched them as they fell to play. The young man seemed to be winning most of the stakes, in spite of the fact that he was manifestly drunk while the other two were quite sober. He was just preparing to settle his own score and leave the tavern, when he noticed that the players' luck was beginning to change; they were at the dice, and the young man who had been winning was now losing every cast. His opponents' throws were amazing; they had already more than retrieved their losses, and the countryman felt convinced they must be using false dice. He gazed keenly to see if he could detect any sleight of hand, but the gamesters, if cheats, were too skillful both for him and for their victim; he could see nothing suspicious. Then his attention was distracted by the entry of two boisterous serving men. They called for drink, kissed the hostess, cursed the drawer for his slowness, and began a vivid narration of a scene they had just witnessed. A young girl had committed suicide in the town-ditch by Moorfields, and they had seen men drawing out the drowned body as they came by.

When they had told their tale the countryman glanced again at his neighbours, but they were gone, and the next moment the two serving men seated themselves at the adjoining table, saluting him in a friendly fashion. Taking advantage of their already loosened tongues and obvious readiness to talk he opened the subject of false dice and cheating at cards. The serving men became voluble at once. There were false dice everywhere, they informed him; there were regular workshops for their production in the King's Bench and the Marshalsea prisons; they could even be bought by any would-be cheater. "Bird in Holborn is the finest workman," one of them interpolated. A favourite device, they told him, was to set a small bristle on one face of a dice, which effectually prevented that face from lying on the table when it fell; another trick was to hollow out one side for the same purpose. From false dice they went on to roguery in general, and the countryman listened with delight— here at last was the London of the conny-catching pamphlets and the ballads, the city where wickedness and cozening stalked the streets. They told him how highway robbers took refuge in the Counters, and how thieves and strumpets could lodge for the night in the prisons on paying fourpence to the gaolers, in order to escape the searches that were made for them by the watch. Then they told him of the places where the rogues of the city were harboured—the Falcon in Grace Street, the Gun at Billingsgate, the Rose at Fleet Bridge, Muggleston's House in Whitechapel, the Pressing Iron in Southwark, and the Bear and Ragged Staff at Charing Cross. The countryman was particularly thrilled at their mention of this last; he had passed it himself, that very afternoon, little guessing the kind of inmates it lodged.

Eager to hear more of this underworld of London, the countryman plied them with a cup of wine apiece, and each vied with the other to produce a more amazing yarn than the last speaker. What astonished their enthralled auditor most, however, was the account they gave him of a training school for thieves, set up at Smart's Quay, so they averred, by one Wotton: "There was a school house set up to teach young boys to cut purses. There was hung up two devices, one a pocket, the other a purse. The pocket had in it certain counters, and was hung about with hawks' bells, and over the top did hang a little scaring bell, and he that could take out a counter without any noise was allowed to be a public hoyster, and he that could take a piece of silver out of the purse, without the noise of any of the bells, he was adjudged a judicial nipper."

The countryman would willingly have listened longer, but the tavern was emptying and his acquaintances offered to put him on his homeward way and see him safely past the watch if he would accompany them. They set out through the dark streets, guiding their steps by a lantern that one of the men had brought with him. Light gleamed occasionally through chinks in doors and window shutters, but most of the houses were already in darkness. Every now and then they passed small parties hurrying home, armed like themselves with lanterns or else with flaring torches. Suddenly one of the men stepped aside and drew the countryman and his companion after him into the darkness of a tiny alley between tall houses. They heard a heavy trampling, and round the corner came the watch armed with their brown bills and a lantern each. Two people, coming in the opposite direction, ran straight into their arms, almost in front of the alley where the three were hidden. "Who goes there?" demanded the constable, and the watch gathered round, holding up their lanterns to get a better view of the night-walkers. "Where have you been so late?" was the next demand, whereupon the hidden watchers heard a woman's voice reply, "At supper, forsooth, with my uncle here, and he is bringing me home." "Are you married?" then came from the constable. "Yes, forsooth," was the reply, and after a few more questions the two were allowed to pass on. Then when the watch too had left the coast clear the three slipped out of their alley mouth and sped on homewards. In Cheapside they parted, and after much knocking at the door of his inn our countryman eventually roused a sleepy ostler, who admitted him with many grumbles and provided him with a candle. A few minutes more and he was in bed, and as he pulled the clothes over him he heard steps coming down the street. Chime after chime rang out from the city churches, and as he settled his head on his pillow the voice of the watchman floated up to him: "Twelve o'clock, look well to your lock, your fire and your light, and so good night."

## *The Magnitude of French Poverty*

ఆ§ *Cecile Augon*

It is impossible to conceive the mental suffering of good men in that cruel age, since even the laconic catalogue of its everyday events inspire more pity and terror than the most Aristotelian of tragedies. Fear was upon every side. There was no safety from men more inhuman than demons, and those who died by the sword and by pestilence were accounted happy by the survivors. As the [seventeenth] century advanced, infection spread gradually from class to class, so that by 1709, that year in which plague, floods and want united to cut France away from among the nations, the old King himself was fain to sell his gold plate and eat the bread of famine in his fast emptying palace.

At first only the poor had suffered. Next, the merchants were ruined. Destitution then spread to the country nobles, many of whom begged their bread in vain along the deserted roads. Finally, those among the rich who had freely spent their substance in feeding the starving, were themselves reduced to the last stage of destitution. Even love of pleasure died of inanition, for people who danced through half the century were compelled to "go softly," when even in the treasury there was no money left. The very framework and safeguards of society were destroyed. Marriage- and funeral-registers were not kept for long periods in certain places. Legitimacy could not be proved, and heirs were unable to claim their inheritance in those rare instances when the wars had left them any to inherit.

The causes of this universal agony were very numerous, and only too well calculated to work as it were into each other's hands.

The wars of religion had effectually emptied the exchequer. During the siege of Paris in 1590, a census was taken of the number of people to be provided for, and the returns showed that the city contained 260,000 people of whom 3000 were refuges from the country. Two months later it was ascertained that of these 123,000 were penniless, while 7000 had money, but could find no bread to buy. The Government could devise no remedy for national poverty, except increased taxation. Of such taxes, that on salt was the most onerous. Each family was forced to buy salt in proportion to the number of its members, at a very high price, and peasants living near the sea were forbidden to use sea-water for cooking.

By 1684, the salt tax had amounted to 26,000,000 livres; that known as the *taille* to 38,000,000 livres, and on the Revocation of the Edict of Nantes, both increased yearly, although the population itself had decreased by one-tenth. As early as 1634, the estates of Normandy complained that "the *taille* has increased to such a point that the poor have been deprived of their very shirts, and in many places women cannot go to church for lack of all clothing." Persons unable to pay were deprived of everything they possessed. When their horses had been taken, the peasants made a last effort to carry on agriculture by dragging their carts themselves. . . .

Warfare was almost continuous throughout the first part of the century. No sooner had the country begun to recover from the effects of the religious struggle, than the Thirty Years' War again plunged it into misery. The French period lasted from about 1635 to 1643, and constant rebellions connected this series of disasters with those of the Fronde, which extended from 1648 to 1653.

All parts of the country were affected, but Lorraine and Picardy suffered more severely, because they were frontier provinces, and thus fell a ready prey to the unspeakable cruelty of the "allies" that each party summoned in turn. In 1632 the Franche-Comté was laid waste by Gaston, and in 1636 Lorraine was devastated by a horde of Swedes, while Picardy fell a prey to a Spanish army. It should be stated that the rapacity of the armies was partly due to the fact that they were never paid. Rosen-Worms, the successor of Erlach, himself writes: "It is now five years since I received either my pay or my pension, so that I have to live like a beggar, and can neither keep a proper table nor dress my servants." The plague, which had broken out in 1606 and 1623, raged without intermission from Easter 1630 to Easter 1635. During that period 600,000 persons met with an unnatural death in Lorraine alone. 1650 was the worst year of the pestilence ever known, and a large number of persons succumbed to the disease, owing to physical degeneration. Most of them had never enjoyed proper or sufficient food, although they toiled all day and nearly all right. The corn was trampled down or stolen by marauding soldiers, who killed the husbandmen, until at last there was no corn left to sow. All through this long period there was great scarcity, but the worst famines occurred in 1631, 1633, 1635, 1648, 1652, 1660, and 1662. In 1651 and 1657 there were terrible floods, and in the latter year so great cold, that the few remaining vines were frozen and the cattle died. In 1709 carts could drive over the Seine and the drinking-water on the royal sideboards froze. Bottles brought up from the kitchen were covered with icicles. Wolves entered villages in broad daylight and carried off women and children. Travellers reaching lonely hamlets and hoping for entertainment found the deserted houses tenanted by wild beasts come to devour the bodies of the dead inhabitants.

The price of food rose ever higher. The day-book of one Hugues Bois de Chesne, citizen of Montbéliard, contains a chart of the prices of corn, beginning in 1618 and carried on through the worst years of famine. The climax occurs in 1636, when the writer states that "on Saturday, 15th September, corn may not be bought for money." In 1652, bread in Paris cost one écu the loaf. In Lorraine the poor were thankful to have acorns and roots and grass to eat. After 1659 corn became cheaper again, but it took many years for normal conditions to be re-established all over the country.

The universal confusion resulting from such a state of things beggars description. The excellent account of it in M. Feillet's *Misère au temps de la Fronde et Saint Vincent de Paul*, or the grim and cruel engravings of Jacques Callot, furnish one with a picture of the vast wilderness that France then was. But perhaps the most faithful because the simplest descriptions occur in the *Relations* published by the Estates of Normandy and other provinces, or by the missionaries sent by Saint Vincent de Paul into the worst districts. Much valuable information is also to be found in the letters of the Abbess of Port-Royal. For instance, on 16th July 1652, she writes: "People massacre each other daily with every sort of cruelty. . . . The soldiers steal from one another when they have denuded every one else, and as they spoil more property than they carry off, they are themselves often reduced to starvation, and can find no more to annex. All the armies are equally undisciplined and vie with one another in lawlessness. The authorities in Paris are trying to send back the peasants to gather in the corn; but as soon as it is reaped the marauders come to slay and steal, and disperse all in a general rout."

In January 1649 she writes: "This poor country is a horrible sight; it is stripped of everything. The soldiers take possession of the farms and have the corn threshed, but will not give a single grain to the owners who beg it as an alms. It is impossible to plough. There are no more horses—all have been carried off. The peasants are reduced to sleeping in the woods and are thankful to have them as a refuge from murderers. And if they only had enough bread to half satisfy their hunger, they would indeed count themselves happy." With regard to the famine bread she says to her Sisters: "I send you a piece of the bread the poor eat, so that you may see to what extremities they are reduced. We do nothing but see poor people who come and tell us that they have not tasted food for two or three days, while others say they have been living on cabbages boiled without salt. I beg you to show this bread to our Sisters, so that they may do all in their power to cut down their own expenses, as I have so often enjoined on you. [Let us do this] so that we may not ourselves need succour at the expense of the poor" (March 1652).

In Paris itself even greater misery prevailed. The agreement made by nearly all the armies to respect the district lying within a radius of ten miles of the capital had not been fulfilled. At Sussy, for instance, the inhabitants had put their household goods into the church for safety, but the Lorraine marauders broke in and destroyed everything. Madame de la Guette, who witnessed the episode, says that they wantonly ripped up the beds, so that one could walk up the nave on feathers reaching half-way up one's legs.

Refugees flocked in from the country, and in 1652 there were 100,000 beggars in the capital. These persons mostly slept in the streets, and the mortality among them was very great. In six faubourgs there were 12,000 destitute families. "I have seen," says La Porte, "on the bridge at Meulun ... three children crawling over their dead mother, one of them still trying to derive food from her."

Armed affrays constantly took place in the dark streets, and the police were quite unable to control the mob. As late as 1709, Monseigneur the Dauphin was attacked on his way from the Opera by a crowd demanding bread. So threatening was its attitude that the royal escort was afraid to force a way through. The prince himself flung handfuls of money into the crowd, and fluently promised everything demanded. The only result of this episode was that the Dauphin did not dare to show himself in Paris for a considerable time, since he was not willing, nor indeed able, to carry out the promises wrung from him in a moment of danger. . . .

Among the many accounts of the state of things found by Saint-Vincent's workers, the following is typical. It is from that part of the *Relations* of 1651, which refers to Saint-Quentin. "Of the 450 sick persons whom the inhabitants were unable to relieve, 200 were turned out, and these we saw die one by one as they lay on the roadside. A large number still remain, and to each of them it is only possible to dole out the least scrap of bread. We only give bread to those who would otherwise die. The staple dish here consists of mice, which the inhabitants hunt, so desperate are they from hunger. They devour roots which the animals cannot eat; one can, in fact, not put into words the things one sees ... This narrative, far from exaggerating, rather understates the horror of the case, for it does not record the hundredth part of the misery in this district. Those who have not witnessed it with their own eyes cannot imagine how great it is. Not a day passes but at least 200 people die of famine in the two provinces. We certify to having ourselves seen herds, not of cattle, but of men and women, wandering about the fields between Rheims and Rhétel, turning up the earth like pigs to find a few roots; and as they can only find rotten ones, and not half enough of them, they become so weak that they have not strength left to seek food. The parish priest at Boult, whose letter we enclose, tells us he has buried three of his parishioners who died of hunger. The rest subsisted on chopped straw mixed with earth, of which they composed a food which cannot be called bread. Other persons in the same place lived on the bodies of animals which had died of disease, and which the curé, otherwise unable to help his people, allowed them to roast at the presbytery fire."

# 8. *Popular Aspects of Army Life*

## *The Extramilitary Activities of Cromwell's Army*
### ❧ *C. H. Firth*

THE ABUSES OF QUARTERING. To prevent open breaches of capitulations and open robbery was not difficult for Cromwell and his officers. It was not so easy, however, to prevent less public breaches of good order, and petty oppression or violence, though that too was attempted. As soldiers were usually quartered in private houses their misbehaviour in their quarters was a continual cause of complaint. Since no barracks existed offences of this kind were bound to occur with great frequency, but every effort was made to put a stop to them. In the reports of the courts held at Dundee there are many examples of punishments inflicted with this object. For instance, a Scotchman living near Dundee complained that there came into his house 'one Richard Walton, a dragoon with six others to quarter; after they had supped, . . . the said dragoon, being full of drink, sent the servants out for drinks, and afterwards beat several of the servants, insomuch that they durst not stay in the house, but were forced to quit it, by which means wanting fire and other accommodations the said dragoon caused the locks of the doors and other wood about the house to be burnt.' Walton was sentenced for this to ride the wooden horse 'with two muskets at each heel, and two pint stoups about his neck.' One soldier was complained of for abusing his host's mother, terming her 'old jade and old witch'; another for saying playfully when his landlady's child cried, 'that he would boil it, and that it would make good broth.' Such occurrences are but examples of what must have occurred in innumerable cases of which nothing is recorded. When the soldiers were unpaid and forced to take free quarters, or to pay for their lodgings in paper tickets instead of in money, the burden on the inhabitants was

253

heavier still, and misconduct was more common. But even when they paid for their quarters and conducted themselves tolerably well soldiers were not agreeable guests for a house-holder. 'My house,' wrote a gentleman in 1647, 'is, and hath been full of soldiers this fortnight, such uncivil drinkers and thirsty souls that a barrel of good beer trembles at the sight of them, and the whole house is nothing but a rendezvous of tobacco and spitting.'

The misbehaviour of regiments on the march from place to place is also often mentioned. The conduct of the old regiments of the regular army was generally good during their marches, for their officers kept them under proper control. But from 1646 to 1649 there were continual complaints from the West of England of the plunderings and outrages committed by the new regiments raised for service in Ireland. A letter written from Cheshire about May 1649 says that the oppression that county suffered from these new raised forces on their way to Ireland was intolerable. 'Several regiments having of late marched through our parts take free quarter, though we are nothing in arrear in our assessments; ten, fifteen and twenty are quartered together in a poor man's house; and when we bring them good beef, bacon, cheese, butter, and other good fare, they tell us they must have such joints of mutton and veal, with poultry, tobacco, and strong beer provided for them. Some of the abler sort give them considerable sums of money to quarter elsewhere, which no sooner done but they go to the next village, and get there perchance as much if not more, and so impoverish the country.' Fairfax issued a severe proclamation against these disorders, confessing that soldiers on their march for Ireland 'have and still do harass, plunder and act great violences and insolences in the country,' and ordering all officers and soldiers that quartered in or near such places to assist the country people in the forcible repression of such outrages. . . .

POACHING AND MARRIAGE. There were two minor breaches of discipline very prevalent amongst the soldiers of the period which must be mentioned in any account of life in the army. One was poaching, the other marriage without leave. The propensity of the soldiers for poaching, noticeable in 1647 and 1648, came to its height in 1649. On 5th September, in that year, Fairfax published a proclamation against it. 'Daily complaints are made,' said he, 'that some disorderly soldiers under my command, contrary to the laws of the nation and discipline of the army, have and still do commit very great outrages and riots, with their arms, entering into parks, chases, and warrens, and thence stealing all sorts of deer and conies, menacing the death of the keepers, and all such who any ways oppose them.' In future, therefore, all field-officers and captains were desired 'that forthwith they cause to be taken from their soldiers, all such hounds, greyhounds, and other dogs which may any ways be hurtful to deer or conies.' Soldiers, moreover, were not to enter any park or warren or to pass through it without a written permission from their officer, and any future transgressors were to be punished in an exemplary manner.

These measures were apparently successful, at least little or nothing is heard of this particular offence in England after 1649. But it appears once more amongst the army of the occupation in Scotland. It is evident that the British privates of the period had a taste for sport. In 1653 the commander-in-chief in Scotland issued a proclamation which recited that soldiers 'do straggle at a great distance from their colours with their muskets, and kill and destroy rabbits belonging to warrens and house-pigeons,' and prohibited the practice as 'contrary to the laws of Scotland, dishonourable to the discipline of the army, and the cause of frays with the country people.' Soldiers, however, could obtain leave to go shooting. In Monck's *Order-Book* there is a pass for a private in his own regiment 'to carry a fowling-piece for the killing of fowls for his game, provided he kill no tame pigeons and rabbits.' Such passes are frequent, and in one order hares and partridges are added to the list of exceptions. In another order Monck prohibits the regiment in garrison at Dundee from keeping more than two greyhounds per company.

As to the other point, the marriage of soldiers, there were originally no restrictions imposed upon it. A large proportion of the rank and file must have been married men, especially so long as the army was recruited by the process of impressment. The wives and the widows of soldiers are frequently mentioned, and soldiers absent on foreign service were sometimes allowed to assign a portion of their pay for the support of their wives and families. In many cases the wives of the soldiers followed their husbands to Ireland, Scotland or Jamaica, and were encouraged to do so, because they were regarded as the best nurses for the sick and wounded. There are even authentic instances of women who enlisted as soldiers to follow their husbands or lovers. In 1657 the colonel commanding the garrison of Ayr reports that a young Lincolnshire woman, named Anne Dymoke, had served for some weeks past in the ranks of his regiment. 'I can perceive,' he adds, 'nothing but modesty in her carriage since she has been with us.' A ballad written in 1655, called 'The Gallant She-Soldier,' celebrates the prowess of a lady who served some years in the same regiment as her husband under the name of Mr Clarke. Incidentally the ballad shows what the usual amusements of the soldiers were.

*With musket on her shoulder, her part she acted then,*
*And every one supposed that she had been a man;*
*Her bandeleers about her neck, and sword hang'd by her side,*
*In many brave adventures her valour have been tried.*

*For exercising of her armes, good skill indeed had she,*
*And known to be as active as any one could be,*
*For firing of a musket, or beating of a drum,*
*She might compare assuredly with any one that come.*

*For other manly practices she gain'd the love of all,*
*For leaping and for running or wrestling for a fall,*
*For cudgels or for cuffing, if that occasion were,*
*There's hardly one of ten men that might with her compare.*

*Yet civill in her carriage and modest still was she,*
*But with her fellow souldiers she oft would merry be;*
*She would drink and take tobacco, and spend her money too,*
*When as occasion served, that she had nothing else to do.*

At last the secret is betrayed, and her military career interrupted by the birth of a young soldier (July 1655). The ballad concludes with the following advertisement:

"All that are desirous to see the young souldier and his mother, let them repair to the sign of the Blacksmith's Arms in East Smithfield, neere unto Tower Hill in London, and inquire for Mr Clarke, for that was the woman's name.'

The causes which led to the restraint of marriage in the army seem to have been entirely political. As soon as Cromwell's first campaign in Scotland was over and the army went into winter quarters, marriage set in. A letter from Edinburgh dated 1st December 1650 says that 'our English lads and Scotch lasses' begin to marry with great frequency. 'So that there is scarce a day but the bagpipes are heard at a marriage; some private soldiers have married knights and lairds' daughters, and others of them marry maid servants of the great citizens of Edinburgh who are absent, so that we are like to stock ourselves of a new generation.' After the second campaign, when Scotland was practically subdued, this epidemic commenced again. On 16th October 1651 the governor of Edinburgh and Leith issued a stringent order that no soldier in his regiment should 'presume to be married to any woman in or of Scotland' without the consent of the governor, deputy-governor, or major of the regiment in writing. If he did he was to be cashiered from the regiment, and the minister who performed the ceremony was to be brought before a court-martial.

The reason for this severity was apparently the fear lest these Scottish wives might make Royalists of their husbands, or give intelligence of military movements to the Scots still in arms.

In Ireland the same thing happened. The Cromwellian soldiers long before the war ended began to intermarry with the Irish women. To a Puritan a Papist was little better than a pagan, and, indeed, much more dangerous. Ireton, the commander-in-chief, published on 1st May 1651 a proclamation against all such marriages. 'I judge it to be displeasing to God,' he declared, 'to join in near relations with the people of such abominations, persons whose principles have led them to the shedding of so much innocent blood as they have done.' It was also, he said, 'a great hazard to the cause and work we are engaged in.' Men faithful before their marriages might be 'led aside by such temptations as they have thereby run themselves into, either to the deserting or betraying their trust.' At all events their union with the enemies of the cause justly rendered such men objects of suspicion. These Irish women, it was true, pretended to be converts to Protestantism, but the general feared it was 'only for some corrupt and carnal ends.'... And the result of these marriages generally was that the children became Irish in feeling and education and forgot their father's language. A pamphleteer, writing in 1697, laments over the number of children of Oliver's soldiers then in Ireland who could not speak a word of English....

THE SOLDIERS' RELIGIOSITY. It is often said that in Cromwell's army every man had a Bible in his knapsack, and some sceptical persons, struck by the inherent improbability of this statement, have asserted that what they carried was the little *Soldiers' Pocket Bible*. There is no evidence in favour of either statement, and much that contradicts both. If the soldiers habitually carried Bibles, the officers of the army in Ireland would not have made the following petition to Parliament in June 1651.

'And lastly, that in regard your poore souldiers there have few to instruct them in the feare of the Lord, who alone (not for your sakes, but for the iniquity of the inhabitants, and his owne free mercy to you) hath hitherto beene your strength in the three nations, this honourable councell would be pleased freely to bestowe upon them four thousand Bibles, or to every six men one, which would not cost above £500, to reade in their tents or quarters, which would probably prevent a greate deale of idlenesse, and, through the blessing of the Lord, might doe much good amongst the poore ignorant souldiers and natives; especially comeing from you, who I am sure, of any generation since the world beganne, have cause to sanctifie God as your strength and praise by all meanes possible.'

The request was acceded to and some Bibles were sent. On 3rd August 1652 Bibles were ordered to be issued by the commissary of stores to the several companies of foot and troops of horse within the precinct of Dublin, one Bible to every file. On the 17th of the same month a hundred Bibles were issued for the use of the forces in the precinct of Galway, for the propagation of the Gospel. The commissaries of musters were ordered to see that these books were periodically accounted for by the officers of the troops and companies. . . .

Much better founded is the popular view that the Parliamentary soldiers were great psalm singers. Sir Henry Slingsby describes how before the battle of Marston Moor began the Roundheads in Marston cornfield fell to singing Psalms, and Lord Saye mentions the 'psalm of praise sung to God after the victory.'

Vicars in his *Parliamentary Chronicle* relates an incident which took place during the fight.

'In the rout of the enemy, and in their flying and scattering about, many of them ran most frightedly and amazedly to the place where some of the regiments of horse of the Parliament side were standing on their guard, and all or most of their riders were religiously singing of Psalms, to whom as the aforesaid runawayes of the enemy came near and by their singing of Psalms perceiving who they were, they all most fiercely fled back again, and cryed out, "God damn them, they had like to have been taken by the Parliament Roundheads." For they only knew them, I say, to be the Parliament soldiers by their singing of Psalmes. A blessed badge and cognisance indeed.'

To take another instance, a Royalist account of the second battle of Newbury says, "the rebels came singing of psalms.' Best known of all, thanks to Carlyle, is Captain Hodgson's story how Cromwell, chasing the flying Scots after Dunbar, called a halt and sang the hundred and seventeenth psalm.

Equally well founded is the popular view that a good deal of the preaching done in the Cromwellian army was done by the soldiers themselves. . . .

Such unauthorized preaching was prohibited by law when the New Model was first established. On 25th April 1645 Parliament passed an order that no person should be permitted to preach who was not an ordained minister in this or some other reformed Church, and sent the order to Fairfax with instructions to see it strictly observed in the army and all transgressors properly punished. The soldiers of the New Model, however, paid little attention to this order.

## *French Corruption and Incompetence*
∽§ W. H. Lewis

When Louis XIV took over the reins of government in 1661, it was merely a polite fiction to speak of the land forces as "the King's army"; they were nothing of the sort. It was an army in which the King was, at best, one of the principal shareholders, and in the control of which the traditional status of the Crown gave him a casting vote. But as the majority of the regiments were not his property, his control was by no means absolute, and that of his War Secretary was practically non-existent. The armies which under Louis XIII and Mazarin had fought Spain, were a hard-bitten, hard-fighting, undisciplined, ill-fed, badly paid rabble, held together by the prestige of famous generals and colonels, living by loot and extortion, things of horror and terror to the civilian population, friend and foe alike. Such discipline as existed was maintained by sudden wholesale hangings, alternating with long periods of absolute licence in which even officers' persons and property were not secure against the attacks of their own men. The officers, generally speaking, were as insubordinate as the troops, and once an army had been got together and sent to the front, the control of the central government often practically ceased to operate; indeed the government's most obvious and urgent care was to get the army out of the metropolitan provinces with all possible speed, before their presence raised a revolt.

Hand in hand with indiscipline went corruption; it was the golden age for the military peculator, and there were few officers who did not see in a campaign a heaven-sent opportunity to reimburse themselves for their considerable capital outlay. Nor was there any efficient method of checking and punishing the officer's dishonesty, for he was not in our sense of the word a King's officer at all; he was an investor, who had bought a regiment or company as another man might buy a farm or a block of Paris municipal bonds; and ratification of purchase, and the subsequent grant of a commission lay not in the hands of the King but in those of two military viziers, the Colonel-General of Cavalry and the Colonel-General of Infantry, both of whom, by the way, had as likely as not bought their posts, and were now recouping themselves by collecting a brokerage on the purchase and sale of commissions. Like stock exchange values, the prices of commissions fluctuated considerably; only a very few *corps d'élite* were maintained in peacetime; so when peace was in the air, the price of all commissions fell heavily, while the market value of those in the new regiments fell to nothing. For the state admitted no obligation to recompense the

holders of commissions in disbanded regiments; as on the stock exchange, the rule was *caveat emptor*. It would have been odd in the
circumstances if every officer had not joined his unit determined to
make hay whilst the sun shone; for his expenses were high, and the
legitimate return on his investment low. For instance, in 1689 companies in the French guards were selling at rather over 3,000 louis d'or;
it is true that a guards captain held the honorary rank of colonel in
the army, and his pay seems to have been 12 louis d'or odd a month,
as against some 4 louis d'or in the line infantry. And there was the
further advantage that when army funds ran out, as they had a habit
of doing in that unorganized age, it was the guards who got any
money that was going, while the line was left to live as best it could;
or in other words at the expense of the district in which they were
quartered. But even when we take into consideration the relative
security of tenure of the guards officer, a return of under five per cent
on a highly speculative investment is a poor one.

Still, it was not pay but peculation that formed the bulk of an
officer's income, and his opportunities for making a little on the side,
as the Americans say, were many. To begin with, it must be understood that the state did no recruiting; that was the business of the
captain. The state paid the soldier's pay, more or less irregularly, into
the hands of the captain, who, in return for a recognized percentage
of the sum received, and his recruiting grant, undertook to enlist,
equip, clothe and feed say a hundred men. But though he received a
fixed rate of pay per man, he in fact made the most advantageous
bargain he could with his recruits, and when he had enlisted a hundred of them, marched his company to the assembly quarter to be
inspected by the commissioner of war. For each recruit on parade he
received about 2 louis d'or in the infantry, and nearly 10 louis d'or in
the cavalry; and there appears to have been no check that the company
which joined the regiment was of the same strength as that which had
appeared on the muster parade. An arrangement better calculated to
promote fraud could hardly be devised, and most officers took full
advantage of it; as late as 1668 Luxembourg reports that if swindles
were perpetrated by a few officers, he could take disciplinary action
against them, but that he has in fact hardly one honest officer serving
under him. And Rochefort, in the same year, ends a report on the same
subject with the airy consolation that it is an evil which time alone
can cure.

An obvious fraud was that the company commander could and did
retain more than his legal percentage of the pay, and, in extreme cases,
pocketed the lot. But this rather elementary swindle had the inconvenient result that the company usually deserted *en masse*, and

even a seventeenth-century colonel was apt to object to a company whose captain was its only member. So the more intelligent contented themselves with the profit to be made out of *passe volants*. Under this system, the captain who was receiving pay for a hundred men, would in fact pay and maintain perhaps sixty, annexing the money of the imaginary forty. Inspections were few and far between, commissioners of war were conveniently blind, and their visits well advertised beforehand; on the day of the muster a collection of valets, grooms, and beggars would be issued with musket and bandolier, and would shuffle along behind the real soldiers. The commissioner would sign the muster roll, the stage soldiers would be dismissed with a *pourboire,* and the captain could put the whole matter out of his mind for another twelve months. If word came down that the commissioner was of a tiresomely observant and inquisitive disposition, it was merely necessary to give what Pooh-Bah calls a touch of artistic verisimilitude to an otherwise bald and unconvincing narrative by borrowing forty real soldiers from the nearest regiment; for as there were no uniforms, there was nothing to expose the deception which was being practised, especially as all the men on parade were obviously soldiers. The fraud was not, one must admit, peculiar to the French service; Montecuculi, the Austrian commander, in his memoirs, complains bitterly of it, and advises that the captain who employs *passe volants* be "chastiz'd with the utmost rigour": but he is silent as to the means to be employed.

There is some excuse for the juniors in that the examples set in the most exalted circles were not calculated to promote professional integrity; in 1641 that curious ruling prince, Charles IV de Lorraine, found himself short of cavalry horses, and without means of buying any. Nothing daunted, he raised the cry of the Church in danger, convened his clergy, and made them an eloquent address in the principal church of his capital. While he was so doing, his troopers stole all the horses of the assembled ecclesiastics. Again, the raising of contributions in enemy territory was a legal and normal method of subsisting an army in wartime; but it was notorious that many generals remitted to the War Office much smaller sums than they had extorted from the occupied area. And, of course, where the general was known to be feathering his nest, naturally each collecting officer did likewise.

The military aspect of the *passe volant* abuse was an even more serious matter than the financial, for it meant that a commander took the field in complete ignorance of the effective strength of his army. To be sure, he had the daily strength returns; but what percentage of the men inscribed thereon really existed? Was his army ten, twenty, or even forty per cent below its nominal strength? It follows from this state of affairs that we must be very cautious in accepting battle casualty figures in the early part of the century; for the captain whose company had a nominal strength of a hundred and an effective strength of seventy would undoubtedly, if he could manage to get his men under fire at all, report that he had lost thirty men in action when perhaps he had had no losses at all.

Sometimes the ingenious company commander would turn his attention from his men to their equipment; two company commanders would decide that in peacetime, with a little management, one set of muskets and bandoliers would suffice for both companies. They would then sell one set for their common profit, lending each other what was necessary for muster days. Then too, some little assistance could be got from the use of the soldiers' rations in garrisons where these were provided by the King and not the company commander; a pack of hounds, for instance, was found to thrive on soldiers' biscuit. And, of course, the immediate consequences of such a theft was a further outbreak of the chronic evils of desertion and looting. In the cavalry, the wide-awake officer found that there were pickings to be made out of the forage ration; it was a simple matter to loot corn for the horses from the countryside, and sell the King's corn to the commissary, who in turn sold it to the army bread contractor. Well may a contemporary complain that the ill-conduct of the officers "frequently produces very fatal inconveniences." . . .

And the same attitude was taken towards the feeding of the troops. The staple ration of the French soldier was bread, and on the march, biscuit, the latter baked hard, with a hole in the middle, so that the ration could be strung on the bandolier. Of these biscuits, a soldier could carry enough for six days. But it never seems to have occurred to the officers to check consumption; at the first night's halt the men would barter their biscuit for wine, with the result that a formation badly wanted at the front would be found immobile and three days' march from its destination, having run out of rations. One French general suggests as a remedy that the men should be given an allowance in cash instead of the biscuit ration; but it would seem unlikely that the French, or any other soldier of the period, would have wasted the money on bread. The Austrian Montecuculi is a strong advocate of the system of supply by contract; which suggests that either Montecuculi was very lucky in his contractors, or else took very little interest in his supply problems. If the regimental officer was careless about the conservation of rations, he could point to an equal and more criminal carelessness on the part of his superiors. When Boufflers defended Lille in 1708, he had to surrender for lack of provisions; but the shortage was caused by the issue of rations throughout the siege for the same number of men as on its opening day, no regard being paid to the very heavy casualties sustained by the defence. Indiscipline as well as negligence played its part in complicating the work of the French supply service; in 1673 the whole of Luxembourg's army was put under stoppages of pay as a punishment for looting their own magazines. And where the troops did not loot, there was the ever present difficulty of the dishonest contractor; Berwick, commanding on the Spanish front in 1704, complains that his bread comes up bad, by reason of the contractor only half-baking it so as to make it weigh more.

Ration scales varied considerably according to the troop's tasks and the resources of the *terrain*; the army in Lorraine in 1670 had an issue of fresh meat daily, Fridays excepted, but the general is told to make it clear to the men that meat is an extra to which they have no right, and which is given them by the King, and not by their captain. Again, in 1677, on the Rhine, the order is that each infantryman is to have one-third of a pound of meat daily, and each cavalryman a quarter: but while the infantry get a free issue, the value of the cavalryman's ration is to be stopped from his pay. And the issue of meat is to cease as soon as there is an abundance of peas and beans. In 1690 the authorized meat issue is three pounds a week, free to the infantry, and at a reduced rate to the cavalry, while the *Maison du Roi* pay full contract price. Louis XIV is himself credited with one contribution towards solving the problem of rations in the field, that of introducing the portable oven, which in one day's halt could bake enough bread for the next six days. I am inclined to suspect that this is truly his own idea; it is just the sort of administrative detail at which the King, nothing of a general, but an excellent junior staff officer, excelled.

Wherever we turn, we find the generals hampered by having to rely on the contract system for the performance of duties which are now regarded as an integral part of the functions of an army; even the artillery was, until 1672, a civilian commercial enterprise, in which the contractor hired soldiers to mount his batteries, and was paid so much for each gun brought into action, a system only one degree less bad than that obtaining in the contemporary Spanish army, where the contractor was paid for every time he moved a gun. The result naturally being that Spanish artillery was constantly on the move, and hardly ever in action. The supply and transportation of rations was organized also on a contractual basis, with results which were sometimes disastrous. In 1675 Maréchal de Créqui was beaten at Consaarbruck without having succeeded in bringing a single gun into action; the post mortem revealed the fact that the artillery contractor, expecting a quiet day, had lent his horses to the commissariat to bring in a convoy. And where were the commissariat contractor's own horses? We are not told, but I have a strong suspicion that they were out on hire to the neighbouring farmers. The whole system cried out, not for more detailed supervision from Versailles, but for the appointment of a general officer charged solely with the duties of administration in the field: and this solution seems to have occurred to no one.

# 9.  From Renaissance to Baroque: The Enrichment of Popular Culture

## The Advent of Printing
❧ Henry J. Chaytor

In the early middle ages the production and distribution of books was chiefly carried on by monastic establishments; copyists and book-dealers working on their own account were not numerous. Peter of Blois was outbid for a parcel of law books which he attempted to secure from a Paris dealer about 1170. Universities controlled the book trade with more or less stringency in the interests of their pupils; this organisation was closer at Paris than elsewhere, probably as a result of the large number of students who resided there. In the fourteenth century the book trade included stationers or writers, booksellers, parchment makers, illuminators and binders. One concern might combine two or three of these avocations. The stationer, so called from the fact that he had a settled place of business and did not travel from town to town, was the medieval counterpart of the modern printer and publisher; he managed the copying of books and employed illuminators to decorate them and binders to finish them when required. The bookseller (*librarius*) sold books or lent them on hire; with this business he might combine the functions of the stationer. The members of this trade were in the position of university officials; they were formally licensed, took an oath to observe university regulations and enjoyed a monopoly which outside traders could not infringe. As a guarantee of respectability, they had to pay caution money, which might be as much as £200, a very considerable sum in those days. As university officials, they were exempt from municipal jurisdiction and taxation, and had their place in university processions and public functions. They were not allowed to engage in other trades or professions, except those of a

literary character—notary, advocate or cleric; in Italy reference is made
to them as *bidelli*. The *bidellus* was a public official who acted as
town crier, or huissier, in support of the dignity of the municipality;
hence probably our university Esquire Bedell.

Books were very expensive, and from the thirteenth century onward
the supply never seems to have equalled the demand. Hence the object
of a university was to secure the necessary supply of books for its
students at the cheapest possible rate. The organisation described was
not suddenly imposed upon the trade by the university; it was of
gradual growth, emended from time to time in order to secure the
object in view. The books required by students were almost entirely
concerned with law and theology; the fact that monastic establishments
did not usually copy law books, and were in many cases forbidden to
do so, gave a stimulus to outside production which became a public
trade. The universities were not concerned with contemporary belles-
lettres, and producers and sellers of these were probably not interfered
with, as they did not infringe the monopoly of legal and theological
publication. The stationer who wished to issue a book was obliged to
submit it to the university officials, who saw that it was correct and
complete and fixed the price of sale. If this regulation may be regarded
as containing the germ of copyright law, it was one which protected
the purchaser, did nothing for the vendor, except to restrict his profit,
and entirely disregarded the existence of the author. The bookseller
would not buy unwanted copies, for, if he did, he could sell them only
at the taxed price; if he moved elsewhere, he was obliged to leave his
stock for his successor, presumably at a valuation. His real profits were
gained from the lending of books upon a monetary deposit. Poor
students who could not buy a text would pool their resources and buy
or hire one for their use during a university session. Books were also
lent in sheets, *peciae*, and the copying of these or of whole books by
students was a practice both regular and encouraged. Public and, under
conditions, monastic libraries were also accessible for study or for
copyists.

During the two centuries before the invention of printing, independent booksellers increased in number.... In England the book
trade was more independent of the universities than on the continent;
the London stationers had formed the inevitable guild by 1403, and
had established themselves in the vicinity of St Paul's, where they
remained until German barbarism recently destroyed their establishments. It was to such booksellers that customers would go who wanted
literature other than law or theology, and the demand for such literature grew steadily, as it was bound to do with the spread of education.
Even theologians and lawyers require some relaxation; as the middle

classes increased in wealth and importance, they discovered the necessity of education for business purposes and saw that their children were taught to read and write; so a demand for popular literature became steadily more general. Book prices were also lowered by the discovery of rag paper, and the invention of mechanical means of reproduction was the natural sequel. A very cursory examination of early *incunabula* will show that the printer did his best to reproduce the text in manuscript form; there will be no title nor title-page, the scribe's abbreviations will be reproduced, his proportion of text to margin observed and so on. There is some reason to believe that the primitive printed text was regarded by the reading public with a certain contempt, as electroplate is considered in comparison with silver. Fashions change and many *incunabula* are now more expensive than any existing manuscript of the text which they reproduce....

Few historians would care to contest Bacon's statement that the inventions of printing, gunpowder and the mariner's compass have changed the form of civilisation, and all would probably agree that he placed these inventions in the order of their relative importance. While much has been written upon the importance of printing as accelerating the diffusion of culture and knowledge, few attempts have been made to contrast the mental attitude of the scholar and the literary man in the ages before print with that of the reading and writing public when print had superseded manuscript as a medium for communicating ideas. The difference is that between the medieval and the modern world. Book collectors have agreed to regard 1500 as the date after which *incunabula* begin to lose their scarcity value and their interest as illustrating the development of the printer's art. This choice of date is arbitrary and somewhat misleading; printing began later in some countries than in others, and in Spain, for instance, the dividing line might be placed some thirty or forty years later. But in 1492 Columbus made his great voyage, in 1494 Charles VIII invaded Italy, in 1500 Copernicus was lecturing in Rome, Erasmus and Luther were at work and in 1521 the Diet of Worms was held, while in the previous year Magelhaẽs had circumnavigated the globe. In the effects of such events the difference between medieval and modern is apparent, in the enlargement of outlook upon the world and the interpretation of man's place and powers in it. That extension of view would have unfolded much more slowly than it did, if the printer had not already been at work for half a century.

## AN AGE OF CURIOSITY AND EXPLORATION

### The Passion for Discovery
ᘒ§ J. H. Parry

The fifteenth century was remarkable for the spontaneous growth, among a few gifted and highly-placed men, of a genuine disinterested curiosity. Like the passion for classical learning (and, of course, associated with it) this spirit of curiosity was among the leading characteristics of the Renaissance. It can hardly, at first, be called scientific, for it was undisciplined and quite unsystematic. The men of the Renaissance were concerned to absorb knowledge rather than to digest it, to amass rather than to select. Their curiosity was far stronger in inquiry than in arrangement; but it was omnivorous, lively, uninhibited; and while it corroded and gradually weakened the accepted medieval systems of knowledge, it collected, with avid and apparently random enthusiasm, the materials of which new systems would eventually be constructed. It was shared not only by scholars, but by princes and by men of action in their *entourage*, especially in Italy, but also in Portugal and Spain. Geography and cosmography were prominent among the objects upon which it seized, but it had many others. The attention paid to medical research at the time, especially to anatomy, is well known. Less obvious, but also important in the growth of the idea of discovery, is a new and more observant attitude towards natural history. How far explorers and promoters of exploration were directly and consciously moved by scientific curiosity, is impossible to say on the scanty evidence which remains; but the explorers' attitude towards what they saw, and the reception of their reports by the public at home, were both profoundly affected by the new spirit. Bernal Díaz, for example, was greatly impressed, but not particularly surprised, by the extensive collections of plants and wild animals kept in Montezuma's compound; botanical gardens and menageries were common among the hobbies of Renaissance princes, and it seemed to him perfectly natural that Montezuma should have similar interests. Alvarado, who climbed to the crater of Popocatépetl, partly to get sulphur to make gunpowder, partly out of bravado, but also partly out of curiosity, was emulating—consciously or not—the celebrated exploit of Petrarch on Mont Ventoux in an age when mountain climbing was unheard of. One of the earliest books about America, written by an eye-witness—Ovicdo's *General History of the Indies*—admirably illustrates this Renaissance interest by the clarity and detail of its account of animals and plants. Of geographical curiosity—the disinterested desire to know what lay beyond the horizon—the outstanding fifteenth-century expression was the *De Orbe Novo* of Peter Martyr, significantly written by a cultivated Italian who found a congenial home in Spain. . . .

The trans-Atlantic migrations of the Reconnaissance brought Europeans into close daily contact with utterly unfamiliar peoples, peoples with whom they had initially few points of contact, but for whose spiritual and material welfare they found themselves in some degree responsible. They had usually little to fear from these peoples, after the initial uncertainties of conquest and settlement, and much to gain as missionaries, as administrators or as exploiters of labour, from understanding them. The rich, strange and varied cultures of the settled Amerindian peoples appealed strongly to Renaissance curiosity, and the desire to study them and write about them acquired urgency because of the possibility, recognized by some of the more perceptive and sympathetic Spaniards, that they might disappear.

### *America and the Appearance of Venereal Disease*
≈§ Will Durant

It is often the fatality of medicine that its heroic advances in therapy are balanced—almost pursued—by new diseases. Smallpox and measles, hardly known in Europe before the sixteenth century, now came to the fore; Europe experienced its first recorded influenza epidemic in 1510; and epidemics of typhus—a disease not mentioned before 1477—swept Italy in 1505 and 1528. But it was the sudden appearance and rapid dissemination of syphilis in Italy and France toward the end of the fifteenth century that constituted the most startling phenomenon and test of Renaissance medicine. Whether syphilis existed in Europe before 1493, or was brought from America by the return of Columbus in that year, is a matter still debated by the well informed, and not to be settled here.

Certain facts support the theory of an indigenous European origin. On July 25, 1463, a prostitute testified in a court at Dijon that she had dissuaded an unwelcome suitor by telling him that she had *le gros mal* —not further described in the record. On March 25, 1494, the town crier of Paris was directed to order from the city all persons afflicted with *la grosse verole*. We do not know what this "great pox" was; it may have been syphilis. Late in 1494 a French army invaded Italy; on

February 21, 1495, it occupied Naples; soon afterward a malady became rampant there, which the Italians called *il morbo gallico*, "the French disease," alleging that the French had brought it into Italy. Many of the French soldiers were infected with it; when they returned to France, in October, 1495, they scattered the disease among the people; in France, therefore, it was called *le mal de Naples*, on the assumption that the French army had contracted it there. On August 7, 1495, two months before the return of the French army from Italy, the Emperor Maximilian issued an edict in which mention was made of *malum francicum*; obviously this "French disease" could not be ascribed to the French army not yet returned from Italy. From 1500 on, the term *morbus gallicus* was used throughout Europe to mean syphilis. We may conclude that there are suggestions, but no convincing evidence, that syphilis existed in Europe before 1493.

The case for an American origin is based upon a report written between 1504 and 1506 (but not published till 1539) by a Spanish physician, Ruy Diaz de l'Isla. He relates that on the return voyage of Columbus the pilot of the admiral's vessel was attacked by a severe fever, accompanied with frightful skin eruptions, and adds that he himself, at Barcelona, had treated sailors infected with this new disease, which, he says, had never been known there before. He identified it with what Europe was calling *morbus gallicus*, and contended that the infection had been brought from America. Columbus, on his first return from the West Indies, reached Palos, Spain, on March 15, 1493. In that same month Pintor, physician to Alexander VI, noted the first appearance of the *morbus gallicus* in Rome. Almost two years elapsed between the return of Columbus and the French occupation of Naples —sufficient time for the disease to spread from Spain to Italy; on the other hand, it is not certain that the plague that ravaged Naples in 1495 was syphilis. Very few bones whose lesions may be interpreted as syphilitic have been found in pre-Columbian European remains; many such bones have been found among the relics of pre-Columbian America.

In any case the new disease spread with terrifying speed. Caesar Borgia apparently contracted it in France. Many cardinals, and Julius II himself, were infected; but we must allow the possibility, in such instances, of infection by innocent contact with persons or objects bearing the active germ. Skin pustules had long since been treated in Europe with mercurial ointment; now mercury became as popular as penicillin is in our day; surgeons and quacks were called alchemists because they turned mercury into gold. Prophylactic measures were taken. A law of 1496 in Rome forbade barbers to admit syphilitics, or to use instruments that had been employed by or on them. More frequent examination of prostitutes was established, and some cities tried to evade the problem of expelling courtesans; so Ferrara and Bologna banished such women in 1496, on the ground that they had "a secret kind of pox which others call the leprosy of St. Job." The Church preached chastity as the one prophylaxis needed, and many churchmen practised it.

The name syphilis was first applied to the disease by Girolamo Fracastoro, one of the most varied and yet best integrated characters of the Renaissance. He had a good start: he was born at Verona (1483) of a patrician family that had already produced outstanding physicians. At Padua he studied almost everything. He had Copernicus as a fellow student, and Pomponazzi and Achillini to teach him philosophy and anatomy; at twenty-four he was himself professor of logic. Soon he retired to devote himself to scientific, above all medical, research, tempered with a fond study of classic literature. This association of science and letters produced a rounded personality, and a remarkable poem, written in Latin on the model of Virgil's *Georgics*, and entitled *Syphilis, sive de morbo gallico* (1521). Italians since Lucretius have excelled in writing poetical didactic poetry, but who would have supposed that the undulant spirochete would lend itself to fluent verse? Syphilus, in ancient mythology, was a shepherd who decided to worship not the gods, whom he could not see, but the king, the only visible lord of his flock; whereupon angry Apollo infected the air with noxious vapors, from which Syphilus contracted a disease fouled with ulcerous eruptions over his body; this is essentially the story of Job. Fracastoro proposed to trace the first appearance, epidemic spread, causes, and therapy of "a fierce and rare sickness, never before seen for centuries past, which ravished all of Europe and the flourishing cities of Asia and Libya, and invaded Italy in that unfortunate war whence from the Gauls it has its name." He doubted that the ailment had come from America, for it appeared almost simultaneously in many European countries far apart. The infection

> did not manifest itself at once, but remained latent for a certain time, sometimes for a month ... even for four months. In the majority of cases small ulcers began to appear on the sexual organs.... Next, the skin broke out with encrusted pustules. ... Then these ulcerated pustules ate away the skin, and ... infected even the bones.... In some cases the lips or nose or eyes were eaten away, or, in others, the whole of the sexual organs.

## *The New World's Impact on English Culture*
❧ A. L. Rowse

The New World was making its impact upon the life and mind of
Englishmen. The date and channel by which the potato was introduced
have been much disputed. But it looks as if it was probably brought
home by Hariot, on board Drake's ship, from the sojourn of the first
Virginia colony upon Roanoke. And it seems that the tenacious tradition
that Ralegh introduced the potato into Ireland is probably true.
Tobacco had reached this country earlier, about the beginning of the
reign. Apparently the first English description of its uses comes from
Hawkins' second voyage, of 1565. The most striking feature in its
conquest of the Old World is the rapidity of it; and yet perhaps one
should not be surprised considering the strength of the addiction once
acquired. The Elizabethans thought it as useful medically as pleasurable. By the end of the reign it had conquered the English upper class,
at any rate the menfolk at Court and among nobility and gentry. (Too
expensive for others!) Again, it was Ralegh who was chiefly responsible
for introducing the habit and patronising the cult—another score
against him in the mind of King James, who detested it: "it seems a
miracle to me how a custom springing from so vile a ground and
brought in by a father so generally hated should be welcomed upon
so slender a warrant."

We [can see] something of the place taken by America in the
practical intellectual interests of the time, but the leaven was beginning to work in the imagination of the poets. As More's *Utopia* is the
first work of genius to reflect the impact of the New World upon the
early Tudor mind, so we may take *The Tempest*, a century later, as
the latest at the end of it all. It is not only that the imagination of the
dramatist was set off by the circumstance of Somers's wreck on the
Bermudas, that the details—the cries, the howling, the island inhabited
by devils, St. Elmo's fire flaming along the mast and yards—come
straight from Strachey's account, but that the whole atmosphere of the
play is drenched in the voyages; or we may say that it distils them into
a magical transparency. The conception of Caliban (=cannibal) comes
from reading about the New World....

It was an Elizabethan situation, frequent enough, to voyage into the
wilderness to avoid creditors and escape from debt. It was the motive
of the novelist Lodge's joining Cavendish on his last journey to the
Straits of Magellan. When he published his novel, A *Margaret of
America*, he pretended that "some four years since, being at sea with
Master Cavendish ... it was my chance in the library of the Jesuits in

Santos to find this history in the Spanish tongue. . . . The place where I began my work was a ship." . . .

It was Donne into the passion of whose mind the excitement and inspiration of a New World most intimately entered. A follower of Essex, he was a voyager himself, to Cadiz in 1596 and on the Islands Voyage in 1597. From the latter he has left two famous verse-letters, describing "the Storm" at the beginning and "the Calm" that followed. But it is the images and metaphors that spring up in that heated Celtic mind that reveal how much he was touched by the influence:

> Let sea-discoverers to new worlds have gone,
> Let maps to others worlds on worlds have shown,
> Let us possess one world, each hath one, and is one.

In addressing his mistress, going to bed, he rhapsodises:

> O my America! my new-found-land,
> My kingdom, safeliest when with one man manned,
> My mine of precious stones, my empery,
> How blest am I in this discovering thee!

Everywhere in Donne there are these extraordinary images and suggestions, revealing how much his mind was fired by thoughts of geography and the sea, continents and planets; sun and moon, and the new worlds of knowledge opening up:

> That unripe side of earth, that heavy clime
> That gives us man up now, like Adam's time
> Before he ate; man's shape, that would yet be
> (Knew they not it, and feared beasts' company)
> So naked at this day, as though man there
> From Paradise so great a distance were . . .

Perhaps we may, in the end, turn back to the hopes of our stock and of our name, expressed by the Elizabethan poet in his "Ode to the Virginian Voyage," which have not been without reverberation and fulfilment in our own time:

> And in regions far
> Such heroes bring ye forth,
> > As those from whom we came,
> > And plant our name,
> Under that star
> Not known unto our north.

# THE SOCIAL SIGNIFICANCE OF HUMANISM

## The Power and Influence of the Florentine Humanists

≈§ Lauro Martines

By whatever route one approaches the humanists, one finds that they tend to be—like their disciples, friends, associates in office, and relatives by marriage—men of remarkable political and social importance in the city. . . .

Let us distinguish the professional from the amateur (in Florence, at all events) by holding that the first devoted most of his time or energies to humanistic interests and studies, whereas the second pursued these mainly in his spare time. Keeping this definition in mind, once I defined the objectives of the present inquiry and started to look to the possible bond between humanism and the social groups which disposed of power, a number of highly pertinent observations began to emerge. I found that the amateur humanists were recruited from the ruling class in almost every case. They were merchants, lawyers, noblemen, bankers, *rentiers*, statesmen, or their sons. Apart from seeking a humanistic education, these amateurs cultivated the friendship of the professionals and studied under the same masters, men such as Malpaghini, Chrysoloras, Guarino, Filelfo, and Marsuppini. Moreover, both amateurs and professionals served in the same political magistracies, contracted marriage in the same circles, and frequented persons of the same social class. And if some professionals were far from having the wealth of many amateurs, neither could many amateurs match the wealth of some professionals. In short, while an occupational distinction was discernible here, the distinction passed from sight when the humanists as a whole were viewed in terms of a wider context. For amateur and professional alike belonged to the governing class—a class which naturally included differences with regard to role, income, rank, and antiquity of family stock. It seems clear, accordingly, that stress on occupational differences would have diverted attention from interest in the relations between intellectual movement and social class, one of my chief concerns.

Owing both to its social recruitment and its point of view, once humanism became associated with the dominant groups in Florentine society, then—by the force of that association—it quickly began to share in the dignity that went with political and economic power. . . .

Thus the great propriety of Garin's observation that in the large industrial and commercial cities of Italy the celebrated teachers of humanistic studies catered almost exclusively to the sons of the great families. For it is this combination, this link between power and a given cultural program, which finally assured the success of humanism. Needless to say, a wealthy Florentine statesman with a humanistic education did not derive his social eminence from the study of humanism. But it might well endow him with brilliance in oratory, or clarity and grace of expression, an ease with words, a fund of historical examples, and a certain urbane *contegno*. Probably one would be right to suppose that in the eyes of the multitude prominent figures like Palla Strozzi and Piero de' Pazzi lent some sort of dignity to the *studia humaniora*. In the world of their peers, however, this was viewed the other way: Palla and Piero were the ones who stood to gain luster from their contact with humanism. . . .

In the optimistic climate of these years (the 1380's and after), the ruling class produced a group of men profoundly interested in the study of antiquity and its literature. Owing to their place in Florentine society, it was *their* social point of view, rather than another, which naturally prevailed in the new program of study. The names which have come down to us are Roberto de' Rossi, Jacopo da Scarperia, Palla Strozzi, Antonio and Angelo Corbinelli, Bartolommeo Valori, Jacopo Corbizzi, and Niccolò Niccoli. Coluccio Salutati, of course, was in his way a preceptor to all. Deeply involved as he was in politics, like the families of most of these men, his civic outlook was one to which they were accustomed. Ugolino Pieruzzi and Pietro di Ser Mino, men with rich experience in public affairs, were also associated with the new intellectual movement. On the edges of this humanist group, though very much their social peers, were Cino Rinuccini, Filippo Villani, and Gregorio Dati. The next generation of such men, to name only a few, included Domenico Buoninsegni, Alessandro degli Alessandri, Lorenzo Benvenuti, Cosimo and Lorenzo de' Medici, Buonaccorso da Montemagno, Franco Sacchetti, Matteo Palmieri, Jacopo Tornaquinci, Carlo Marsuppini, Giannozzo Manetti, and Francesco del Benino.

It would be unimaginative to suppose that men who are not born into a certain social class cannot adopt or express its point of view. By ambition, association, education, or another route, some men swiftly assimilate the values of others; and those who are mobile, who must be ready to change, do this all the more easily with the values of those who constitute the ruling groups in society. Men who are social climbers follow the ways of power, not some contrary route. When Lionardo Bruni and Poggio Bracciolini arrived in Florence and fell in with the first generation of the men we have named and with many others from the ruling class who were not necessarily their companions in study, they soon took over the dominant political and social values, making them their own. Bruni, indeed, with his extraordinary talent for "fitting in" and for procuring the support of the powerful, soon came to represent the intellectual vanguard of civic humanism, though in a setting where his civic views were—*mutatis mutandis*—a commonplace of practical experience.

According to Hans Baron, humanism in the later fourteenth century "was a literary movement some of whose exponents lacked all identification with any specific group of Italian society, while others began to be attached to tyranny." The movement was furthered "chiefly by grammar school teachers and the chancery officials of a multitude of secular and ecclesiastical princes." Hence "they did not form their minds in the give and take among the citizenry," but rather in more solitary surroundings, or in the princely chanceries and courts.

If true, these observations explain the type of humanism fostered in Florence, where "humanistic *literati* and erudites," as Baron has noted, were formed in the give and take between citizens. Here humanists grew up in households that were intensely political, or they frequented men deeply involved in public affairs, or were themselves drawn into the vortex of public life. Until the last two decades or so of the fourteenth century, civic-minded literati usually appeared in Florence individually or a few at a time at most. But in the 1380's and especially the 1390's, owing to the factors already mentioned, factors essentially connected with the social energies of the ruling class, a whole school of such men suddenly appeared on the scene, and thenceforth the literary culture of the laity became a collective enterprise. It thus appears that civic humanism was born with the emergence of a generation of young men who impressed their social and political viewpoint—already dominant in the Florentine community—on humanistic study. Indeed, it might be more accurate to say that the purity and force of that worldly viewpoint are what induced them to look back and find nourishment and cultural standards in an earlier civilization, a civilization itself thoroughly pervaded by the outlook of men whose interests were turned out towards the world. For to the young Florentines who cultivated the *studia humanitatis* around 1400, to their relatives, and to all the men of their social set, political office was an absolute social and economic—one might almost say moral—necessity. They were bred to a tradition of public service. The survival and success of their families, their position in society, their very fortunes were all directly connected with the privilege of political power. Consequently, the ideal of service to the community was naturally given a prominent place in the roster of humanistic values. Salutati, Rinuccini, Bruni, Benvenuti, and

Palmieri extolled the life of the active citizen, of the man who devotes himself to the welfare of his community and so displays a virtue superior to that of the man who seeks only his own good. The older ideal of the solitary and virtuous sage, as championed by Petrarch, thus gradually lost out to the *vita operosa*.

## The Thirst for Learning
৵ৎ Lawrence Stone

Between 1540 and 1600 there occurred one of the really decisive movements in English history by which the propertied classes exploited and expanded the higher educational resources of the country. By doing so they fitted themselves to rule in the new conditions of the modern state, and they turned the intelligentsia from a branch of the clergy into a branch of the propertied laity. At last it was possible to be an intellectual without having to endure the intolerable hardships of celibacy.

The drive to give a more intellectual training to the children of the nobility and gentry in the early sixteenth century sprang from two sources. The ideals of Italian humanism were seeping in, a century late, through educational reformers like Colet, Vives, and Erasmus; and there was developing a growing anxiety about the prospects of the nobility maintaining their grip on the key positions in the political system. 'The fault is in your selves, ye noble men's sonnes,' said Roger Ascham in 1570, 'that commonlie the meaner mens children cum to be the wisest councellours and greatest doers in the weightie affaires of this Realme. And why? For God will have it so, of his providence, bicause ye will have it no otherwise, by your negligence. Ceasse nobles, therefore, to hate learnynge,' urged Laurence Humphrey. The early sixteenth century saw the 25-year rule of two men of low birth, Wolsey and [Thomas] Cromwell, and the massive upward thrust into positions of honour, wealth, and power of intelligent gentlemen like Russell, Wriothesley, and Rich, Petre, Paget, and Paulet. Rule by clerics of humble birth like Wolsey was familiar enough to the Middle Ages; what was new was the replacement of the clergy in high political and administrative office by talented laymen from the lesser gentry or even below. As this revolution gathered momentum there developed open competition for the seats of power between the hereditary nobility and lower social groups among the laity. This threat to the established order alarmed conservatives everywhere, and stimulated a demand that the old aristocracy should again fill their rightful place in the councils of the nation. What had happened was that the technical require-

ments for public service had altered. The demand for military expertise
had slackened, and the demand for intellectual and organizational
talents had increased. As the state bureaucracy grew and as the modern
diplomacy took shape, the highest public offices went to those who had
been trained to think clearly, could analyse a situation, draft a minute,
know the technicalities of the law, and speak a foreign language. There
was a demand for men who could give a sense of perspective to current
problems thanks to a familiarity with classical and modern history and
with the institutions and economies of the other states of Europe.

These two forces, humanism and the desire to preserve a fixed social
hierarchy, interacted one upon the other, the former being a powerful
support for the latter. What distinguishes the English humanists of the
second quarter of the sixteenth century from their foreign colleagues
is the relative poverty of their scholarship. No great corpus of learning,
no monumental encyclopaedias came from the English presses. Instead
there poured forth a flood of translations for the benefit of gentlemen
anxious to absorb the lessons of the classics without going to the trouble
of mastering the language. The leading educational figures of the middle of the century were not remote and ineffectual dons but academic
politicians and government officials like Sir Thomas Smith and Sir John
Cheke, absorbed in the power struggles of court and university. They
were the Jowetts of their day, who regarded the production of an
educated *élite* to rule the country as a more important objective than
the pursuit of scholarly research. And who is to say they were wrong?

These educational reformers were unable to solve the problems posed
by the waywardness of the laws of heredity operating in a partly closed
society. But at least they could see to it that the number of idle and
ignorant aristocrats was reduced to a minimum, and that chances of
promotion for the talented 'new man' were consequently restricted.
And so there was launched a sustained and in the end remarkably successful attack upon the ignorance of the nobility. Again and again it
was hammered home that the justification of the privileges enjoyed by
the nobility was service to the commonwealth; that the definition of
nobility was not exclusively good birth, but ancestry coupled with
virtue; and that virtue consisted not only in devotion to God and the
Established Church (whichever it might happen to be at the time), not
only in moral rectitude, but also in the mastery of certain technical
proficiencies. Among the latter were now counted book-learning, languages, and history as well as the ancient attributes of good manners
and proficiency in the military arts, for only by acquiring this new
training could the nobility fit themselves to serve the Prince in peace
as well as war.

In their zeal for the new learning, the reformers expressed a passionate contempt for the late medieval and early Tudor nobleman:

> . . . noble men borne
> To lerne they have scorne,
> But hunt and blowe an horne,
> Lepe over lakes and dykes
> Set nothyng by polytykes,

sang John Skelton. Richard Pace reported a conversation with a gentleman who exploded: 'I swear by God's body, I'd rather that my son should hang than study letters. For it becomes the sons of gentlemen to blow the horn nicely, to hunt skilfully and elegantly, carry and train a hawk. But the study of letters should be left to the sons of rustics.' Thomas Starkey thought that the 'first and most principal of all ill customs used in our country commonly . . . is that which toucheth the education of the nobility, whom we see customably brought up in hunting and hawking, dicing and carding, eating and drinking, and, in conclusion, in all vain pleasure, pastime, and vanity.' 'With us,' he concluded, 'gentlemen study more to bring up good hounds than wise heirs.' Thomas Elyot admitted that gentlemen normally despised learning, thinking it a positive disqualification for responsible office, and Edmund Dudley frankly said that he thought that the English nobility were 'the worst brought up for the most part of any realme of christendom.' Not surprisingly, in view of their vigour and persistence, these thinkers impressed their ideas upon posterity. At the end of the sixteenth century the 2nd Earl of Essex (or more probably Bacon) believed that in the old days: 'The nobility of England brought up their sons as they entered their whelps, and thought them wise enough if they could chase the deer.' . . .

By the middle of the sixteenth century peers and gentry were at last convinced, both by the propaganda of the humanists and by the evident success in life of those with education, that it was time to bestir themselves and get some professional training. There resulted an astonishing explosion of higher education in England, and one that temporarily embraced even women among the aristocracy. The mid-sixteenth century was the first great age of the blue stocking: there were the celebrated More, Cheke, and Cooke ladies, there was Lady Jane Grey, and there was Queen Elizabeth herself. The Howards were for generations outstanding for their insistence on giving their children a sound education, which at this period even extended to their daughters. Katherine, daughter of the luckless Earl of Surrey and wife of Henry Lord Berkeley, kept up with her Latin grammar, was skilful in French, perfect in Italian, a student of natural philosophy and astronomy, familiar with globes and quadrants, and was an admirable player on the lute into the bargain. Whether or not she made a good wife is another matter.

In this first, heroic, phase of the educational revolution, peers and gentry possessed an enthusiasm for pure scholarship that far outran the practical needs of an administrative *élite*. They rushed headlong into a course of study that stands comparison in its academic austerity with that of any educational system of twentieth-century Europe. Men like Elyot were well aware that their purpose was to train a governing class, but they tended to exaggerate the academic side of the programme. Elyot himself advised a study of Greek and Latin literature from the ages of 7 to 13, followed by a university course in logic, rhetoric, cosmography, and history, though he admitted the need for physical recreation to strengthen the body. Parents were won over by these ideas, and men like the 4th Duke of Norfolk, the 8th Earl of Northumberland, and the 2nd Earl of Essex under Elizabeth, and Sir William Wentworth and the 9th Earl of Northumberland in the early seventeenth century, all urged upon their children the importance of a sound academic education in the classics, logic and rhetoric, science, modern languages, and the common law. In his enthusiasm Sir Henry Slingsby began to teach his son Latin (by Montaigne's method) at the age of 4. In 1632 Sir John Strode told his son that 'learning to a gentleman is like a diamond set in a gold ring: one doth beautify the other,' and Richard Evelyn successfully instilled into the mind of his son John the notion that it is 'better to be unborn than untaught.' Here is learning exalted not merely as a means to virtue and public service, but as an end in itself.

## ART'S EXPANDING AUDIENCE

### Civic and Private Art in Florence
⊷§ August C. Krey

When the authorities of Florence decided to beautify their city and had the money with which to do so, that was all that was needed. They were not creating something that had not existed before. They were merely giving craftsmen an opportunity to do on a much larger scale the kind of work they were normally doing in industry and for commerce. That these supreme triumphs of Florentine craftsmanship should be singled out as alone deserving of the appellation "art" seems an injustice to the equally artistic work which they were and had been doing in the pursuit of their crafts. Having reached the conclusion that the highly developed crafts practised all the techniques that art required, and that it was therefore natural, rather than strange, that many of the great works of Florentine art were created by Florentine craftsmen, one is tempted to examine the career of other artists of Florence. Such an examination, however, tends only to confirm the conclusion already reached, for every one of the great artists of Florence whose career is known was first trained as a craftsman.

The works of art ... were those of men employed by the public, either directly by the city authorities or indirectly through the sponsorship of the guilds. As the fifteenth century opened, Florence witnessed a widening gap in the prosperity of its citizens. A few families had acquired very great wealth, some of them, like the Medici, controlling private means of princely proportions. These families tended to adopt a standard of living proportionate to their wealth. The modest town houses were replaced with palaces like those of the Pitti and the Medici, and their country estates were provided with attractive villas, like Careggi of the Medici. Some of them, notably the Medici, made generous gifts for the construction of churches, chapels, libraries, and hospitals and for the further adornment of buildings already erected. San Marco, the gift of the Medici to the Dominicans, is an excellent example. These activities gave opporunity for the employment of Florentine craftsmen and added incentive to those supreme achievements which have been accorded the title of art. There is little to indicate that the craftsmen preferred employment by private individuals. Nearly all those noted as great artists during the fifteenth century engaged in both types of employment. Even Leonardo da Vinci and Michelangelo, favorites of the Medici, were drawn by the competition for the decoration of the walls of the Palace of the Seignory to what some regard as the highest point in art which either reached; and the latter finished his career as *capo-maestro* for the city, a fitting close to the great civic enterprise so happily begun under the direction of Arnolfo. Civic pride remained throughout the period a dominant force in the lives of the Florentine craftsmen-artists....

The expansion and multiplication of building operations during the fifteenth century doubtless attracted many able young Florentines into the crafts required for that work. The rivalry as well as the great amount of building both contributed to hasten the technical development of the arts involved. The greater achievements aroused the admiration not only of the Florentines themselves but of travelers, who helped to spread abroad the city's fame. Florence attracted young artists from all parts of western Europe who came there to study its art. The four years that Raphael spent there almost make him a Florentine. As other communities, first in Italy, then beyond the Alps, embarked upon lavish building operations, Florentine artists were in great demand. Thus Cosimo de Medici was able to discharge a portion of his debt of hospitality to Venice by having Michelozzo erect several buildings there. Donatello's equestrian statue of Gattamelata and Verrocchio's similar statue of Colleone represented like services to the Venetians. Leonardo da Vinci served similarly at Milan. Michelangelo and many lesser artists worked much in Rome. Leonardo went finally to the court of Francis of France, and many Florentines, including Benvenuto Cellini, worked in France during the sixteenth century. Fame as well as fortune were lavished upon these Florentine artists.

### Popular Art Exhibitions
⌇§ Francis Haskell

[A most effective way of] bringing the artists into contact with a wider public was the gradual extension of art exhibitions. The principal occasions for these were provided by the many saints' days and processions which were such a feature of seventeenth-century life. The feast of Corpus Domini above all was associated with the display of pictures, but it certainly had no monopoly. No exact spot seems to have been indicated and artists probably exhibited indiscriminately with other craftsmen or merchants showing their wares. Obviously no artist of established reputation would ever think of lowering his dignity in this way, and those that we generally come across are minor specialists in landscape and genre and above all painters newly arrived in Rome or returning after a long absence. For such men exhibitions seem to have been useful and to have attracted connoisseurs of standing. They also inspired other artists: we hear of a young peasant boy who decided to take up painting as the result of seeing a stall covered with pictures at the fair of Sinigaglia, and Claude is supposed to have seen landscapes by the Flemish artist Goffredo Wals at an exhibition in Rome and to have been so struck with them that he went to study under him in Naples—a move which played a decisive part in his career. And another exhibition—though very different in aim and organisation—was actually arranged under pressure from the painters in Rome. In 1607 the Duke of Mantua's agent was forced to satisfy them by putting on view Caravaggio's *Death of the Virgin* which he had just bought for the Duke on Rubens's advice—an occasion which was aparently attended by all the leading artists, who thus provided striking evidence of their growing influence and emancipation. . . .

By the end of the century there were four regular exhibitions in Rome each year—in March, July, August and December—quite apart from a large number of occasional ones arranged for special events and casual affairs spontaneously organised by a particular patron or artist. But none of the regular exhibitions had as its primary aim the opportunity for a painter to show new work, and some deliberately excluded this. Essentially all of them made use of pictures, as of tapestries and banners, for decorative purposes. From the strictly artistic point of view it is probable therefore that the more informal showings were the most fruitful and that it was only gradually that artists managed to turn to their own purposes what had been designed as a religious function. For this reason the importance of regular patronage, and the need to exhibit work on a permanent basis by painting altarpieces in the more frequented churches, were comparatively little affected by seventeenth-century exhibitions. . . .

At the same time, and partly owing to these very circumstances, a very wide and hitherto unimportant range of the general public was beginning to take an interest in painting and consequently to influence its development. We frequently come across references to these anonymous patrons in the artistic literature of the seventeenth century. Giulio Mancini was among the first to address them. In his *Treatise* he devoted a small section to the 'rules for buying, hanging and preserving pictures'. Carefully distinguishing between the rich and the artistocratic on the one hand and the 'huomini di stato mediocre e di stato basso' on the other, he pointed out that the latter would not be in a position to distribute their largesse very freely. If they had to bargain with the painter over the price, they should find out how long the work took him and estimate what his daily earnings should be 'by comparison with the pay of a craftsman engaged on similar work.' They were only likely to have two rooms available for hanging pictures— the bedroom and the reception room. Devotional works should be placed in the former; 'cheerful and profane' ones in the latter.

## *The Popular Appeal of Mannerism*
◄§ *Jacques Bousquet*

There is more than a verbal affinity between good manners and Mannerism. They both take for granted a preoccupation with ritual and with established manners, a certain negation of reality because of its inherent coarseness, a certain effort to construct artificially a strictly

human world. Good manners and Mannerism belong to the same
moment of civilization, the moment when man, having fulfilled his
immediate needs, began to seek refinement. It is natural that good
manners and Mannerism should have been born in the same era and
in the same social environment. . . .

Certainly, the princely courts did not create Mannerism, but they
greatly helped it to develop and they had a tremendous influence on it.
It was these princes and prelates who assured the triumph of a profane
art which, by its very nature, was far more versatile than religious art.
It was these patrons who created the whole climate of distinction, elegance, and concettism in which Mannerism grew up. It was they, above
all, who authorized the extraordinary moral liberty—one might well
say license—of sixteenth century art. The courts were above the law
and above current morality. Sexual perversion—which was one of the
essential characteristics of Mannerism—could never have been treated
openly had the princes themselves not condoned scandalous conduct.
At the court of Henri III, the ladies-in-waiting of the Queen Mother,
Catherine de' Medici, presided over the details of a banquet naked
under diaphanous robes which left their breasts uncovered. At another
banquet, during the same reign the guests all dressed in garments of
the opposite sex, men masquerading as women, and women as men.
The equivocal flowers of Mannerism sprang from this rich, decaying
soil, and flourished.

However strong the influence of aristocratic minorities upon Mannerism may have been, one should nevertheless not forget the role
played by other classes of society.

The fifteenth century had seen the constitution of the bourgeoisie
as an independent social class, distinct from both the common people
and the nobility. By the beginning of the sixteenth century, there
already existed a great number of bourgeois citizens who were no
longer semi-uncouth upstarts, but could boast of a family tradition and
several successive generations which had enjoyed ease and luxury. They
had built richly furnished, sumptuous residences for themselves in the
great trading cities. They had acquired seats in the town councils, their
sons attended the universities, and their business dealings with foreign
countries gave them access to international culture. A new aristocracy
—the aristocracy of money—was in the process of being born. In many
cases, especially in the Netherlands and Italy, it was already eclipsing
the real nobility. The discoveries of maritime explorers brought in new
commodities, opened up new markets, and hastened the flow of
precious metals to Europe (the annual production of silver, which was
about two tons in 1500, had increased tenfold by 1550). Thus, the
means of exchange were multiplied and an intense commercial activity

was set in motion, the chief beneficiary of which was the bourgeois. Hugh commercial and financial fortunes were founded at this time, and certain dynasties of merchants became as powerful as the princely families.

The classical example is that of the Fuggers of Augsburg. . . . The Fuggers, however, were simply the most distinguished members of a whole clan of businessmen and financiers who, behind the façade of emperor, kings, and princes, were fast becoming the real masters of Europe: these families had names such as Welser, Rehlinger, Imhoff, Tucher, Salviati, Strozzi, Grimaldi, Chigi, Kleberger and Van Spangen. Like the Fuggers, most of them were intelligent amateurs who not only commissioned Mannerist works for themselves, but what is more important still, introduced a taste for such painting among the bourgeoisie. Ultimately each one of the great commercial centers also became an artistic center. The artistic schools of the princely courts were now supplemented by the groups or schools of artists who worked in these wealthy cities: the School of Nuremberg with Albrecht Dürer, Hans Baldung Grien and, later, Wenzel Jamnitzer; the School of Augsburg with Christoph Amberger, Hans Rottenhammer, and Georg Penez; the School of Antwerp, or more accurately, the Schools of Antwerp (the first, at the turn of the century, with the so-called Romanists, the second around 1600 with the circle of Jan Bruegel the Elder); the School of Utrecht with Abraham Bloemaert and Joachim Wtewael; the School of Haarlem with Karel van Mander, Cornelis Cornelisz van Haarlem, and Hendrick Goltzius. There is no doubt that many of these artists also worked for the courts, and that on the other hand, many court artists also belonged to a city school. Nevertheless, however complicated the interrelationship may have been, it is unquestionably possible to distinguish in Mannerism, running alongside the aristocratic trend, a specifically bourgeois trend, particularly in Germany, Switzerland, and the Netherlands. This bourgeois Mannerism was, generally speaking, more extremist than the courtly variety. It was both closer to the whimsical oddness of the dying Middle Ages and to the eccentricities of the yet unborn Romantic movement. Elegance of gesture is often so exaggerated here that it becomes affectation (as in the work of Herri met de Bles or Cornelis Engelbrechtsz). In some works by Pieter Aertsen, Jan van Hemessen, and Joachim Beuckelaer, expressionism is transformed into a systematic vulgarity, which reminds one of some of the German Expressionist painters of the 1920's. The erotic element often becomes very crude, sometimes obscene as for instance in some works of Urs Graf, Barthel Beham, or Georg Penez. Subtlety easily degenerates into a bookish pedantry, indulging in ultracomplex symbolism and obscure anecdote. There was a pronounced tendency to glorify everyday objects; hence the many kitchen scenes and still lifes. Finally, as has happened throughout the history of art, bourgeois civilization, being essentially an urban civilization, began to feel a tremendous need for escape into nature. From this era and this social environment there sprang the first pure landscape artists: Joachim Patinir, Jan Bruegel the Elder, Gillis van Coninxloo, Gillis Mostaert, Paul Bril, and Roland Jacobsz Savery.

During the sixteenth century, there existed a small number of cultured members of the working class who played a more important role in the development of art than may be imagined. The great mass of the people, consisting of the peasantry, was of course completely excluded from any culture, let alone that promulgated by the Mannerists. But among the apprentices and journeymen living in the large towns at that time, there existed a true proletarian élite.

The most original religious movement of the sixteenth century, Anabaptism, was conceived among the urban proletariat, and its prophets and leaders were workers. Many workers made great efforts to acquire learning, some with remarkable success. It may suffice to mention the example of a certain Thomas Platter, from a peasant family, who was first a servant in Alsace, then a rope maker in Basel. He became so fired with enthusiasm for humanism that without aid he learned Latin and Greek and became a distinguished Hebrew scholar. One should also remember that many painters were of modest origin. Jan Gossaert Mabuse was the son of a bookbinder, Jean Bellegambe the son of a cooper, Sodoma the son of a shoemaker, Salviati the son of a weaver; Girolamo Genga, in his youth, was an apprentice wool-stapler, and Girolamo da Carpi a plasterer; Maerten van Heemskerck, Giorgione, and Pieter Bruegel the Elder all belonged to peasant families; Domenico Beccafumi herded sheep as a child. We may well conjecture that the work of these artists reflects, to some extent, the environment from which they emerged. . . .

The populus of the towns also had a certain influence on the evolution of taste. Certainly, sixteenth century workingmen had not the opportunity to really become acquainted with contemporary painting, since most of the artistic output of the time was hidden away in princely palaces or the mansions of the wealthy middle class. It should be remembered however, that it was these laborers who formed the bulk of the audience at the frequent parades, triumphs, and carnivals which were such important events in the town life of the epoch, and were also important factors in molding the forms and feelings of Mannerism.

## Baroque Aesthetics As a Reflection of Social Change
❧ *Hugo Leichtentritt*

The causes for the change of taste leading to the new baroque aesthetics are manifold. They must be sought mainly in events of political history, in changing economic and social conditions, in technical inventions and geographical discoveries, and in the natural growth of artistic ideas. Scientific and artistic tendencies, conditions of life, and the mental atmosphere of Europe in general were, of course, profoundly influenced by such occurrences as the discovery of America, the increase of commerce with India and other parts of Asia and Africa, the invention of printing, the Reformation in Germany, Switzerland, and England, and the combat between Catholicism and Protestantism which reached its climax in the Thirty Years' War. One who understands the meaning of such grave events for the cultural life of a period will not have much difficulty in finding their echoes in the music of the late sixteenth and seventeenth centuries.

Let us survey quickly the literature of music of about 1550 to 1750 in order to see how the style and aims of music changed under the influence of the new aesthetic creed. Chronologically the baroque style almost coincides with the rise of the Catholic Counter Reformation and its systematic organization, as we find it displayed at the Council of Trent. In 1550 Vignola built the splendid Villa de' Papa Giulio outside of Rome and described what he called the new "Jesuit style" in his famous book, *Trattato degli ordini* ("Essay on the Various Styles"). At that time the Jesuit order was only ten years old, but it was already very powerful and influential in the cause of the Counter Reformation, directed against the rise of Protestantism as formulated by Luther, Calvin, and Zwingli. In 1551 the Jesuits founded the Collegio Romano, their Roman headquarters. Two years before, they had made their entrance into Germany in Ingoldstadt in Bavaria, and from there they extended their activities throughout Germany, founding churches and schools. Everywhere the new "Jesuit style," the Roman baroque, followed them, and thus it spread to all parts of Germany, became popular, and was finally accepted even by Protestants. To a certain extent the Jesuit tendencies might almost be identified with baroque tendencies. This order, so shrewd, persistent, and logical in the pursuance of its aims, certainly assigned music a definite part in its policy. Surveying the literature of music from about 1575 through the seventeenth century and a part of the eighteenth, we might say that the greater part of it leans toward the baroque, and a considerable part of it is certainly directly inspired by Jesuit ideals and needs. In other cases the clever Jesuit fathers made skillful use of novel styles of composition that they thought likely to win the ear and the favor of a large public.

The first traces of baroque music become manifest at a time when Renaissance aesthetics seems still to be in full bloom. We can observe them, especially in Italy, from about 1550, at first rarely, later abundantly, until after 1600 they become dominant. Wherever in seventeenth-century Italian music the element of color is accentuated strongly and intentionally, we have the first signs of the baroque attitude. Color effects in Italian music are of two kinds: those of the Venetian polychoral style, with its broad stretches of a certain coloring suddenly changing to another color, and those of the new chromatic harmony of the later Italian madrigals....

Reference has been made to the Counter Reformation, the systematic, cleverly organized defense of the Catholic Church against the powerful and dangerous attacks of the Protestant Reformation. It has also been mentioned that music was used by the Roman Church both in defense and in attack. With profound insight into the propagandistic possibilities of the new concertizing and dramatic style, the Roman Church made a speedy and effective use of the sensational invention of opera about 1600. The opera plots of Monteverdi and the Florentine writers, based on classical mythology and drama, were transformed in Rome into allegorical works with a moralizing Catholic tendency, into a kind of religious drama. This variation of opera was baptized oratorio. In its more primitive form the oratorio goes back a half century earlier to St. Philip Neri of Rome, Palestrina's friend, who about 1552 had founded a sort of organization of priests who met in the oratory (called *oratorio* in Italian) of a convent. At this point the Counter Reformation got hold of the new movement, and in 1575 Pope Gregory XIII sanctioned the constitution of the so-called "Congregazione dell' Oratorio," a carefully organized institute for the education of lay priests, as a means of Catholic propaganda. In 1600 the first opera, *Eurydice*, by Caccini and Peri was performed in Florence. At once Rome felt the importance of the innovation. It was very speedily utilized for the aims of the Church, and in the same year a kind of spiritual allegorical opera, *La Rappresentazione di anima e di corpo*, was performed in Neri's oratory. This was written by Emilio dei Cavalieri, who for years had been in charge of the festive musical performances of the Congregazione dell' Oratorio in the convent of Santa Maria in Valicella, and it is generally called the first oratorio, with a curious misunderstanding of the word *oratorio*. Gradually in the course of the seventeenth century the oratorio was changed from a kind of allegorical religious drama, hardly distinguishable from early opera, to what we now call oratorio. At any rate, the Catholic Church appropriated it and made it a purely Catholic specialty for a long time. ... Oratorio reached its artistic culmination and its greatest popularity, however, only after the great Protestant masters, especially Handel, took hold of it.

# Part Four. ENLIGHTENMENT AND REVOLUTION, 1700 TO 1815

The period between 1700 and 1815 contains some of the great social and cultural contradictions of which men are capable in their social relations. In an era whose philosophy, letters, and political theory set forth the potentialities of human betterment through the marshaling of human reason and will, men continued to live in the most wretched circumstances, and the popular culture of the period, although comprising more varied diversions, was if anything touched by more violence, crudity, and passion than any earlier epoch.

The opening chapter of Part Four deals with the many popular pastimes involving violence and death. Preceding chapters have shown there was no absence of entertainments involving blood and battle in earlier periods, but here the sports and spectacles are raised to a higher level of art by such innovations as the guillotine. Moreover, popular thirst for blood sports was unquenchable, even at the height of the revolutionary period, during which blood, death, and torture were the grim content of everyday life.

In addition to the violent sports, this period was a highwater mark for the pursuits of gambling and hard drinking. Strong liquors were becoming readily and cheaply available for the first time, and the expansion of trade, the agricultural and industrial revolutions, and the early colonial enterprises were supplying the leisure classes with the excess capital for gambling and speculation. These social manias are discussed in the second and third chapters of this part.

Urban development, the advances in education attendant upon the secularization of education in an earlier period, and the increased leisure of larger proportions of the populace, gave rise to the clubs, coffeehouses, and salons. These institutions were the battlegrounds of the great wits, the hangouts of the worst rakes, and the gathering places of the men who would reform and rebuild European society along what they deemed more reasonable lines. A considerable percentage of the free time of men of letters, business, and affairs was spent in one or another of such establishments. The fourth chapter describes these places and their significance.

The eighteenth century witnessed something of a revolution in travel in Europe. Although it did not compare with the rail, steam, automobile, and air travel revolutions that were to follow, it did represent a great advance over what had gone before. Turnpikes and improved carriages meant safer, smoother, longer trips. The building of canals in England and on the continent facilitated much-improved communication. And the development of larger and more commodious ships from the middle of the seventeenth century on meant more and easier travel to more distant points in Europe and the New World. The fifth chapter describes the two most typical kinds of travel in the period: the Grand Tour of the continent, which was an integral part of the training and polishing of the upper classes of Europe; and the tour of one's own country, in this case England, now made far easier and safer by improved transportation.

Ever-greater numbers of people became literate during these years, giving rise to the popular press. This manifestation of cultural expansion, along with the rise of the middle-class novel, are discussed in the sixth chapter. The next chapter deals with the growth of the popular opera in the eighteenth century. Together, these chapters discuss the expansion of the audiences for beauty and excitement or artistic creation in music and writing.

The eighth chapter is devoted to an examination of the daily life of workers in the new towns created by the industrial revolution. These places bred men whose capacity for toil and hard living was exceeded nowhere before or since, and the popular pastimes of these people are characteristic of the toughness of the participants.

In the following chapter Evangelical, or experiential, religion is viewed in its popular dimensions and is seen as a survival of Christian fervor and in part as a prime form of entertainment in the circumstances of eighteenth-century society. The three final chapters touch on the various aspects of revolution which marked the last decades of the era. The life and attitudes of the military man of the period are significant inasmuch as so many people were caught up in the revolutionary and postrevolutionary warfare attendant upon the collapse of the Old Regime. A chapter is devoted to popular uprisings in the revolutionary era. Riot and insurrection consumed a great deal of the time and energy of lower-middle-class and working-class people in the late eighteenth century and became a prime form of leisure activity as well as a means of expressing social and political discontent. Finally, the intellectual revolution in human sensibility which replaced Enlightenment attitudes with Romanticism is described in the concluding selections.

# 1. The Enjoyment of Violence and Death

## Blood Sports
⋖§ E. D. Cuming

COCK-FIGHTING was *the* diversion of the age, as it had been for centuries past and was to be for near a century to come. All classes indulged in it from the peer who bred his Blackreds, Duckwings, Piles, or what not, by the thousand, to the humblest villager who had his 'shakebag.' There is no more convincing proof of the universality of cocking than the number of expressions derived therefrom which have passed into current phraseology—'pit against,' 'clean pair of heels,' 'cut out for,' 'scoot,' to mention a few. County fought county, town fought town, village fought village; peer and gentleman fought among themselves, and ploughman fought cowherd. The stake or prize ranged from 1,000 guineas at one end of the scale to a fat pig at the other. Spurs, steel and silver, had been introduced about the end of the seventeenth century and quickly came into general use among well-to-do cockers; they were expensive—in 1698 the Duke of Rutland paid £3 for six pairs— hence the humbler sort continued to prepare their birds for battle by sharpening the beak and natural spurs with a knife. Race meetings were great occasions for cocking; they brought together men from all the country round, thus offering an unrivalled opportunity for a main: to take an example at random, in 1751: 'At Epsom, on the 14th of May and following Days (being the Time of the Races) Mr. *Bennet senr.* fought Mr. *Howell,* shewing forty-one cocks on each Side, for six Guineas a Battle and an Hundred the Main.'

A main might consist of any odd number of cocks from seven upwards; forty-one was a very usual showing; the object being that one competitor should win a majority of the battles. There were mains of various kinds: a 'long' main lasted four days or more; a 'short' one two or three days. Then there was the 'Welsh' Main fought out on the same system as modern coursing, the winner of each battle being pitted against a fellow winner. In a 'Battle Royal' a number of cocks were pitted together and suffered to fight one another as seemed good to them. Different sorts of spurs were in use—'long heels,' 2 to 2½ inches long; 'short heels' 1½ inches long; 'sickle,' 'lanche,' and 'penknife' spurs; but the one most in use was the simple spur like a stout needle curved, long or short. The results of important mains were regularly published in the *Racing Calendar*, as also were particulars of forthcoming events.

The Rules and Orders for Cocking framed during the reign of Charles II were still in force, but the old method of matching birds by measurement had now given place to matching by weight; and in duly organized mains they were matched to an ounce. A graphic description of cocking is given by a French visitor to England in a letter dated February 23, 1728:

> The animals used are of a particular breed; they are large but short-legged birds, their feathers are scarce, they have no crests to speak of, and are very ugly to look at. . . . The stage on which they fight is round and small. One of the cocks is released, and struts about proudly for a few seconds. He is then caught up, and his enemy appears. When the bets are made, one of the cocks is placed on either end of the stage; they are armed with silver spurs, and immediately rush at each other and fight furiously. It is surprising to see the ardour, the strength, and courage of these little animals, for they rarely give up till one of them is dead . . . the noise is terrible, and it is impossible to hear yourself speak unless you shout . . . Cocks will sometimes fight a whole hour before one or the other is victorious.

With regard to that first remark: the cock 'cut out for battle' was certainly no beauty, but M. de Saussure evidently did not know that the comb and wattles had been cut off as soon as the sex of the young bird was recognized, or that the neck feathers from neck to shoulders were clipped, the tail cut to the rump and the wing feathers cut 'slopewise' to sharp points, to prepare the cock for the pit. He writes as though the lack of plumage and comb were natural.

Country folk carried on the sport with little regard for Rules and Orders; a patron of the village public-house would come in with a bag containing his cock and offer to pit it against that of any one present; a friend might take him up, fetch his own bird, and each man shook out his champion on the floor; hence the term 'shake-bag,' formerly 'turn-poke.' Organized cockings often took place in the village churchyard, more particularly on church festivals. There were indoor and outdoor pits; some of the latter still exist in their original shape —an amphitheatre, seats cut in the turf rising in tiers round the central plot whereon the battle took place. Space forbids reference to the many superstitions surrounding the cockpit, but mention may be made of the rural practice of putting gamefowls' eggs in a magpie's nest to be hatched; the magpie being the special protégé of the Evil One, it was thought that chicks so hatched were the fiercer. Inconsistently enough, the cocker who swept dust from the Communion Table and sprinkled it on the pit felt assured that evil influences had been thereby dispelled and the best bird (his own, naturally) must win.

COCK-THROWING and GOOSE-RIDING were 'diversions' in favour with the proletariat. The former was properly a Shrove Tuesday institution; its devotees, however, were not strict about the occasion. It was a brutal business, but in spite of efforts to put an end to it, cock-throwing survived until the end of the eighteenth century.

Some unfortunate bird, usually one trained by its owner to dodge a missile, was tied by the leg with a length of cord to a peg, and for twopence any one might have three throws with a broomstick from a a distance of 22 yards. If the thrower knocked the cock over and could run in and seize it before it rose the bird was his. The well-trained victim became clever in evading the stick, and thus was a source of profit to the owner. The street was often the scene chosen, and then cock-throwing ranked as a nuisance; in 1759 the lieges of Newbury lodged an objection to cock-throwing in the street. Goose-riding does not appear to have been peculiar to any season or festival: the bird with neck well greased was hung by the legs to a bough or to a rope stretched between two poles, and the competitors, riding at speed beneath, tried to pull off the head.

BULL-BAITING was very popular. The bullward, or bullard, led his beast about the country, stopping at any town or village to enlist the patronage of local 'bull-hankers'. The animal was fastened by a rope or chain to a stake, and any one who cared to pay a shilling might set his dog at him. Bull-hankers sometimes carried long staves with which to break the fall of a dog when tossed—a frequent happening. Near the stake was dug a hole of size sufficient to admit the bull's muzzle, the experienced dog always trying to seize that most tender part of the anatomy. The condition of such a bull was pitiable; continually baited, his head and neck were covered with scars, and wounds part-healed and new. The Stamford and Tutbury Bull-runnings were peculiar to those towns; the former was less objectionable than bull-baiting; the

latter was abominably cruel. The Stamford institution endured until
1840, when respectable rate-payers raised effective objection to it—on
account of the expense. It was costing £300 a year to bring in troops to
reinforce the local police and keep rowdyism within bounds.

BULL-RACING was popular; when cattle were used for draught, trials
of speed naturally grew therefrom; any bull, bullock, or cow might be
entered, and the race often took place in the street. That at Lyndhurst
was celebrated; it was run over a two-mile course, and in heats.

BADGER-BAITING was another sport (save the mark!) to which the age
was addicted. The yard of a public-house was commonly the venue;
here, in a hole dug for the purpose, a stake was fixed and the badger
being secured thereto by a chain passed *through* his tail, dogs were set
on him. The jaws and teeth of the badger being exceptionally strong,
he might maim or kill half a dozen dogs before he succumbed himself.

FALCONRY was now far advanced in its decline, ousted by the gun.
True, the Royal Mews was still maintained by George II, and his son
Frederick, Prince of Wales, used to fly his hawks on Epsom Downs; but
those who indulged in this oldest of sports were few. Establishment of
the Falconers' Club in 1770 is indicative of endeavour to keep it alive.
In 1781 the club counted fifty-six members; these held a meeting every
year at some chosen spot, Alconbury Hill in Huntingdonshire being
a favourite resort by reason of the many kites still to be found in the
locality. Hawking was always the sport of the rich man; a falcon to be
properly 'manned' must be ever on the fist of him who flies her, hence
a professional falconer who devoted all his time to his charges was
indispensable. The gun, as already said, did much to make an end
of falconry, and the increase of hedges, walls, &c., brought about by
Inclosure Acts, contributed to the same result, providing cover for the
quarry when the falcon stooped.

PUGILISM, as carried on until this time, has been described as 'downright slaughtering'; and, to say truth, introduction of scientific methods
did little to improve it. To Jack Broughton, who succeeded Tom Pipes
as Champion of England in 1740, is due credit for what was at least an
attempt to redeem the Noble Art from reproach. In 1743 Broughton
framed the first Rules for prize-fighting, and sought to elevate boxing
to a science at the Academy he opened in the Haymarket four years
later. A wise man, he thoughtfully provided his pupils with 'mufflers',
later known as boxing-gloves—'that would effectually secure them from
the inconveniency of black eyes, broken jaws, and bloody noses'. 'Inconveniency' applied to a broken jaw seems an understatement, but let
that pass. Broughton's well-meant efforts were not generally appreciated,
nor was his example everywhere followed, for fighting in booths at fairs
and kindred resorts continued in all its savagery. In 1749 boxing and

cudgel play at Southwark Fair were suppressed as a public nuisance, such a pitch of barbarity had they reached; and we need not suppose that Southwark was worse than other places.

The pugilist who fought his way to fame usually became the protégé of some peer who took interest in the Ring; such a patron found the money for a prize-fight and backed his man: thus, the Duke of Cumberland was the patron and backer of Broughton for several years until, on April 10, 1750, that hero was defeated by Jack Slack in a fight which lasted only fourteen minutes; a blow between the eyes blinded Broughton and thus brought the battle to an end. The defeat of his protégé and consequent loss of his bets, said to amount to some thousand pounds, caused the Duke to withdraw his support; a step which compelled Broughton to close his academy, and withdraw from the Ring. Ten years later the Duke bestowed his patronage on Slack, who won the championship in 1750, backing him for £100 against Bill Stevens, the champion of 1760. From 1761 to 1783 the championship was in a very unsettled state, several men holding it in turn; and so matters continued till the appearance of Tom Johnson, a corn-porter, whose defeat of Jarvis in 1783 brought him into notice. Johnson, whose real name is said to have been Jackling, was a man of very unusual strength; he could take up a sack of corn and swing it round his head; also he possessed great courage; and to these advantages he added 'most minute attention to Art'; in other words, displayed science; and thus it came about that he defeated every man who came against him during the 1780's, his opponents including Bill Warr, Michael Ryan, Bill Darts, who had held the championship for six years from 1765, and Peter Corcoran, who claimed it in 1771, but whose title to the honour for some reason was considered doubtful. Johnson held the championship for eleven years from 1783. Another famous pugilist was George Taylor, Champion in 1734. This man fought numerous battles before he entered the ring against Tom Faulkener at St. Albans in 1758; he had lost an eye in a former fight, and after an hour and seventeen minutes a blow from Faulkener closed the other; thus blinded he had to accept defeat. It would seem that he sustained other injuries not suspected at the time, for he died three months afterwards. Men were sometimes so badly punished that it was necessary to support them from the ring.

For many years prize-fights were brought off on the ground, a rope holding, or intended to hold, off the crowd; but fights were too often marred by the misconduct of onlookers; backers of the man who seemed to be losing would force their way into the ring and with kicks and blows strive to disable his opponent. Hence the introduction of a stage raised 6 feet or more above the ground. Johnson's fight with Bill Warr at Oakhampton, Berkshire, in 1787 took place on such a stage.

Displays of boxing were common attractions at the country fairs; a professional would go the round of these, advertising by handbills his readiness to meet the local talent; and it is very improbable that such bouts were conducted with any regard for rules.

CUDGEL PLAY was also to be seen at the fairs; the weapon was a stout stick with basket-handguard; he who first drew blood from his adversary's head won the bout. There is no better description of cudgel play, though at a much later date, than that in *Tom Brown's Schooldays*.

WRESTLING was a popular exercise, especially in counties where a particular style had been evolved. The wrestlers of Cornwall and Devon were the most celebrated; after them those of Cumberland and Westmorland; then the Norfolk and Bedfordshire men. Other districts adopted one or other of these styles; thus, Sir Thomas Parkyns of Bunny Park, Notts, was an enthusiast who organized an annual wrestling meeting in his park, the Cornish style being favoured. Sir Thomas died in 1741, but the meeting was regularly held for many years afterwards.

CRICKET underwent important changes. In its very early days the game was confined to the humbler classes, and perhaps we see in the method of scoring—cutting notches on a stick—evidence of illiteracy; but in Johnson's time men of all classes were playing, and exciting adverse comment by so doing: says one such critic: 'Noblemen, gentlemen and clergy have certainly a right to divert themselves in what manner they think fit, nor do I dispute their privilege of making butchers, cobblers or tinkers their compaions...'

## Upper-Class Devotion to the Hunt
ⅇ§ G. M. Trevelyan

Nothing marked more clearly the growing power of squirearchy in the House of Commons and in the State than the Game Laws of the Restoration period. By the Forest Laws of Norman and Plantagenet times, the interests of all classes of subjects had been sacrificed in order that the King should have abundance of red deer to hunt; but now the interests of the yeomen and farmers were sacrificed in order that the squire should have plenty of partridges to shoot. Even more than politics, partridges caused neighbours to look at one another askance: for the yeomen freeholder killed, upon his own little farm, the game that wandered over it from the surrounding estates of game preservers. And so in 1671 the Cavalier Parliament passed a law which prevented all free-holders of under a hundred pounds a year— that is to say the very great majority of the class—from killing game, even on their own land.

Thus many poor families were robbed of many good meals that were theirs by right; and even those few yeomen whose wealth raised them above the reach of this remarkable law, were for that reason regarded with suspicion. The best that even the good-hearted Sir Roger de Coverley can bring himself to say of the 'yeoman of about a hundred pounds a year,' 'who is just within the Game Act,' is that 'he would make a good neighbour if he did not destroy so many partridges'—that is to say upon his own land.

For many generations to come, grave social consequences were to flow from the excessive eagerness of the country gentlemen about the preservation of game. Their anxieties on that score had grown with the adoption of the shot-gun. During the Stuart epoch shooting gradually superseded hawking, with the result that birds were more rapidly destroyed, and the supply no longer seemed inexhaustible. In Charles II's reign it was already not unusual to 'shoot flying.' But it was regarded as a difficult art, the more so as it was sometimes practised from horseback. But the 'perching' of pheasants by stalking and shooting them as they sat on the boughs, was still customary among gentlemen.

The netting of birds on the ground was a fashionable sport, often carried on over dogs who pointed the game concealed in the grass. It is written that Sir Roger 'in his youthful days had *taken* forty conveys of partridges in a season' probably by this means. To lure wild duck, by the score and the hundred, into a decoy upon the water's edge was a trade in the fens and a sport on the decoy-pond of the manor house. Liming by twigs, snaring and trapping birds of all kinds, not only pheasants and wild duck but thrushes and fieldfares, had still a prominent place in manuals of *The Gentleman's Recreation*. But the shot-gun was clearly in the ascendant, and with it the tendency to confine sport more and more to the pursuit of certain birds specifically listed as *game*. In that sacred category a place had recently been granted by Statute to grouse and blackcock; already the heather and bracken where they lurked were protected from being burnt except at certain times of the year, and the shepherd transgressing the law was liable to be whipped. Addison's Tory squire declared the new Game Law to be the only good law passed since the Revolution.

Foxhunting, under the later Stuarts, was beginning to assume features recognizably modern. In Tudor times the fox had been dug out of its earth, bagged, and baited like a badger, or had been massacred as vermin by the peasantry. For in those days the stag was still the beast of the chase *par excellence*. But the disorders of the Civil War had broken open deer-parks and destroyed deer to such an extent that at the Restoration the fox was perforce substituted in many districts. As yet there were no county or regional packs supported by public subscription, but private gentlemen kept their own packs and invited their nearer neighbours to follow. The idea that gentlemen should hunt 'the stag and the fox with their own hounds and among their own woods,' was gradually yielding to the chase across the country at large, irrespective of its ownership.

In some counties earths were stopped and the endeavour was made with frequent success to run the fox down in the open. Under these conditions runs of ten or even twenty miles were not unknown. But in Lancashire and probably elsewhere 'the hunters ran the fox to earth and then dug him out; if he refused to go to earth he generally got away. It is possible that there had not yet been developed as tireless a breed of hounds as today.'

The chase of the deer, with all the time-honoured ritual of venery, still continued as the acknowledged king of sports, but it was steadily on the decline, as the claims of agriculture of more land reduced the number of forests and set a limit to the size of the deer park that a gentleman was likely to keep enclosed round his manor-house.

More widely popular than the hunting of deer or fox was the pursuit of the hare, with a 'tunable chiding' of hounds, the gentlemen on horseback, and the common folk running, headed by the huntsman with his pole. This scene partook of the nature of a popular village sport, headed indeed by the gentry but shared with all their neighbours, high and low. . . .

Older forms of the chase were yielding to the pursuit of the fox. The hunting of deer, the King of sports in all past ages, became a memory, except on Exmoor and in a few other regions. As early as 1728 some Hunts had already come down to the ignominious 'carting' of deer, the beginning of the end. The reason is evident: the destruction of forests, the enclosure of wastes and the encroachments of agriculture caused the continual decrease of the herds of wild deer that used to roam the countryside at large. In the reign of George III, stags browsing under the oaks were an ornament to a gentleman's park, safely enclosed within its pales, but were no longer beasts of the chase. The owner or his gamekeeper would shoot them in season, for the table.

Hare hunting, beloved of Shakespeare and of Sir Roger de Coverley, went out more slowly. Although fox-hunting was gaining ground throughout the Eighteenth Century, as late as 1835 a sporting magazine enumerated 138 packs of harriers as against 101 packs of fox hounds. The harriers had this advantage, that the countryman on foot could keep within view of the shorter circles of the hunted hare, more easily than he could follow the longer and straighter run of the fox. But although the democratic and pedestrian element formed a smaller part of the field in fox-hunting, 'the hunt,' with its red or blue coats, its hounds and horn, caught the imagination of all classes in the country-side; spirited fox-hunting songs were shouted as loudly and as joyously on the ale bench as round the dining table of the manor.

In the reign of George III fox-hunting had become in its essential features what it has been ever since, except that very few then joined a Hunt who were not resident in the County. But it had ceased to be an affair of one or two neighbours riding over their own lands. The hounds now ran over a whole district, and great Hunts like the Bad-minton, the Pytchley and the Quorn carried the science to the point where it has remained ever since. The runs became longer as the Cen-tury advanced, and the Enclosure Acts, by cutting up the open fields with hedges in the hunting shires of the Midlands, made a greater call on the qualities of the horse and its rider. But even as early as 1736, Somerville, the squire-poet of *The Chase*, describes jumping as an im-portant part of the game:

> with emulation fired
> They strain to lead the field, top the barred gate,
> O'er the deep ditch exulting bound, and brush
> The thorny-twining hedge.

Shooting in the Eighteenth Century was rapidly taking the place of the hawking, netting and liming of wild-fowl. Its procedure was mov-ing towards present-day practice, but more slowly than that of hunting. 'Driving' the birds had not yet come in. The long, hand-cut stubble still made it easy for sportsmen to get near partridges, walking up to them behind the faithful setter. Pheasants were not driven out of covers high over the heads of the 'guns,' but were flushed out of the hedgerows and coppices by packs of yelping spaniels and shot as they rose. In northern moorlands, grouse were less numerous than today, but less wild. Blackgame and duck were very numerous on suitable land, and everywhere troops of hares did much injury to the farmers; rabbits were not quite such a pest as they are now (1939), because the proportion of grass land to arable was smaller. Ruffs and reeves, bittern, plovers, wheatears, landrails and other wild birds were shot as freely as more regular game.

The muzzle-loading flint-and-steel gun of slow ignition was very different from the modern ejector; its action being slower, it was neces-sary to shoot much further in front of the bird, a fact reflecting all the more credit on the performance of Coke of Norfolk, who on more than one occasion killed 80 partridges in less than a hundred shots. Reload-ing was a matter of time, and, if carelessly done, of danger; therefore after each shot the sportsman had to halt and the dog was bidden 'down charge' while the 'charging' of the gun took place. In the middle of the Eighteenth Century, gamekeepers, like Black George in *Tom Jones*, were not so generally respectable a class of men as their successors of a later day. They were often 'the worst of poachers, taking one brace for the master, and two for themselves.' But neither the gentry nor their keepers were the only people who took game; there was never a truce to the poaching war in old England.

## *The Attractions of Public Executions*
⊷ Leon Radzinowicz

THE EXECUTION AUDIENCES. In the crowd which usually assembled to witness executions there were people from all walks of life. Griffiths observes that what 'was a morbid curiosity among a certain section of the upper classes became a fierce hungry passion with the lower. . . . It was a ribald, reckless, brutal mob, violently combative, fighting and struggling for foremost places, fiercely aggressive, distinctly abusive. Spectators often had their limbs broken, their teeth knocked out, sometimes they were crushed to death. Barriers could not always restrain the crowd, and were often borne down and trampled underfoot.' The number of women and adolescents was very considerable; even children were brought there to witness the scene. The underworld of London was of course well represented, as were the lower strata of society. But many persons belonging to the higher ranks were also known to be keenly interested, George Augustus Selwyn, Thomas Warton, and the Duke of Montagu being frequent visitors.

'Frightful scenes were witnessed at executions in those days', writes John Laurence, 'the crowd standing awestruck as it watched the convulsions of the strangling culprit. Every contortion of the limbs was hailed with a cheer or a groan, according as the sufferer was popular or not; appalling curses and execrations occasionally rent the air and rendered the last moments of the unfortunate criminal more odious; hawkers boldly sang the praises of their wares the while a fellow creature was being done to death. Rich and poor, thief and lord, gentle and simple, attended to see "the hanging," and cracked jokes at the sufferer's expense.' The assemblage of so prodigious a crowd naturally offered excellent opportunities to thieves. Magistrates' offices were later thronged by people who had lost their watches, pocket-books, or purses. . . .

Public interest in executions was greatly stimulated by the widespread sale of publications known as 'last dying speeches and confessions'. The confessions were usually obtained by prison officials—

and particularly by the Ordinary—who exerted all their influence to induce the delinquent to admit his guilt. These efforts, which were by no means always successful, were continued even at the very scaffold at Tyburn. Thus when the hangman was fastening the rope round the neck of Richard Patch—sentenced for murder—the Rev. Mann, who attended Patch 'for the last time, attempted to draw from him a confession, but with no success. The sheriff then went to him, and entreated him to confess; but he steadfastly refused'. The effect and indeed the purpose of these endeavours were not necessarily praiseworthy. At that time the prestige of the prison chaplain was not very high, a fact which in itself may have accounted for the obstinacy with which so many offenders refused to make a confession, and may have stimulated them to make false statements about themselves and their associates. Another no less important reason, already mentioned, was that since the confessions were later printed and sold in pamphlet form, a suspicion was created that the chaplains were acting from mercenary rather than charitable motives. . . .

THE HANGMEN. William Andrews quotes a local newspaper for the following account of the execution of two housebreakers in 1738: 'At the tree, the hangman was intoxicated with liquor, and supposing that there were three for execution, was going to put one of the ropes round the parson's neck, as he stood in the cart, and was with much difficulty prevented by the gaoler from so doing'. Influenced by the general atmosphere prevailing at Tyburn, hangmen often behaved like actors on the stage. Thus when William Brunskill, for twelve years a deputy-hangman, became the principal one and on the first day of his new office was called upon to execute seven criminals, he performed his task with exemplary efficiency and then advanced to the front of the platform and, with his hand on his breast, made a profound bow to the assembled crowd. Hangmen were allowed to receive money from the offender whom they were about to hang, a practice which sometimes gave rise to undignified scenes.

Many hangmen had several offences on their record and some were executed. Thus Derrick had committed a rape and would have been hanged but for the interposition of the Earl of Essex, whom some years later he was called upon to decapitate. Richard Brandon was committed for bigamy. John Price (1714–1715) served several prison sentences and was ultimately executed at Bunhill Fields for the murder of an old woman. His successor, Pasha Rose, was among the first offenders to be executed at Tyburn. William Marvell (1715–1717) was both an insolvent and fraudulent debtor and an inveterate drunkard, and was afterwards found guilty of a capital larceny; John Thrift (1735–1752) was found guilty of murder; Thomas Turlis (1752–1771) was indicted for a capital larceny and Edward Dennis (1771–1786) took part in the Gordon Riots.

In their defence it must be said that the influence of their duties, both as hangmen and as the executioners of such other sentences as whipping and standing in the pillory, was bound to be brutalising. In 1731 John Hooper, known as the laughing Jack, was called upon to execute the sentence of cutting both ears, slitting the nostrils and branding the nose, which had been passed on Joseph Crook, *alias* Sir Peter Stranger, found guilty of the forgery of certain deeds of conveyance. 'Dressed in overalls of butcher blue, Jack Hooper came up behind him and severed his (Stranger's) ears with an "incision knife", after which he held them aloft so that the mob could see, and then delivered them to Mr. Watson, a Sheriff's officer. . . . Although he endured his punishment with undaunted courage, the wretched man could not help flinching from the final act of torture. When both his nostrils had been slit with a pair of scissors and the hangman was proceeding to sear his nose, he sprang from his chair at the first touch of the red-hot iron . . .'. Roger Gray, a seventeenth century Exeter hangman, hanged among others his own brother.

GALLOWS CUSTOMS AND SUPERSTITIONS. One of the effects of public executions was to encourage the growth of certain superstitions. The crowd would thus storm the gallows after an execution to touch the body of the hanged. Women were observed to approach the scaffold to be stroked by the hands, still quivering in the agony of death; 'I remarked'—writes Meister—'a young woman, with an appearance of beauty, all pale and trembling, in the arms of the executioner, who submitted to have her bosom uncovered, in the presence of thousands of spectators, and the dead man's hand placed upon it'. Another object of superstition was the rope. For many years it was customary for the hangman to hold a reception after the execution at a tavern in Fleet Street, and there to sell the rope at the rate of sixpence an inch. After Earl Ferrers had been put to death there was a fight between Turlis and his deputy for the rope; and after Corder had been hanged for murdering Maria Marten the scuffle spread to the spectators. After the execution of Colonel Wall in 1802, the hangman was selling the rope at a shilling an inch at the same time as a woman and a man were selling the 'authentic' rope at a somewhat reduced price in two other districts of London.

The bodies and clothes of executed delinquents were the property of the hangmen, from whom the relatives or friends of the dead could purchase them, if they wished; otherwise the bodies were sold to surgeons to be dissected. The bargaining was often hard and not necessarily peaceful. Scuffles between the surgeons' messengers and the crowd, who resented the practice of dissection, were very frequent. People fought even for the privilege of carrying the bought corpses to parents and friends waiting in coaches and cabs to receive them, for the carriers were well paid for their trouble. Silas Told, who, under the influence of Wesley, took upon himself the thankless mission of bringing spiritual comfort to prisoners, relates that after the execution of John Lancaster no one claimed his body for interment. However, when it became known that the 'surgeons' mob' had secured it and had taken it to Paddington for dissection, a party of sailors recovered the body and carried it in state through Islington and Hounsditch; when they became tired they dropped it on the doorstep of an old woman, who recognised in it the body of her own son. After the execution of Richard Turpin the people whom he had selected to be his mourners took all possible care to secure his body, which they deposited in a grave. The next day some persons were discovered to be moving the body, 'and the mob having got scent where it was carried to, and suspecting it was to be anatomised, went to a garden in which it was to be deposited, and brought away the body through the streets. . . .

When the death of the hanged delinquent was not instantaneous, his friends would pull him down by the legs to shorten his agony. Zetzner notes that sometimes they would beat his heart with heavy stones, to make him die quicker. The *Gentleman's Magazine* thus describes the execution of an offender condemned under the Waltham Black Act: 'Monday 26 (July 1736) one, Reynolds, . . . was hanged at Tyburn. He was cut down by the executioner as usual, but as the coffin was fastening, he thrust back the lid, upon which the executioner would have tied him up again, but the mob prevented it, and carried him to a house where he vomited three pints of blood, but on giving him a glass of wine, he died'.


## *Popular Responses to the Guillotine*

&§ Alister Kershaw

At half past three on the afternoon of April 25th, 1792, [Nicolas-Jacques] Pelletier, red-shirted as required by the law of his time, was led onto the scaffold. Before . . . a large crowd [executioner] Sanson operated the guillotine in dead earnest for the first time. Pelletier's head was whipped off without a hitch.

Press reaction was one of sober approbation, typified by the contented observation of one newspaper that the new device "in no way stained any man's hand with the murder of his kind, and the speed with which it struck is more in accordance with the spirit of the law, which may often be severe but which should never be cruel".

But that large crowd, indifferent to or unaware of all the philanthropy around, was distinctly disappointed. The deliciously affrighting scenes of the old days were gone. One had to go back to 1626 for such an epic decapitation as that of the comte de Chalais, whose head was only hacked off at the twenty-ninth stroke of the sword and who was still living at the twentieth; but even in modern times there had been some marvellously messy spectacles. But now ... with this new-fangled apparatus: one hardly got a glimpse of anything. And the speed ... which the newspapers would next day applaud—it was sickening! The whole business was over before one had had a chance to enjoy it. . . .

The execution of Louis XVI has tended to obscure subsequent guillotinings of equal, although less epic, interest. And the Queen, apologising to Sanson when she accidentally trod on his foot; the Dubarry, pleading with the executioner (as if he, poor brute, could arrest the process) for a few seconds' stay; the long procession of unnamed aristocrats, derisively acknowledging the execration of the crowd, laughing among themselves as they stood on the scaffold waiting their turn, taking urbane leave of each other when Sanson beckoned—these have overshadowed occasions well worth attention, perhaps even more indicative of the thoroughgoing enthusiasm which characterised the Terror.

It has not been possible to confirm the legend that a dog which had been taught to howl whenever it heard the word "republican" was guillotined along with its master; but there is nothing inherently improbable in the story. It is no more ridiculous, for instance, than the decapitation of Valazé. He was guilty of a crime still graver than that of howling at a word; he had picked the wrong side. Arrested as a Girondin, he and his accomplices were (what else?) condemned to death, but Valazé—and it was additional confirmation of his deviationism—would not accept the idea of dying at the hands of the enemy. On the eve of his execution, he committed suicide. He was sadly ingenuous in thinking that it was as easy as that to deprive the Government of its fun; his corpse was bundled into the cart which was to take his associates to the scaffold; and the dead Valazé was triumphantly decapitated with the rest.

And if a dog, if a corpse, why not children? The omission was rectified at Nantes on December 17th, 1793, when two children of fourteen and two of thirteen were included among the twenty-four individuals selected for summary execution that day.

Why limit the treatment to members of the canine or human race at all? The rationalists of the Revolution reflected briefly; then wooden figures of the saints were carted from the churches and guillotined; Lejeune chose the birds for his dinner-table and had them guillotined; to celebrate the anniversary of the King's death, Albitte assembled effigies of reigning monarchs and had them guillotined; the Breton schoolteacher, Guillaume Kerhouant, built dummies of notorious *émigrés* and, for the instruction of his pupils, had them guillotined. The machine provided endlessly varied entertainment.

# 2. The Extent of Drinking and Gambling

## The Twin Vices of the Leisure Classes

ᵛᶳ A. S. Turberville

Drinking and gaming were the prevalent vices of the eighteenth century. Hard drinking among the upper classes sensibly decreased during the century, but that only means that at the beginning the practice was almost incredibly bad. Oxford, Bolingbroke, Carteret, Walpole were all heavy drinkers. 'They tell me', George III once said to Lord Chancellor Northington, 'that you love a glass of wine.' The reply was, 'Those who have informed your Majesty have done me great injustice; they should have said a bottle'. And although Northington spoke of *one* bottle, he probably meant *two*. The eighteenth century boasted its two-bottle men, who were accustomed to consume that amount of wine at a single sitting. At the end of the previous century, owing to the prohibition of French imports, the headier wines of Portugal began to displace the lighter French clarets; and this tendency was strengthened by the Methuen Treaty of 1703 with Portugal, which admitted her wines into England at a specially low rate. Port drinking spread the ravages of gout, which is the characteristic malady of the eighteenth century. Its numerous victims succeeded in persuading themselves that its tortures, however unpleasant, were rather beneficial to general health than otherwise. George III with sturdy common sense refused to believe in the validity of this comforting reflection. In truth there can be no doubt of the devastating results of the prevalent hard drinking on most constitutions; many men, as the result of their intemperance, were quite worn out and elderly before they reached fifty; some showed visible signs of decay at the age of thirty. The middle classes did not indulge in port, and the tendency among them to substitute the drinking of wine for ale probably aided sobriety. Such at any rate was the opinion of Dr. Johnson, who tells us that in his early days 'all the decent people in Lichfield got drunk every night, and were not the worse thought of'. That was in the ale-drinking days. French visitors to England in the 'sixties ascribe the 'melancholy' which they professed to discover in the people to their drinking not French wines, but home-made concoctions, compounded of sloes, blackberries, or cherries with the juice of turnips, slightly fermented and sometimes sold as port wine in London taverns.

From the reign of Anne till the beginning of the nineteenth century gambling was a national disease among the leisured classes of both sexes. Games of skill and games of chance, horse racing, lotteries, and commercial speculations—all made an irresistible appeal. While the men spent most of the day, and sometimes of the night also, round the card-tables at the fashionable clubs of Almack's, White's, and Boodle's, the ladies occupied themselves in similar fashion in their own drawing-rooms. Thousands of pounds would be won or lost at a single sitting. It is recorded that Charles James Fox would occasionally sit for nigh twenty-four hours at play, losing £500 an hour. Before he was twenty-five he had squandered £140,000, mostly at cards. He played whist and piquet very well, but it was the element of chance that really attracted him, and it was in such a purely gambling game as the popular 'faro' that he lost most of his money. Men would take wagers on anything—that X would not be made a vice-admiral by such and such a date, that Y would be found wearing a certain suit on a particular occasion, that Z would, although seriously ill, be still surviving on the first of next month, and so forth.

## Hard Drinking in London
❧ M. Dorothy George

The fact that a high death-rate and low birth-rate should have combined between 1720 and 1750 is strange, because during this time London was spreading itself over a wider area and the narrow streets and courts of the City were becoming less crowded as tenements made way for warehouses and counting-houses. The price of corn was very low; in the forty years between 1715 and 1755 there were only three bad seasons, 1727, 1728, and 1740. Meat in London was cheap and plentiful, the market and stalls were being increasingly well supplied with fruit and vegetables from the neighbouring market gardens. Trade was growing—apart from a set-back after 1739—and the country was financially prosperous. The sanitary condition of London was of course very bad, but there is no evidence that it was deteriorating—on the contrary, it must have tended to improve with the spreading out of the population. The constant fires and the rebuilding which followed them must have had on a small scale something of the effects of the Great Fire [1666]. The appearance of the plague at Marseilles in 1720 roused a salutary terror in London. As a matter of fact the effects of an improved diet and some sanitary progress are seen in the decline since the seventeenth century in the mortality from scurvy, dysentery and intermittent fever.

The only explanation seems to be that usually given by contemporaries—the orgy of spirit-drinking which was at its worst between 1720 and 1751, due to the very cheap and very intoxicating liquors, which were retailed indiscriminately and in the most brutalising and demoralising conditions.

> "The diminution of births," wrote Corbyn Morris in 1751, "set out from the time that the consumption of these liquors by the common people became enormous. . . . As this consumption hath been continually increasing since that time, the amount of the births hath been continually diminishing. . . . Can it be necessary to add to this shocking loss . . . the sickly state of such infants as are born, who with difficulty pass through the first stages of life and live very few of them to years of manhood? . . . Enquire from the several hospitals in this City, whether any increase of patients and what sort, are daily brought under their care? They will all declare, increasing multitudes of dropsical and consumptive people arising from the effects of spirituous liquors."

A representation to the House of Commons in 1751 on the effect of spirituous liquors estimates the annual loss in London since 1740 by the premature deaths of weakly children under five, and by fewer births as 9323: "Other trivial reasons for this great mortality, which in some degree have always subsisted, may possibly require some abatement; but still the real grand destroyer is materially evident."

Other reasons of course there were—among them the effects of dearth and fever in 1740 and 1741 are apparent, but it is probable that the reason why these were so calamitous in those years, as compared with similar years before and after, was that they were aggravated by the effects of spirit-drinking. Distilling was a new trade in England and one which received special favours from the Government. It produced a revenue and gave farmers a market for cereals at a time when prices were low. It was supposed to be favourable to the balance of trade, though as a matter of fact foreign spirits, even if smuggled, were too dear for general mass consumption. Large vested interests were created, and Lord Hervey (or rather Samuel Johnson) said in 1743 "that the great fortunes recently made were to him a convincing proof that the trade of distilling was the most profitable of any now exercised in the kingdom except that of being broker to a prime-minister." . . .

The cheapness of British spirits caused a new demand and altered the tastes and habits of the people. Brandy shops and geneva shops multiplied in the poorer parts of London. Almost every shop daily resorted to by the poorer classes also embarked upon the selling of spirits. Employers, including the numerous middlemen who worked in cellars and garrets, sold gin to their work-people. The result was an orgy of spirit-drinking whose effects were seen in the streets of London, in the workhouse, in the growing misery of the poor, in an increase of crimes of violence.

The great increase in the consumption of spirits showed itself in the excise returns about 1721 at the same time that its effects begin to be discoverable in the Bills of Mortality. From this year also dates the beginning of the campaign against gin-drinking which at last forced restrictive measures upon the Government. But the dangerous tendencies of spirit-drinking had been seen twenty years earlier. Davenant said of the drinking both of foreign brandy and of strong waters made in England: " 'Tis a growing vice among the common people, and may in time prevail as much as opium with the Turks, to which many attribute the scarcity of people in the East."

In April 1721 the Government was concerned to discover certain "scandalous clubs and societies of young persons" whose object was blasphemy and the denial of religion, as to which there was much rumour and little evidence. The Westminster justices were ordered to investigate, and to take proceedings against all profaneness, immorality and debauchery. They failed to find the clubs, but took occasion to represent that in their opinion the immorality of the times was due to gaming-houses, play-houses and the great increase of alehouses and spirit-shops. "Nor is there any part of this town wherein the number of alehouses, brandy and geneva shops do not daily increase, though they were so numerous already that in some of the largest parishes every tenth house at least sells one sort or another of those liquors by retail." This, they "humbly offer," is "the principall cause of the increase of our poor and of all the vice and debauchery among the inferior sort of people, as well as of the felonies and other disorders committed in and about this town."

From this time onwards the Sessions repeatedly showed its concern with the evils of spirit-drinking. In the same year owing to fear of the plague, a committee of justices was appointed by the Sessions to consider sanitary nuisances under certain heads, one being "persons retailing brandy, geneva and other distilled liquors." The committee take notice "of the great destruction made by brandy and geneva-shops whose owners retail their liquors to the poorer sort of people and do suffer them to sit tippling in their shops, by which practice they are not only rendered incapable of labour . . . (but by their bodys being kept in a continual heat) are thereby more liable to receive infection.' . . .

The effects of unlimited sale became more appalling than ever. In 1735 the Middlesex Sessions appointed another committee which reported in January 1735-6 much on the lines of the report of 1726, but showing, as do the excise returns, that the evil had spread in the past ten years. The number of retailers—7044 (4939 licensed and 2105 unlicensed)—the justices consider very far short of the truth, as the returns were made by the constables, about half of whom were retailers themselves. The "inferior trades" which sold spirits had increased to "above fourscore . . . particularly all chandlers, many weavers, several tobacconists, shoemakers, carpenters, barbers, taylors, dyers, labourers and others. . . ." The weavers of Bethnal Green who sold spirits had increased to "upwards of ninety," besides

> "other persons of inferior trades concerned in our manufactures . . . and as they generally employ many journeymen . . . this liquor being always at hand . . . they are easily tempted to drink freely of it, especially as they can drink the whole week upon score, and too often without minding how fast the score runs against them; whereby at the week's end they find themselves without any surplusage to carry home to their families, which must of course starve, or be thrown on the parish. . . . With regard to the female sex, we find the contagion has spread even among them, and that to a degree hardly possible to be conceived. Unhappy mothers habituate themselves to these distilled liquors, whose children are born weak and sickly, and often look shrivel'd and old as though they had numbered many years. Others again daily give it to their children . . . and learn them even before they can go, to taste and approve this certain destroyer."

To the inflaming character of gin the committee ascribed the many crimes of violence, the drinkers being often "carried to a degree of outrageous passion." Neglected children "starved and naked at home . . . either become a burthen to their parishes or . . . are forced to beg whilst they are children, and as they grow up learn to pilfer and steal."

The Government was moved to a heroic remedy. The Middlesex justices presented a petition to the House of Commons against the excessive use of spirituous liquors; resolutions supporting the petition were carried unanimously, and an Act was passed which was intended to stop the retailing of British spirits. A duty of 20s. a gallon was laid on spirits and retailers were required to take an annual licence costing £50. This step is almost more eloquent of the evils of gin than the reports of the justices. That a land-owning Parliament should attempt to suppress the home consumption of British spirits at a time when corn prices were still low suggests something of the incredible state of things when gin was threatening to destroy the race. Moreover the prohibition of retailing was generally expected to lead to riots, and the Jacobites were ready to take advantage of any discontents. The Bill was opposed on this ground, and on that of the unfairness of destroying a trade which had been deliberately fostered for forty years. The "regulation will raise great disaffection to the present Government," said Pultency, "and may produce such riots and tumults as may endanger our present establishment, or at least cannot be quelled without spilling . . . blood . . . and putting an end to the liberties of the people." The loss to the revenue was estimated at £70,000.

The Act could not be enforced. It did at first check the consumption of spirits, but these were sold illicitly, at first secretly, then openly; riots broke out, informers were hunted down and murdered, and the law became a dead letter. In seven years only three £50 licences were taken out, but the quantity of spirits sold progressively increased and reached its maximum of over 8,000,000 gallons in 1743.

# 3. The Popular Mania for Financial Speculation

## The Big Bubble
ↆ *John Carswell*

Paris had become the financial capital of Europe. Speculators and speculative capital were pouring into France, where Mississippi stock stood at 2,000 and the word 'millionaire' had just been invented. It is inconceivable what wealth there is in France now', wrote the Duchess of Orleans. 'Everybody speaks in millions. I don't understand it at all, but I see clearly that the god Mammon reigns an absolute monarch in Paris'. Joseph Gage, one of the most theatrical speculators of the century, was contemplating the purchase of a kingdom with his vast paper fortune, and Law himself was unwearying in his readiness to place funds subscribed by British aristocrats. During September 1719 the Duke of Chandos alone put £40,000 at the disposal of Drummond's Bank, to be invested under Law's personal direction. The Pay Office official, William Sloper, was said to have made £80,000.

Speculative fever was not the only stimulus coming from across the Channel. Profits were beginning to seep back into England to inflate the domestic boom, of which Secretary Cragg's office had plain evidence in a steady flow of applications for patents. Two rival insurance subscriptions for capitals amounting to £3 million were opened on successive days, 22 and 23 December. The South Sea project was not to blame for these promotions. They presaged the tide on which it was possible to launch it. The anxiety of its promoters was that they might miss that tide. . . . It did not escape the notice of the market that when the great Chandos bought Mississippi he sold South Sea. . . .

The certainty of profit by investing in the South Sea [Company] was the talk of all the drawing-rooms in London during the early weeks of March, when the Earl of Sunderland's daughter Anne was married with great pomp to William Bateman, son of the late Sub-Governor. The great Duke of Chandos himself had decided to cut his losses in the Mississippi and go in for what he called 'one of the best funds in Europe'. Three days before the Bill was published on 17 March, the Earl of Halifax, Auditor of the Receipt of the Exchequer, laid out £4,000 at 184½. The Duchess of Rutland wrote about the same time to her stockbroker:

> ... this comes to good Mr. Warner, to lett him know that I am allmost sure, I can mack an advantage by bying today in the South Seas with the hundred and four score pounds is still in your hands ... so I would bye as much as that will bye today, and sell it out agane next week, for tho I have no oppinion of the South Sea to contineue in it I am allmost certine thus to mack sum litell advantage to her that is good Mr. Warner's reaell freind. . . .

Hoare's Bank, which had been buying steadily since early February, increased its buying tempo right up to the 22nd, when it brought its total holding of South Sea stock to £17,000, acquired for an average price of about 160. . . .

James Windham, of the Salt Office, was a typical carrier of the infection when he wrote to his Norfolk relatives that he had grown so rich he would soon be buying an estate. Soon the relations, in their turn, were writing back begging him to stake their fortunes as well, and getting credit down in Norfolk on the strength of their luck.

Fortunes already 'made' were beginning to break out in spectacular displays as the fashionable London season ran to its climax. In the middle of the conversion week itself Sunderland was installed at Windsor as Knight of the Garter, and the customary feast is said to have cost him £2,000. Four days later the biggest crowd Lady Cowper had ever seen at Court celebrated the King's birthday at St. James's. A hundred dozen of claret were drunk, and the bulky Duchess of Kendal far outshone the Duchess of Bolton by appearing in a dress covered with jewels valued at £5,000. The congratulatory ode offered to the King by the Reverend Laurence Eusden boldly referred to the source of it all:

> Hence (for in his peculiar reign were laid
> Schemes, that produc'd the sure increase of trade)
> Shall generations, yet unborn, be told,
> Who gifted them with silver mines and gold;
> Who gave them all the commerce of the Main,
> And made South Seas send home the wealth of Spain.

The directors, fresh from their triumph, made a gala appearance at their Governor's birthday, and 'had much more court paid to them than the ministers themselves'. One was said to have made £3 million in three months. Janssen, whose South Sea holding was valued at a million, was presented with a diamond ring by the Prince of Wales. He was knocking down the old Tudor mansion at Wimbledon, which had once belonged to the Cecils, to build afresh, and even his housekeeper had compiled a dowry of £8,000 in the South Sea. Grigsby, who had just bought a country house in fashionable Wanstead and was said to be worth £50,000, was helped out of his coach on arrival by the new senile master of Blenheim. Both the Marlboroughs had been early in the market, and this was the moment the Duchess had decided to sell out and put her money into Bank and insurance shares.

The boom in insurance had been even more spectacular than in the South Sea. When Walpole and Craggs had been buying them back in February Chetwynd's insurance could be had for as little as 4, and at the beginning of May could still be had for 20. By the end of May they had gone to 50. Onslow's too more than doubled in price during May. The new equipages in the Park were labelled 'Insurance' or 'South Sea' by the crowds, and there were as many of one as of the other. Secretary Craggs, with typical kindliness, had distributed the proceeds of well-sold parcels to his servants and his clerks, tipped his old tutor £1,000, and was acquiring a row of houses at the bottom of Whitehall, which he proposed to demolish and replace with an impressive mansion. Walpole was systematically buying land down in Norfolk.

The crowd in Exchange Alley was as thick, and almost as aristocratic, as it was at St. James's. More than one sword was drawn there—a thing almost unknown. A Scotch peer had his pocket picked in Garraways, and an Irish earl lost his wallet coming out of South Sea House. Jonathan Wild's lost property office at the Old Bailey throve on retrieving missing portfolios containing papers said to be 'of no value to any but the owner'—4,000 shares in the Sail Cloth Company, 3,000 in Shales's Insurance, 6,000 in Baker's Annuities, 2,000 in Salter's Hall Remittances, 1,000 Wyersdale's Turnpike, 2,000 in the Company for Insuring Seamen's Wages, Sword Blade notes of large denominations, and 1,000 in Arthur Moore's Royal Fishery 'to be transferred to a Lady of Quality'.

Although several South Sea directors—notably Sir John Lambert—were individually concerned in these 'Lower Alley' bubbles, those in control of the Company watched their spawning with growing alarm. More than 100 were advertised in May and the first fortnight of June, despite the steady progress of Hungerford's Bill designed to suppress them. The newspapers doubled in size to carry the notices—twenty-three on 7 June, twenty-four on the 9th, fifteen on the 10th. There was the Company for trading in hair, the Company for improving and trading in the truly national commodity of woad; a Company for purchasing disputed titles to land, and one for manufacturing hats and caps; companies for importing broomsticks from Germany, for fixing quicksilver, for extracting silver from lead, and for 'settling the country on a desolate river more than seventy miles up the main continent in Acadia'.

Almost more than the South Sea itself, this tail to the comet has caught the historical imagination. Swindles, in the sense of being primarily money-getters, most of these companies undoubtedly were; but they illustrate far more than the gullibility of the age. They sprang from a vision of material progress in advance of the technical capacity to achieve it. The 'desolate river' was the gateway to North America, and the site proposed for settlement was Montreal. There really were goldmines in Terra Australis, which the irrepressible Captain Welbe was again raising a subscription to discover. The 'Grand Dispensary' designed to 'serve all families, shipping and poor in Great Britain with medicine at reasonable rates and the constant advice of able physicians' was not always to be a chimera. . . .

The economic confusion of the last three months of 1720 has perhaps no parallel in the history of England. A tangle of ruined credit sprawled over the country like a vast, overgrown beanstalk, withering. The gentleman in Exchange Alley who said he had bilked his cabman 'on account of having been bilked himself' stands for a universal picture of default. In some cases the default was genuine; in others it was a panic-stricken clinging to cash. Each aggravated the other.

It was not merely that the bubble had burst, with a consequent evaporation of surplus credit and the ruin of a group of speculators. The whole system of credit which had gradually grown up with the expanding economy since the middle of the previous century had suddenly collapsed. . . .

The cry that hundreds of families had been ruined had gone up on every side and has echoed down the centuries. 'There never was such distraction', wrote poor William Windham three days after the crash of the Sword Blade. 'You can't imagine the number of families undone . . . many a £100,000 man not worth a groat, and it grieves me to think of some of them'.

This must be accepted with reservations. For many the 'ruin' they now bewailed was simply the converse of the 'wealth' on which they had been congratulating themselves only a few weeks before. Pulteney wrote philosophically that ' 'Tis ridiculous to tell you what a sum I might have been master of; but since I had not discretion enough to secure that, 'tis some comfort to me to have put my affairs in such a way that let what will happen I shall be no loser by it'. But it was not easy for the Duke of Chandos to be philosophical when he found, in a review of his portfolio on the very day Windham wrote his *cri de cœur*, that although he was still £200,000 up, its total value had shrunk over the past month by more than £700,000. Chandos was the biggest money giant of his day, and could afford to hang on in the hope of better times; but even he was finding it difficult to raise an urgently required £70,000, either at home or abroad, and for a poorer man like the South Sea director Edmundson the collapse meant penury. In June he had reckoned himself worth £50,000; at the end of September £10,000, if that.

Such losses in fairy gold, and the innumerable public and private adjustments that were later made, limited the real losses. Nevertheless, the shock was felt by every family of any consequence in England, even if it was far beyond the immediately speculating circle; and on some the effects were crippling and permanent.

# 4. The Clubs, Coffeehouses, and Salons

## The Golden Age of Clubs
&#x2983; Donald McCormick

"If two Englishmen were to be cast aside on an uninhabited island," wrote the brothers Goncourt, "their first consideration would be the formation of a club."

Since this observation was made in the eighteenth century it has been borrowed, cribbed and improved upon by so many tedious after-dinner speakers that today it is little more than an outdated cliché. Nonetheless, it is a cliché which is an unconscionable time in burying itself. The English still like to think of themselves as a race of clubmen whether on the elevated level of White's or Boodle's, or on the homelier and more bucolic plane of the working man's institute, or an Oddfellows' lodge. The myth that England was ruled by "clubmen" lived throughout the nineteenth century; it flared into reality at the celebrated Carlton Club meeting in 1922, when the Coalition Government was brought down. It has even been suggested by an august, if not Augustan Sunday newspaper that Mr. Macmillan [had] shown his "greatness" as a Premier by "occasionally walking from No. 10, Downing Street, to meet old friends at the club."

But in the eighteenth century such polite condescensions to a juvenile conception of democracy were happily unnecessary. It was not the Cabinet Minister who deigned still to find time to visit his club, but the rakish clubman who graciously quaffed his tankard and condescended to give a portion of his time to the affairs of State.

This was truly the golden age of the English club. "These were not the 'co-operative palaces of luxury,' which exist now in Pall Mall or St. James's Street," wrote R. B. Mowat. "They were simply groups of mutually congenial men who agreed to meet once a week or once a fortnight in a certain coffee-house or tavern. They met in order to enjoy the society and conversation of one another.... There were thousands of such clubs all over the country."

There was no snobbish nonsense about memberships; the clubs of the eighteenth century were an aristocracy of the spirit, not of blood. A good clubman needed to have no inhibitions, none of that narrow orthodoxy which a century later was to become the death rattle of the aristocracy, blending it into an unholy alliance of middleclass snobbism and a decadent and self-deprecatory élite. The eighteenth century had no time for that modern phenomenon, the well-bred bore. A capacity for being elegantly outrageous was of more importance than a talent for polite insincerities.

Club life had been known spasmodically in England since the Middle Ages. The earliest known club in London was Le Court de Bone Compagnie, which existed in the reign of Henry IV. It was described in detail by the medieval poet, Occleve, and seems to have possessed a spirit of Chaucerian cameraderie. Sir Walter Raleigh is reputed to have founded the Friday Street Club which met at the Mermaid Tavern in Cheapside, while Ben Jonson was a member of the Apollo, whose meetings were at the Devil Tavern, close by Temple Bar. But club life in its modern form—in something more carefully organized than spontaneous tavern gatherings—only began to flourish with the coming of the chocolate and coffee-houses of the seventeenth century. The traditions of Liberal journalism may have arisen from the cocoa trade, but the seventeenth-century cup of chocolate was the beverage on which radical pamphleteering was most truly founded. Pepys, that inveterate preserver of private thoughts, was a member of the Coffee Club and White's (founded in 1693) was really evolved from the Chocolate House Club.

As the coffee and chocolate-houses were used as a serious source of news gathering and for exchanging opinions, it is understandable that the first clubs which sprang up at this time were mainly of a literary character. For, perhaps, the only period in English history the political and social scene was dominated by men of literature. Never before or since have literary men been held in such great respect in a country supposed to be influenced mainly by Philistines. But in the eighteenth century London society accepted, almost without question, what amounted to a dictatorship by men of letters. Swift formed the literary coterie known as the Scriblerus, which provoked Pope— because of feeble health a *salon* visitor rather than a clubman—to write his satires on dullness, *The Works of Dr. Scriblerus*.... Later the supreme literary arbiter of the day arose in the argumentative but entirely lovable person of Dr. Samuel Johnson, who described the faithful Boswell as "a very clubbable man." In fact, it is said that the word "clubbable" is Johnsonian in origin. Certainly he was club-minded, founding one club in Ivy Street, Paternoster Row, and another at the Essex Head Tavern in Essex Street. Most famous of all these literary organizations, which fulfilled a valuable role in moulding opinion and stimulating the cut and thrust of civilized argument, was the Literary Club, sponsored by Sir Joshua Reynolds, and including Dr. Johnson, Edmund Burke and Dr. Goldsmith among its members.

Not only writers started these literary clubs. One of the best known, the Kit Cat, was founded by Christopher Cat, a cook who was better known for his mutton pies than his literary aspirations. The writers and artists did not have it all their own way for long. Politicians quickly realized the advantages of organizing themselves into similar groups. By the end of the seventeenth century the Sealed Knot, a royalist institution, had aroused considerable controversy, and in 1710 "150 staunch Tories" met at the Bell in Westminster to launch the October Club. Lord Bolingbroke's Saturday Club, the Green Ribbon and the Hanover were other politically inspired bodies, and as the eighteenth century progressed so the nomenclature of clubs became more eccentric. The Calves' Head, started shortly after the execution of Charles I, for the purpose of ceremoniously deriding his memory, lasted until 1734, when it was suppressed after a riot. The dishes served at its annual dinners included a cod's head, symbolizing "Charles Stuart," a boar's head, said to denote the King's tyranny over his subjects, while the calves' heads depicted the adherents and descendants of the Stuarts.

New clubs sprang up to vie with one another in the oddness of their titles. There was the Golden Fleece in which every member had to assume a characteristic pseudonym, such as Sir Boozy Prate-All, Sir Whore-Hunter and Sir Ollie-Mollie. The last-named eventually broke away from his hearty, wenching, brandy-swilling companions with their robust and Rabelaisian brand of humour to form, by way of contrast, the first of the Mollies' Clubs, which, for a few years, became à la mode for young men. At these gatherings male memberes dressed up as women, sipping gin and simpering in satins as giggling behind fans, they cooed to one another:

> 'Tell me, gentle hobdehoy,
> Art thou girl, or art thou boy?'

But this preview of the Green Carnation era of the eighteen-nineties did not predominate in the eighteenth century. The "Mollies" were merely a reaction from the empty-headed and exaggerated masculinity of the Roaring Boys. They were quickly ridiculed out of existence, for even in the most sophisticated circles it was held that there was an infinite variety of permutations in normal sexual relations without borrowing from Plato and Hadrian.

The quest for perversity was in the realm of ideas rather than of passion. It was exemplified in the Ugly Club, whose members had to pass a test for possessing extreme viciousness of countenance and unpleasing features before election was sanctioned. Those who thirsted for the latest news at the earliest possible moment joined the Wet Paper, which met at the Chapter Coffee House in Paternoster Row, a condition of membership being that they had to read newspapers fresh from the press and before the ink had dried on them. It is noteworthy and perhaps socially significant that the clubs with the eccentric names survived longest, while those which laid claims to omniscience, immortality and pompous grandeur came to a speedy end. Humbug was regarded as the supreme vice of the century, and the Everlasting, which started with the idea that it should go on for ever, soon dissolved, while the Ace of Clubs, aimed at becoming the most exclusive in London, closed down in under a year.

On the other hand the Lying Club, in which downright tergiversation was the essential qualification for membership, flourished exceedingly, most of its members being lawyers! Doubtless it was with a wistful nostalgia that Oscar Wilde, in his memorable essay on *The Decay of Lying*, recalled this club and invented the "Tired Hedonists ... to wear faded roses in our button-holes when we meet, and to have a sort of cult for Domitian." Wilde's lament was that one of the chief causes of the "curiously commonplace character of most of the literature of our age is undoubtedly the decay of lying as an art, a science and a social pleasure." Wilde would have loved the golden age of clubmanship and one can picture him starting the Tired Hedonists in some cupid-canopied, marble folly and telling his polished and impossible stories to an enthralled gathering.

To appreciate fully the reasons for this passion for club life one must understand that it marked the birth pangs of the Romantic Movement in Britain. The seventeenth century had been one of bawdry, brawling and nauseating brutality which not even its veneer of sophisticated manners could disguise. A reaction from this was long overdue, and it took the form of a passion for style. Many factors had been at work to bring about the first glimmerings of Romance. The Goncourts wrote: "The century has embraced the realities; it has restored activity to the senses; it has done away with sham and affectation." This may not sound like the birth pangs of romanticism, but one must remember that this wasn't Daphnis and Chloe experiencing romance through innocence;

it was worldly wise men sniffing out the dangers of the romantic spirit before they sampled it. The rakes learned the joys of romance the hard way. Their education, carefully rounded off by the Grand Tour, taught them early on that Romance may call from the hilltops to invoke the early riser in the name of beauty, but that it brings with her an incongruous and unseemly retinue. There is her consort, Mephistopheles, her maid, Mischievousness, and her Ticket Collector, Love. But they were practical men. They did not sermonize about tedious and uninspiring stones, nor were they led astray by so utterly depraved a bird as the cuckoo, as was William Wordsworth a century later. They approached Romance, as they saw her in Italy, as uninhibited hedonists, yet taking care to guard their choicest discoveries by preserving a certain amount of awe. They realized that while life might be lived joyously and rumbustiously, it contained an element of melancholy and mystery that was worth nurturing. So they sought to have the best of both worlds—the world of carnal carnival and bacchanalian revelry against a background of wild grandeur and Poesque grotesqueries. It was romance as it might be practiced by Jean-Paul Sartre, should the founder of Existentialism ever seek to found a new school in the romantic mood. . . .

The Grand Tour gave to the sons of squires an appreciation of culture that had not previously been known in the English countryside. The squires of the beginning of the century were little better than farmers in their tastes and manners. They lived to hunt and to till. They improved their lands, but failed lamentably to improve their minds. But their sons changed all that. After the Grand Tour they took back to England a passion for Italian architecture. But what seemed aesthetically right in Italy did not fit into the English pattern of life. These young men sensed the need for a more sympathetic background to the Palladian columns and statuary which they sought to reproduce in the slumberous shires. To them rusticity was synonymous with domesticity and they felt that neither provided the right environment for the Italianate. Thus began a soon-to-be-fashionable cult for making gardens resemble nature in the raw. A garden, they decided, must not be a cosy, neat domestic paradise, but a broad splash of rugged grandeur, a landscape that had the wildness of a Scottish moor, a plot of ground that could be converted into acres of hillocks dotted with artificially contrived ruins, giving an atmosphere of genteel decay. It has been argued that these young patrons of the arts were anticipating Wordsworth. But, as we have already seen, they were too logical for that. They possessed none of Wordsworth's combination of narrow Anglicanism and romantic pantheism. Instead they tempered their romantic enthusiasms with agnosticism.

The truth was that Italy had given them a taste not only for Palladian architecture, but for romantic love. The blend of the two led them to believe that love-making required a new background. The pleasure gardens of Ranelagh and Vauxhall were all right for Roaring Boys to indulge their crude seductions and hoydenish flirtations, but serious wooing demanded a more secluded setting, remote from the mob, somewhere that exuded exoticism. So it was with one eye on creating a seduction ground that, with the aid of "Capability" Brown and other artist-gardeners, they turned their country estates into a cross between the House of Usher and Wuthering Heights, a Heathcliffian blend of artificial mountains, lonely moors and decaying ruins....

It may be argued that it is wrong to keep referring to the rake-ruler class as "they." Surely, one may ask, these men were individualists and varied tremendously in opinions and outlook. While the answer is in the affirmative, it cannot be denied that there was a remarkable uniformity about them. It was this uniformity which their passion for club life induced. Few, if any, of these young men did not belong to some club or other, and membership give them a common outlook. The rake of this period had become conscious of the need for some organization in his quest for pleasure. He had outgrown the crudities of earlier generations when the Roaring Boys terrorized whole neighbourhoods and kidnapped respectable housewives, rolling them down the streets in barrels—"matrons poop'd in hogsheads," as Gay so aptly put it.

So the fastidious rake slowly took the place of. the boasting, prattling, empty-headed Roaring Boy. He became more selective in his choice of companions, less willing to tolerate noisy bores, even seeking friends among the middle-class intelligentsia which was just emerging. And selective companionship was more easily achieved by forming clubs than by wandering from tavern to tavern in drunken, marauding bands.

Puritanically minded historians have made much foolish condemnation of the eighteenth-century rake. The portrait of a dissolute, hard-drinking, profane and lecherous society is merely one side of the coin. On the reverse is a very different picture, revealing that, by and large, the rake of this period was a more honest man than his Victorian counterpart, less empty-headed than the Edwardian masher (perhaps the nadir of rakemanship), club-minded, yet imaginative and individualistic, a progressive landlord, a patron of arts, politically active and a cultured and knowledgeable fellow. Whatever his faults and excesses, his vices and political chicaneries, he was a man who had a social conscience more often than not and one who helped to make history. At the worst he may have been an amoral politician, or a third-rate statesman, but it is to his credit that he not only tippled, but found time to govern, not only devoted himself to the arts of seduction, but toppled the nobility from their perch as arbiters of the nation's destiny.

Doubtless the literary traditions of the coffee and chocolate houses contributed to the spirit of clubmanship, but, as the country squires and their sons outnumbered the literary men, so they set the tone to the new clubs. And the half-understood spirit of romanticism which they brought from the Continent was an ever more vital factor. They began to organize their devotions to Bacchus and Venus into a club ritual. Formal dinners, with toasts to Bacchus, and sonnets specially composed for the occasion took the place of spontaneous, drunken orgies. As for seduction, the new method was to escape from the crowd, to practise their talents in their own lonely gardens and in man-made caves. Instead of wenching in the taverns, they would hold week-end orgies for club members on their own estates, or in private rooms at club headquarters. And those of the young bloods who had included Turkey in their Grand Tour borrowed ideas of oriental splendour and set up harems for themselves.

Indeed, Turkey appealed to this generation as Greece did to the Byronic Age which was to follow. The passion for harems led to the setting up of private bordellos. The Divan Club, which met at the Thatched Tavern in St. James's Street, was a direct result of Turkish influence. Its members wore daggers and turbans when they dined.

Travelling in Italy had brought about a craze for paganism as well as the classics and a realization that the Englishman's reputation as a lover was far from high on the Continent. He was regarded as stiff and boorish, clumsy in his amorous approaches. The truth was that for more than half a century seduction had been too easy for him. The ruling classes had been getting their own way without having to exercise any technique. They had not had to contend with the agents of the Inquisition like Casanova and lack of opposition makes Cupid a dull dog.

London's morals were probably the loosest in Europe. Easy virtue had become a bore. So, to be really à la mode, the new fashion was to set love-making on a more grandiose, if not a higher plane. But the reason why the age failed to produce any notable romantic lovers in England was that clubmanship called for team work rather than individual efforts at seduction. There were few "lone wolves," few attempts at romantic monogamy. Seduction was a sport to be shared, analysed and duly debated by club members. It was generally, though not always, accepted that marriage was a matter of financial arrangements convenient to both parties, and that sexual adventure was to be sought outside the sphere of matrimony. There was a juvenile attitude to this quest for adventure, and club members not only compared notes and exchanged mistresses, but kept lists of approved harlots, with detailed  memoranda of their qualities and foibles. These were exchanged within a limited circle.

Romantics though they might have been, they had a mania for comparing notes both verbally and by letter on their sexual escapades and were always giving one another advice. Thus John Wilkes, writing to his friend, Charles Churchill, the poet, enjoining him that "you should not fail to make yourself known to Effie when at Tunbridge Wells. By all means mention my name and you will find her both pliant and pliable. She is gifted with a capacity for translating the language of love into a rich, libidinous and ribald phraseology which lends enchantment to her amoristic acrobatics."

The Society for the Propagation of Sicilian Amorology contained in its records these notes on its "feminine accessories": "Antonina, Priscilla and Evadne have this day passed the most rigorous tests of the Brotherhood and have been accepted as Sisters according to the laws of the Society. I hereby testify that they are virgins all and have been instructed in the arts and sciences in which they will be expected to give satisfaction to members. Signed, Brother Tiberius."

Even so sedate a scholar as Benjamin Franklin was sufficiently the child of his age, when in England, to write these words of advice to an acquaintance who was cogitating whether to seek a mistress. While urging that matrimony was undoubtedly the ideal state, Franklin suggested that if his friend must take a mistress he should avoid young virgins, but seek "a discreet and older woman": . . . "because in every animal that walks upright, the deficiency of the fluids that fill the muscles appears first in the highest part, the face. Covering all above with a basket and regarding only what is below the girdle, it is impossible of two women to know an old one from a young one. And as in the dark all cats are grey, the pleasure of corporal enjoyment with an old woman is at least equal, and frequently superior."

Meanwhile many clubs specialized in copying pagan ritual on their convivial evenings. There was the Sunday Night Club, which practised corybantic orgies, and occultism was occasionally introduced to heighten the atmosphere and relieve the monotony. It has already been explained that visits to Italy, while producing a love of classicism and paganism, also inspired a revolt against Papist customs. This revolt became so intense that it developed into an aesthetic reaction against anything that smacked of Rome, and clubs sprang up which prided themselves on their blasphemousness and vied with one another in sneering at religion. There was a spate of clubs bearing the name "Hell-Fire," one of the most prominent of which was founded in 1720 by Lord Wharton (later the Duke of Wharton). A menu of this club included in its dishes "Hell Fire Punch," "Holy Ghost Pye," "Devil's Loins" and "Breast of Venus," the latter being two pullets arranged to resemble a woman's breasts and garnished with cherries for nipples.

On 28 April, 1721, a royal proclamation was issued against "blasphemous clubs in London," and for another twenty years nothing more was heard of them. In the late 'twenties of the century the tone of clubs tended to change again, and the emphasis was on ritualistic dinners, patronage of the arts and dressing up in oriental costumes. There was the Sublime Society of Beefsteaks, which met each Sunday at the top of Covent Garden Theatre, of which John Wilkes was a member, and the Dilettanti Society in 1732, devoted to "eating, drinking and discussing the arts."

Once again members became more selective in their choice of feminine society, though judging from the correspondence of Boswell, Wilkes, Churchill, Lord Sandwich and others, this does not seem to have saved them from the dangers inherent in promiscuity. They were for ever telling each other of their venal casualties. Bluntly Lord Sandwich told John Wilkes: 'You will either die from the pox, or be hanged.' To which Wilkes spontaneously replied: 'That depends on whether I embrace your principles or your mistress.'

But more often the rakes referred to their ailments in a roundabout way—"*Monsieur la croix de Venus*," or "Signor Gonorrhoea."

Tiring of the lists of harlots which were circulated among club members (one club actually printed a *Guide to a Whoremonger's London*), the young rakes advertised for amorous adventures. The newspapers of the period contained many examples of this....

"Wanted. A Woman in the poet's sense with a capital W. With soft lips, expressive eyes, sweet breath, bosom full and plump, firm and white, lively conversation and one looking as if she could feel delight where she wishes to give it." ...

By the 'forties clubmen were becoming weary of formal gatherings and the desire for some new element of sensation to titillate their jaded palates made itself felt. Among the older clubmen there was much sighing for the old-time orgies of the Hell-Fire clubs, but no one dared to revive them until Sir Francis Dashwood surreptitiously founded the Brotherhood of "Saint Francis of Wycomb." Perhaps it was a whim with a double purpose when he gave the new club this name; at least it sought to disguise the real activities of the "Brothers." Though history and legend has re-named this organization the "Hell-Fire Club," the title was never used by any of its members. Only towards the end of the eighteenth century and in the early nineteenth, when its exploits were publicized, did this name come to be adopted. No contemporary figure ever referred to it as such, though the Brothers were variously mentioned as "The Monks of Medmenham," "The Medmenham Friars," "The Franciscans," "The Order of Saint Francis" and "Dashwood's Apostles".

Doubtless the club was often confused with the original Hell-Fire clubs like that founded by Lord Wharton. Nevertheless, in popular legend it remains the most notorious society ever to be formed in Britain and has been painted in truly satanic colours. Gossip and wild tittle-tattle about Dashwood and his followers grew with the years and in the early nineteenth century Hell-Fire clubs were formed in places as far apart as Dublin, Edinburgh and Paris, while in 1828 a society modelled on the Franciscans was started at Brasenose College, Oxford.

A North County version of the Brotherhood was formed by John Hall Stevenson, a friend of Sterne, and the author of a Rabelaisian collection of fables and verse published under the title of *Crazy Tales* in 1772. This society was named the Demoniacs and there is evidence that Dashwood was consulted and asked for his advice on the rituals which it should adopt. But the Demoniacs never achieved the same fame as the Franciscans, nor did their bogus ruined castle in Yorkshire attract members as illustrious as those who gathered first at Medmenham Abbey and later in the caves beneath West Wycombe Hill.

For it is not surprising that the Brotherhood should have become a lurid legend. Its members included at least one Prime Minister, a Chancellor of the Exchequer, a First Lord of the Admiralty, various Cabinet Ministers, a Lord Mayor of London, a general and an Oxford professor, not to mention two or three of the best-known poets of the day and in Hogarth the age's greatest satirical painter. So the myth arose in the twilight of Victorian prudery that in the previous century England had been ruled by a gaggle of wicked, satanically minded rakes from chalk caves cut deep into the heart of a Buckinghamshire hill.

## The Significance of the French Salons

◆§ Albert Guérard

Monarchy had abdicated leadership; the court, more numerous and more lavish than ever, had become a mob torn into cliques; the scepter fell to a new sovereign, Public Opinion. That phantom power, amorphous, ubiquitous, irresponsible, *Monsieur Tout-le-Monde*, the collective mind, proved mightier than the king and wittier than Voltaire.

A unique phenomenon without exact equivalent in our days. Under the Second Empire opinion, although officially curbed, had a definiteness, a quiet authority, which it has lost in our vociferous, bewildered age; yet Alexis de Tocqueville, comparing ancient France and the France of Napoleon III with its daily press, its legislative body, its plebiscites, could say, "France today is muffled, echoeless: then it was vibrant. It was sufficient to raise one's voice to be heard afar."

The key to this paradox is "society." Information was transmitted, opinions vented, measures suggested or opposed, ministers made or unmade by word of mouth—an epigram, a song, perhaps even a glance, a smile, a shrug. By society we should not understand in this case a formal, exclusive set, the "Four Hundred": society had no single center and no recognized hierarchy. It simply meant conversation. Wherever people gathered informally and talked—in a public garden like the Palais-Royal, in the pit of a theater, in a coffee house like Procope or La Régence, in a club like l'Entresol or Clichy—there a cell of society came into being and went into action. Between a chance conjunction of idlers at the fair and the exclusive *salon* of Madame du Deffand there was apparently an abyss, but between the most remote circles there existed innumerable channels of communication. The rumor that originated among the newsmongers of *La Petite Provence*, a sheltered spot in the Tuileries gardens, would be discussed the same evening in an aristocratic company; the song that amused the Pont-Neuf would at once proceed to the Faubourg Saint-Germain, bastion of ancient pride; and conversely, a witticism whispered under a crystal chandelier in the Faubourg Saint-Honoré would find its way, with mysterious swiftness, to the workshops of the Faubourg Saint-Antoine. Paris, high or low, was curiously cohesive in those days. In spite of social barriers, there existed a freemasonry of wit, which the Revolution, industry, science, democracy have actually weakened and all but destroyed. It was that unorganized and invisible empire that was called society.

Public opinion, struggling for consciousness, found in the drama a powerful instrument. A theater was an open club. Not only did the common people have their own spectacles in the farces at the fair, particularly that of Saint-Laurent, but they thronged the Théâtre-Français. The pit was open to all those—and they were innumerable in Paris—to whom the language of the classics was not a sealed book. They were not seated: this made that part of the audience, thus jammed together, more responsive and more irresponsible. A joke, a jibe, a biting allusion, and the offender, in the confusion of laughter, applause, or protest, would duck under the sea of heads and elude the police. Allusions were found even in Racine's biblical *Athalie*. Playwrights knew the possibilities of this incomparable instrument. Even Marivaux, the sophisticated analyst of love, was not averse to a "philosophical" touch in the midst of his badinage. The "lachrymose comedy" of Nivelle de La Chaussée, the "middle-class tragedy" of Diderot and

Sedaine were social manifestoes, the glorification of bourgeois virtues. Voltaire, who wrote plays for sixty years, never failed to preach against abuses, prejudices, superstitions, intolerance. The performance of Beaumarchais's *Marriage of Figaro* (1784) was a victory against the tottering world of privilege.

The *salon* was not therefore the only temple of society, but it shows society in its perfection; and the eighteenth century saw the unquestioned reign of the *salon*. It was not a literary or political institution: the pleasure of meeting congenial acquaintances was its essential aim, *philosophie* only a by-product. If a secondary purpose existed, it was flirtation, the highly expert fencing of wit and sentiment so well reported by Marivaux. Society did not allow itself to be infected with the pedantry of *philosophie*: it was *philosophie* that was tinged with what may be called the pedantry or convention of society, a tone of artificial levity, a gesture of apology for every lapse into boorish seriousness. It was this tone, first consistently practiced by Fontenelle, that Montesquieu carried to perfection in his *Persian Letters*. He could never discard it altogether: even in his masterpiece, *De l'esprit des lois* (*On the Spirit of Laws*), we find at times *de l'esprit sur les lois* (witticisms about the laws). The deep earnestness of Voltaire is often veiled in graceful flippancy.

The great hostesses of the time would repay detailed study: we can merely mention the most prominent, from Madame de Tencin, the resolute adventuress who conquered the regent and Dubois, gambled heavily in the days of Law's "system," and managed to make her brother a cardinal, to Madame Necker, the virtuous wife of the Genevan banker called *in extremis* to save the finances of the monarchy. The two most impressive, and the most sharply contrasted, were Madame du Deffand and Madame Geoffrin.

Madame du Deffand was a great lady, cool and sharp; Voltaire respected her as an equal. She derided the romantic eloquence and sentiment of Rousseau: yet, at seventy, and blind, she fell in love with Horace Walpole, to the infinite embarrassment of that middle-aged worldling. Madame Geoffrin, at fourteen, married Money, forty-eight years of age. After a long apprenticeship and with marvelous pertinacity the modest bourgeoise turned her *salon* into "the Kingdom of Rue Saint-Honoré," the most brilliant social empire of the time. She could not be presented at court, but she counted Catherine of Russia and Gustavus III of Sweden among her friends. Stanislas Poniatowski, King of Poland, with many other celebrities in Europe, loved to call her "Maman."

The leaders of the Enlightenment, the *philosophes* of the *Encyclopedia*, had their favorite *salons*: those of Julie de Lespinasse (who had seceded from her protectress, Madame du Deffand), Madame d'Épinay, Holbach, Helvetius, Necker. It was in that exhilarating atmosphere that Germaine Necker was brought up, who was to be the redoubtable Madame de Staël; all through the Revolution and the Empire she yearned incurably for that lost Paradise.

Society not *philosophie* was the queen of the age, but *philosophie* was one of its favorite games. The social, the conversational, nature of eighteenth-century thought must ever be kept in mind. It was lively, daring, amusing; it shunned jargon like a plague; it spurned the lone wrestling of the metaphysician with the Absolute: for the Absolute is not fit for polite society. It was tolerant, except of intolerance, the archmonster, "the Infamous One to be crushed," to quote Voltaire's famous battle cry; for fanaticism is the deadly enemy of urbanity.

This drawing-room or coffee-house character explains both the popularity of *philosophie* at the time and the discredit in which it fell in later ages. For conversation is evanescent. Even if we had a full record of the words, if we could follow the dazzling bout of paradox, irony, and repartee, the setting would be lost, the animated scene, the soft lights, the exquisite decorations, the tones, undertones, and overtones, and especially the smile—that unique eighteenth-century smile, shrewd, mocking, and tender, preserved in the marvelous pastel portraits of La Tour.

# 5. The Character of Eighteenth-Century Travel

## The Grand Tour
⁂ J. H. Plumb

To learn manners, to learn the only trades open to an aristocrat—war and diplomacy—to learn the culture of his class made a Grand Tour a necessity for the young English or German peer. Fortunately the new wealth that was seeping into Europe enabled him to afford what was the most expensive form of education ever devised by European society. The young nobleman resided abroad usually for three, but often for four, and at times even five years. More often than not he was accompanied by two tutors: one for bookish study, the other for riding, fencing, the arts of war. Often the former were men of distinction—Adam Smith, the economist, accompanied the Duke of Buccleuch; William Coxe, the historian, tutored Lord Herbert. Usually one personal servant was taken from England, the others hired as necessary. The grandest people shipped their own coaches, but the enterprising hotelier, Monsieur Dessin of Calais, ran a highly profitable coach-hire business and had a virtual monopoly of it.

Usually the Tour started very modestly with a stay in a French provincial town, preferably where the English were few, so that the boy was forced to speak French. Strasbourg, Dijon, Lyons were favoured because they afforded convenient places for short tours to Germany and Switzerland. Others preferred the towns in the Touraine because the purest French was spoken there. A boy's day was meticulously regulated. William Coxe was instructed to make 'a return of the occupations of every day in the week and at what hours' to the Earl of Pembroke. Both Coxe and Captain Floyd, young Lord Herbert's second tutor, and the boy himself had to give an account of themselves on the first, tenth and twentieth of every month. The young man's hours of riding, fencing, dancing, tennis and billiards were as keenly regulated as his mathematics, history and geography. He was ordered to a dentist twice a year, commanded to take a purge of camomile tea every morning before eating, and to have the tips of his hair trimmed on the second day of every new moon. This vigorous, almost remorseless system could be kept up only whilst the boy was young, the society in which he moved alien and strange, and the tutors still in awe of the noble father at home. Paris with its salons and sophistication usually proved irresistible and the tutors' resistance easily overcome.

Paris either entranced or disappointed; the incurable Anglophiles saw it as a meaner, shabbier London, but the majority were delighted by the clean streets, brilliant lighting and the lovely royal gardens designed by Le Nôtre; gardens made for elegant lounging and discreet flirtation. Here the young Englishmen, Germans and Russians came to gape at fashion and to grow accustomed to the new French clothes it was *de rigueur* to buy on arrival in Paris. Even Dr. Johnson, who made his Grand Tour very late in life, gave up his brown fustian and went into silk and lace the day he arrived. Naturally the wellborn were amply provided with introductions to aristocratic circles and usually they were presented at Court. Weeks of balls and parties followed, interspersed with sightseeing and buying luxurious gewgaws—gold snuffboxes, seals of carnelian and agate, the lovely porcelain of Sèvres; fine velvets, silks and damasks; screens, fans, *étuis*, clocks in ormulu and marble; watches framed in diamonds; daring terra cottas by Clodion and bronzes by Bouchardon. All were boxed, packed, insured, and dispatched against the day when the exile returned to his distant province. Before Paris endangered the morals or ruined the finances, the young nobleman's steps would be diverted towards Italy. Until 1780, the usual routes were either through Savoy and over the Mont Cenis to Turin or by boat down the Rhone and by felucca—a coastal sailing craft—from Antibes to Genoa. Both could be exciting. The Mont Cenis route necessitated taking the coach to pieces and carrying the traveller in a chair over the steepest part of the path, a formidable undertaking in winter when bad weather might endanger everyone's life. During his passage, Horace Walpole had his favourite lap dog seized from under his nose by a wolf. The danger of the other route lay in the treacherous nature of the swift-flowing Rhone, particularly at Pont-Saint-Esprit, and after that there was always the possibility that the felucca would be seized by the Barbary corsairs who roamed the Mediterranean: rich Christians fetched a good ransom. After 1750, however, mountains became fashionable and the sea route grew neglected. The marvels of nature—particularly glaciers and above all the *Mer de Glace* on Mont Blanc—

began to be admired and no Grand Tour was complete without a mountaineering adventure. So, on the way to Italy, many stopped off at Chamonix. Armed with guides and loaded with barometers, tea kettles to boil water on the glacier and so determine heights, luncheon baskets, tents and servants (the Empress Josephine took sixty-eight guides in 1810!) they braved the mountainside. Sometimes even an artist was hired to render the scene immortal—Lord Palmerston took a famous water-colourist, William Pars; so did William Beckford, who had with him J. R. Cozens. Their drawings are some of the earliest we have of romantically viewed mountain scenery. Amidst the towering peaks of snow and ice all felt a proper sense of fear, of man's insignificance, of the majesty and indifference of Nature. More than twenty years after his visit, Dr. Howard of Baltimore, one of the early travellers to the *Mer de Glace*, said: 'I cannot even now think of some of the situations without a feeling of dread.' Earlier generations, like that of Addison and afterwards of Gibbon, had ignored these mountains and concentrated in Switzerland on a course of comparative constitutional study for which the multiplicity of states and free cities provided ample material. But it was of the nature of the Grand Tour to increase in entertainment and diminish in education as time passed; also romanticism, through Rousseau, was making the transition easier by insisting that the feelings needed education as much as the mind.

Italy was, perhaps, the most important part of any tour and a far longer time was usually spent in it. As Dr. Johnson said: 'A man who has not been in Italy is always conscious of an inferiority.'

Italy was the land of marvels, the antique shop of Europe. Speculators dug feverishly for Roman marbles and bronzes, and the discoveries of Herculaneum and Pompeii inflamed the imagination still further. All Englishmen were expected to return festooned with works of art and they became dilettantes overnight, talking with assurance of patina and of significant form. They ransacked palaces, abbeys and convents, employed spies and informers, and were easily, too easily, gulled by fakes. But throughout the century an ever-increasing stream of works of art—good, bad and indifferent—flowed into the country houses of England, Germany, Scandinavia and Russia. Italy, however, offered more than art. 'Indeed,' pontificated Dr. Johnson, 'if a young man is wild, and must run after women and bad company, it is better this should be done abroad, as, on his return, he can break off such connections and begin at home a new man.' Better an Italian countess, Catholic and married, than an English actress, marriageable but impossible. Furthermore the Italian countess was likely to improve his style not only in the arts of elegant flirtation but also in training him for the marriage bed. And the worldly-wise parents expected their young to lose their hearts in Italy; some, like Lord Pembroke, recommended their old flames to their sons and wrote sentimentally about their own past. Strenuous sight-seeing days followed by nights, equally strenuous, of amorous dalliance completed the education of the young nobleman abroad. But it was a leisurely finish—Turin, Milan, Rome (the Jacobite Court carefully avoided), Naples for the ruins and the opera, and then Vicenza for Palladio's sake, and Venice for its Carnival. The pictures of Longhi—suggestive, raffish, elegant—recall for us the dissolute nature of Venice's charm. Here the mask permitted licence.

After one or two years in Italy, the long voyage home began. The traveller had left England as a stripling unversed in the arts of life; he returned sophisticated, urbane and a *cognoscente*. His portrait painted by Batoni, Rosalba or Mengs; one or two pictures of the first rank, sometimes genuine, sometimes false; a collection of water colours, drawings and lithographs; the latest volumes on Pompeii from the royal press of Naples; marbles, bronzes, Genoa velvet and Capodimonte porcelain that would embellish his state rooms were packed in their great crates and sent home via a warship for safety's sake. On his return to Paris, the success of his Grand Tour could be measured by the ease with which he bore himself in the *salons*. Back at home, he joined a magic circle. By turning the conversation to stories of Madame du Deffand, or by mention of a picture in the Pitti, or the prices charged by Busiri, he could quickly get the measure of each new acquaintance and discover whether he belonged to his own aristocratic world. This prolonged, extravagant education was achieved only at great cost—a young nobleman abroad could easily run his father into three or four thousand pounds a year—in gold. Expensive though it might be, the Grand Tour drew more and more people into its orbit; indeed, not only the young and aristocratic but also the middle-aged and the middle class. The fascination of a European tour even began to intrigue the well-to-do in the American States and the West Indies. By the end of the century, English, Germans, Scandinavians, bourgeois as well as aristocrats, began to swarm to the warm south. Philip Thicknesse pioneered and popularized the idea of making the Grand Tour cheaply. In 1790 William Wordsworth, the poet, and his friend Robert Jones were perhaps the first undergraduates to make the tour on foot with their belongings strapped to their backs. As steamships and railways replaced the sailing ship and the coach, the swarm became a flood and finally submerged the Grand Tour. Under the pressure of middle-class values, aristocratic standards of education began to give way and the tutor and the Grand Tour were replaced by the public school and university. Entertainment became the aim of foreign travel rather than education and fine manners.

During its heyday, however, the Grand Tour had influenced social life to a remarkable degree; it also created the basic structure of foreign travel which later generations were to adopt and to extend. Some of the diaries and journals, which all travelers tended to keep, got into print; others stayed in the family archives to warn and exhort and advise youngsters. As the eighteenth century progressed, descriptive literature gave way to practical guides. Thomas Taylor's *The Gentleman's Pocket Companion for Traveling into Foreign Parts*, which provided maps, advised on roads, and gave distances, also printed tables of money and weights for conversion, listed a huge variety of information, and gave as well simple dialogues in Italian, French, German and Spanish. It quickly became every traveller's *vade mecum* and spawned a vast brood of guides that have never ceased to pour from publishing houses.

Nor were the journalists, publishers, amateur writers the only men to see that money was to be made out of the passion for the Grand Tour. Fencing masters, dancing masters, riding masters did so excellent a trade in Paris that their professions became over-crowded. The least successful drifted to Moscow, Budapest, Edinburgh and Stockholm to take the education in manners to the *petite bourgeoisie* who could not afford either the time or the money to leave their native heath, but wanted their sons and daughters to ape the airs of the aristocracy. Language masters often pioneered the way, for it became a mark of gentility in all countries to be able to interlard conversation with a few phrases in Italian or French. Although moralists might denounce the corruption of native manners that French and Italian airs always produced, there can be little doubt that the rage for southern European culture softened the barbarity and increased the civility of countries in the west, north and east of Europe. Yet when carried to excess, as it was in some German courts and amongst the aristocracy of Russia, it possessed dangers. The noblemen of Russia spoke French, dressed in French clothes, sat on French furniture, mostly employed French servants, and became alien to their own people and their problems; and the cleavage between classes in Russia was immeasurably widened. In Germany the nationalistically minded *bourgeoisie* turned under the influence of the *Aufklärung* from emulation to envy and hate, and cultivated Teutonic customs—crude, absurd, cloudy with bourgeois romance—as a sort of protest against the aristocratic attitude of international culture derived from Greece and Rome and kept alive in France and Italy, of which the Grand Tour was the symbol. Perhaps both these disruptive effects were natural responses to the greatest achievement of the Grand Tour. This was to give a homogeneity never achieved since by any class on such an international scale: James Boswell had no difficulty in slipping into the best aristocratic society in

Utrecht, Berlin, Darmstadt, Geneva, Florence, Venice, Milan, Naples, Paris; yet he was, as Scottish gentlemen went, rather a raw youth of no great family distinction. Horace Walpole, a youth of twenty, fitted into the highest circles in France and Italy with instinctive ease: taste, knowledge, background and education were the same—whatever their race—for young men of his birth and breeding. Their early years had been spent in learning those arts of living which the Grand Tour brought to perfection. It made for ease not only in the transmission of taste but also of ideas. Voltaire, Rousseau, Diderot, Gibbon, Hume were read as quickly in St. Petersburg or Naples as in their native lands. Yet the Grand Tour probably had its most profound effect in two spheres—travel and taste. The rudimentary foundation upon which the huge structure of modern European travel has been erected came into being very largely to fulfill the needs of the young aristocrats setting out on their tours. Hotels, couriers, foreign exchange facilities, specialized transport to beauty spots—the whole paraphernalia by which the aristocrats were housed, fed and informed came into being in eighteenth-century Europe. By and large these early travellers found and fixed upon what were to become the playgrounds of Europe. They discovered the delights of the Alps and made Switzerland a tourist centre of Europe; they recommended the French and Italian Rivieras for their climate and cheapness. Before the end of the century the old and delicate from northern Europe were infesting Nice, Menton and San Remo; the unmarried aunts of the European peerage drifted into the resorts—throughout France and Italy—which their noble ancestors had discovered on their Grand Tours.

Yet the greatest influence of the Grand Tour was in art and taste. Every museum in northern Europe owes something to the wealth and skill of those young aristocrats who made the Grand Tour, and bought on the strength of their taste—or rather the taste of that small band of Anglo-Roman expatriates who devoted themselves to the British nobility's passion for sight-seeing and for art. Usually they were failed architects or artists like Colin Morrison, James Byres and John Parker. They usually could be found hanging about the English coffee-house in the Piazza di Spagna, waiting for their custom. They gave good value. James Byres took the historian Edward Gibbon on a tour of Roman antiquities that lasted eighteen weeks without a day's intermission, and left Gibbon exhausted. Even the indefatigable Boswell, who in a fit of enthusiasm insisted that he and Morrison speak Latin as they visited the Forum, discovered that he lacked the stamina and the spirit to maintain a passionate interest as Morrison remorselessly plodded in the Roman heat up and down the hills and in and out of the ruins, leaving nothing undescribed. Usually these *cicerones*, as they were called, kept a close contact with Italian painters and art dealers, collecting a double commission from the patron and the patronized. Byres was responsible for the Portland Vase reaching England, and the sale of Poussin's *Seven Sacraments* was negotiated by him. Obviously the young noblemen felt much safer if buying through one of their own countrymen: a weakness which a shrewd Welshman, Thomas Jenkins, turned to his own great profit. He became the leading art dealer in Rome. Often the aristocrat could not raise the huge sums Jenkins demanded for his statues, so he lent money for the purchase and thus took a double profit. Jenkins's histrionic powers were highly developed: he wept with emotion at parting with an object on which he was making several thousand per cent profit. His head, however, was equal to his heart and no one could match him in the technique of restoration; under his skilful hands a battered antique torso quickly achieved arms, legs and head with the finest nicotine staining to give them an age worthy of the price that he charged. Nor was he humble to his clients. He underlined their ignorance, paraded his own virtuosity, and plucked their pockets in the mood of humility so induced. And, of course, there were far less reputable sharks than Jenkins, eager to catch the gullible nobleman with a bargain at an exorbitant price. The standards of professional honesty were low and the skill in copying old masters high, and many a Raphael was born to blush when seen in the cold, critical, northern light.

No traveller came back empty-handed: pictures, statuary and bronzes, ranging from antique Greek marbles to fashionable Italians, were brought back in thousands to enable English, Dutch, Germans, Russians and Scandinavians to appreciate and enjoy the great aristocratic inheritance of Europe. The astonishing virtuosity of these young men can be seen from a recent exhibition held at Norwich which displayed works collected on the Grand Tour during the eighteenth century, principally by the leading Norfolk families. This not only contained old masters, but also illustrated the patronage they brought to eighteenth-century Italian artists. No Italian artist of real merit was absent and the quality of many of their works was exceptional; there were magnificent examples of Canaletto, Guardi, Piranesi, Zuccarelli, Batoni, Rosalba, Pannini, Busiri and the Riccis.

This passion for all things Italian, whether antique or modern, forced painters and architects to make their own pilgrimages to Rome, for they stood little chance of making a living in England unless they could parade a recognizable virtuosity to the returned tourists. So off they went: some, like Reynolds, by man-of-war, in the luxury of great patronage; others, like Thomas Patch, on foot in poverty. They reached Italy in droves; some died there, some stayed, most returned with improved techniques and many splendid canvases to stimulate the powers and imagination of those who stayed at home. Strangely few Italian artists attempted to exploit the English market in its homeland; the most outstanding of these was Canaletto whose pictures of London, Windsor and Alnwick Castle are amongst the finest topographical pictures of the eighteenth-century English scene.

Passionately preoccupied as tourists were with art, few developed a keen critical judgment or displayed much independence of mind. They were willing to pay huge prices for Veroneses and Titians, they prized Caravaggios and eagerly bought early Bolognese painters—Guido Reni, Guercino and the Caraccis—artists who are now regarded as far, far inferior to Tintoretto or Botticelli whom they consistently ignored. As in painting, so in architecture: they confined themselves strictly to the limits of the fashionable, thought St. Mark's at Venice barbarous, and kept their praise for Caserta by Vanvitelli or for Bernini's colonnades at St. Peter's. Their classical education, however, gave them a profound interest in the discoveries at Pompeii and Herculaneum. Sir William Hamilton with his lovely wife Emma, afterwards Nelson's mistress, acted as host to a whole generation of the British aristocracy and not only taught them the beauties of classical design, but often secured objects for them that were both authentic and beautiful. Indeed the pilgrimage to Pompeii strengthened considerably the adoption of classical motives in architecture and decoration which marks the last half of the eighteenth century. The wily Josiah Wedgwood was quick to exploit this acquired taste of returned aristocrats, and he manufactured for them huge quantities of pottery in Pompeiian shapes festooned with classical reliefs. Indeed, he called his factory 'Etruria'.

The ideas, the attitudes, the tastes fostered and extended by the Grand Tour imbued the aristocracy with more than sophistication. They regarded themselves as the true heirs of the Augustans. They came, in consequence, to believe passionately in the virtues of courage and stoicism. They thought nothing became them so well as heroic death in the service of their country, and in the wars against Napoleon they died as well as many a Roman. Furthermore they regarded an interest in classical literature and a capacity to judge the decorative arts as essential qualities of a gentleman. At least these were the standards in which they believed, even though many fell short of them; for all did not respond, as Adam Smith realized, to the educational values of the Grand Tour. He thought that the boy 'commonly returns home more conceited, more unprincipled, more dissipated and more incapable of any serious application, either to study or to business, than he could well have become in so short a time had he lived at home'. True of some, it was not the common experience. The

country houses of England, its museums and galleries, the vast literature of travel, the increased urbanity and the growth of civility of
English social life in the late eighteenth century, reflected in the correspondence of Horace Walpole, show that this fabulously extravagant
education for a ruling class—more costly than any invented before or
enjoyed since—paid fat dividends. The rich are not always remarkable
for taste, wit or elegance, but the eighteenth-century aristocracy
throughout Europe insisted on these virtues. Thanks to the Grand
Tour, taste acquired in Italy, combined with the breeding acquired
in France, brought sophistication to the remoter outposts of European
society which had previously lived close to barbarism. It also gave to
the Western world a love of ancient Europe and its artistic heritage
that has long ceased to be confined to the aristocracy. What was once
the unique privilege of a nobleman is now the common experience of
the English-speaking peoples.

### *Touring England*

  ◄§ Dorothy Marshall

As travelling facilities grew better and roads were improved by the
exertions of the turnpike trusts, the most comfortably circumstanced
and educated section of the middle class, as well as the gentry, became
more mobile, though it was said of the majority of the well-to-do in
Birmingham, even by the end of the century, that they did not travel
far from home except on business. 'Comparatively few had ever seen
London, near as it was; fewer still had ever seen a mountain or the
sea, or had any idea of a ship, except from pictures. These things were
read about and talked of as very wonderful indeed.' Many middle-class
families were more mobile. Though the educational advantages of the
Grand Tour were not for them they broke the monotony of life and
added to their own information by exploring their native country. The
eighteenth century was the century of the watering-place and the Spa.
Bath in particular was the very essence of the genteel and the civilized.
Here persons of fashion, the minor gentry, the prosperous middle class,
all accepted the discipline of its social routine. This was very largely
the work of Beau Nash. A visit to Bath was a much more exciting and
formative event to an ordinary middle-class family than it ever could
be to the regular man of fashion, and did much to spread the observances of polite society among those who would otherwise have had
little chance of such contacts. That there could be this intermingling,
this apparent harmony of social life was itself highly significant of the
place that the middle-class were coming to assume in the social struc-

ture of their country. They were no longer content to accept a purely utilitarian role in the national life: they wanted more than merely material satisfactions. By now they were claiming the more artificial pleasures of polite society. A visit to Brighton, that centre of Regency life, came into the same category, though here the social round was more informal and the fashionable cure sea-bathing rather than taking the waters, a practice assisted by the new-fangled and experimental bathing-van.

The North had similar, if less sophisticated, resorts of its own. A journey to the South was a more formidable undertaking to most people than a trip to the Continent would be to-day. In Yorkshire both Harrogate and Scarborough rose to more than local fame. A visit to one of these places was an event important enough to be thought worthy of print and there seems to have been a steady demand for 'travel' books like Hutton's *A Tour to Scarborough*, describing for mere stay-at-homes both the incidents of the journey and life at the watering place, and in particular the new routine of sea bathing.

> There are thirty six machines for sea bathing, [wrote Hutton] which is a sufficient proof of their frequent use. I have often observed eight or ten in the water at the same time. The place is extremely convenient. The bathers are fond of a full tide; but I can see no evil in bathing at low water except the length of the way; for, as no river runs into the sea to weaken it the water must at all times have the same effect. Each time you bath is sixpence exclusive of perquisites.

As for all new practices, much was claimed for this one; and sea-bathing was thought to be helpful for such varied complaints as epilepsy, palsy, disorders of the heart, debility, cutaneous complaints, gout, rheumatism and scrophile scurvy. It is little wonder therefore, that a class of persons not sufficiently wealthy or experienced to enjoy the experience of the Grand Tour should flock to avail themselves of amenities at once so novel, so pleasurable and so beneficial! Both Harrogate and Scarborough, because of their situation, were essentially more middle-class in their clientele than either Bath or Brighton, for they lay further from the hub of the polite world, London, and therefore attracted less attention from the world of fashion. Even so, they too helped to spread some of the conventions of polite society to a wider circle, for local families of good standing were among their patrons, and by their example helped to set a new standard of urbanity for those who frequented, either for pleasure or for health, the spas and seaside resorts of the North.

Some travellers were more adventurous in their search for air and scenery. Elizabeth Bennet, it may be remembered, exclaimed 'What delight! What felicity!' when invited to join her uncle and aunt on a tour of pleasure to the Lakes. Catherine Hutton took her mother to Aberystwyth, and left an amusing record of the trials, and even perils of the journey: roads left much to be desired and the accommodation at some of the Welsh inns was more than primitive, even by eighteenth-century standards. On another occasion they went to Blackpool, which made no very favourable impression on her. She described it as 'situated on a level, dreary, moorish coast, the cliffs are of earth and not very high. It consists of a few houses, ranged in a line with the sea and four of those are for the reception of company; one accommodating 30, one 60, one 80 and the other 100 persons.' Of her fellow guests she has some amusing comments to make. 'The Boltoners', she declared, 'are sincere, good humoured, and noisy, the Manchestrians reserved and purse proud; the Liverpoolians free and open as the ocean on which they get their riches. I know little of the gentry but believe them to be generous, hospitable and rather given to intemperance'.

## English Inns
⚜ E. W. Bovill

[Travel] would have [been] pleasanter ... had the roadside inns been less unreliable. Donne, writing in the middle of the nineteenth century and looking back nostalgically to the days of his youth when England was famous for the excellence of its inns, tells us that 'indifferent roads and uneasy carriages, riding post, and dread of highwaymen, darkness or the inclemency of the seasons, led, as by a direct consequence, to the construction of excellent inns in our island'. That was not so. The good inns Donne recalled remained very rare until travelling became easy, and that was not till after the close of the eighteenth century.

Few men of culture and gentle birth knew the inns of England as well as John Byng who, between 1781 and 1794, spent several weeks a year travelling in the country on horseback. And none knew better how to guard against the discomforts of the average country inn. He always took a servant with him, partly to give himself consequence, thus ensuring a little extra attention, but chiefly to send on ahead 'to pre-pare for me, & my horses, proper accommodations at night. This is the true use of servants on the road, tho but selldom what their masters require of them; trusting to the waiter, and chambermaid for dirty glasses, and ill made beds, and confiding the care of their horses to drunken, roguish, hostlers; & whilst their own genteel followers are regaling themselves in a genteel parlour, the horses are neither clean'd, nor fed. As for my sheets I allways take them with me, knowing that next to a certainty, 5 sheets must be dirty, and 3 damp, out of number ten: these with a very few other necessaries, travell behind my servant; as for my night cap, great coat, and such other etceteras, they travell behind my own person, in & upon, a small cloakbag.'

At Oxford, in 1781, he reached the conclusion that 'the imposition in travelling is abominable; the innkeepers are insolent, the hostlers are sulky, the chambermaids are pert, and the waiters are impertinent; the meat is tough, the wine is foul, the beer is hard, the sheets are wet, the linnen dirty, and the knives are never cleaned!! Every home is better than this!'

A visit to the Crown at Ringwood started fairly well—'I was well waited upon'—but he did not like having to sup off grey mullet—'he is strong, and oily, . . . nor would any dressing, (even from a receipt of Mr. Walton's,) render him palatable'—but he had a terrible night. 'Of all the beds I ever lay in, that of last night was the very worst, for there could not be more then fifty feathers in the bolster, and pillow, or double that number in the feather-bed; so there I lay tossing, and tumbling all night, without any sleep, or place to lay my head upon, tho' I rowl'd all the bolster into one heap.'

At the Bull's Head, Manchester—'Oh! what a dog hole is Manchester'—the bill of fare was encouraging, but the dinner was a sad disappointment. 'My dinner, (order'd magnificently) was a salmon-peal, —lamb chops, and peas:—look to the product; peas were not to be had; the salmon, serv'd to me, was too stale to be eaten; and the thick, raw, fry'd chops swam in butter! "God sends meat; but the devil sends cooks".—I could not eat; I try'd to drink of the port wine, but could not; the bread was intolerable, and the cheese was in remnants;—I said "Take away, I cannot eat!" '

One of Byng's fads, which irritated one of his companions, was a dislike of being waited upon at meals. For this he seems to have had some slight excuse. 'Instead of a nasty, dirty wench,' he wrote, 'watching you all the time, picking her nails, blowing her nose upon her apron, and then wiping the knives and glasses with it; or spitting and blowing upon the plates. Surely . . . there is nothing so comfortable for a small company as dumb waiters; as for myself, I am uneasy when a fellow stands behind me, watching me, running away with my plate, and winking at his fellows.'

But he had one great advantage over most travellers: 'I am never stung by bugs, or fleas; and when I enter a bed, I believe that they all quit it.'

# 6. The Expansion and Transformation of the Reading Public

## The Growth of the Popular Press
ᦂ *Raymond Williams*

The story of the foundation of the English Press is, in its first stages, the story of the growth of a middle-class reading public. The first half of the eighteenth century is a critical period in the expansion of English culture, and the newspaper and periodical are among its most important products, together with the popular novel and the domestic drama. The expansion is significant, in that it took place over a wide range and at many different levels. The development of the press fully reflects the range and the levels, and sets a pattern in this kind of expansion which is vitally important in all its subsequent history.

The cultural needs of a new and powerful class can never merely be set aside, but the ways in which they are met may be determined by various legal, technical and political factors. The factors which most clearly affected the press, in the late seventeenth and early eighteenth centuries, were, first, the state of communications, in particular the postal services, and, second, the passage from State-licensed printing to conditions of commercial printing for the market. State control over printing was, in its turn, an obvious political control over the powerful new means of disseminating news and opinions.

There had been many efforts, in the sixteenth and early seventeenth centuries, to use printing for this obvious social purpose, but all had been hampered by direct political censorship. In one form or another, the *Corantos*, *Diurnalls*, *Passages* and *Intelligencers* did their best to break through, yet all these were still, essentially, books or pamphlets. The establishment of the weekly public post in 1637 made possible a new technique, that of the news-letter, which was circulated by sub-

346

scription to booksellers, and which, being handwritten by scriveners in the booksellers' employ, escaped the restrictions on printing. This advance in freedom was, however, obviously technically regressive, and when the same freedom found a progressive technique the news-letters were left far behind. This was not to happen, however, until nearly the end of the century.

The important technical advance, the development of a news *paper* instead of a book or pamphlet, in fact took place under official direction. This was in 1665, when an official *Oxford Gazette* was 'published by Authority', in the new single-sheet form. This later became the *London Gazette,* now only an official publication, but then a true newspaper. In the same period, however, State control of printing was being put on a new basis. The Licensing Act of 1662, to prevent 'abuses in printing, seditious, treasonable and unlicensed books and pamphlets', limited the number of master printers to twenty; and in 1663 a Surveyor of the Press (L'Estrange) was appointed, with a virtual monopoly in printed news. Thus, while the right technical form was being found, the conditions for its exploitation were firmly refused.

Yet the balance of political power was now evidently changing, and as 1688 is a significant political date, so 1695 is significant in the history of the press. For in that year Parliament declined to renew the 1662 Licensing Act, and the stage for expansion was now fully set. In addition to the new freedom, there was also an improved postal service, with country mails on Tuesday, Thursday and Saturday, and a daily post to Kent. The expansion was not slow in coming, for in the years between 1695 and 1730 a public press of three kinds became firmly established: daily newspapers, provincial weekly newspapers, and periodicals. Between them, these new organs covered the whole range of the cultural expansion.

The first daily newspaper, the *Courant,* appeared in 1702, and was followed by the *Post* (1719), the *Journal* (1720), and the *Advertiser* (1730). Many thrice-weekly morning and evening papers began publication in the same period, on the days of the country mails. At the same time, provincial weekly papers were being established: two in 1695–1700; eight in 1701–1710; nine in 1711–1720; five in 1721–1730. In periodicals, Defoe's *Weekly Review* began in 1704, and Steele's *Tatler* in 1709. Almost immediately, however, a new form of State control was attempted, with the imposition of a Stamp Duty (½d. or 1d. according to size) and an Advertisement Tax (1s. on each insertion), not to raise revenue, but as the most 'effectual way of suppressing libels'. The new form of control is characteristic of the new conditions: the replacement of State licensing by a market tax.

The pressures of the expansion in fact fairly easily absorbed these impositions. The daily press, in particular, was serving so obvious a need of the new class that hardly anything could have stopped it. A glance at its contents makes this clear, for the commercial interest could hardly have been better served. The news at first is mainly foreign, including news of markets and shipping. Of home news, a principal item is 'the Prices of Stocks, Course of Exchange, and Names and Descriptions of Persons becoming Bankrupt'. Lists of exports and imports are given, and after these come a few miscellaneous items of such other news as marriages, deaths, and inquests. Finally comes the material which was in fact to sustain the eighteenth-century newspaper: the body of small commercial advertisements. With the growth of trade, this last item became for a time the principal feature, and the *Advertiser*, 1730, conveniently marks this emphasis. It began as a strictly commercial sheet, and then broadened itself, when advertisements were short, to include 'the best and freshest accounts of all Occurrences Foreign and Domestick'. It became the leading mid-eighteenth century newspaper, and the priority it gave to advertisements, in putting them rather than news on its front page, initiated a format of obvious subsequent importance.

At the same time, however, the broader interests of the rising class were being served, at many levels, by the periodical press. The daily newspapers ordinarily abstained from political comment, not because comment was thought unnecessary but because this could obviously be more conveniently done in periodical publications. Defoe's *Weekly Review* is the first of these political periodicals, and it had many successors and imitators. There was also, however, the need for social commentary, on manners and polite literature and the theatre. This was met by the *Tatler*, which again was widely imitated. After the first phase of establishment of these classes of periodical, a wide expansion took place between 1730 and 1760. The word 'magazine' conveniently marks the expansion, beginning with the *Gentleman's Magazine* in 1730 and going on, in rising scale, to the *London Magazine*, the *Universal Magazine*, the *Town and Country Magazine*, the *Oxford Magazine*, the *Magazine of Magazines*, and the *Grand Magazine of Magazines*. These publications illustrate very clearly the broadening cultural ambitions of the class of readers they served. Their contents vary in quality and intention: from original work that can properly be classed as literature, through polite journalism, to an obvious 'digest' function. It is what one has learned to recognize as characteristic of such a stage of expansion in a culture: a range of publications serving everyone from those who want a first-hand acquaintance with facts, literature, and opinion, to those who want these in summary and convenient form as a means of rapid cultural acquisition. In the whole field it is an

impressive record of work, though it must not be idealized. There is
much good writing, but also much self-conscious 'pre-digested' instruction in taste and behaviour, and some exploitation of such accompanying interests as gossip and scandal about prominent persons. There
is not only Steele's *Tatler*, but Mrs de la Riviere Manley's *Female
Tatler* (Mrs Manley was the author of *Secret Memoirs and Manners
of Several Persons of Quality, of both Sexes*); not only Johnson's essays
in the *Universal Chronicle*, but also the *Grand Magazine of Magazines,
or Universal Register*, 'comprising all that is curious, useful or entertaining in the magazines, reviews, chronicles . . . at home or abroad'.
The fact is that when a culture expands it does so at all its levels of
interest and seriousness, and often with some of these levels exploited
rather than served.

Meanwhile, the daily newspaper was changing, alike in contents,
organization, and ambition. Increasingly, features that had been left
to the periodical press were being absorbed into the daily papers: comment, general news, and 'magazine interest' such as theatrical notices,
light literature, and reviews. This expansion took place on the basis of a
solid and growing commercial function. Since the 1740s, advertising
had grown in volume, and a successful newspaper was an increasingly
profitable business enterprise. One mark of this development is the
beginning of a new type of ownership. Ordinarily, the first papers had
been the property of printers, who had welcomed their regular printing
as a way of keeping presses fully occupied. From a sideline, papers were
becoming in some instances a main activity—a development which as
a whole is not complete until the early nineteenth century. In this situation, the floating of joint stock companies to run newspapers, the
printers being hired agents rather than proprietors, was a natural commercial development of the times. The first such company was formed
in 1784, to run the *London Gazetteer*, and the change was later to be
of considerable importance.

Circulations continued to rise. A total annual sale of 2,250,000 in
1711 had become 7,000,000 in 1753. Readership was much larger
than sales, for more papers were taken in by coffeehouses and similar
institutions than by private individuals. The raising of the Stamp Duty
in 1757 did no more to check the expansion than had the original imposition. The time was coming, in fact, when with increased prosperity
the papers would aspire to a higher political status. Their political importance was already sufficiently recognized to make them the objects
of persistent Government bribery: Walpole, for example, paid out more
than £50,000 to newspapers and pamphleteers in the last ten years of
his administration. But the time was coming when the freedom of the

press, as a political institution in its own right, would be seriously claimed. The key issue in this was the freedom to report Parliamentary proceedings, and here the periodicals had been in the van. Cave began to report Parliamentary debates in 1736, in the *Gentleman's Magazine*. When in 1738 this was declared a breach of privilege, Cave continued to publish reports, as of the 'Senate of Lilliput', and in 1752 resumed direct reports, with only the first and last letters of speakers' names. The battle was not yet won, but the claim had been staked. For the next three-quarters of a century, the freedom and political status of the press were to be dominating issues in its development. For the newspaper had broken out into the market, and had prospered: it now sought, with all those whose history had been similar, to take a greater share in the government of the country. . . .

The press as a whole was buoyant in these years. Two very important newspapers, the *Morning Chronicle* and the *Morning Post*, were founded in 1769 and 1772 respectively. With these, the London daily press had reached the beginnings of its political establishment. *The Times* followed, in 1785. Although the Stamp Duty had been again raised, in 1776, circulation continued to grow. The 7,000,000 total annual sale of 1753 had become 12,230,000 in 1776, and by 1811 was to reach 24,422,000. In 1784 there were eight London morning papers, in 1790 fourteen. Distribution had been improved, first by the coming of the Mail Coach, in 1784, and then, in 1785, by the separation of newspaper distribution from the ordinary mails. The first regular evening paper appeared, as a result of these improvements, in 1788: the *Star*, which gained a circulation of 2,000. The *Courier* followed, in 1789, and reached a circulation of 7,000. The leading morning newspapers at this time had circulations varying between two and three thousand, and a profit could be shown on this. When the *Morning Post* temporarily declined, in the 1790s, circulation fell to 350 before closure was threatened. Meanwhile, in 1779, the first Sunday paper, the *Sunday Monitor*, had appeared, and was followed by many short-lived imitators and by others destined for success, *The Observer* (1791), *Bell's Weekly Messenger* (1796), and *The Weekly Dispatch* (1801). In every direction, the press was expanding, but at just this time taxes on it were sharply increased. In 1789 Stamp Duty was raised to 2*d.*, and the Advertisement Tax to 3*s.* In 1797, Stamp Duty went up to 3½*d.* In 1789 the practice of hiring out papers was forbidden, though not stopped. These measures produced a temporary decline in circulation, though demand continued to grow. In the excited political atmosphere following the French Revolution, the influence of the press was deeply feared by the Government.

# The Novel As a Reflection of Middle-Class Attitudes

❦ *David Daiches*

The English novel, destined to become the most popular and prolific of all English literary forms, first fully emerged in the eighteenth century. It was in large measure the product of the middle class, appealing to middle-class ideals and sensibilities, a patterning of imagined events set against a clearly realized social background and taking its view of what was significant in human behavior from agreed public attitudes. From Richardson until the early twentieth century the plot patterns of English fiction were based on the view (shared by reader and writer) that what was significant was what altered a social relationship—love followed by marriage, quarreling and reconciliation, gain or loss of money or of social status. The class consciousness shown by the novel from the beginning, the importance of social and financial status and the use of the rise or fall from one class to another as reflecting critical developments in character and fortune, indicate the middle-class origin of this literary form. Like the medieval *fabliau*, also a product of the urban imagination, the novel tended to realism and contemporaneity in the sense that it dealt with people living in the social world known to the writer. . . .

Certain *Spectator* papers, the writings of Defoe, and Swift's *Gulliver's Travels* provide the . . . immediate and obvious background for the emergence of the English novel, and the story of the novel in the modern sense of the term properly begins here.

Whether Defoe was "properly" a novelist is a matter of definition of terms, but however we define our terms we must concede that there is an important difference between Defoe's journalistic deadpan and the bold attempt to create a group of people faced with complex psychological problems. Defoe's interest in character was minimal, and the novel only grew up when it learned to combine Defoe's sense of social and material reality with some awareness of the complexities of human personality and of the tensions between private moral and public social forces, between morality and gentility. With the novels of Samuel Richardson (1689–1761) we first find this combination.

Richardson was a prosperous London printer, who discovered his talent as a novelist at the age of fifty-one when he was in the process of compiling a volume of letters designed to serve as models for humble people not sufficiently educated to be able to write easily and confidently on those occasions when letters night be called for. He was working on this collection in 1739—probably writing letter number 138, entitled "A Father to a Daughter in Service, on hearing of her Master's attempting her Virtue"—when it occurred to him that he might work up a complete novel out of a series of letters written by a virtuous servant girl to her parents in the intervals of dodging her master's attempt at rape. He remembered a true story of a virtuous servant girl who eventually married her master after succcessfully repulsing his more irregular approaches, and this exemplary combination of prudence and virtue appealed to him. He temporarily dropped his collection of letters and in two months produced *Pamela* (1740). The theme of the novel is basically a folk theme, but the treatment is very different from anything to be found in folk literature. The class background is far from being the simple one of low-born maiden and high-born lord. Richardson's class was committed to the view that worth depended on individual effort rather than on status, yet they were fascinated by status and could not help admiring and envying it. This gives an ironic ambivalence to the whole moral pattern of the novel (which is presented in the form of letters from Pamela to her parents). Squire B., whose mother had employed Pamela as her maid, is bent first on seduction and then on rape; he is dishonest, malevolent, cruel, and persecuting. He does everything he can to get Pamela into his physical power, and at one stage is on the point of committing rape when Pamela providentially falls into fits and scares him off. Yet, after Mr. B. has relented and sent Pamela home, she returns voluntarily when he sends for her, loving and admiring him all the time, though disapproving of his attempt to dishonor her. Whenever he relaxes his attempts for a moment, she is all respect and admiration for him; and when he finally convinces her that her continued successful resistance has led him to offer marriage, she is all humble love and passionate gratitude. Successful resistance turns lust to love; once Squire B. has got over his weakness for seduction and rape he is seen by Richardson as a wholly admirable person, not only worthy of the love of a virtuous girl like Pamela but deserving of her humblest obedience and veneration. If a man is a wealthy landowner, and handsome and graceful in manner to boot, he must be considered wholly good so long as he is not being actively bad. Printers do not become angels by merely ceasing to threaten girls with sexual violence, but evidently squires do. Richardson, of course, would have been horrified by such a comment. He claimed that he was showing a genuine reformation of character, wrought by Pamela's virtue in a young man who had the advantage of an excellent moral grounding in childhood. But the reader knows better. . . .

*Clarissa* appeared in eight volumes in 1748. It is a subtler and profounder work than *Pamela,* and by general agreement Richardson's masterpiece. The deployment of the plot is a remarkable achievement. Clarissa, the virtuous, beautiful, talented younger daughter of the wealthy Harlowes, with a fortune of her own left her by her grandfather (but which she has filially surrendered to her father), is manipulated from a position which combines the height of virtue with the height of material good fortune to one in which she is despised and rejected, becoming an almost Christlike figure of the Suffering Servant. This is achieved by no sudden and dramatic reversal of fortune, but by a brilliantly deployed series of little incidents which combine to deny Clarissa, the virtuous, beautiful, talented younger daughter of the prudent character and eventually close in on her to prevent any return to the world of material happiness. Clarissa is maneuvered into sainthood by a cunningly woven mesh of circumstance which seems always until almost the very end to allow the possibility of escape back into the world of lost prosperity. She is given the appearance of guilt without real guilt; she is made to appear to fall without having really fallen; almost everybody comes at one time or another to doubt the purity of her motives or the perfection of her character. Then, in the end, when public opinion seems to have disposed of her for ever, she rises in death from her degradation to shine on high in glorious resurrection.

The first major phase of the action concerns the Harlowe family's sustained attempt to force Clarissa to marry the stupid, ugly, and mean-spirited Mr. Solmes. The leading spirit here is her contemptible brother, who sees financial advantage to himself in the match, while her jealous sister Arabella, suspicious that Clarissa is in love with Lovelace (whom Arabella loves but pretends to hate), is equally determined to have her married off to Solmes. Her father, a gouty autocrat, finds his authority and what he calls his honor involved, and insists on the match. Her mother, weakly giving in to pressure from the rest of the family, adds her persuasions. Meanwhile, Clarissa's brother has insulted Lovelace, who has overcome and wounded him in a duel, while Clarissa reluctantly consents to a clandestine correspondence with Lovelace in order to prevent him from taking a bloody revenge on the Harlowe family. Clarissa is in continuous correspondence with her friend Anna Howe, to whom she recounts each day's events.

The situation here developed enables Richardson to unfold a much richer moral pattern than anything to be found in *Pamela*. Clarissa, the perfection of whose character is made clear from the beginning, finds herself obliged to disobey her parents and at the same time involved in a clandestine correspondence with a rake. Richardson is here exploring, as fully as he can, the borderland of his moral universe. Children must obey their parents; but on the other hand parents must never force a child into marriage against the child's inclinations. These principles Richardson had already made clear elsewhere, but they are clear enough in the story. Clarissa offers to give up all thoughts of marriage and to live single either on the estate her grandfather had left her or anywhere else acceptable to her parents. She is suspected of being really in love with Lovelace, but she protests that she will have nothing more to do with him or any other man if she is allowed to remain free of Solmes. But her brother has organized the family to press for her marriage with Solmes, and she is confined to her room and subjected to every kind of pressure in the hope that she will consent to the marriage, in connection with which the most elaborate and (to the Harlowe family) favorable settlements have been drawn up. The picture of family pressure operating on Clarissa is drawn with magnificent vividness. The spiteful brother and sister, the tender but insistent mother, the hectoring uncles, and in the background the father egotistically insistent on his parental rights—all this comes through with vividness and immediacy from Clarissa's letters to Anna Howe. At the same time Anna herself is revealed in her replies as a sprightly and witty girl whose chief pleasure in life (to Clarissa's distress) is teasing the worthy gentleman whom her mother wants her to marry and whom, it is clear, she will eventually marry.

We also get occasional glimpses of Lovelace, who is revealed as the master mind behind the preposterous behavior of the Harlowe family. By bribing servants to report his intention of performing various rash acts in pursuit of his vengeance against the Harlowes and his love for Clarissa, he whips the family into a fury of determination that Clarissa shall marry the odious Mr. Solmes at the earliest possible moment. Pressure on Clarissa grows stronger and stronger; Lovelace presents himself continually as a source of refuge, offering to provide unconditional sanctuary for the persecuted girl among the ladies of his family (who, of course, all adore her, though by reputation only). Finally, when it looks as though Clarissa is to be forced by physical compulsion into marriage with Solmes, she momentarily yields to Lovelace's suggestion of rescue, only to revoke her acceptance of his offer shortly afterward. But Lovelace refuses to take cognizance of her letter of revocation and awaits her at the garden gate with all necessary equipment for her escape. On her going out to inform him that she cannot take advantage of his offer, he contrives a scene which enables him to whisk her off, and henceforth she is in Lovelace's power.

The second movement of the novel deals with the struggle between Clarissa and Lovelace. He is a rake, and therefore is reluctant to marry, though he adores Clarissa. He contrives matters so that she is made more and more dependent on him, and eventually brings her to Lon-

don, to an apparently respectable lodging house which is in fact a
brothel run by an old friend of his and staffed by girls whom he has
ruined. After much coming and going, and a complex series of movements in Clarissa's heart toward and away from Lovelace—the docu-
mentation of this shows us Richardson at the height of his powers—
he attempts her virtue by arranging a mock fire and bringing her out
of her room in her nightdress to escape the supposed conflagration. She
sees his purpose, discovers his trick, and successfully repulses him,
shaken to the core by his villainy. He is repentant, and offers immediate
marriage, which she proudly rejects. She despises him now, and will
not marry a man whom she despises. He plays a variety of tricks in
order to try to regain favor in her eyes and succeeds to the point of
maneuvering her back to the house of ill-fame, and there, with the
cooperation of the inmates, he first drugs and then violates her. Now
that he has won his bet with himself, as it were, and scored up another
triumph for rakery, he is prepared to concede Clarissa's true virtue and
to marry her. (He had pretended to be dying to marry her all the time,
but had adroitly phrased his offers so as to compel her refusal on each
occasion.) After illness and hysteria she escapes from him, and ignores
his frenzied appeals for forgiveness and immediate marriage. Meanwhile her friends and relations consider her a ruined woman who has
wilfully contributed to her own dishonor. Her family regard her as a
wicked runaway who deliberately chose ruin at the hands of a rake.

The third and final movement of the book deals with Clarissa's
vindication and sanctification. By means of letters appropriately copied
and circulated, the truth begins to emerge. But her family are prevented
from knowing the truth until after her death, while her dear friend
Anna Howe is kept from her by a number of contrived circumstances,
and even her sympathetic cousin Morden, who finally arrives home from
Italy, is not allowed to come to see her until her death is inevitable.
All this time the unfortunate Lovelace is frantically pleading for forgiveness and marriage, backed by his powerful family. But Clarissa
remains alone, in lodgings, befriended by strangers, cut off from friends
and relations. And there, having made all suitable preparations, she
dies, before an audience of new-found admirers. Her death is a studied
presentation of *ars moriendi*, a high example of the art of dying like
a Christian. Her family, on finally learning the whole truth about her
conduct, are consumed by remorse, and her funeral is the occasion of
its exhibition. Every single wicked character in the book then meets
with an appropriate sticky end.

Before her violation Clarissa had been prepared to consider marriage
to the fascinating Lovelace for the purpose of reforming him, and
Lovelace himself cunningly played on his need for reformation by

such means. But that temptation is over once the rape has taken place; marriage is henceforth unthinkable to Clarissa (but not to her friends), whose thoughts are more and more centered on the next world. Attempted violation is one thing; successful violation is another. Richardson is not as clear as he might be on the relation between guilt and misfortune. Sometimes he suggests that Clarissa (though through no fault of her own) is "ruined," made permanently unfit for matrimony by having been forcibly rendered a fallen woman. Like so many of his generation and later, Richardson had a purely technical view of chastity. Clarissa, though a saint, had lost her chastity, so she must give up hope of accommodation with this world. She could not, of course, consider marriage with her violator (Richardson is a cut above many nineteenth-century moralists in this), but neither could she respect any other man willing to marry a woman who had lost her "honor," however innocently. . . .

This, then, is what is meant by the claim that Richardson's novels enshrine an eighteenth-century bourgeois morality. Virtue is consistently related to prudence on the one hand and to reputation on the other, and the arena of moral struggle is the stratified society of contemporary England. Further, in the eyes of Richardson and his fellows the aristocracy is still a class to be envied and aspired to. Pamela, the serving maid, has her virtue rewarded by marrying into the squirearchy; Clarissa's upper-middle-class family want to consolidate their position as property owners and achieve a title, and Clarissa's pursuer, the aristocratic Lovelace, has never any doubt that marriage to him is a desirable thing for her. Prosperous tradesmen and master craftsmen may have believed that their class was the sole repository of true virtue and respectability in the nation, but the aristocracy was still admired and looked up to as the class which the successful bourgeois hoped ultimately to enter. The implications of this double view of the aristocracy as representing both rakishness and the heights of that worldly felicity which was the proper reward of a life of combined prudence and virtue—can be seen again and again in the working out of Richardson's plots.

# 7. The New Popularity of Opera

## Composers and Audiences
ﻬﺺ Donald J. Grout

The amount of music written by eighteenth-century opera composers testifies to the popularity of this entertainment. A tabulation of forty leading composers of the period shows nearly two thousand works, or an average of about fifty operas apiece. The sum total of the production of all composers would, of course, be much greater. One reason for this was that audiences insisted on new music each season, though they welcomed the old familiar librettos year after year. Then, too, the writing out of the score was not the time-consuming process that it is in modern days, since so much was left to be improvised. The score was really little more than a memorandum of the composer's intentions, to be filled in by the performers. A composer commonly completed a score in a month or six weeks, and received for it a sum amounting to $100 or $150, plus the price of the first copy of the arias—in manuscript usually, though favorite airs of popular operas were often published in London. Once the first copy was sold, the composer's income from his work ended, for there was no copyright protection for him.

Contemporary audiences, far from regarding the opera as a serious dramatic spectacle, looked upon it merely as an amusement. De Brosses reports that the performances in Rome began at eight or nine in the evening and lasted to midnight. Everyone of any consequence had a box, which was a social gathering place for friends. "The pleasure these people take in music and the theatre is more evidenced by their presence than by the attention they bestow on the performance." After the first few times, no one listened at all, except to a few favorite songs. The boxes were comfortably furnished and lighted so that their occupants

357

could indulge in cards and other games. "Chess is marvellously well adapted to filling in the monotony of the recitatives, and the arias are equally good for interrupting a too assiduous concentration on chess." Dr. Burney mentions the faro tables at the Milan opera; at Venice, where the pit was usually filled with gondoliers and workmen, "there is a constant noise of people laughing, drinking, and joking, while sellers of baked goods and fruit cry their wares aloud from box to box"; at Florence it was the custom to serve hot suppers in the boxes during the performance.

Some understanding of the circumstances under which these operas were performed will explain why we of today often fail to see what there was in the music to arouse enthusiasm on the part of the audiences. We must realize that those things which were the very life of the performance were just the things which could never be written in the score—the marvelous, constantly varied embellishments by the singers, the glamour of famous names, the intoxication of the lights and scenery, above all the gay, careless society of the eighteenth century, the game of chess during the recitatives, and the gabble of conversation, hushed only for the favorite aria and the following rapturous applause.

## The New Paris Opera
∽§ Norman Demuth

The new Salle du Palais Royal opened its doors on January 20th, 1770, with Rameau's *Zoroastre*. The building contained many novel features, several of which have remained in use ever since. The erection was directed by Moreau to the plans of Soufflot. A full and detailed description may be found in the *Dictionnaire historique de la Ville de Paris*, by Hurtault and Magny, from which the following facts have been gleaned.

The new theatre was three times as large as the original, for Moreau extended it as far as the Rue des Bons-Enfans, which ran parallel to the site, at a distance. It was the first French theatre to be built on an oval plan. The earlier buildings, which had often started life as tennis-courts, were rectangular. The Salle des Machines des Tuileries was intended more for circus performances than for opera or vaudeville. One feature of the new design was the *baignoire*; in this, four people sit in the utmost discomfort in a space made for two, on hard wooden chairs, with a diagonal view of the stage. Moreau ordered three reservoirs containing two hundred *muids* (hogsheads) of water in case of fire, and for the first time the stage was fitted with a fireproof curtain.

The seating capacity was 2,500, and the four rows of boxes were constructed of wood and iron. The decoration was lavish, if not to say garish, with marble and plush. The foyer contained busts of Quinault, Lully, and Rameau, while four empty niches stood ready to receive the effigies of any future great men. . . .

A Royal Decree instituted the queue system for admission, again insisting that everyone, without exception, should pay for his seat. Each had to take his chance at the Box Office, regardless of rank. Nobody was to wear a hat during the *entr'actes*. . . .

The prices of seats were:

| | | | |
|---|---|---|---|
| First Balcony | . | . | . | 10 livres |
| Amphitheatre | . | . | . | 10 livres |
| Second Balcony | . | . | . | 7 livres 10 sous |
| First-Row Boxes | . | . | . | 7 livres 10 sous |
| Second-Row Boxes | . | . | . | 4 livres 10 sous |
| Third-Row Boxes | . | . | . | 3 livres 10 sous |
| Gallery ('Paradis') | . | . | . | 2 livres 10 sous |
| Pit ('Parterre') | . | . | . | 2 livres 10 sous |

Seats could be rented for a year at the following rates:

| | | |
|---|---|---|
| Front Boxes ('Timbales') | . | . | 3,600 livres |
| Side Boxes ('Chaises de poste') | . | . | 2,400 livres |
| Baignoires ('Crachoirs') | . | . | 1,000 livres |

A properly regulated Box Office Agency was appointed. The responsible officials were Le sieur Levy, from whom seats for the Opera might be obtained (his orders were to reply to no letters sent unfranked), and M. de la Porte, a 'marchand perfumeur,' who sold the tickets for the Opera Balls. . . .

The prices were doubled for a first performance, and quadrupled when the King attended.

In accordance with what had become almost a tradition, all was confusion on the opening night, January 26th, 1770. The police had to be reinforced; there was the usual trouble over tickets and priority of admission, and the pathetic attempt to practise the 'first come, first served' principle fell to pieces. Eventually, the Académie was given its own special troop of soldiers, chosen from the élite of the Guards, and it was all they could do to stem the onrush of people who, every night, 'étaient obligés de se créer de vive force une place qui n'existait pas'.

Once inside, the audience passed the time shouting across the auditorium and making uncensored comments on the people in the more expensive seats. It was not uncommon for a person to appeal to the public for 'justice' when someone claiming the same ticket-number tried to eject him. The first-comer was usually supported so whole-heartedly that the rival claimant had to beat a hasty retreat. It would seem that the holders of tickets paid no attention to the numbers on them, but sat exactly where they wished.

# 8. Proletarian Life in the New Industrial Towns

---

## Adjustment and Survival in the Early Machine Age
≈§ J. L. and Barbara Hammond

Perhaps the best way to describe the new [industrial] towns and their form of government would be to say that so far from breaking or checking the power of circumstances over men's lives, they symbolised the absolute dependence and helplessness of the mass of the people living in them. They were not so much towns as barracks: not the refuge of a civilisation but the barracks of an industry. This character was stamped on their form and life and government. The mediæval town had reflected the minds of centuries and the subtle associations of a living society with a history; these towns reflected the violent enterprise of an hour, the single passion that had thrown street on street in a frantic monotony of disorder. Nobody could read in these shapeless improvisations what Ruskin called "the manly language of a people inspired by resolute and common purpose," for they represented nothing but the avarice of the jerry-builder catering for the avarice of the capitalist. It would be as reasonable to examine the form and structure of an Italian *ergastulum* in order to learn the wishes and the characters of the slaves who worked in it. Nobody could find a spell of beauty or romance to supply the pieties of the old city, or to kindle a civic spirit in the great tide of human life that poured in from the villages that had lost their commons or the distant towns that had lost their trade. Their towns were as ugly as their industries, with an ugliness in both cases that was a symptom of work and life in which men and women could find no happiness or self-expression; the brand of a race disinherited of its share in the arts and the beauty of the world.

361

"The singers have sung and the builders have builded,
    The painters have fashioned their tales of delight;
For what and for whom hath the world's book been gilded,
    When all is for these but the blackness of night?"

And these towns were precisely what they looked. They were settlements of great masses of people collected in a particular place because
their fingers or their muscles were needed on the brink of a stream here
or at the mouth of a furnace there. These people were not citizens of
this or that town, but hands of this or that master. Often the houses
where they lived, and the shops where they bought their food, were
supplied by their employers.

The extreme type of this organisation was the mining village. The
Society for Bettering the Condition of the Poor described with great
enthusiasm the arrangements made by the Duke of Bridgewater for the
management of his collieries near Manchester. The colliers were all his
tenants at will ("an encouragement to good conduct" as the Society
puts it), and when they were paid their wage each month, the shopkeeper, also the Duke's tenant, brought their bills to the colliery agent,
who paid the bill and handed the surplus to the collier. "Thus the collier always has credit for necessaries and reasonable comforts; and, at
the same time, is not able to squander the mass of his gains, to the injury of himself and his family." A rather different view of this arrangement was put before the public in the course of the coal strike on the
Tyne in 1765, when a correspondent wrote to Lloyd's *Evening Post*,
giving a picture of the colliery economy: "This Overseer, who by the
by is seldom distinguished for the amiableness of his character, constantly keeps a shop contiguous to the Pit where he lays in every necessary both for the belly and the back, and obliges the poor men to buy
whatever they want from him, stopping it out of their wages at a stip-
ulated sum a week till the whole is discharged." Even Lauderdale, the
most inflexible of doctrinaire economists, supported the extension of the
early and not very effective Truck Acts to mines in 1817, declaring that
he knew of cases of the grossest fraud, miners being compelled to pay
12s. for 6s. worth of flour. But even if this system was administered with
absolute honesty and good faith, it remained true that this society was
a society depending entirely on the industry, living under its shadow,
immersed in its economy, with no life or interest outside. And, of
course, the colliery owners were the masters of the situation: in the
Northumberland strike of 1832 one clergyman owner evicted all his
tenants during a raging cholera.... The *Annals of Agriculture* give a
picture of the plight of one of these towns when this avalanche of population swept into it. The writer is describing Preston and its neighbour-

hood in 1791: "Sudden and great call and temptation for hands from the country, of this county and others, and many distant parts; crowded of course in their lodgings; tempted, by extra gain, to long continued application at sedentary work, in air contaminated both by the exhalation and breathing of many people together, and also the effluvia of the material used, in confined places; and, though getting good wages at what they think easy work, yet (by the natural consequence of so many different manufactures, flourishing all over the county, and so suddenly increasing, provisions being dear, as you would see from my last) perhaps living but poorly in diet, these people are frequently visited, especially in autumn and beginning of winter, with low and nervous fevers; in short, putrid and gaol distempers, that often cuts off men, leaving families behind; and who by the high rent that all the above must cause on houses, gain settlements, come from where they will." Nassau Senior has drawn a picture of those parts of Manchester that were inundated by the Irish tide: "As I passed through the dwellings of the mill hands in Irish Town, Ancoats, and Little Ireland, I was only amazed that it is possible to maintain a reasonable state of health in such homes. These towns, for in extent and number of inhabitants they are towns, have been erected with the utmost disregard of everything except the immediate advantage of the speculating builder. A carpenter and builder unite to buy a series of building sites (*i.e.* they lease them for a number of years) and cover them with so-called houses. In one place we found a whole street following the course of a ditch, because in this way deeper cellars could be secured without the cost of digging, cellers not for storing wares or rubbish, but for dwellings of human beings. Not one house of this street escaped the cholera. In general the streets of these suburbs are unpaved, with a dungheap or ditch in the middle; the houses are built back to back, without ventilation or drainage, and whole families are limited to a corner of a cellar or a garret." Chadwick summed up the conditions under which the working classes lived with an apt illustration: "Such is the absence of civic economy in some of our towns that their condition in respect of cleanliness is almost as bad as that of an encamped horde or an undisciplined soldiery." It looks as if all the creative and organising enthusiasm and spirit of the age had gone into the making of machinery and those conquests over fire and water that had produced the new industry. Men were so engrossed in building mills that towns were left to build themselves.

These towns, too, were now losing their last glimpse of nature. Formerly the men and women who lived in the English town, like those who lived in Pisa or Verona, were never far from the open country: their town life was fringed with orchards and gardens. But as the Industrial Revolution advanced, a Manchester was growing up in which the workmen would find it harder and harder to escape out of the wide web of smoke and squalor that enveloped their daily lives. . . .

For the workman, Manchester was a prison: he was excluded from all the amenities that other classes enjoyed. "The commons on which the labourers indulged in healthful sports are enclosed; policemen guard the streets and keep the highways clear; high walls enclose demesnes, and even the iron palisades that surround ornamental grounds are jealously planked over to prevent the humble operative from enjoying the verdure of the foliage or the fragrance of the flowers." "Have we not seen the commons of our fathers enclosed by insolent cupidity—our sports converted into crimes—our holidays into fast days? The green grass and the healthful hayfield are shut out from our path. The whistling of birds is not for us—our melody is the deafening noise of the engine. The merry fiddle and the humble dance will send us to the treadmill. We eat the worst food, drink the worst drink—our raiment, our houses, our everything, bear signs of poverty, and we are gravely told that this must be our lot." Dr. Hawkins had remarked to the Factory Commission the effect of this on the health of Manchester. "It is impossible not to notice the total absence of public gardens, parks, and walks at Manchester: it is scarcely in the power of the factory workman to taste the breath of nature or to look upon its verdure, and this defect is a strong impediment to convalescence from disease, which is usually tedious and difficult at Manchester." Meanwhile the same process that swept the colour from the town swept the colour too from the sky. In the middle of the eighteenth century the smoke was so thick in Arnold Bennett's Five Towns on a Saturday afternoon that people had to grope their way in the streets of Burslem. It is true that some observers had found an extraordinary poetry in this new atmosphere, and one critic of the day, anticipating the triumphs of the art of Muirhead Bone, wrote in rhapsody of the black streams and the chimney tops, but this was an acquired taste, and it was human nature to prefer the lost rainbow to all the gorgeous canopy of mill or furnace.

Life in such a town brought no alleviation of the tyranny of the industrial system; it only made it more real and sombre to the mind. There was no change of scene or colour, no delight of form or design to break its brooding atmosphere. Town, street, buildings, sky, all had become part of the same unrelieved picture. The men and women who left the mill and passed along the streets to their homes did not become less but more conscious of that system as a universal burden, for the town was so constructed and so governed as to enforce rather than modify, to reiterate rather than soften the impressions of an alien and unaccommodating power. The town was as little their own as the mill. For the working classes had no more control over their own affairs outside than inside the factory. The weaver of Burnley or the spinner of Rochdale had less to remind him that he counted in the life of a society than his grandfather who had helped to administer the little affairs of the village and to regulate the use of its common pastures. . . .

Whatever the form of government here or there, there was a general agreement about the needs of the working classes. The town which at one time in English history had provided artists, players, minstrels, great pageants and guild festivals, represented now the meanest and barest standards of life. Scarcely a year passed without some improvement in the arts of manufacture and production, but for the great armies of men, women, and children harnessed to the thunder and lightning of the new science, the art of living had been degraded to its rudest forms. These towns illustrated, indeed, a remark made by Windham when defending a bad cause, in the debate on bull-baiting, that men of his own class were apt to think of the common people as people whose only business it was to eat, sleep, and work. The working classes were regarded as persons incapable of profiting by leisure, and fit only for the long discipline of factory hours. There were conspicuous exceptions to this general spirit, and exceptions among employers. No man fought harder for a shorter working day and a more humane life for the factory workers of Lancashire than John Fielden, the great cotton spinner of Todmorden, and the crusade against the cruelties of the woollen factories was launched by John Wood, the worsted manufacturer of Bradford. Rathbone Greg, one of the family of that name, wrote in favour of reducing hours. Some employers provided schools and libraries for their workpeople, and the Strutts of Derbyshire supplied not only schools and library, but a swimming-bath with an instructor and a dancing-room. But, generally speaking, the employing class, though perhaps they would not have said of all the labours of mine and mill, with Bishop Berkeley addressing the Irish peasants, *"Labor ipse voluptas,"* would certainly have thought that any *voluptas* that the poor could enjoy would do them more harm than any labour their masters could impose on them. It was a favourite argument for long hours in the mill that the hours spent elsewhere would be spent in drinking, and the favourite argument for low wages was based on the same general view of the working classes. The employing class were not of course peculiar. It was a commonplace in the speeches in Parliament, though many members must have known very little of the industrial districts, and Pitt summed up the artisan population of the northern towns as "ignorant and profligate." The working men of Manchester were fond of music, and Cooke Taylor, who visited the public houses, found that there was a marked difference between the manners of the workmen in houses where music was allowed and those where it was forbidden. "The operatives of Manchester have shown their taste and capability for higher enjoyments than smoking and drinking. I have gone into some of the concert-rooms attached to favoured public-houses which they frequent, and I have never been in more orderly and better-behaved company. The music was well selected, the songs perfectly unobjectionable; the conversation, in the intervals between the pieces, not only decorous, but to some degree refined, and the quantity of liquor consumed by each individual very trifling. But I have also been in houses where music was prohibited, and the scenes which I witnessed will not bear description." Yet Cooke Taylor found that it was the practice of the magistrates, as a rule, to refuse licences to public-houses where concerts were held. It was generally agreed that drunkenness was particularly common in Lancashire, and in 1819 Norris, the Stipendiary Magistrate of Manchester, wrote to the Home Office to recommend that an Act of Parliament should be passed to make it compulsory on employers to play their workpeople singly and at the factory. It was the general practice to pay a lump sum to one of the workpeople, who took it to the public-house where there were regular pay-tables. In this way the children had to go to the public-house to be paid, and of course they were expected to drink. Thirteen years later Detroisier, a witness before the Factory Commission, pointed to the same practice as an important cause of early drinking: the piecers had to go to the public-house for their wages.

It was not surprising, as Detroisier said, that the working classes who were offered little else took their pleasures in vicious and brutal amusements. These included bull-baiting and cock-fighting, practices that were still legal down to 1833. There was a regular trade connected with the latter sport, men appearing as cock-feeders and cock-heel makers in the Directories of the time. It was stated in the House of Commons that bull-baiting was a favourite sport in Lancashire, Staffordshire, and Shropshire, but that it was unknown in Yorkshire and Northumberland. Attempts were made in 1800 and 1902 to put down these practices, but without success. It is not always easy to trace the line that divides a noble from a barbarous pleasure in the treatment of animals, or to ascertain the exact ratio that prowess must bear to suffering if a sport that involves the infliction of pain is to rank as a sport that gentlemen ought to enjoy. In the debates in Parliament in 1800 and 1802 a good many speakers, and some, at any rate, of the promoters of the Bill, were preoccupied with the effects of bull-baiting in making workmen disorderly and idle. It was unfortunate for the Bill that it was in the hands of Sir Richard Hill, a typical representative of the school that rarely supports a good proposal except for bad reasons. So far as the question of cruelty was concerned, there were three lines of argument. It was possible to distinguish bull-baiting from stag-hunting and fox-hunting, or to approve of both or to condemn both. Windham, for example, who opposed legislation strongly, argued that bull-baiting was no more cruel than hunting, and that though he was not a sportsman himself, he was not prepared to forbid the sports of his friends. He would, however, introduce such a Bill himself if Parliament interfered with the pleasures of the poor. Canning extolled the sports of all classes, declaring of bull-baiting that "the amusement was a most excellent one; it inspired courage, and produced a nobleness of sentiment and elevation of mind." On the other side, speakers like Sheridan contended that the poor were capable of enjoying other amusements, that there was nothing to prevent them from playing cricket, and that though the magistrates were far too ready to suppress innocent diversions, this particular cruelty was generally recognized as a scandal. Sheffield had apparently at one time a cruel amusement of its own that disappeared under the pressure of public opinion. Cocks were tied to a stake and then used as targets by men and boys who pelted them with large billets of wood. Mackenzie, describing the Northumberland pitmen, mentioned that they dressed in gaudy colours on holidays, with variegated patterns, and that their amusements were cock-fighting, bowling, foot-races, handball, quoits, cards, and when possible hunting or fowling. Yorkshire was pre-eminently the county for horse races. The "Lancashire way of fighting" was the common description of a particularly violent kind of single combat, of which Baines gives an account in his *History of Lancashire.* "At almost every Assizes at Lancaster several individuals are tried for murder or manslaughter, arising out of battles, when, to the astonishment of strangers, evidence is given of parties mutually agreeing to fight 'up and down,' which includes the right of kicking (or purring, as it is called) on every part of the body, in all possible situations, and of squeezing the throat or 'throttling' to the very verge of death. At races, fairs, and on other public occasions, contests of this nature are witnessed by crowds of persons who take part on each side, with as much interest as is excited by the regular boxing matches of the south. That death often occurs in such battles will not be thought extraordinary, especially when it is considered that clogs or heavy wooden-soled shoes, with iron plates and studded with large nails, are commonly worn in the districts where this barbarous custom prevails."

# 9. Evangelism: The Religion of Experience and Emotion

---

## The Fervent Popular Response to Methodist Preaching
⋄§ R. A. Knox

In the September of 1654 two Quakers, Audland and Camm, went to preach at Bristol. And we are told that Audland 'opened the way of life in the mighty power of God with such effect, that they [the congregation] were seized in the soul and pricked at the heart; and some fell on the ground and foamed at the mouth, while others cried out, while the sense of their states of sin was opened to them'. Some eighty years afterwards, on 17 April 1739, John Wesley was in the same town, not preaching but conducting a sort of Bible class. He expounded the fourth chapter of the Acts, and then

> We called upon God to confirm his word. Immediately one that stood by (to our no small surprise) cried out aloud, with the utmost vehemence, even as in the agonies of death. But we continued in prayer, till a new song was put in her mouth. . . . Soon after, two other persons . . . were seized with strong pain, and constrained to roar for the disquietness of their heart. But it was not before they likewise burst forth into praise to God their Savior. The last who called upon God as out of the belly of hell was I.E., a stranger in Bristol. And in a short space he also was overwhelmed with joy and love.

What had happened? Was there something in the air or the soil of Bristol which produced these transports? Did memories of the Quaker visit linger in the memory? Or had the convulsions of the French

preachers, who had recently 'run a pitch' in the same district, predis-
posed men's minds to such a method of welcoming the gospel? All such
questions are beside the mark, and for a simple reason. The Methodist
paroxysms, although they are usually referred to as if they started on
the occasion named, began in fact not at Bristol, but in London. Three
months before 'we were surprised in the evening, when I was expound-
ing in the Minories. A well-dressed, middle-aged woman suddenly cried
out as in the agonies of death.' Admittedly the woman had been told
by her minister that she was stark staring mad; perhaps Wesley had
slight doubts about her, though he expresses none. But he cannot have
been altogether taken by surprise when the same thing happened at
Bristol in April.

It was Bristol, however, that first witnessed in large numbers those
instances of 'Shriekings, Roarings, Groanings, Gnashings, Yellings,
Cursings, Blasphemies and Despairings' which so shocked Bishop Lavington. Little more than a week later, during a sermon at Newgate
(Bristol), 'one, and another, and another sunk to the earth; they dropped
on every side as thunderstruck'. The same thing happened in the
evening; 'almost before we called upon him [Christ] to set to his seal,
he answered'; it will be noticed that by now a deliberate prayer-tech-
nique is used for the evocation of the symptoms. It would be easy for the
historian to cumber his pages with endless quotations; a précis of the
manifestations must suffice. There is a cry, or a roar; usually (not always) the afflicted person drops to the ground; you can see that he or
she is something in the position of the demoniac healed after the Trans-
figuration; Satan is letting his prey go, with the utmost reluctance. The
bystanders fall to prayer; if there is no immediate deliverance the inter-
rupter is carried out, and prayer goes on, often till late at night. We do
not hear, commonly at least, of people foaming at the mouth; but in
these as in other cases of religious convulsions we are often told that it
took so many strong men to hold the energumen down. (Six or seven
in the case of Thomas Maxfield.) Sometimes the interior struggles of
these people who could not yet 'find Christ' were prolonged for several
days, though in such cases the outward manifestations were only intermittent. Whether the re-converting of backsliders was accompanied by
exactly the same symptoms as accompanied the 'new birth' of the un-
awakened is nowhere made sufficiently clear.

'The power of the Lord was present, both to wound and to heal';
I think that Wesley, whenever he uses the word 'wound' in such con-
texts, means an outward manifestation of spiritual crisis, more or less
sensational. But he attached great importance, also, to the inward experiences of the people concerned, and shows obvious disappointment
when they can 'give no clear, rational account' of these. They seem to

have tallied with the outward behaviour of those who underwent them; a sense of despair, sometimes vividly representing itself as slavery to the devil, was followed by a conviction that Christ's blood had now conquered, and they were free. 'She saw her Saviour, as it were, crucified before her eyes'; what virtue is there in the 'as it were'? Wesley does not tell us, but it seems clear that some of the new converts claimed to have been favoured with visions. Others were less precise; 'her case was peculiar. She felt no fear of hell, but an inexpressible sense of the sufferings of Christ, accompanied with sharp bodily pain.' These pangs of the new birth did not occur only during sermons; they might be caused by a dispute about Justification in a private house, or even by reading a sermon to yourself. Convulsive motions of the body, like those at St. Médard, are mentioned sometimes, but not often. It was not long before Newcastle followed the lead of Bristol. 'There seemed in the evening to be a deeper work in many souls than I had observed before. Many trembled exceedingly; six or seven (both men and women) dropped down as dead. . . . In the evening, God was pleased to wound many more who were quiet and at ease. . . . Several of these were now constrained to roar aloud. . . . I never saw a work of God, in any other place, so evenly and gradually carried on.' (Wesley, no doubt, is not thinking *merely* of the paroxysms when he talks about 'the work', like Carré de Montgéron and his friends, who called the convulsions *l'œuvre*.)

If it was the work of God, how did the devil come into it? Clearly he was allowed—we may suppose, for evidential purposes—to give outward proof of his vain efforts to keep souls under his dominion; that was all. It may be observed that the afflicted persons sometimes spoke in the character of the devil, in the proper tradition of exorcism. Thus, a woman at Bristol cries out: 'No power, no power; no faith, no faith. She is mine; her soul is mine.' Sometimes the very technique of the exorcist was imitated. When a Bristol woman lay on the ground, roaring and gnashing with her teeth, 'one who from many circumstances apprehended a preternatural agent to be concerned in this, asking *How didst thou dare to enter into a Christian?* was answered, *She is not a Christian; she is mine. Q. Dost thou not tremble at the name of Jesus?* No words followed, but she shrunk back and trembled exceedingly. *Q. Art thou not increasing thy own damnation?* It was faintly answered, *Ay, ay*', and so on. Another Bristol woman, while 'the thousand distortions of her body shewed how the dogs of hell were gnawing her heart', cried out 'I am the devil's now. . . . I will be his . . . I must, I will, I will be damned'. In this and in other cases mentioned, Wesley confines himself to prayer, and hymn-singing is the only incantation. On one occasion he writes 'I felt as if I had been plunged into cold water'; this was with a woman who 'reared up in bed, her whole body moving at once, without bending one joint or limb'. He does not often claim success in dealing with such extreme cases—indeed, anybody but Wesley was content to write them down as lunatics. But it must be admitted that Lavington is nearer the target than usual when he compares the scenes in question to the exorcisms performed by Ignatius and other Popish enthusiasts.

All through those early years of the forties, even when there is no suggestion of diabolic interference, you feel the atmosphere to be one of Pentecostal visitation. 'About three in the morning, as we were continuing instant in prayer, the power of God came mightily upon us, insomuch that many cried out for exceeding joy, and many fell to the ground.' 'Forty or fifty of those who were seeking salvation desired to spend the night together, at the Society room.... Between two and three in the morning I was waked, and desired to come downstairs. I immediately heard such a confused noise, as if a number of men were all putting to the sword.' 'The words God enabled me to speak there, and afterwards at Bristol, ... were as a hammer and a flame.... A cry was heard from one end of the congregation to the other, not of grief, but of overflowing joy and love.' 'Our Lord was gloriously present with us at the watchnight, so that my voice was lost in the cries of the people.' 'Great indeed was the shaking among them; lamentation and great mourning were heard.' 'Men, women and children wept and groaned and trembled exceedingly; many ... cried with a loud and bitter cry.' 'One of the old colliers began shouting amain ... for the mere satisfaction and joy of heart.' 'God darted into one and all, I believe hardly one excepted, the melting flame of love, so that their heads were as water.' 'Almost every person who was present at the meeting of the Society seemed to be broken in pieces.'

What were the critics to make of it all? Southey offers a heroic solution: 'Like Mesmer and his disciples [Wesley] had produced a new disease, and he accounted for it by a theological theory instead of a physical one.' More commonly, the Wesleyan manifestations were dismissed as coming under one or other of two heads—lunacy or hysteria. Thus Lavington contemptuously refers to people who 'were scarce in their senses when they went among them, and have quite lost their senses since'. It was alleged that Whitefield's first sermon had driven fifteen people mad. But, so far as lunacy was concerned, Wesley was content to answer the objectors in their own kind. They claimed that all diabolical possession was lunacy; he claimed (for practical purposes) that all lunacy was diabolical possession. Once he seems to have hesitated; it was when he was considering (in Cornwall) 'the darkness which was fallen on many who lately rejoiced in God.... One or two persons . . . seemed to be indeed lunatic, as well as sore vexed. But while I was mus-ing, what would be the issue of these things, the answer I received from the word of God was, *Glory to God in the highest*', &c. There was no arguing with him; when he is told a few days later, that some of the people concerned have gone quite distracted, he adds: 'That is, they mourn and refuse to be comforted, till they have redemption through his Blood.' Yet even Wesley must sometimes have put two and two together; had he really no inkling of the true situation when he wrote of the 'immense scandal which has been given [at Dudley] by those who lately rejoiced in the love of God. One of these has lately killed his own child, by a blow upon the head'? On the question of hysteria, he is content to say (apropos of the convulsionaries at Wapping) that theirs are like none of the many hysterical and epileptic fits which he has seen. But here again, with the great honesty which characterizes him, he has put on record certain manifestations which suggest that hysteria, sometimes at least, haunted those early gatherings. 'I was a little surprised by some, who were buffeted of Satan in an unusual manner, by such a spirit of laughter as they could in no wise resist.' This was at Bristol; a few days later the same epidemic recurred, and two people who had maintained laughter could always be controlled were themselves overtaken by it. They 'laughed whether they would or no, almost without ceasing. Thus they continued, a spectacle to all, for two days; and were then, upon prayer made for them, delivered in a moment.' Lavington assures us that *fou rire* of this kind was common among the French prophets in their convulsions....

The question naturally suggests itself, Was it only Wesley's preaching and Wesley's influence that produced these strange phenomena? Or was it a common experience of his fellow Evangelists? The question is evidently of importance, for if Wesley stood alone in this respect, we might be led to conjecture that there was some literally hypnotic power in the man which carried his audiences away. But it seems clear that other preachers of the Revival were accustomed to similar interruptions. Daniel Rowlands's sermons in Wales made many 'cry aloud in the most awful manner'; a heckler at Bristol, on being called 'a contemptible little worm' by Howell Harris, fell down in a trembling fit from which (it is said) he never recovered. Cennick, when he was a lay preacher at Bristol in Wesley's own connexion, had people lying before him with swollen tongues and necks, held down sometimes, and with difficulty, by as many as seven men. You meet the same thing in the works of Jonathan Edwards, that flinty-minded Calvinist whose account of the Great Awakening in America was in Wesley's hands as early as 1738 (he read it on a walk from London to Oxford, before his own field-preaching began). 'There have been several instances here', Edwards writes, 'of persons waxing cold and benumbed, with their hands clinched, yea, and their bodies in convulsions.' And after Whitefield's visit to Northampton (U.S.A.) in 1741: 'The whole room was full of nothing but outcries, faintings and the like.... The children there were very generally and greatly affected with the warnings and counsels that were given them, and many exceedingly overcome ... and when they were dismissed, they almost all of them went home crying aloud through the streets.' Do we grudge him the children? We shall find, later, that Wesley himself was no less edified by their distress.

## The Great Revival in America

ᷝ Bernard A. Weisberger

If Satan kept close track of human affairs in 1797, he might have taken a warning from the experience of a certain Kentucky hunter who one day trapped a bear at the foot of a tree and swung at him with an ax. The bear knocked the ax away and sank his teeth into the hunter's left arm. Promptly the Kentuckian plunged *his* teeth into the bear's nose and his free thumb into the animal's eye socket. At that point, friends came up and dispatched the beast. Later, the hunter was asked if bears gave him much trouble generally. His answer was no. "They can't stand Kentucky play," he said. "Biting and gouging are too much for them."

The portent would have been plain for Satan. When he met with Americans on the frontier, there was going to be gouging and biting. From 1798 to about 1810, certain communities of the half-tamed forest met the enemy in Christian battle, in what was sometimes called the Western or Kentucky or Great Revival. This revival was not the first on the American continent. A so-called "Great Awakening" had lit fires of religious zeal along the seaboard in the seventeen-forties. But holy enthusiasm among the squirrel hunters of Kentucky, western Virginia, the Carolinas and Tennessee was something special. They had concepts of pious experience that went with braining bears and battling Indians. Theology was presented to them by men whose faith was strong, but who "murdered the king's English almost every lick." They received it with tears and shouts and such wild dances as David performed before the ark of the Lord. For a few passionate years, something amounting to godly hysteria crackled and smoked in the backwoods settlements. But this was only the flash of initial combustion. Within a decade the Western revival was institutionalized, more or less, in the camp meeting, which abounded in demonstrative energy, certainly, but kept within control. Its enthusiasm was carried through the clearings in the saddlebags of a traveling, evangelistic ministry, mostly of the then "lower-class" Methodist Church. These men were native timber, with the bark on. They were undistinguishable in dress, manner or rhetoric from the rest of the pioneers, except that they brought to the job of converting sinners the same quick-triggered zest which their neighbors directed against the British, or land speculators, or excise men. Yet they, too, for all their individuality, preached mostly within the bounds of rule and discipline.

Therefore, by 1830 the *genuinely* frenzied and spontaneous frontier revival was largely a memory. It survived where settlement was brand new, and in islands of population, mostly Southern, where frontier attitudes somehow never quite changed—in the remoter mountain counties, and among certain Negroes. What remained was still lusty, but somewhat more ritualized and predictable. Yet the early binge of unharnessed emotionalism left its mark on part of American Protestantism. It bequeathed a tradition of unpolished preaching by plain men, lay exhorters in all but name. It left another pattern, of mass participation in special meetings gotten up exclusively to save souls. It shaped a kind of religious thinking that was intensely individual, making the apex of Christian experience for each separate man and woman a *personal* change of heart which came about suddenly and publicly and under excruciating emotional pressure.

These things were part of the frontier revival, and when the settled churches embraced a brand of revivalism, they became part of the nation's religious life. The churches of the older regions did not plan it that way. They did their best to domesticate and polish whatever it was they took from the wilderness, but afterwards they were never quite the same. However indirectly they borrowed from the camp meeting, they were touched with the frontier spirit. In every public exercise carried on in that spirit there was just a suspicion of the circus. The camp meeting, though it might be frontier religion's "harvest time," flourished along with the "militia muster, the cabin-raising, and the political barbecue." The whole history of American revivials would lightly or heavily underscore that fact.

# 10. Soldiers and Sailors of the Revolutionary Era

## The Morale of the Napoleonic Armies
◄§ David G. Chandler

By using the principles of offensive action, speed, security, assembly and concentration, Napoleon as often as not succeeded in surprising his opponent; and a surprised enemy was often a demoralized one. Napoleon was always aware of the vital importance of morale in warfare, and another of his best-known maxims declared that in war, the moral is to the physical as three is to one. Again at St. Helena, he restated his conviction that "Moral force, rather than numbers, decides victory." For Napoleon, the military principles of morale and leadership were carefully fostered and, if necessary, artificially created. Here again he was fortunate in his time and the nation of his adoption, for the basic enthusiasm and general intelligence of the Revolutionary citizen-armies provided a sound basis and newly forged tradition which could inspire the conscript armies of the Consulate and Empire—the terrors of Europe.

In order to obtain the unquestioning obedience of his rank and file, Napoleon unhesitatingly set out to gain their affection as well as their respect. He wished to develop two main qualities in his officers and men: "If courage is the first characteristic of the soldier, perseverance is the second." Bravery was needed in the field and at the moment of crisis; perseverance and endurance at all other times. Napoleon was aware that "Bravery cannot be bought with money" and deliberately aimed to create the illusion of *La Gloire* by playing on the vanity and underlying credulity of his men. "A man does not have himself killed for a few half-pence a day or for a petty distinction," he once declared; "You must speak to the soul in order to electrify the man." A carefully

375

graded system of military awards—ranging from the coveted Cross of the *Légion d'Honneur*, swords of honor, monetary grants and nomination to a vacancy in the Imperial Guard for the rank and file, to the award of duchies, princedoms and even thrones to the elect among the leaders—was one aspect of this policy; the rewarding of talent and proven ability by accelerated military promotion another; the creation of an air of *general bonhommie* with the ordinary soldiers, yet a third.

Napoleon knew his men and what appealed to them, their virtues and their vices, their hopes and fears. On the credit side were their intelligence, reckless bravery and sense of humor; on the debit side was their tendency to unruliness, resentment of discipline and discouragement in defeat. He carefully assessed the needful balance between praising them and censuring them. On the one hand he would wander round their campfires, using his encyclopedic memory for faces to pick out here and there a veteran. "You were with me in Egypt. How many campaigns? How many wounds?" The men loved him for his apparent interest in their records and care for their well-being: the ultimate accolade was to have the Emperor seize the lobe of an ear between forefinger and thumb and give it a good tweak. He listened seriously to complaints—and usually made sure that they were looked into. He was often prepared to overlook even the most flagrant acts of indiscipline—providing they did not compromise his plans.

On occasion, however, Napoleon could turn into a martinet whom even the bravest grenadier would quail to confront. His large grey eyes would harden and seem to spit fire. "Have it inscribed on their colors," he declaimed once in Italy while reviewing a recalcitrant *demi-brigade*, "that they no longer belong to the Army of Italy." Few among even the marshalate dared stand up to him when he was in a rage; he would swear profanely at the object of his wrath, make liberal use of the riding crop he habitually carried on his victim's head and shoulders, and was even, on occasion, known to have kicked his victims in the stomach. And although he undoubtedly cared for his men in a peculiar way, he was also capable of sending large numbers of them to certain death without a twinge of emotion and was quite prepared to abandon whole armies (as in Egypt, 1799, or West Russia, 1812) when they had failed his purposes or been hopelessly compromised. First and foremost he was a hard realist and a ruthless opportunist, but occasionally the man broke through the hardened shell of the general and emperor. "The sight of a battlefield, after the fight, is enough to inspire princes with a love of peace and a horror of war," runs one of Napoleon's maxims. After Eylau in 1807 he wrote to Josephine: "The countryside is covered with dead and wounded. This is not the pleasant part of war. One suffers, and the soul is oppressed to see so many sufferers." And when his torn legions were commencing the long trek home from Moscow, Napoleon enjoined Mortier to "Pay every attention to the sick and wounded. Sacrifice your baggage, everything for them. Let the wagons be devoted to their use, and if necessary your own saddles. . . ." And yet it was the same man that could cold-bloodedly order mass executions in disaffected areas, butcher the Turks at Jaffa or remark to the Austrian diplomat Metternich that "a man like me troubles himself little about the lives of a million men."

Clearly Napoleon's attitude toward his men—like so much else—was an enigma, but there is no doubt at all that he had the power to inspire men and bind them to his service. "If I want a man I am prepared to kiss his a—," was the way he once described it. If this attitude was a coldly deliberate act of policy, it was no less effective. As Wellington remarked: "I used to say of him that his presence on the field made a difference of 40,000 men." The reception he received when passing a unit on the battlefield—even in the later days when the number of veterans was low and the ranks were filled with *les Marie-Louises*, mere boys of sixteen years—is incontrovertible evidence of his power over men and his ability to inspire a high state of morale. . . .

Napoleon inherited from the Revolution the idea of "living off the countryside." From the earliest times armies had always relied to a greater or lesser extent on supplies seized, requisitioned or (very occasionally) bought locally for their subsistence, but in the seventeenth- and eighteenth-centuries the practice had grown up of relying on long, slow-moving convoys of wagons, operating from pre-stocked depots and arsenals, as the primary source of supply. This was for two reasons: firstly, in the "Age of Reason" there had been a reaction against the totality and horrors of war as demonstrated by the Wars of Religion, and opinion had set its face against indiscriminate looting; in the second place, most armies were made up of very unwilling material—pressed peasants, freed convicts and the like—who could not be trusted to go out and forage for themselves for fear of widespread desertion. In the early Revolutionary Wars, however, the whole attitude of the French Government and populace toward warfare had undergone a great change. Huge armies (at one point as many as 600,000) were raised of volunteers (and later conscripts), and it proved impossible to provide them with "conventional" logistical support. Hence, *de rigueur* rather than as a matter of policy, the French armies resorted to almost complete dependence on local supplies; what convoys existed were reserved for munitions. This act of desperation, however, proved workable. Because of the intelligence and revolutionary fervor of the new-type popular soldier, the threat of mass desertions proved illusory. At first every Frenchman was imbued with a sense of defending *la Patrie et la Revolution* against foreign reactionary forces; later, the proselytizing mission of the Revolution—the need to spread the new gospel of *Liberté, Egalité, Fraternité* to other submerged peoples and "liberate" them from their chains, provided a new incentive. As a result, it proved possible to operate whole armies on a shoestring, administratively speaking, and Napoleon inherited the system—or rather the lack of a system—of supplying forces in the field. Again typically, he improved and regularized an already existing practice. Although by 1805 the First Empire could have provided as much food for its troops as was needed, Napoleon deliberately adopted the old, desperate methods; the army that marched to the Danube carried merely eight days' rations with it—and these were issued only when the enemy was close at hand and it was consequently impractical to send the men out to forage for themselves. Only in 1812, faced by the immense wastes of plain and forest in Holy Russia, did Napoleon attempt to resort to the old convoy system( and without conspicuous success, be it noted). At all other times he made the fullest use of the improved mobility afforded by dispensing with cumbrous convoys, associating the divisional and corps system with this policy of "living off the countryside"; to facilitate foraging, the French army could move in widely spaced, self-contained formations, each with its allotted foraging area, and then concentrate rapidly for battle. This was the essence of Napoleonic *blitzkrieg* and it proved fatally baffling to the reactionary governments of Europe. . . .

The Revolution provided Napoleon with a promotion system open to talent. The importance of this legacy cannot be overestimated; it was the caliber of the truly "natural" leaders who emerged from the ranks of the Revolutionary Armies to command battalions, *demi-brigades*, divisions, corps and armies, that made Napoleon's achievements possible. He himself was of course the greatest product of this aspect of the Revolution. Without distinction of birth or influential connections, it is doubtful whether Napoleon would ever have been permitted to rise to high position outside his own arm of the service; it is absolutely certain that he would never have risen so fast—nor ever have attained a position from which he could coordinate and control every aspect of France's war effort. Similarly, he could have achieved little without the able aid of soldiers like Lannes, Davout, Massena or Murat, his righthand men. If Napoleon provided the inspiration, the brains and the will power, his subordinates provided the brawn, muscle and courage—and, to a lesser extent, the intelligence as well—that transformed theory into fact. As we shall see at a later stage, Napoleon eventually misused this system of promotion by merit by discouraging even his ablest generals from indulging in original thought, but to the end of his meteoric career the way to promotion for every soldier in the French Army lay through proven courage and ability. The proverbial *baton* was in "every soldier's knapsack."

## *The British Sailor*
&§ Arthur Bryant

The Royal Navy had made its entry onto the world stage under Drake and the Elizabethans, had sunk into insignificance under the early Stuarts, recovered under Cromwell and the second Charles to wrest the sceptre of ocean commerce from Holland, and, given administrative discipline by the life-long labours of Pepys, became during the eighteenth century the chief arbiter of human affairs at sea. Yet until the age of Nelson its ascendancy was never undisputed. For over a hundred years monarchical France, with its much greater population and resources, contended with Britain for command of the sea and, on more than one occasion, all but attained it. Britain's danger was greatest when France and the Atlantic empire of Spain joined hands against her, as they did during the American War, when, with her fleets outnumbered, she had had to fight for her very existence.

Yet Britain had always triumphed in the last resort because the sea was her whole being, whereas with her Continental rivals it was only a secondary consideration. "The thing which lies nearest the heart of this nation," Charles II had written, "is trade and all that belongs to it." Being an island, her commerce was maritime and its protection an essential interest of an evergrowing number of people. They were ready to make sacrifices for the Navy which they would never have done for the Army or any other service of the Crown. For it was on the Navy, as the Articles of War put it, that under the Providence of God the safety, honour, and welfare of the realm depended.

Because of these things the Navy touched mystic chords in the English heart which went deeper than reason. The far sails of a frigate at sea, the sight of a sailor with tarry breeches and rolling gait in any inland town, and that chief of all the symbolic spectacles of England, the Great Fleet lying at anchor in one of her white-fringed roadsteads, had for her people the power of a trumpet call. So little Byam Martin, seeing for the first time the triple-tiered ships of the line lying in Portsmouth harbour, remained "riveted to the spot, perfectly motionless, so absorbed in wonder" that he would have stayed there all day had not his hosts sent a boat's crew to fetch him away. From that hour his mind was "inflamed with the wildest desire to be afloat." Bobby **Shafto** going to sea with silver buckles on his knees was an eternal theme of eighteenth century England: of such stuff were admirals made.

They had a hard schooling. Flung, like Nelson, at twelve into an unfamiliar world of kicks and cuffs, crowded hammocks and icy hardships, or after a few months under "Black Pudding," the omnipresent horsewhip of the Naval Academy, Gosport, apprenticed as midshipmen to the cockpit of a man-of-war, they learnt while still children to be Spartans, dined off scrubbed boards on salt beef, sauerkraut and black-strap, and became complete masters before they were men of a wonderful technical skill in all that appertained to the sailing and fighting of ships.

They were as inured to roughness and salt water as gulls to wind. Boys in their teens would spend days afloat in the maintop, ready at any moment to clamber to the masthead when top-gallant or studding sail needed setting or taking in. They grew up like bulldogs, delighting to cuff and fight: in some ships it was the practice while the officers were dining in the wardroom for the midshipmen to engage regularly in pitched battles on the quarterdeck, Romans against Trojans, for the possession of the poop, banging away, "all in good part," with broomsticks, handswabs, boarding pikes and even muskets. Midshipman Gardner of the *Edgar*, being pinked in the thigh by a comrade with a fixed bayonet in the course of one of their friendly scraps, retaliated by putting a small quantity of powder into a musket and firing at his assailant, marking "his phiz" for life. So toughened, they faced the world on their toes ready for anything and everyone. Such were the high-spirited midshipmen who pelted the British ambassador with plums at the Carnival at Pisa and, as he looked angry, hove another volley at his lady, observing that she seemed better tempered than his Excellency. So also the officers of the wardroom, dining at the best inn in Leghorn and growing somewhat merry, rolled the waiter among the dishes in the table-cloth and pelted the passers-by with loaves and chicken legs.

These were the permanent cadre of the Navy; the officers of the establishment, "born in the surf of the sea," who, unlike the lower deck, coming and going as occasion demanded, lived in the Service and died in it. They were bound together by the closest ties of professional honour, etiquette and experience. Socially they were of all sorts: one high-born captain filled his frigate with so many sprigs of aristocracy that his first lieutenant—no respecter of persons—was wont to call out in mockery to the young noblemen and honourables at the ropes, "My lords and gentlemen, shiver the mizen topsail!" The majority were of comparatively humble origin, occasioning Sir Walter Elliot's remark that, though the profession had its utility, he would be sorry to see

any friend of his belonging to it. Few had much of this world's goods
nor, unless exceptionally lucky over prize money, could hope for much.
Some were scholars—for it was a literary age—and read their Shakespeare or discoursed learnedly on the classical associations of the foreign
ports they visited: more often they were simple souls, "better acquainted with rope-yarns and bilge water than with Homer or Virgil."
But one and all were masters of their profession, proud in their
obedience to king and country and ready to give their lives and all
they had whenever the Service demanded. "A bloody war and a sickly
season!" was the closing toast of many a jovial evening in the wardroom: it was so that men rose in their calling.

Such men not only officered the fleet: they gave it their own tone
and spirit. They were often rough teachers, full of fearful oaths like
the master's mate of the *Edgar* who ended every sentence with a
"Damn your whistle," and too fond of enforcing their commands with
the lash. But the men they commanded were rough too; hard-bitten
merchant seamen and fishermen, brought into the Service for the dura-
tion by the pressgangs, with always a sediment in every ship of jailbirds
and incorrigibles whose only chance of freedom was the hard life of the
sea. The unresting, automatic discipline which the handling of wind-
propelled warships in northern waters demanded could not have been enforced by gentler souls: it was that which gave Britain command of the
waves and kept the Royal Navy from the slovenly, helpless degradation
which befell that of revolutionary France. From the admiral, piped on
board, to the boatswain's mate with his colt ready to "start" the lower
deck to action, strictly ordered subordination and readiness to obey
were the hallmarks of the Service.

The life of the seamen was a life apart; something that was of England and yet remote from it. A king's ship was a little wooden world of
its own, with its peculiar customs and gradations unguessed at by lands-
men; its proud foretopmen, the aristocrats of the sea, and far down out
of sight its humble waisters: pumpers and sewermen, scavengers and
pigsty keepers. In such a community, often years together away from
a home port, men learnt to know each other as they seldom can on
shore: to love and trust, to fear and hate one another. There were
ships that became floating hells, ruled by some sadistic tyrant, with
drunken, flogging officers "crabbed as fiends," and savage, murderous
crews such as that which flung Bligh of the *Bounty* to perish in an
open boat in a remote sea. There were others commanded by captains
like Nelson, Pellew and Duncan, where the men looked on their
officers as fathers and were eager to dare and do anything for them.
Here something of the unspoken sympathy between experienced rider
and horse entered into the relationship between quarter and lower deck.

The nation honoured its rough, simple seamen, as it had cause to, though it usually saw them at their worst: ashore on their brief spells of leave, with discipline relaxed and their hard-earned money riotously dissipated on brandy and the coarse Megs and Dolls of the seaports. But it saw too, as we also can glimpse from the prints of the old masters, the fine manly faces, the earnest gaze, the careless attitudes so full of strength and grace for all the gnarls and distortions of weather, accident and disease: symbols of rugged-headed courage, manly devotion and simple-hearted patriotism. They were children—generous, suspicious, forgiving, with the fortitude and patience of men: rough Britons tempered by the unresting sea into virtue of a rare and peculiar kind. The sight of a Monsieur's sails roused in them all the unconquerable pugnacity of their race: the whine of Johnny Crapaud's shot whipped their quick tempers to savagery. Though chivalrous and generous victors, they were not good losers like the courtly Spaniards and the aristocrats of the old French navy; they had to beat their adversary or die. As they waited at quarters before a fight, "their black silk handkerchiefs tied round their heads, their shirt-sleeves tucked up, the crows and hand-spikes in their hands and the boarders all ready with their cutlasses and tomahawks," they reminded an eye-witness of so many devils.

Yet from such scenes the British sailor could pass in a few hours to the buffoonery and practical jokes dear to the lower deck, the fiddler's lively air, the droll or pathetic ballads with their rhythm of the waves, while the seas broke over the forecastle and the ship pitched and rolled; and to those tenderer moments when, homeward bound, hearts panted with the anticipated happiness of meeting wives and sweethearts and the headwind's moping contrariness was lulled by the chorus of "Grieving's a folly, Boys!"

> "And now arrived that jovial night
> When every true bred tar carouses,
> When, o'er the grog, all hands delight
> To toast their sweethearts and their spouses."

History loves to linger over the good-humoured jollity between decks when port was reached: the girls on the seamen's knees with sturdy, buxom arms around their necks; the reels and gigs as Susan's bright eyes promised her Tom Tough his long-awaited reward; the grog and flip that passed about under the light of the flickering lanterns. And judging by the popularity of Dibdin's songs, the nation liked to think of such scenes too and took deep comfort in the thought of the hearts of oak and jolly tars that kept its foes at bay.

# 11. Popular Uprisings

## Eighteenth-Century Mobs
&s George Rudé

In Paris the food riot was not the predominant type of popular disturbance. There were other forms of protest in which the poorer classes, though by no means challenging the existing order, laid claim to better living standards or to a fuller measure of social justice. In July 1720, the crisis provoked by the Scotsman John Law's financial operations touched off massive riots in the business quarter: 15,000 people gathered in the Rue Vivienne, sixteen were trampled to death, Law's coachman was lynched, and the Palais Royal, home of the Regent, was threatened with destruction. In 1721, a succession of disturbances was caused by the severity of the punishments inflicted on domestic servants: on one occasion, a crowd of 5,000 formed to protest at the whipping, branding, and exhibition in the stocks of a coachman; five were killed and several were wounded. In 1743 in Paris and nine years later at Vincennes, riots broke out in protest at the manner of balloting for the militia. In 1750, a panic followed the arrest of a large number of children, rounded up by the *archers* (armed police) on charges of vagrancy. It was widely believed (and with some justification, as this had in fact happened thirty years before) that the children of the poor were being shipped to the colonies. In the course of a week's rioting four to eight *archers* were killed; and, after sentence by the *parlement* of Paris, three men were executed in the Place de Grève amid scenes of violent disorder. There was even talk—such were the feelings aroused—of marching to Versailles to burn down the royal château.

On this last occasion, the Marquis d' Argenson, who had witnessed the disturbances, deplored the fact that the *parlement*, which had ordered the executions, must now have lost all credit with the common people. His fears proved to have little substance. It was, in fact, the *parlement* which, more than any other body, first drew the Parisian *menu peuple* into political agitation and taught them political lessons that they later, in 1789, turned against their teachers. Quite apart from its judicial functions, the Paris *parlement* claimed, by ancient usage, to be the guardian of the nation's "liberties" and under weak or indolent monarchs refused to register royal edicts until its "remonstrances" were satisfied. It became the firm champion of the Gallican Church against the Jesuits and Ultramontanes; it resolutely opposed the operation of the Bull *Unigenitus* against Jansenist heresy within the Church; and, in the name of "liberty" (a term often synonymous with "privilege"), it resisted the government's attempts to reform the finances by encroaching on the fiscal immunities of aristocracy and clergy. But the magistrates, though largely concerned to safeguard their own particular interests, were past masters at playing on popular passions in their war on Ultramontane claims or ministerial "despotism." Already in 1727, the *parlement* headed a common front, composed of the parish clergy, the Parisian *bourgeoisie*, the lawyers, and the common people of the streets, against the Jesuits. The next popular explosion of this kind came in 1752, when the Archbishop of Paris was condemned by the *parlement* and mobbed in the streets of the city for ordering the refusal of the sacrament to dying nuns and clergy who were not prepared to make formal renunciation of their Jansenist beliefs. Soon after, the political battle of the *parlement* against the royal government, largely dormant since the 1720's, began again in earnest. Having studied the "philosophers" (first Montesquieu and later Rousseau), the magistrates translated their political speculations, hitherto reserved for the more fashionable society of the *salons*, into a language intelligible to the streets and markets, and, in the course of a protracted pamphlet war, indoctrinated Parisians in the use of such catchwords as "citizens," "nation," "social contract," and the "general will." The *parlement's* remonstrances of 1753, 1763, 1771, and 1776 evoked a considerable response among the people. These years were studded with minor disturbances in support of the *parlement's* claims; they reached a climax on the very eve of the Revolution when, in 1787 and 1788, great demonstrations of city craftsmen and journeymen from the faubourgs rioted in sympathy with the exiled *parlement* and acclaimed its return to the capital.

In London, too, the typical eighteenth-century riot was either a form of social protest or a political demonstration; but more often it was compounded of the two. Apart from industrial disputes, the undiluted social protest without political undertones was comparatively rare:

probably rarer than in Paris, at least before the 1750's. There were, however, such occasions: in July 1736, the dismissal of English workmen and the employment of cheaper Irish labor touched off violent rioting against the Irish in Shoreditch, Spitalfields, and Whitechapel; and in August 1794, "a mixed multitude of men, women, boys and children" (to quote one of the Lord Mayor's dispatches) defied the militia and Guards for three days and attacked and destroyed "crimping houses," or houses used for recruiting to the army, in Holborn, the City, Clerkenwell, and Shoreditch. On both occasions, there were sinister rumors of enemy agents at work—in the first case Jacobites, in the second Jacobins—but in neither case do the motives for rioting appear to have been any other than those that were proclaimed.

More often, however, London riots were attached to a political cause. Even if there was no such thing as a "Tory mob" (a term used by some historians), it seems evident that Tory influences were at work behind the riots of 1715 and 1716, when London crowds paraded the streets of the city, Holborn, and Whitechapel to shouts of "High Church and Ormonde," smashed the windows of government supporters, and attacked a Presbyterian Meeting House in Highgate. Yet it was not the dwindling band of Tory politicians, but the Common Council of the City of London, that most often gave the lead. The city, which prided itself on its political independence, opposed the policies of Westminster and St. James's almost continuously throughout the century, and more particularly between 1730 and 1780; and, like the *parlement* in Paris, it became the real political educator of London's "lower orders." It was the city that, in 1733, led the campaign against Sir Robert Walpole's Excise Bill and forced him to withdraw it, after London crowds had besieged Parliament and mobbed the minister to cries of "No slavery—no excise—no wooden shoes!" Three years later, a similar fate befell Walpole's Gin Act, which, though passed by Parliament, became impossible to operate. This time, riots were only threatened—in the form of mock funerals to celebrate "Madam Geneva's lying-in-state"—and actually came to nothing. The same thing happened in 1753, when a combination of City interests, country Tories, and opposition Whigs compelled the Pelham Ministry, by means of a nationwide agitation and the threat of London riots, to defeat its own Bill for the easier naturalization of alien Jews.

Up to now, the City Corporation had been allied, in order to wage its political battles, with a group of opposition Tory leaders: to that extent, at least, each one of these movements, if not wholly Tory, may be said to have had Tory undertones. This was no longer the case after 1756 when, in clamouring for war with France (and later Spain), the Common Council adopted William Pitt as its champion, helped him into office, and after his dismissal in 1761 conferred on him the City's Freedom, while London's "lower orders" hailed Pitt and booed and pelted the King's favorite, the Earl of Bute. The same year, Pitt's principal lieutenant in the City, William Beckford, in standing for election to Parliament, denounced "rotten boroughs" and thereby fired the opening shot in the City's campaign for electoral reform. Thus City radicalism, which challenged the principles of both parliamentary parties, came to birth. From the City's radicalism there stemmed, in turn, the wider movement that rallied to the cause of John Wilkes; and "Wilkes and Liberty" became for a dozen years the political slogan uniting the diverse activities of City merchants, Middlesex freeholders, and the small shopkeepers, craftsmen, and workmen in the London streets and boroughs. After the Wilkite riots came the last and the most violent of London's great upheavals, the Gordon Riots of 1780, when "No Popery" crowds held the streets of the metropolis for a week and caused widespread destruction of both private and public property. This last outbreak was not strictly speaking "political"; but in this case too the rioters drew their initial inspiration, though not their mode of behavior, from a solid body of respectable City opinion.

## *The Rising of the Paris Masses*

*Alfred Cobban*

The revolt of Paris, in which culminated the nation-wide disturbances of 1789, and the general collapse of royal administration, confronted the members of the Third Estate with the problem of taking steps to protect property and restore some semblance of law and order to France. In their turn, like the privileged classes before them, they were to find that they had started something they could not stop, and that a movement which they had envisaged as one of moderate constitutional and social reform was to become a revolution of a very different nature and scope....

The Parisian populace, which by its rising had frustrated the plans of the court and saved the Third Estate, was not moved solely by altruistic political emotion; it had its own grievance in the high price and shortage of bread. A week after the fall of the Bastille, Bertier de Sauvigny, intendant of Paris, and his father-in-law, Foulon, who were responsible for food supplies, were seized by a mob besieging the Hôtel de Ville and massacred. Their heads—it was an *ancien régime* custom—were stuck on the end of pikes. A man in the uniform of a dragoon, followed by a large crowd, pushed his way into the meeting of the municipal body with a chunk of bleeding flesh, saying, 'Here is the heart of Bertier.' When it was proposed to bring in the decapitated head also, messengers were sent out to inform the populace that the council was engaged on important business and preferred not to have the head of its former intendant on the agenda. The electors, who had been chosen in the first place as secondary electors for Paris to the States-General but had never dissolved, now constituted themselves the municipal authority, appointed Bailly, the eminent scientist, as mayor in place of the murdered Provost of Merchants, and took over such government as the city was capable of....

Towards the end of July ... sporadic risings were caught up in a different and more extensive movement which has come to be known as the Great Fear—a panic terror of brigands who were supposed to be descending on the peaceful villages of France. Over large areas the Great Fear raged like a forest fire. The legendary brigands were never clearly identified. In the north-east, where there had been the troubles of the Fronde, they were called the Mazarines, and in the centre 'la bande anglaise'—shades perhaps of the Black Prince and the White Company still surviving in the age-old peasant memory. The association of an aristocratic plot with the menace of rumoured brigands set a pattern that was to be repeated more than once in the Revolution. At the time of the September massacres it was the criminals of the Paris prisons who were expected to be let loose by the aristocrats on the wives and children of Patriots. Given the picture of the Revolution as a rising of the riff-raff of the towns and the landless proletariat of the country, such fears are meaningless. When it is realized that the revolutionary masses were not these, but rather the master craftsmen, shopkeepers and the like in the towns, and the peasant proprietors in the country, they become easily explicable.

The prosperous professional men and officials of the Third Estate, who had seized control of the Revolution from the privileged classes, had no intention of letting it slip from their hands, but the game they were playing, even if unconsciously, was a dangerous one. After the affair of the Bastille they regained control of Paris with the aid of the new municipal authorities and the National Guard. The countryside presented a more difficult problem. The peasants rarely attacked individuals, their objective was usually to burn the manorial rolls, overthrow enclosures and restore common lands, kill game, and 'have fires out of the Grand Duke's wood.' Regular troops and National Guards were sent out from the towns to repress such disturbances and protect property rights. Where effective action was possible the rioters were seized and, after trial before summary courts, hanged. In most areas, however, the authorities were powerless before the resistance of the peasantry. Unless something was done rapidly to remedy the situation, it was evident that it would soon be completely out of control. But from what quarter could a lead be given? . . .

For the National Assembly the unrest of the towns and the peasantry was a diversion from its proper task, which was to give France a new Constitution. Royal co-operation in this task was still less than half-hearted, and aristocratic opposition vigorous and vocal. The king, it was feared, had not drawn the necessary lesson from the fourteenth of July and the Patriots came to think that only another dose of the same medicine would make him fully amenable to their wishes. In Paris, popular agitators and journalists were keeping the people in a fever of political excitement with denunciations of aristocratic plots. Neither the respectable leaders of the Patriot party in the Assembly, nor the less respectable agitators in the streets, could have taken effective action, however, if it had not been for the continuing and even increasing economic distress of the populace. The incident which set fire to this inflammable material was so petty as to give ground for the suspicion that it was merely the occasion and not its cause.

On October 1st a dinner was held at Versailles for the officers of the Flanders Regiment newly arrived there. When the king and queen appeared to acknowledge their loyal acclamations, Blondel's song 'O Richard, O mon roi, l'univers t'abandonne,' from Grétry's opera, was sung amid enthusiastic demonstrations. Nothing happened for four days, which is odd if this episode is to be regarded as the provocation which led to the October Days, but indeed the whole story of what did happen is an odd one. On October 5th women gathered before the Hôtel de Ville demanding bread: this was quite normal. Getting no satisfaction the cry was raised—by whom?—that they should make their way to Versailles to appeal to the king. Several thousands set out, gathering numbers as they went. It was a gloomy, wet, October day, hardly the best one for a spontaneous demonstration. Now, however, the tocsin was being rung through Paris, district assemblies were meeting, National Guards and others were gathering, especially before the Hôtel de Ville, where La Fayette, on horseback, was trying unavailingly to control the situation. The watchword still seemed to be to march on Versailles. At four o'clock in the afternoon the Municipal Council authorized La Fayette to move off with the National Guard, and now there appeared for the first time a definite objective: the king was to be brought back to Paris. With a mixed body of National Guards and others, La Fayette set out. At Versailles Louis XVI, who as usual had been out hunting, returned in the afternoon, interviewed a deputation of the women who by now were congregated before the palace, and promised them a supply of bread for Paris. That evening the main body of the Parisians arrived, settled down for the night as best they could or ranged about the streets of Versailles and the courts of the palace. At early dawn on the next day a few hundred of the demonstrators found a way into the palace, slaughtered some of the royal bodyguard whom they encountered and penetrated nearly to the queen's apartments before they were repulsed.

Morning saw serried masses in the courtyard before the palace, now with one cry, 'To Paris!' Was resistance to an armed mob of some 20,000 possible? It seems not to have been contemplated. The idea of flight had again been urged on the king and queen, only to be rejected by them, perhaps for fear of leaving the throne vacant for Orleans, whose inspiration was suspected behind the march on Versailles. The only course left was to yield as graciously as possible in the circumstances. In the afternoon of October 6th the triumphal procession set out on the muddy march back to Paris: National Guards armed and royal bodyguard disarmed, wagons laden with corn and flour lumbering, market men and women straggling along, Regiment of Flanders and Swiss Guard, La Fayette riding alongside the carriage bearing the royal family, also beside them the heads of two of the Royal Guards on pikes, a hundred deputies in carriages as evidence that the National Assembly would keep the king company, and, trudging along in the rapidly failing twilight, the dark shapes of thousands of nameless Parisians. At ten o'clock on a gloomy autumnal night the royal family, having first for two hours listened to speeches before the Hôtel de Ville, at last reached the Tuileries, whence Louis XIV had departed for Versailles 118 years earlier, and camped down in hurriedly cleared rooms as best they could for the night.

In the October Days the capital took possession of king and Assembly. For the next five years Paris was to dictate the course of the Revolution, and the Paris mob, which the Patriots of 1789 had used for their purposes, was to prove, as they were to discover in due course, a weapon that could be employed by more than one party and to more than one end.

# 12. The New Sensibility

## The Coming of Romanticism
ເຈົ້ David Daiches

It is perhaps no great oversimplification to say that people of the earlier eighteenth century, in their gratitude for what civilization had achieved by way not only of making life agreeable but also of making men more amenable to regular observation, tended to think of the arts as a product of conventional urban society and of the function of literature as the representation of general aspects of human nature expressed in the language of that society and with all the resources of that society's traditional culture. One of the shifts in attitude that produced the new movement was the questioning of that very point. A generation that had survived the religious and civil disputes of the seventeenth century might well have accepted with relief and gratitude a norm of urbane moderation operating within strictly defined conventional limits, but a later generation, which had no memory of those disputes and no feeling of relief at having escaped from the perpetual conflicts between single-minded religious or political enthusiasts, came to feel a sense of constraint rather than a sense of freedom in the demands of urban gentility. They lifted their eyes from the gentlemanly limitations imposed on their horizon to contemplate with a certain fascination the world of Gothic superstition or heroic violence or primitive behavior of one sort or another. (It is worth noting that the Jacobite movement became a fertile source of literary inspiration in Scotland only *after* it had become a safely lost cause.) And of course the great paradox was that at the very core of eighteenth-century genteel culture lay two venerated works dealing with life in a very ungenteel society—the Bible and Homer. Sooner or later neoclassic culture would have had to come to terms with primitivism. Actually, it turned to investigate the "primitive" back-

390

ground of the Bible and Homer rather earlier than might have been expected—in Robert Lowth's *De Sacra Poesi Hebraeorum* (1753) and Robert Wood's *Essay on the Original Genius and Writings of Homer* (1769).

The extension of the horizon was social as well as chronological. Primitive and heroic societies became more and more objects of interest, and at the same time the life of men living outside the pale of urban gentility was coming to be regarded as legitimate, even as the most proper, subject matter for poetry. "Since it often happens that the most obvious phrases, and those which are used in ordinary conversation, become too familiar to the ear and contract a kind of meanness by passing through the mouths of the vulgar, a poet should take particular care to guard himself against idiomatic ways of speaking." So wrote Addison in 1712. By 1800, Wordsworth was writing: "Humble and rustic life was generally chosen, [as the subject of his poems] because, in that condition, the essential passions of the heart find a better soil in which they can attain their maturity, are less under restraint, and speak a plainer and more emphatic language; because in that condition of life our elementary feelings coexist in a state of greater simplicity, and, consequently, can be more accurately contemplated, and more forcibly communicated; . . ." Dryden and Pope had insisted that the language of poetry should be based on the conversation of gentlemen; Wordsworth held that it should be based on the conversation of peasants. Between the two views lay generations of gradual exaltation of the primitive (as opposed to the polished and highly civilized) as a state peculiarly favorable to poetry.

To look beyond the polished life of educated men in cities to wilder and cruder ways of living, to investigate ballads and folk poetry as representing something more genuinely poetic than modern literature (and Thomas Percy's *Reliques of Ancient English Poetry*, 1765, was only one of many eighteenth-century signposts in this direction, and not the clearest), to include as proper subject matter for serious poetry aspects of life which neoclassic critics would have considered "low" or "mean" ("men who do not wear fine clothes can feel deeply," said Wordsworth—a proposition Dr. Johnson would not have denied, but which he would have considered irrelevant to the production of poetry), and in general to hold that the conventions of contemporary civilization did not represent the only guarantee of valuable human behavior —we can at least say that these were attitudes which became increasingly common as the eighteenth century advanced. One might add to this list the desire to explore kinds of emotion and sensibility which someone like Lord Chesterfield would have carefully shunned as simply inviting trouble. The result of the application of these attitudes was that poetry which has come to be called "romantic" can exhibit either a calculated simplicity or an equally calculated exoticism. Coleridge, looking back many years later on the *Lyrical Ballads*, produced by Wordsworth and himself in 1798, explained that his own endeavor had been "directed to persons and characters supernatural, or at least romantic; yet so as to transfer from our inward nature a human interest and a semblance of truth sufficient to procure for these shadows of imagination that willing suspension of disbelief for the moment, which constitutes poetic faith." Wordsworth's task, Coleridge added, had been "to propose to himself as his object, to give the charm of novelty to things of every day, and to excite a feeling analogous to the supernatural, by awakening the mind's attention to the lethargy of custom, and directing it to the loveliness and the wonders of the world before us; . . ." Here we see the poet's glance directed away from the world of social politeness in two different directions—to the imaginative world of the supernatural, and to the everyday world of ordinary people outside "society." Both poets were seeking a deeper reality than they considered any account of the urbane, conventional world of men and manners could yield. (Not, of course, that the neoclassic writer necessarily made the contemporary world of polite society his *subject matter*; but he addressed it as his audience.)

Thus the term "Romantic movement" has been used to cover such different literary phenomena as the studied rustic realism of Wordsworth's *Michael*—whose most often quoted line is the impressive matter-of-fact

And never lifted up a single stone,

and the deliberate indulgence of an exotic imagination that we find on occasion in Coleridge and Keats and which reaches its sometimes fantastic culmination in such a poet as Beddoes.

New political and social ideas helped to complicate the picture. The French Revolution, the developing Industrial Revolution in England which changed the physical appearance and the social structure of the country, and new notions in psychology and metaphysics, all played their part. Wordsworth, enthusiastic about the French Revolution when it first broke out, suspicious of "the increasing accumulation of men in cities," and eager to find the fundamental truths about man and the universe through a contemplation of external nature, interested in the way in which "we associate ideas in a state of excitement," showed the effect of these new ideas no less than Shelley, who moved from the atheistic rationalism of William Godwin to a passionate Platonic idealism. Byron, who combined an antisocial irony with an equally antisocial self-pity, and Keats, who understood what the individual life of the imagination could do for a poet more clearly, perhaps, than any other English creative writer, developed their own characteristic poetic themes, modes and techniques—but they, too, like the early Wordsworth and like Shelley, were in some sense alienated from polite society; they rejected the earlier eighteenth-century view that polite society was what made man capable of civilized achievements, and explored areas of the imagination and the sensibility to which their readers had access only by reading and surrendering to their poems. Keats' "Eve of St. Agnes" distills the purest essence of passionate living in a society that is symbolically violent and magical, and his "La Belle Dame sans Merci" broods with strange beauty over the fact that we can love to despair what is nevertheless horrible: society as Pope or Prior saw it is wholly ignored in these poems. The poet is on his own, drawing nourishment from his solitary reading and imaginings. This means that each poem must create its own world and present it persuasively to the reader. In Keats' odes, as in Wordsworth's "Tintern Abbey," the mood and ideas of the poet are generated from a sensitive brooding over natural objects, and the poem becomes an organic unity wholly different in meaning and effect from any paraphrase or summary of its content. . . .

Whether the romantic poet moves out into the country with Wordsworth, or into a symbolic Middle Ages, as Keats sometimes did, or proceeds to have a passionate Platonic love affair with the universe such as we find in Shelley, he is illustrating in one way or another his isolation, his inability to draw nourishment from the conventional attitudes and culture patterns of a select society, his desire to escape from his loneliness not by normal human companionship but by discovering man in general through external nature. In referring the poem back to the poet, we also associate it in a new way with the external world, which the poet's mind intuits and to which the poet's mind corresponds in a special way:

> No outcast he, bewildered and depressed:
> Along his infant veins are interfused
> The gravitation and the filial bond
> Of nature that connect him with the world.

The poet escapes from his fellows to find man through nature ("For I have learned /To look on nature, not as in the hour /Of thoughtless youth; but hearing often-times /The still, sad music of humanity"), and this is often the same thing as finding himself:

> There is a pleasure in the pathless woods,
> There is a rapture on the lonely shore,
> There is society where none intrudes,
> By the deep Sea, and music in its roar,
> I love not man the less but nature more,
> From these our interviews, in which I steal
> From all I may be, or have been before,
> To mingle with the Universe, and feel
> What I can ne'er express, yet cannot all conceal.

The voice of Byron here, for all its individuality, is also the voice of the romantic poet in his alienation from society.

## Napoleon As a Romantic Hero
✍ *Pieter Geyl*

The first to provide a portrait in which there was nought but unblemished beauty, endearing humanity, greatness and virtue, was Napoleon himself. On St. Helena he set about the task of shaping his reputation for posterity. The *Mémorial*, in which the Marquis Las Cases noted his conversations, a book which had an immeasurable influence in France, and which was the first and foremost source of what is called the Napoleonic legend, was peculiarly suited to become a popular classic. Anecdotes and reminiscences chosen at random from the whole miraculous life are interwoven with speculations, the whole within the framework of the Longwood tragedy and the bitter struggle with Sir Hudson Lowe, which Las Cases describes from day to day. This plan gives the book its human note. It catches the emotions as well as the interest of innumerable readers. It presents Napoleon not just as the aloof, mighty Emperor, but as somebody who, for all his incomparable cleverness, greatness and luck, is nevertheless accessible, one of ourselves.

From this living, variegated backcloth emerges the political Napoleon. He is before everything else the son of the Revolution, the man who consolidated the possession of equality, and made good his country's escape from feudalism by restoring order, by ridding France of those factions which had practically dissipated the fruits of the Revolution, and by wresting peace from the monarchs who hated France and the Revolution. That peace (Lunéville, 1801, Amiens, 1802, when Bonaparte had only just become First Consul) was a breathing space, which brought sudden overwhelming popularity to the victorious hero. There was nothing Napoleon liked better to recall after his downfall, and the fact could hardly be denied, but how brief was that respite! How endless, bitter and bloody were the compaigns which followed, up to the disasters and the final collapse! It was all the fault, so the Napoleon of the *Mémorial* would have us believe, of those self-same monarchs, and of envious Britain. His conquests had adorned the name of France with undying fame—*gloire,* that word dear to the Frenchmen of the period—but they had been forced upon him. He had been obliged to conquer Europe in self-defence. And even this conquest was fraught with benefits. After the French it was the turn of the Dutch, the Swiss, the Germans, the Italians, the Spanish, to receive the blessings of the codes of laws and other revolutionary reforms. Had he been allowed to go his own way, or had he remained victorious, Europe would have become a federation of free peoples, grouped round enlightened and fortunate France in an eternal peace. It was the hatred of the monarchs and the envy of England, the mischief-maker, the pirate swayed only by low, materialistic motives, which had destroyed his noble future for France and for Europe.

Such is Napoleon's apology. But I would give an incomplete outline of the *Mémorial,* and would fail to account for the impression it made, were I to omit to add that not only is this apology embedded among anecdotes, reminiscences and daily particulars of the mournful exile, but that no sense of inconsistency prevents the fallen Emperor from enlarging with inexhaustible complacency on his military achievements. The whole work glows with the glory which surrounds Napoleon even in his fall, and which the people of France share with him. The glory of France is the thought to which he constantly returns; and what he did, he did for France.

# INDEX OF AUTHORS

# Index of Authors